DEVELOPING COUNTRIES AND PREFERENTIAL SERVICES TRADE

WTO law sets the global minimum standards for trade regulation, while allowing some regulatory flexibility for developing countries. The exact scope of regulatory flexibility is often unclear, and, at times, flexibility may be counterproductive to sustainable economic growth in developing countries. Undisputedly, developing countries would have some flexibility with respect to tailoring preferential services trade agreements to their individual economic needs and circumstances, but empirical data from over 280 preferential services trade agreements worldwide show that this flexibility is rarely used. This volume clarifies the regulatory scope of flexibility for preferential services trade agreements between developing countries by linking the legal interpretation of WTO law with evidence from research in economics and political sciences. The book suggests that the current regulatory framework leaves room for meaningful flexibility for developing countries and encourages policymakers and scholars to take these flexibilities into consideration in their design and study of trade policies.

CHARLOTTE SIEBER-GASSER studied law in Bern and Fribourg, Switzerland, and Development Studies in Manchester, UK. She works currently as a senior visiting research fellow at the Graduate Institute for International and Development Studies in Geneva and as a senior research fellow at the World Trade Institute of the University of Bern, Switzerland.

CAMBRIDGE INTERNATIONAL TRADE AND ECONOMIC LAW

As the processes of regionalisation and globalisation have intensified, there have been accompanying increases in the regulations of international trade and economic law at the levels of international, regional and national laws.

The subject matter of this series is international economic law. Its core is the regulation of international trade, investment and cognate areas such as intellectual property and competition policy. The series publishes books on related regulatory areas, in particular human rights, labour, environment and culture, as well as sustainable development. These areas are vertically linked at the international, regional and national level, and the series extends to the implementation of these rules at these different levels. The series also includes works on governance, dealing with the structure and operation of related international organisations in the field of international economic law, and the way they interact with other subjects of international and national law.

Books in the series

Developing Countries and Preferential Services Trade
Charlotte Sieber-Gasser

WTO Dispute Settlement and the TRIPS Agreement: Applying Intellectual Property Standards in a Trade Law Framework
Matthew Kennedy

Establishing Judicial Authority in International Economic Law
Edited by Joanna Jemielniak, Laura Nielsen and Henrik Palmer Olsen

Trade, Investment, Innovation and Their Impact on Access to Medicines: An Asian Perspective
Locknie Hsu

The Law, Economics and Politics of International Standardisation
Panagiotis Delimatsis

The WTO and International Investment Law: Converging Systems
Jürgen Kurtz

Export Restrictions on Critical Minerals and Metals: Testing the Adequacy of WTO Disciplines
Ilaria Espa

Optimal Regulation and the Law of International Trade: The Interface between Societal Values and WTO Law
Boris Rigod

The Social Foundations of World Trade: Norms, Community and Constitution
Sungjoon Cho

Public Participation and Legitimacy in the WTO
Yves Bonzon

The Challenge of Safeguards in the WTO
Fernando Piérola

General Interests of Host States in International Investment Law
Edited by Giorgio Sacerdoti, Pia Acconci, Mara Valenti and Anna De Luca

The Law of Development Cooperation: A Comparative Analysis of the World Bank, the EU and Germany
Philipp Dann

WTO Disciplines on Subsidies and Countervailing Measures: Balancing Policy Space and Legal Constraints
Dominic Coppens

Domestic Judicial Review of Trade Remedies: Experiences of the Most Active WTO Members
Müslüm Yilmaz

International Organizations in WTO Dispute Settlement: How Much Institutional Sensitivity?
Marina Foltea

Public Services and International Trade Liberalization: Human Rights and Gender Implications
Barnali Choudhury

The Law and Politics of WTO Waivers: Stability and Flexibility in Public International Law
Isabel Feichtner

African Regional Trade Agreements as Legal Regimes
James Thuo Gathii

Liberalizing International Trade after Doha
David Gantz

Processes and Production Methods (PPMs) in WTO Law: Interfacing Trade and Social Goals
Christiane R. Conrad

Non-discrimination in International Trade in Services: 'Likeness' in WTO/GATS
Nicolas Diebold

The Law, Economics and Politics of Retaliation in WTO Dispute Settlement
Edited by Chad P. Bown and Joost Pauwelyn

The Multilateralization of International Investment Law
Stephan W. Schill

Trade Policy Flexibility and Enforcement in the WTO: A Law and Economics Analysis
Simon A.B. Schropp

DEVELOPING COUNTRIES AND PREFERENTIAL SERVICES TRADE

CHARLOTTE SIEBER-GASSER

CAMBRIDGE
UNIVERSITY PRESS

CAMBRIDGE
UNIVERSITY PRESS

University Printing House, Cambridge CB2 8BS, United Kingdom

Cambridge University Press is part of the University of Cambridge.

It furthers the University's mission by disseminating knowledge in the pursuit of education, learning and research at the highest international levels of excellence.

www.cambridge.org
Information on this title: www.cambridge.org/9781107147560

First published 2016

A catalogue record for this publication is available from the British Library.

Library of Congress Cataloging-in-Publication data
Sieber-Gasser, Charlotte, 1982– author.
Developing countries and preferential services trade / Charlotte Sieber-Gasser.
Cambridge, United Kingdom : Cambridge University Press, 2016.
Series: Cambridge international trade and economic law Based on author's thesis (doctoral – University of Bern, 2014) issued under title: South-South Preferential Trade Agreements in Services : Exploring the Scope for Development in International Economic Law. Includes bibliographical references and index.
LCCN 2016008233 ISBN 9781107147560 (hardback)
LCSH: Service industries – Law and legislation – Developing countries.
Foreign trade regulation – Developing countries.
LCC K3973.S56 2016 DDC 343/.124087 – dc23
LC record available at http://lccn.loc.gov/2016008233

ISBN 978-1-107-14756-0 Hardback

To Nils and Miro

CONTENTS

FIGURES

TABLES

ACKNOWLEDGEMENTS

The following pages are the result of a long journey and would not have been possible without the most precious support of many kind and inspiring people. I consider myself fortunate to be surrounded by many brilliant minds and open hearts; they facilitated not only this research but also combining it with a young family and to engage in related consultancy and academic work. One year after submitting the Ph.D. thesis, it is with great pleasure that I cease this opportunity to thank those, who made these past four years such an extraordinary, rich and successful journey.

That I was provided with a considerable amount of support and trust was a key to the successful completion of the Ph.D., in particular during times when new insights were rare. Therefore, I am most grateful and indebted to my supervisor, Thomas Cottier, for this opportunity and for sharpening my understanding of the overarching, systemic implications of what may appear like small legal details. Along the way, I have had the chance to meet and interact with a number of scholars, who inspired the outcome of this journey, each in their own way. Thank you for your inspiring work and the insights I gained from it, Rudolf Adlung, Lorand Bartels, Tomer Broude, Edwini Kessie, Markus Krajewski, Debra Steger, Sherry Stephenson and Marion Panizzon. Thank you for helping me to structure my work and for engaging with my ideas, Mira Burri, Nicolas Diebold, Manfred Elsig, Joseph Francois, Matthias Oesch, Joost Pauwelyn, Anirudh Shingal, and Judith Wyttenbach. Finally, even if they did not directly translate into this work, numerous discussions with fellow researchers and friends have been increasing my understanding of the overall complexity of South-South economic integration. In particular, I am grateful for the opportunity to exchange views with Anoushka Boodhna, Mariana Dias Simpson, Dominik Gerber, Irene Grohsmann, Karolis Gudas, Malebakeng Kohere, Rodrigo Polanco, Victor Saco, Clarence Siziba, Alaa Tartir and Cyrill Zosso.

For me personally, the completion of this manuscript is not only special because of its content, but also because during the process of writing it, our two sons were born. It takes a whole village to raise a child, a famous saying goes. In these first months and years in the life of our sons, it took in particular my parents and my parents-in-law who supported us along the way and took good care of them on the occasional weekends and late afternoons, when our working schedules and childcare did not add up. But it also took the support and understanding of the people at the World Trade Institute who tolerated the occasional meeting with a toddler present in the room and my being tired after yet another sleepless night. And it took the consideration of the people at Obviam, when my husband jumped in to take care of a sick child or to have my back when a deadline was (over)due. Thank you!

This is not the most relaxed and easy-going choice of career for a lawyer. Therefore I thank my husband for encouraging me nevertheless to continue along this path, for appreciating my curiosity and my critical spirit. We did rock this (sometimes) rocky road; thank you for being my brave and forbearing travelling companion! I thank my parents, Armin and Christa Sieber, who accompanied and supported me on my many explorations of the world and beyond, and who continue to help me understand the true meaning of unconditional love in all of its beauty. I also thank my parents-in-law, Adrian and Camille Gasser, whose support and encouragement throughout the process was invaluable and not to be taken for granted and therefore fills me with tremendous gratitude.

I gratefully dedicate this book to our beloved sons, Nils William and Miro George. Thank you for putting work into a healthy perspective, for the opportunity to explore this world once again through your eyes, and for all the traces and marks you leave in our lives.

ABBREVIATIONS

Art.	Article
AB	Appellate Body
ANZCERTA	Australia New Zealand Closer Economic Relations Trade Agreement
appr	approach
ASEAN	Association of Southeast Asian Nations
BIT	Bilateral Investment Treaty
BRIC	Brazil–Russia–India–China bus business and professional services
CARICOM	Caribbean Community
CARIFORUM	Forum of the Caribbean Group of African, Caribbean and Pacific
Ch.	Chapter
com	communication services
COMESA	Common Market for Eastern and Southern Africa
cons	construction services
CRTA	Committee on Regional Trade Agreements
CTS	Council of Trade Services
DAC	Development Cooperation Directorate of the OECD
DESTA	Design of Trade Agreements
DR	Dominican Republic
Dr.	Doctor
DSB	Dispute Settlement Body
DSU	Dispute Settlement Understanding
EAC	East African Community
EC	European Community
Ed.	Editor
edu	education services
Eds.	Editors
EFTA	European Free Trade Association
e.g.	for example
EPA	Economic Partnership Agreement
et al.	and others
etc.	et cetera

EU	European Union
FDI	Foreign Direct Investment
fin	financial services
G77	Group of 77
G8	Global-8
GATS	General Agreement on Trade in Services
GATS+	GATS-plus
GATSx	GATS-extra
GATS–	GATS-minus
GATT	General Agreement on Tariffs in Trade
GDP	Gross Domestic Product
GNI	Gross National Income
GSP	Generalised System of Preferences
horiz	horizontal commitments
IEL	International Economic Law
IIA	International Investment Agreement
incl	included
inv-chap	chapter on investment
IT	Information Technology
lab mode	4 supply of services
lib	iberalisation
lit.	litera
LDC	Least-Developed Country
LDCs	Least-Developed Countries
MA	Market Access
MERCOSUR	Southern Common Market
MFN	Most-Favoured Nation Treatment
MNCs	Multinational Corporations
move-	plus more than GATS level of commitments in mode 4 supply
NA	Not Available
NAFTA	North American Free Trade Agreement
NCCR	National Centre for Competence in Research
neg	negative list approach
no.	number
NT	National Treatment
NZZ	Neue Zürcher Zeitung
ODA	Official Development Aid
ODI	Outward Foreign Direct Investment
OECD	Organisation for Economic Co-operation and Development
OECS	Organisation of Eastern Caribbean States
p.	page
para.	paragraph

pp.	pages
PTA	Preferential Trade Agreement
PTAs	Preferential Trade Agreements
Ph.D.	Doctor of Philosophy
Prof.	Professor
recogn	mutual recognition
ref	reference
SADC	Southern African Development Community
sects	sectors
sep	separate
S-S	South-South
SDT	Special and Differential Treatment
TISA	Trade in Services Agreement
T-TIP	Transatlantic Trade and Investment Partnership
tou	tourism services
TPP	Transpacific Partnership
tran	transportation services
TRIPs	Agreement on Trade-Related Aspects of Intellectual Property Rights
UAE	United Arab Emirates
UN	United Nations
UNCTAD	United Nations Conference on Trade and Development
US	United States of America
USD	US Dollar
VCLT	Vienna Convention on the Law of Treaties
vol.	volume
WAEMU	West African Economic and Monetary Union
WTO	World Trade Organisation

TABLE OF AGREEMENTS

Complete list of agreements provided by DESTA in 2013:

* If services are mentioned in these treaties at all, it is not in the context of services trade

Additional agreements to DESTA (dataset):

TABLE OF CASES

Foundations

"The worst form of inequality is to try to make unequal things equal."

Aristotle

In the past twenty years, the world has seen unprecedented globalisation of markets and production, along with a more integrated governance of their operations. The pace and scope of globalisation that we currently witness is linked with new technologies and the fact that firms were able to take advantage of the new – and more global – opportunities. Ramifications of globalisation were not predicted ten or twenty years ago, and demand from governments increasing coordination of policies beyond external affairs.[1] But the regulatory framework of global trade has not yet fully accommodated this need for coordination. While businesses and other economic forces continue to cooperate and coordinate closer, governments lack the right institutions to follow suit. Some say, therefore, that progressive globalisation is weakening state institutions and, thus, strengthening economic forces.[2]

In line with this argument, concerns are raised over the remaining authority of states in today's globalising world. The main concern is that while it was the state, which defined the rules in the market before, it is now the market that dictates the rules to the state.[3] Assuming this assessment is correct, implications for inequality across the globe are distinct. And

[1] See, e.g. Dunning, John H. (2015) *The Globalization of Business: The Challenge of the 1990s*, Routledge Revivals, Routledge, New York, p. 73.

[2] E.g. Nullmeier, Frank (2009) 'Formen der Staatlichkeit: Zu einer Analytik politischer Einheiten', In: Nicole Deitelhoff and Jens Steffek (eds.), *Was bleibt vom Staat?: Demokratie, Recht und Verfassung im globalen Zeitalter*, Campus Verlag, Frankfurt am Main, pp. 35–56; Dingwerth, Klaus, Blauberger, Michael and Schneider, Christian (2011) *Postnationale Demokratie*, VS Verlag, Wiesbaden.

[3] Strange, Susan (2015) The Declining Authority of States', In: Frank J. Lechner and John Boli (eds.), *The Globalization Reader*, 5th edition, John Wiley & Sons, West Sussex, pp. 232–238, p. 233; Rodrik, Dani (2011) *The Globalisation Paradox*, W. W. Norton & Company, Inc., New York, p. 77.

indeed, most recent economic evidence suggests that globalisation is not necessarily benefitting all: inequality is on the rise globally,[4] the so-called trickle-down effect proved to be working only in theory.[5] Reversing free trade and with it economic globalisation appears, however, neither feasible nor desirable.[6]

While the reasons for the negative implications of globalisation for global welfare are numerous, it is widely agreed that the regulatory framework governing globalisation is a key factor. This is where this book comes into play: By assessing the scope for economic development inherent in WTO law and in preferential trade agreements, this book is shedding light on one possible avenue to consider when targeting inequality resulting from globalisation.[7]

4 Goldberg, Pinelopi K. and Pavcnik, Nina (2007) 'Distributional Effects of Globalization in Developing Countries', *Journal of Economic Literature*, vol. XLV, March, pp. 39–82, p. 54.

5 See, e.g. Krugman, Paul (2008) 'Trade and Wages, Reconsidered', *Brookings Papers on Economic Activity*, Spring, pp. 103–37.

6 E.g. Rodrik (2011, p. 88).

7 Slaughter, Anne-Marie (2004) *A New World Order*, Princeton University Press, Princeton; Dunoff, Jeffrey L. and Trachtman, Joel P. (eds.) (2009) *Ruling the World?: Constitutionalism, International Law, and Global Governance*, Cambridge University Press, Cambridge; Posner, Eric (2009) *The Perils of Global Legalism*, University of Chicago Press, Chicago.

1

Special and Differential Treatment in the WTO

About two-thirds of WTO members – and therewith the majoritiy – are developing or least-developed countries (LDCs). Contrary to other international organisations,[1] the votes of all members of the WTO – whether LDC or industrialised – have the same weight, and decisions are taken by consensus only.[2] While the political reality of differing economic and political strength certainly impacts on decisions taken by the WTO,[3] it is nevertheless remarkable that the WTO's organisational structure treats developing countries as full members, on equal footing with industrialised members. Consequently, developing countries have a decisive shaping power today in all decisions taken by the WTO.[4]

In balance for the equal rights and treatment, the WTO provides neither financial support nor permanent exemptions from legal obligations to developing countries. Nonetheless, the obligations of developing countries have been eased to some extent in comparison with industrialised members of the WTO. For instance, developing countries are typically offered longer time frames for meeting their legal obligations, in addition to administrative and technical assistance. The WTO treaties reflect their concern about the difficult economic and social circumstances by

[1] E.g. the UN has a two-chamber system with the Security Council and its permanent members; the weight of the vote depends on the money transferred to the organisation both within the IMF and the World Bank, which marginalises the vote of developing countries.

[2] See Agreement Establishing the World Trade Organisation Art. IX.

[3] See for a critical note on the consensus decision making: Steinberg, Richard H. (2002) 'In the Shadow of Law or Power? Consensus-Based Bargaining and Outcomes in the GATT/WTO', *International Organisation*, vol. 56, no. 2, pp. 339–374.

[4] It has been observed that developing countries used to be reluctant or unsuccessful with respect to shaping the decisions within the WTO in the past. This may have changed, given that developing countries are now organised in interest groups and manage to exert considerable pressure on industrialised countries. See also Ismail, Faizel and Vickers, Brendan (2011) 'Towards Fair and Inclusive Decision-Making in the WTO Negotiations', In: Carolyn Deere Birkbeck (ed.), *Making Global Trade Governance Work for Development*, Cambridge University Press, Cambridge, pp. 461–485, p. 478.

providing for the additional flexibility – the aim being to facilitate trade liberalisation in these poorer countries suffering from economic insecurity and a weak institutional environment.[5]

Munin (2010) states that this reflects the principle of teaching developing countries how to fish, rather than sending them the fish.[6] While this is one possible view and conceptual explanation of the legal status of developing countries within the WTO, arguably, the equal treatment as manifested by the WTO is also a strong commitment to the concept of free trade, which in theory should be more efficient in alleviating poverty than any form of foreign aid.[7] Seen this way, demanding equal rights and obligations from developing countries is in their interest: structural adjustment, a trade- and competition-friendly policy and the sheer power of economic activity should have a sustainably positive impact on economic growth in the poorer countries of this world.[8]

The following paragraphs discuss the legal status of developing countries in the WTO. They take a critical look at the legal implications of the concept of self-declaration and explain why there is a legal difference between the status of a developing country and the status of an LDC in the WTO. After providing a general overview of the debate concerning the legal status of developing countries in the WTO, they discuss different avenues for the future of the concept of special and differential treatment of poorer countries in the WTO. The practical consequences of the unspecific legal status of developing countries within the WTO are illustrated well by the search for a meaningful list of developing countries for establishing the sample of PTAs for this study. The part concludes with describing the theoretical framework of this study with respect to the legal definition of South-South and the concept of special and differential treatment of developing countries.

I. Developing Countries in the WTO

The term 'developing country' in WTO law is legally difficult to grasp, because WTO law itself does not provide a definition of 'developing

[5] See, e.g. KECK, ALEXANDER AND LOW, PATRICK (2004) Special and Differential Treatment in the WTO: Why, When and How?, Staff Working Paper ERSD-2004–03, WTO, Geneva.

[6] MUNIN, NELLIE (2010) *Legal Guide to GATS*, Kluwer Law International, Alphen aan den Rijn, p. 323.

[7] See, e.g. MORRISSEY, OLIVER (2006) 'Aid or Trade, or Aid and Trade?', *Australian Economic Review*, vol. 39, no. 1, pp. 78–88.

[8] See, e.g. WINTERS, ALAN L. (2004) 'Trade Liberalisation and Economic Performance: An Overview', *The Economic Journal*, vol. 114, no. 493, pp. F4–F21.

country'. While WTO law frequently uses the term 'developing country', belonging to the group of developing countries within the WTO officially is a matter of self-declaration: When joining the WTO, countries declare themselves to be either developing or developed. This self-declaration has, however, mainly political implications and is not legally binding. It is up to the rest of the WTO members whether they accept a country as a developing country or not, and the status of 'developing country' does not necessarily force others to provide, e.g. more preferential treatment.[9]

Until recently, the issue of defining the group of developing countries within the WTO was of limited relevance. Members seem to agree that the discussion on the definition and categorisation of developing countries in the WTO has come to a hold because a conclusion of this discussion within the WTO seems unlikely, and because the system of self-declaration seems to be working fairly well, despite its impreciseness.[10] Kennes (2000) points out how challenging introducing new regulation of the definition and treatment of developing countries within the WTO would be:[11]

> It should be kept in mind that the developing countries are a very heterogeneous group, often with divergent interests. They range from countries with very small population and economic size to large emerging economies.

In the report of the Panel on Defining the Future of Trade (2013), convened by then WTO director-general Pascal Lamy, the question of the legal status of developing countries and the balance of rights and obligations was, however, prominently brought up:[12]

> We believe it is time to embrace a new perspective on managing reciprocity and flexibility. We do not question differentiation and consider it an essential feature of a fair and effective trading system. [. . .] But in recognizing the legitimacy of differentiation, we consider that policy effectiveness is crucial. We need a dynamic approach to flexibility, tailor-made for specific needs and supported by appropriate capacity-building programmes.

The panel suggests that flexibilities should in the future be based on needs and capacities, they should target specific challenges, they should be time-specific, and finally, the manner in which flexibilities help countries to

9 Eberhard, Torsten (2008) *Diskriminierende Gleichbehandlung von Entwicklungsländern in der WTO?*, Mendel Verlag, Witten, pp. 92–93.

10 Eberhard (2008, p. 93).

11 Kennes, Walter (2000) Strategies for Effective Participation of Developing Countries in the World Trading System, PSIO Occasional Paper, WTO Series No. 06, Geneva, p. 9.

12 Panel on Defining the Future of Trade (2013) *The Future of Trade: The Challenges of Convergence*, WTO, Geneva, p. 30.

converge should be monitored. The issue of the legal status of developing countries in the WTO should, thus, be seen rather as a process than as a static categorisation.[13] In sum, Jean (2013) points out that:[14]

> The defects of the SDT system are not new, but they are increasingly glaring, up to a point where an update now appears inevitable, if the negotiating capacity of the WTO is to be preserved.

Regardless of the differences among them, developing countries have nevertheless since the 1960s stood together in order to raise their voice and provide their interests with greater weight, given their – still occurring – marginalisation in global trade and politics.[15] Within the WTO, developing countries demonstrated their political weight impressively when their firmness provoked the breakdown of the WTO's ministerial meeting in Seattle in 1999. Ties among developing countries have grown stronger in the meantime and they are organised in mainly three different groups of interest,[16] having also developed a considerable weight in multilateral trade negotiations.

Keet (2006) wrote the following about memberships in more than one group of developing countries and about the general implication of this new form of cooperation among developing countries within the framework of multilateral trade negotiations:[17]

> Such cross-cutting memberships, co-operation and mutual support could, more significantly, contribute towards gradually shifting the overall balance of power within the WTO, and possibly more widely.

However, with multilateralism having stalled since 2008, these new pressure groups of developing countries in the WTO have not yet achieved

[13] Ibid., p. 31.

[14] Jean, Sébastien (2013) WTO: Rethinking the Special and Differential Treatment Granted to Developing Countries, CEPII, le blog, 8 October 2013.

[15] See for instance Agreement on the *Global System of Trade Preferences among Developing Countries*, UNCTAD, GSTP/MM/BELGRADE/10 (12 April 1988), which takes advantage of the GATT Enabling Clause and is a direct result of the grouping of developing countries referred to as 'G-77+China'.

[16] The G-20, which emerged in 2003, consists of mainly Latin American countries in addition to China, India, Egypt and South Africa. The G-20 presses for the removal of agricultural tariff barriers in the North. The second group is called G-33, which has a main focus on agricultural export dumping and its damage to small producers in LDCs. And finally, the Group of 90, which is a larger group of developing countries spanning all global regions, which insists on the full recognition of development needs in WTO agreements.

[17] Keet, Dot (2006) *South-South: Strategic Alternatives to the Global Economic System and Power Regime*, Transnational Institute, Amsterdam, p. 22.

their goals,[18] other than preventing additional imbalances in the multilateral trading system. The Bali Ministerial Conference in December 2013 was, thus, concerned with the demands from developing countries and supposed to revive the Doha round through a new decision involving special treatment of LDCs and developing countries.[19]

At the Bali Ministerial Conference in December 2013, WTO members adopted the Bali Package,[20] which covers measures to simplify customs procedures, including assistance for developing countries and LDCs to update their infrastructure and for implementing the agreement.[21] Furthermore, an interim solution was adopted in the area of food security, which allows developing countries to pursue trade-distorting domestic support through public stockholding programmes for food security.[22] With a focus on LDCs, the Bali Package also includes decisions on duty-free and quota-free access for LDCs to richer countries' markets,[23] simplified rules of origin for LDCs[24] and a 'services waiver', which allows LDCs preferential access to richer countries' services markets.[25] Finally, with respect of developing countries, a 'monitoring mechanism' was adopted, which is targeted at monitoring special treatment given to developing countries.[26]

Nearly all the decisions of the Bali Package are targeting improved integration of developing countries and LDCs in the global market and have a development objective. While this illustrates the strength of developing countries and LDCs in the WTO, the decisions adopted arguably are of

18 See also Ismail, Faizel (2011) 'Rediscovering the Role of Developing Countries in the GATT', In: Y-S. Lee, G. N. Horlick, W-M. Choi and T. Broude (eds.), *Law and Development Perspective on International Trade Law*, Cambridge University Press, New York, pp. 130–160, p. 132.

19 See WTO (2013b) Ninth WTO Ministerial Conference.

20 WTO (2013a) 'Days 3, 4 and 5: Round-the-Clock Consultations Produce, Bali Package', Ninth WTO Ministerial Conference, 5–7 December 2013.

21 Agreement on Trade Facilitation, WT/MIN(13)/36 – WT/L/911.

22 Public Stockholding for Food Security Purposes, Ministerial Decision, WT/MIN(13)/38 – WT/L/913.

23 Duty-Free and Quota-Free (DFQF) Market Access for Least-Developed Countries, Ministerial Decision, WT/MIN(13)/44 – WT/L/919.

24 Preferential Rules of Origin for Least-Developed Countries, Ministerial Decision, WT/MIN(13)/42 – WT/L/917.

25 Operationalisation of the Waiver Concerning Preferential Treatment to Services and Service Suppliers of Least-Developed Countries, Ministerial Decision, WT/MIN(13)/43 – WT/L/918.

26 Monitoring Mechanism on Special and Differential Treatment, Ministerial Decision, WT/MIN(13)/45 – WT/L/920.

limited effect for economic growth in poor countries: most concessions to developing countries depend on the readiness of richer countries to offer preferences,[27] are introduced as interim solution[28] or are non-binding.[29] Given that developing countries and LDCs have an imminent interest in reviving multilateralism, they have to carefully balance the pressure they apply in the WTO. While demanding more flexibility and technical assistance, they should keep in sight of their strong interest in the WTO remaining the most influential forum for global trade policy and regulation. It remains to be seen whether the Bali Package can serve as a stepping-stone in this direction.

The role of developing countries in the WTO – both on the legal and the political side – is matchmaking for the future of world trade. It is said that, if the Bali Ministerial Conference had failed to foster an agreement, WTO members would have lost interest in multilateral trade negotiations and turned towards preferentialism. More than for industrialised countries, such a development would not have been in the interest of developing countries.[30] In particular, the so-called mega-regionals, such as the Transatlantic Trade and Investment Partnership (TTIP) and the Transpacific Partnership (TPP) are a considerable challenge to trade policy in poorer economies.

A general turn to mega-regionals by industrialised countries would weaken the impact of developing countries on global trade policy quite dramatically as decision-taking would be shifted away from the WTO in which developing countries currently have the advantage of being a majority. A shift to mega-regionals would also negatively impact on the level of inequality among WTO members, given that mega-regionals cover substantial shares of total global trade, and that therefore trade distortion and potential spill-over effects for countries outside of the agreements are considerable. While industrialised countries will likely benefit from

[27] E.g. the Operationalisation of the Waiver Concerning Preferential Treatment to Services and Service Suppliers of Least-Developed Countries, Ministerial Decision, WT/MIN(13)/43 – WT/L/918.

[28] E.g. the Public Stockholding for Food Security Purposes, Ministerial Decision, WT/MIN(13)/38 – WT/L/913.

[29] E.g. the Monitoring Mechanism on Special and Differential Treatment, Ministerial Decision, WT/MIN(13)/45 – WT/L/920.

[30] See, e.g. Murphy, Sophia (2013) 'The Road to Bali: The WTO's Ninth Ministerial', IATP; Helble, Matthias and Wignaraja, Ganeshan (2013) 'Bali Ministerial a Turning Point for the WTO?', East-Asia Forum; Priyadarshi, Shishir and Rahman, Taufiqur (2013) 'Build Up to the Ninth WTO Ministerial Conference: Issues of Interest to LDCs', *Commonwealth Trade Hot Topics*, no. 98, Commonwealth Secretariat, London.

spill-over effects of mega-regionals through voluntary regulatory alignment and access to larger markets with a single standard,[31] it is probable that developing countries will suffer from both trade distortion based on discriminatory tariffs and rules of origin and from the fact that they cannot benefit from spill-over effects through voluntary regulatory alignment like industrialised third countries.[32] Additionally, because of the share in global trade covered by mega-regionals, decisions taken by the industrialised partner countries of mega-regional trade agreements on WTO-plus regulation may eventually have to be incorporated in WTO law as well. With respect to regulatory convergence and trade liberalisation in general, multilateral negotiations are, thus, likely to be negatively affected by mega-regionals. Sheer practical need could force developing countries to accept – and potentially even implement – regulation established in mega-regionals if multilateralism is not catching up quickly enough with the new regulatory dynamics emanating from them. Therefore, contingent on the reaction of WTO members to mega-regionals, again, developing countries are currently at risk of substantial restrictions to their potential impact on international trade regulation in the future.

A. *Self-declaration*

When joining the WTO, members have the right to declare whether they wish to belong to the group of developing countries or not. This self-declaration, however, cannot be made entirely without basis: the country in question has to provide a reasonable justification, and the definition as a developing country within the WTO may come with consequences in other international organisations, such as the OECD.[33]

During negotiations over accession to the WTO, a country normally establishes the commitments it is ready to accept in its schedule of commitments, which includes the decision on its status as developed or developing country. If the proposal is accepted, the country will then receive

[31] See, e.g. Cottier, Thomas, Egger, Peter, Francois, Joseph, Manchin, Miriam, Shingal, Anirudh and Sieber-Gasser, Charlotte (2014) *Potential Impacts of a EU-US Free Trade Agreement on the Swiss Economy and External Economic Relations*, Rechtsgutachten erstattet Staatssekretariat für Wirtschaft SECO, available at: www.wti.org.

[32] Impact of TTIP on third countries, see Sieber-Gasser, Charlotte (2016), 'TTIP and Swiss Democracy', In: M. Bungenberg, C. Herrmann, M. Krajewski and J. P. Terhechte (eds.), *European Yearbook of International Economic Law 2016*, European Yearbook of International Economic Law, vol. 7, 2016, Springer, Basel.

[33] Munin (2010, p. 319).

the corresponding treatment. Until today, only in the case of China, a proposal by a country to classify itself as developing country was not fully accepted.[34]

Aside from the differentiations in the schedules of commitments, WTO law also knows additional preferences for developing countries granted by developed countries. These preferences – although linked to the term 'developing country' – neither provide substantially more clarification regarding the definition of the term 'developing country' nor do they depend on the self-declared status alone. For instance, an indication for the profile of developing countries within the GATS may be found in GATS Art. XVIII:1, which refers to members as developing countries if their economies 'can only support low standards of living and are in the early stages of development'.[35] However, given the lack of a general definition of the term 'developing country', it is in fact up to developed countries to decide on a case-by-case basis whether or not they will grant the preferences for developing countries to a particular member.

Preferences for developing countries are listed in the Generalised System of Preferences (GSP) or may be found in bilateral agreements. Complementing the WTO, the United Nations Conference on Trade and Development (UNCTAD) collects the list of beneficiaries of the GSP on the basis of country-schemes submitted to UNCTAD.[36] In 2011 schemes of Australia, Belarus, Canada, the EU, Japan, New Zealand, Norway, Russia, Switzerland, Turkey and the US were collected. Table 1 shows a selection of donors and beneficiaries and illustrates well how relative benefits under the GSP are.

The list of beneficiaries includes countries, which have declared themselves as developing countries at different occasions under WTO law. Following the general logic of WTO law, they may, thus, also benefit from preferential treatment. However, even though all of them could be considered as developing countries under WTO law, by far not all of these beneficiaries are actually treated as such by developed members of the WTO under the GSP.

[34] Kasteng, Jonas, Karlsson, Arne and Lindberg, Carina (2004) *Differentiation between Developing Countries in the WTO*, Swedish Board of Agriculture, International Affairs Division, Jönköping, p. 12.

[35] GATS Art. XXVIII:1.

[36] See UNCTAD (2011) *Generalised System of Preferences: List of Beneficiaries*, UNCTAD, Geneva.

Table 1 *Selected GSP donors and beneficiaries*[a]

	GSP donors							
GSP beneficiaries	Australia	Canada	EU	Japan	New Zealand	Norway	Switzerland	US
Albania				x	x	x		x
Armenia		x	x	x			x	x
Belarus			x	x			x	
Brazil		x	x	x	x	x	x	x
Chile		x	x	x	x			
China		x	x	x	x	x	x	
China, Hong Kong		x				x		
China, Macao		x	x		x	x	x	
Taiwan (Province of China)								
Kosovo							x	x
India		x	x	x	x	x	x	x
Occupied Palestinian Territories				x	x			x
Russia		x	x					
South Africa		x	x	x		x		x
Turkey		x		x	x			x
West Bank and Gaza Strip								x

[a] Derived from UNCTAD (2011).

Whether benefits are granted may depend on country-level policy,[37] on political ties[38] or on the perceived level of economic development in the respective country.[39] The system seems to work in an unpredictable way: for instance, the BRIC countries are not treated the same as other countries in terms of GSP benefits. Additionally, while Chile is a member of the OECD and still benefits from GSP, the West Bank and Gaza Strip, clearly a poor region, is more or less excluded from GSP benefits. Not even LDCs are given the same treatment by all GSP donors, even if such

[37] Without further looking into this, it is interesting that Australia grants benefits mainly – but not exclusively – to LDCs.

[38] Close political ties between Switzerland and Kosovo might explain why Switzerland grants benefits to Kosovo, while most others do not.

[39] This may be read into the fact that the number of countries granting benefits to China and its neighbours is decreasing if GDP per capita is increasing.

discrimination seems strongly counter-intuitive and might contradict commitments made by developed countries under WTO law.[40]

Therefore, while countries have the right to self-declaration under WTO law and therewith have the means to adjust their own schedules of commitments, this declaration remains of little consequence as long as other countries do not adapt their schedules of preferences accordingly.

B. *Conceptual Issues of Self-Declaration*

The principle of self-declaration has paradoxical consequences. In general, one would assume that countries desire to become 'developed countries', but WTO members seem to prefer remaining within the group of 'developing countries'. This can be illustrated by compiling lists of all WTO members who drew the 'developing country'-card at some point recently.[41]

In these lists, some – undoubtedly developed countries – appear as developing countries under the WTO institutions, when other international organisations or authorities list them as 'developed countries'. In addition, the fact that relatively rich countries under certain circumstances belong to the group of 'developing countries' contributes to increasing the heterogeneity of the 'developing country' group in the WTO: for example, Israel (with a GDP per capita of 32,800 USD), Singapore (with a GDP per capita of 61,400 USD) and the United Arab Emirates (with a GDP per capita of 49,600 USD) are all listed as developing countries under WTO law, together with countries such as Honduras (with a GDP per capita of 4,700 USD) or Tunisia (with a GDP per capita of 9,900 USD).[42,43]

The heterogeneity of the group of developing countries under WTO law poses a problem for the effectiveness of special and differential treatment (SDT) rules: developed countries are in general not prepared to offer substantial preferences to the entire group of developing countries, because they point out that some of the countries belonging to this group are well off and do not depend on special treatment. Developed countries are, thus, reluctant to agree on embedding general, substantial preferences for the group of developing countries in the legal body of the WTO.[44]

[40] See UNCTAD (2011, pp. 1–11).

[41] See e.g. Bosco, David (2011) 'Who's a "Developing Country"? You'd be Surprised', 18 February 2011, FP Voices.

[42] GDP per capita as provided by the World Bank. [43] See Kasteng et al. (2004).

[44] See, e.g. IPC (2004) A New Approach to Special and Differential Treatment, 15 September 2004, IPC Position Paper, Washington and Brussels.

Thus, holding onto the self-declaration principle provides for flexibility, not only when countries join the WTO, but also later when countries are offered to decide on a case-by-case basis whether they are prepared to commit to full schedules or whether they need more time or additional protection in a specific case. This flexibility would, in theory, allow for sector-based SDT if countries only referred to their 'developing' status in particularly difficult situations.

This case-by-case approach to SDT is, however, part of the reason why SDT does not deliver the results that it promised. Because WTO members have limited control over the composition of the group of 'developing countries', it is difficult to predict the consequences of substantial preferences generally granted to 'developing countries' under WTO law. Therefore, a more meaningful definition – or a better-equipped SDT regime – is of imminent importance for the future of developing countries' rights in the WTO.

II. Least-Developed Countries in the WTO

Within the group of developing countries, WTO law also distinguishes between LDCs and other developing countries. The commitment to continue paying special attention to this distinction was reaffirmed at the First Ministerial Conference in Singapore in 1996:[45]

> In this connection, we recall that the WTO Agreement embodies provisions conferring differential and more favourable treatment for developing countries, including special attention to the particular situation of least-developed countries.

Before the establishment of the WTO, little legal reference was made to the special status of LDCs under IEL. Hawthorne (2013) describes a 'cascade' of the norm of special treatment for LDCs in the 1990s, resulting in the norm's institutionalisation through its reflection in WTO law, and through the explicit inclusion of LDCs as a category under WTO law. In addition, the reference of WTO law to the UN definition of LDCs helped consolidating the category of LDCs at the international level.[46] In this sense, the WTO can be seen as a key contributor to the establishment of

[45] Singapore Ministerial Declaration, Ministerial Declaration, WT/MIN(96)/DEC, para. 13.

[46] Hawthorne, Helen (2013) *Least Developed Countries and the WTO: Special Treatment in Trade*, Palgrave Macmillan, Basingstoke, p. 53.

an internationally acknowledged norm according to which LDCs deserve favourable treatment.

While the group of developing countries is composed on a self-declaration basis, the constitution of the LDC group is less controversial, as the LDC designation is taken over from the UN.[47] The idea of splitting poor countries into groups – one group requiring urgent help from the international community, and another group deserving special treatment – dates back to the 1970s. UNCTAD then played a key role in promoting and establishing the criteria for defining LDCs and drawing up the according list of countries. Distinguishing between poor and even poorer countries helped the international community to better target aid and development assistance.[48]

The UN list of LDCs was initially composed of twenty-five countries in 1971. In four decades, only four countries graduated from the status of an LDC (Botswana in 1994, Cape Verde in 2007, the Maldives in 2011 and Samoa in 2014), while the number of countries on the list nearly doubled (from 25 in 1971 to 48 in 2015).[49] In 2015, of the forty-eight LDCs, thirty-four were members of the WTO, with eight more negotiating to join. Hence, within the nearer future, it is expected that almost all LDCs will have joined the WTO. This fact confirms the importance of trade regulation for development policies in LDCs. Even though aid and donations are crucial for LDCs in the short term, the 'solution [to end poverty sustainably,] should come from economic development'.[50] History shows that countries, which successfully escaped poverty in the last fifty years, did so through economic development. This underlines the role of trade regulation in eradicating poverty around the world.

LDCs are currently given more flexibility and more favourable treatment in relevant key areas of trade regulation than other developing countries. The Uruguay Round Agreements alone established seventeen

[47] In 2015, the UN counted forty-eight countries as LDCs, with the bulk of countries located on the African continent. See UN Office of the High Representative for the Least Developed Countries, Landlocked Developing Countries and Small Island Developing States (UN-OHRLLS) [online], available at: http://unohrlls.org.

[48] Hawthorne (2013, p. 28).

[49] UN Office of the High Representative for the Least Developed Countries, Landlocked Developing Countries and Small Island Developing States (UN-OHRLLS) [Online], available at: http://unohrlls.org.

[50] Lee, Yong-Shik (2011a) 'Law and Development for Least-Developed Countries: Theoretical Basis and Regulatory Framework for Microtrade', In: Y-S. Lee, G. N. Horlick, W-M. Choi and T. Broude (eds.), *Law and Development Perspective on International Trade Law*, Cambridge University Press, New York, pp. 7–28, p. 8.

additional provisions applicable exclusively to LDCs. In general, LDCs are given the opportunity to limit their commitments to the 'extent compatible with their individual development' and financial and trade needs.[51] In 1997, the 'twin track approach' was adopted regarding the SDT of LDCs in the WTO.[52] This approach arguably provides the basis for many of the current demands in multilateral trade negotiations and consists of one track emphasising the limited commitments of LDCs to liberalisation and of another track encouraging increased commitments by developed countries regarding market access and technical assistance for LDCs.

A. *Conceptual Issues Related to the Least-Developed Country Status*

In 2000, Michalopoulos asked:[53]

> The key issues that need to be addressed in the context of the special provisions for the LDCs are much the same as with developing countries [. . .]: are commitments for preferential market access and treatment offered by developed countries meaningful relative to the constraints these countries face in integrating in the world trading system? Is the international technical assistance in support of these countries effective? And does the flexibility offered to these countries in meeting their WTO commitments contribute to their long term trade and development objectives?

Little has changed since then: scholars and policymakers alike struggle with identifying the appropriate set of flexibilities versus commitments in trade regulation for LDCs. Obviously, membership in the WTO did not immediately result in substantial increases in welfare for LDCs. Most of them have remained on the list of LDCs, irrespectively of the duration of their membership in the WTO.

While flexibilities at times may be crucial for economic growth in LDCs, at other times, flexibilities may even develop detrimental effects on economic growth, as they can hamper structural change and distract the focus of policymakers away from designing the best trade policy to achieving the highest level of flexibility. This discussion is very similar in

[51] Michalopoulos, Constantine (2000) Trade and Development in the GATT and WTO: The Role of Special and Differential Treatment for Developing Countries, Working Paper, World Bank, Washington DC, p. 22.

[52] High-Level Meeting on Integrated Initiatives for Least-Developed Countries' Trade Development, Note on the Meeting, WT/LDC/HL/M/1 (26 November 1997).

[53] Michalopoulos (2000 p. 23).

nature to the issue surrounding the legal status of developing countries in general in the WTO.[54]

A few LDCs – despite being generally very poor – have strong industries-specific sectors, such as services or pharmaceuticals.[55] In some instances, these industries are competitive on the global market. It has, thus, been questioned whether it was still justified to grant an LDC special and more favourable treatment across the board, or whether specific industries, in which an LDC is in fact a global competitor, should be excluded.[56] Some argue that it could be in the interest of LDCs to waive preferences for sectors, in which they are globally competitive, assuming that this would allow them to negotiate additional preferences in sectors, in which they are weakly positioned on the global market. In analogy to the case of preferences for developing countries, this might ease the fear of richer countries from additional competition and induce them to grant more substantial preferences.[57] However, this proposition would have to be subjected to closer economic analysis, in view of determining the importance of LDCs' most competitive economic sectors as motors of economic development and poverty reduction, as well as the impact of SDT on them.

[54] See, e.g. Michalopoulos (2000); Kleen, Peter and Page, Sheila (2005) *Special and Differential Treatment of Developing Countries in the World Trade Organisation*, Global Development Studies No. 2, Overseas Development Institute and Ministry for Foreign Affairs Sweden, London, pp. 39–41.

[55] E.g. Bangladesh is a global leader behind only China in the apparel industry, see Lewis, David (2011) *Bangladesh: Politics, Economy and Civil Society*, Cambridge University Press, Cambridge; Rwanda has a highly developed tourism industry, see Nielsen, Hannah and Spenceley, Anna (2011) The Success of Tourism in Rwanda – Gorillas and More, Background Paper, World Development Report 2011, The World Bank, Washington DC; Togo and Benin have a highly developed sector in distribution services, see Golub, Stephen (2010) *The Role of Transit and Re-export Trade in Togo's Economy* [Online], available at: www.swarthmore.edu/Documents/academics/economics/Golub/Togo-reexports.pdf; and, finally, Angola actually is a leading country in oil- and diamond export, see, e.g. Burgos, Sigfrido and Ear, Sophal (2012) 'China's Oil Hunger in Angola: History and Perspective', *Journal of Contemporary China*, vol. 21, no. 74, pp. 351–367.

[56] E.g. because there are other countries, with similar difficulties, which are not in the group of LDCs, see Grynberg, Roman (2000) The Pacific Island States and the WTO: Towards a Post-Seattle Agenda for the Small Vulnerable States, Global Conference on the Development Agenda for Small States, London; similarly, Ismail, Faizel (2006) 'How Can Least-Developed Countries and Other Small, Weak and Vulnerable Economies also Gain from the Doha Development Agenda on the Road to Hong Kong?', *Journal of World Trade*, vol. 40, no. 1, pp. 37–68; or more generally, see Brennan, Anna Marie (2011) 'The Special and Differential Treatment Mechanism and the WTO: Cultivating Trade Inequality for Developing Countries?', *Trinity College Review*, vol. 14, pp. 143–160.

[57] On the general discussion on protectionism of infant-industries, see Slaughter, Matthew J. (2004) Infant-Industry Protection and Trade Liberalisation in Developing Countries, Research Report, USAID, Washington DC.

Part of the reason why LDCs do not (yet) seem to economically benefit from the membership in the WTO may finally be found in the twin track approach itself: if flexibilities are manifold and hamper necessary structural change, while the preferences granted by developed countries on a voluntary basis remain marginal, LDCs may after all suffer more from their legal status than if they had to commit to more open markets.

III. Special and Differential Treatment

SDT, which denominates the provisions of international trade regulation enabling the beneficial treatment of certain groups of countries, constitutes a departure from the principle of formal equality of states. SDT applies to a specific group of states, usually developing countries or LDCs. Such rules acknowledge the different stages of development and the particular challenges of developing countries and LDCs in complying with international standards. SDT may also take into consideration the different capabilities of a group of countries to contribute to a certain goal, such as climate change.[58] SDT appears in the form of modified rules of dispute settlement, technical assistance, or transitional periods for the implementation of substantive obligations of WTO law.

There are three kinds of SDT: first, provisions allowing developing countries to depart from their WTO commitments. These are meant to provide developing countries with a great scope of flexibility and should allow for adequate measures, in the countries, given the special economic needs. The particular flexibilities in GATS Art. V for PTAs among developing countries fall under this category.[59] Second, programmatic provisions, which encourage developed countries to undertake measures to promote economic development in developing countries. The Enabling Clause, which gave a permanent validity to measures such as the GSP, is an example for such a programmatic provision of SDT. The special provisions for LDCs[60] constitute the third and final type of SDT. These provisions

[58] See, e.g. Feichtner, Isabel (2012) *The Law and Politics of WTO Waivers: Stability and Flexibility in International Law*, Cambridge University Press, Cambridge, pp. 294–295; Cullet, Philippe (2003) *Differential Treatment in International Environmental Law*, Aldershot, Ashgate; Rajamani, Lavanya (2006) *Differential Treatment in International Environmental Law*, Cambridge University Press, Cambridge.

[59] Interestingly, Eberhard (2008, p. 59) does, however, not include GATS Art. V into his list of current SDT provisions; also the NUPI Report 2010 does not discuss SDT based on GATS Art. V, see Melchior, Arne, Stevens, Christopher and Johnsen, Åshild (2010) Services and Development: The Scope of Special and Differential Treatment in the GATS, NUPI Report 2010, Norwegian Institute of International Affairs, Oslo.

[60] Eberhard (2008, pp. 5–6).

encompass different measures, such as encouraging developed countries to provide trade opportunities to LDCs or to support them in a particular way (e.g. by providing for tax incentives for knowledge transfer under TRIPs).[61]

Because the provisions did not produce the economic outcome that they were expected to develop, critics now claim that the SDT regime has lost its legitimacy.[62] Therefore, rendering SDT more efficient ranks high on the agenda of the Doha Round. It is generally agreed that action must be taken in order to support and protect weaker industries from poorer countries on the global market, but the outcome of this revision of the SDT concept and regime is not yet foreseeable.

A. *The Logic of Special and Differential Treatment*

While free trade was understood to be created through equal treatment of everyone involved in it, claims started early – referring to Aristoteles among others – that equal treatment is only valid as long as it involves equally strong economies. MFN treatment, the core of equal treatment in the free trade regime, was not seen as a suitable principle for trade regulation involving countries of highly unequal economic strength.[63]

In the – initially successful – attempt to accommodate the different levels of economic development in the WTO, the concept and philosophy of progressive liberalisation was introduced in the early GATT in 1947. Subsequent rounds of multilateral trade negotiations then served the purpose of 'progressively and individually' lowering tariff rates. Both market access and domestic needs of protection were taken into account in this process, as well as needs of social and economic development.[64]

Interestingly, eleven of the initial twenty-five Members of the GATT were developing countries. It appears that they all agreed on the potential gains from multilateral trade, assuming that 'they identified the sectors in

61 Hoekman, Bernard, Michalopoulos, Constantine, and Winters, Alan L. (2003) More Favorable and Differential Treatment of Developing Countries: Towards a New Approach in the WTO, World Bank Policy Research Working Paper, World Bank, Washington DC, p. 5.

62 Kessie, Edwini (1999) 'Developing Countries and the WTO – What Has Changed?', *World Competition*, vol. 22, no. 2, pp. 83–110, p. 92; Low, Patrick (2003) 'Developing Countries in the Multilateral Trading System: The Insights of Robert E. Hudec', *Journal of World Trade*, vol. 37, no. 4, pp. 801–811, p. 803.

63 Eberhard (2008, p. 10).

64 Cottier, Thomas (2006) 'From Progressive Liberalisation to Progressive Regulation in WTO Law', *Journal of International Economic Law*, vol. 9, no. 4, pp. 779–821, p. 779.

which they had comparative advantage'.[65] Requesting trade preferences for developing countries did not occur to them, as they were concerned that it would distort trade and reward inefficient producers. Cottier (2006) writes in this context:[66]

> It is, therefore, not astonishing that the basic rules relating to progressive liberalisation *per se* do not need to take recourse to the concept of special and differential [. . .] treatment for [developing countries]. The same rules can apply to all Members alike as results can be tailored, taking into account highly diverging levels of development.

It was only in the 1950s, when a number of newly independent developing countries joined the GATT, that the treatment of developing countries as equal partners under the GATT was questioned and challenged:[67]

> Most of these countries challenged the very basis on which the GATT was built; that is, as a rules-based, non-discriminatory multilateral trading system. They argued that it was not realistic to expect newly independent countries with fragile economies to compete on a level playing field with established industrial countries at that time.

Subsequent pressure from developing countries and later also the UNCTAD first led to a number of specific measures of SDT and later to the adoption of Part IV of the GATT, which was entitled 'Trade and Development'. These changes formalised the acceptance of the non-reciprocity principle 'under which developed countries gave up their right to ask developing countries to offer concessions during trade negotiations'.[68] Finally, introducing the 'Enabling Clause' during the Tokyo round placed SDT at the core of the GATT system and created a permanent legal basis for a variety of measures that ought to support and protect developing economies.

Before the Uruguay Round, however, the majority of developing countries came to question the effectiveness of the different SDT provisions. They realised that substantial market access to developed countries would by far outnumber the gains from SDT.[69] As developed countries were, however, not prepared to offer substantial commitments in market access

[65] Kessie, Edwini (2007) 'The Legal Status of Special and Differential Treatment Provisions under the WTO Agreements', In: G. A. Bermann and P. C. Mavroidis (eds.), *WTO Law and Developing Countries*, Cambridge University Press, Cambridge, pp. 12–35, p. 16.

[66] Cottier (2006, p. 781). [67] Kessie (2007, pp. 16–17). [68] Ibid., p. 18.

[69] Ibid., p. 21; see also Hoekman, Bernard (2005a), 'Operationalising the Concept of Policy Space in the WTO: Beyond Special and Differential Treatment', *Journal of International Economic Law*, vol. 8, no. 2, pp. 405–424, pp. 410–411.

and National Treatment in sensitive sectors crucial to economic prospects in developing countries, the concept of SDT was held on to as a means to balance inequalities of the world trading system. Finally, on completing the Uruguay Round, SDT was firmly anchored across the board in WTO law.[70]

B. *The Provisions on Special and Differential Treatment*

The majority of the SDT provisions are to be found in the agreements of the Uruguay Round. The number of provisions is high, as pointed out by Lee (2011a):[71]

> One hundred and forty-five such provisions are scattered throughout WTO agreements, understandings, and GATT articles, among which twenty-two are applied exclusively to LDCs.

As mentioned above, there are currently three types of SDT treatment in the WTO. This thesis is mainly concerned with the first kind of provision (exemptions from WTO commitments for developing countries). In particular, this study focuses on GATS Art. V, the provision, which establishes the requirements for a PTA in services to be exempted from MFN.

Without going into detail on each and every one of the SDT provisions, the sheer number of such provisions proves that from a legal perspective, it is relevant whether or not a country belongs to the group of LDCs, developing countries or developed countries. The GATS knows several references and exemptions for developing countries and LDCs. They are already given special attention in the preamble,[72] followed by GATS Art. III.[73] GATS Art. IV is explicitly concerned with the 'Increasing Participation of Developing Countries'.[74] Additional flexibilities are granted in

[70] Cottier (2006, p. 784); Hoekman (2005a, pp. 421–424). [71] Lee (2011a, p. 115).

[72] GATS preamble: [. . .] 'Recognizing the right of Members to regulate, and to introduce new regulations, on the supply of services within their territories in order to meet national policy objectives and, given asymmetries existing with respect to the degree of development of services regulations in different countries, the particular need of developing countries to exercise this right;' [. . .] 'Taking particular account of the serious difficulty of the least-developed countries in view of their special economic situation and their development, trade and financial needs;' [. . .].

[73] GATS Art. III:4: 'Appropriate flexibility with respect to the time-limit [. . .] may be agreed upon for individual developing country Members.'

[74] GATS Art. IV:1: 'The increasing participation of developing country Members in world trade shall be facilitated through negotiated specific commitments [. . .]'; GATS IV:3:, 'Special priority shall be given to the least-developed country Members [. . .]. Particular account shall be taken of the serious difficulty of least-developed countries in accepting

GATS Art. V to PTAs involving a developing country[75] and to South-South PTAs in services.[76] With respect to subsidies, GATS Art. XV:1 establishes more flexibility for developing countries.[77] Furthermore, GATS Art. XIX provides for flexibility with respect to the individual level of development for further rounds of liberalisation.[78] GATS Art. XXV:2, finally, constitutes a legal basis for technical assistance provision to developing countries.[79] Further flexibility is to be found in the Annex on Telecommunications.[80] In 2011 members have agreed to an additional LDC waiver for commitments under the GATS.[81] Since no member took advantage of the waiver, a Ministerial Decision on the operationalisation of the LDC services waiver was adopted in 2013.[82]

As mentioned before, the number of different flexibilities and preferences for developing countries and LDCs is vast. Provisions and flexibilities generally refer to developing countries, which encompasses the group of LDCs. In addition, there are a smaller number of additional provisions that explicitly provide preferences to the LDC group. These SDT provisions are incoherently scattered around the different legal texts of the WTO, which makes it challenging to keep the overview. It seems important to keep in mind that this may negatively affect the ability

negotiated specific commitments in view of their special economic situation and their development, trade and financial needs.'

75 GATS Art. V:3(a): 'Where developing countries are parties to an agreement [. . .] flexibility shall be provided for regarding the conditions set out [. . .]'.

76 GATS Art. V:3(b): '[. . .] in the case of an agreement [. . .] involving only developing countries, more favourable treatment may be granted [. . .]'.

77 GATS XV:1: 'Such negotiations shall recognize the role of subsidies in relation to the development programmes of developing countries and take into account the needs of Members, particularly developing country Members, for flexibility in this area.'

78 GATS XIX:2: 'There shall be appropriate flexibility for individual developing country Members for opening fewer sectors, liberalising fewer types of transactions, progressively extending market access in line with their development situation [. . .]'; GATS XIX:3: 'Negotiating guidelines shall establish modalities [. . .] for the special treatment for least-developed country Members [. . .]'.

79 GATS XXV:2: 'Technical assistance to developing countries shall be provided at the multilateral level by the Secretariat [. . .]'.

80 Annex on Telecommunications 5:(g) and 6.

81 See WTO Briefing Note on the 8th Ministerial Conference in Geneva, 17 December 2011 [Online], available at: www.wto.org/english/news_e/news11_e/serv_17dec11_e.htm; Schloeman, Hannes (2012) 'The LDC Services Waiver: Making It Work', *Bridges Africa Review*, vol. 1, no. 4.

82 See WTO on the Bali Ministerial Declaration and Decisions [Online], available at: www.wto.org/english/thewto_e/minist_e/mc9_e/balipackage_e.htm; and also Stephenson, Sherry and Pfister, Anne-Katrin (2013) 'The LDC Services Waiver beyond Bali', *Bridges Africa Review*, vol. 2, no. 8.

of developing countries and LDCs to apply them in their best interest when interpreting the results of the assessment of the use of SDT in this study.

C. *De Jure versus De Facto*

Some suggest that it would serve developing countries more if they were to assume full responsibilities at the WTO, as this would help locking in domestic reforms and assist sustainable economic growth and development. Developing countries themselves, however, do not agree with the view that SDT has failed to achieve its objective and therefore should be eliminated. Rather than being concerned with the ineffectiveness of the measures, developing countries see a problem in the fact that many SDT measures are 'best-endeavour' clauses, which are in essence voluntary for developed countries. They would instead prefer strengthening SDT provisions by giving them the force of law.[83]

Today, the problem may be that the key issues of multilateral trade liberalisation are no longer centred on tariff reduction but are concerned with the unification of regulation of domestic legislation and other behind-the-border regulatory barriers to trade. Thus, the risk of multilateral rules having a negative impact on economic growth in developing countries has increased, since they may not be capable of guaranteeing and following the same standards as developed countries.[84]

As mentioned before, the group of developing countries in the WTO encompasses some relatively advanced economies such as Singapore, Israel, or Chile. *De jure* there is no doubt that SDT treatment is available to these economies. *De facto* however, it is in some cases questionable whether SDT applies to the right countries. In a way, this contradicts the very idea of SDT and therewith risks eroding the whole concept.

Hoekman, Michalopolous and Winter (2003) therefore suggested to introduce an 'LDC+' group, which would capture those countries in need of SDT, but exclude those countries which are in fact better off by assuming full responsibilities under WTO law.[85] They argue that the fewer countries are eligible for SDT, the more substantial the concessions are likely to be.[86]

[83] Kessie (2007, pp. 34–35).

[84] See also Low, Patrick (2007), 'Is the WTO Doing Enough for Developing Countries?', In: G. A. Bermann and P. C. Mavroidis (eds.), *WTO Law and Developing Countries*, Cambridge University Press, Cambridge, pp. 324–357.

[85] Hoekman et al. (2003). [86] Ibid., p. 27.

Others suggest country-specific evaluations, which would result in tailored packages of individual commitments, temporal exemptions and technical assistance for each developing country in the WTO.[87] Other ideas are rather concerned with a country's capabilities of implementing and enforcing WTO law and suggest that the criteria of who qualifies for SDT be redefined depending on a threshold specific to the application of individual rules. General pre-defined economic needs would, following this idea, automatically identify the countries eligible for and most likely to benefit from SDT.[88]

Many more suggestions on how to fix the gap between the *de jure* system of SDT and the *de facto* outcome have been put forward in recent years.[89] One of the more recent suggestions is to rethink the concept of single undertaking. In a way, this could replace the current SDT system and allow for more of a 'pick and choose membership' in the WTO for those countries that cannot afford to or are not yet capable of complying with the entire body of WTO law.[90]

Cottier (2006) follows a similar logic by introducing the concept of graduation to WTO law: taking into account the different levels of development in the structure and content of the rules themselves would enable a return to the concept of progressive liberalisation and the equal application of single, uniform rules to all members. This would allow abandoning the relatively tiring debate about how to define and depict different groups of countries based on their respective level of development. Rather than opting out of obligations, the concept of graduation aims at gradually phasing in. WTO law would, thus, serve as the basic regime defining the manner and direction of regulatory development and trade liberalisation, but countries' individual social and economic level of development would be factored in as determinant of the individual speed of liberalisation and commitment.[91]

[87] E.g. Prowse, Susan (2002) 'The Role of International and National Agencies in Trade-Related Capacity Building', *The World Economy*, vol. 25, no. 9, pp. 1235–1261.

[88] E.g. Stevens, Christopher (2002), 'The Future of Special and Differential Treatment (S&D) for Developing Countries in the WTO', IDS Working Paper 163, Institute of Development Studies, Sussex; Keck and Low (2004)'.

[89] See for an overview also Hoekman (2005a).

[90] See, e.g. Cottier (2006); Levy, Philippe I. (2006) 'Do We Need an Undertaker for the Single Undertaking? Considering Angles of Variable Geometry', In: S. J. Evenett and B. M. Hoekman (eds.), *Economic Development and Multilateral Cooperation*, The World Bank/Palgrave Macmillan, Washington DC, pp. 417–438; Cornford, Andrew (2004) Variable Geometry for the WTO: Concept and Precedents, Discussion Paper, UNCTAD, Geneva.

[91] Cottier (2006).

Strikingly, the issue of re-thinking the concept of SDT and the pursuit of ideas brought forward by the pre-cited authors have largely disappeared from scholarly publications after 2005. Thus, we are left today with not much more than the insight that the legal position of developing countries in the WTO needs to be reconsidered and that the specific measures targeting at helping developing countries and LDCs to participate in and gain from the global market have so far not led to the results that were intended.

IV. In Summary

Essentially, the distinction in WTO law between LDCs, developing countries and developed countries is arbitrary, arguably with the exception of the group of LDCs. Even though the groups of developing and developed countries are not legally defined categories, WTO law is nevertheless building upon these distinctions. However, in an age of emerging and transforming economies alongside with countries with highly developed and competitive industries in one sector and industries heavily depending on subsidies and imports in another sector, such distinctions are increasingly difficult to substantiate and justify.[92]

Cottier (2006) states that the 'basic idea of looking at countries as whole is increasingly flawed'. He points out that this is a concept, which dates back to the idea of uniform and homogeneous nation states and fails to reflect the fact that through progressive liberalisation of trade and enhanced interdependencies of economies, countries can no longer be captured 'in simple terms of individual uniform nation states'.[93]

This work follows the concept of interdependent, internally heterogeneous countries and departs from perception of single and uniform nation states, which seems inadequate in the 21st century. It takes into consideration that nation states are no longer single, uniform units and that when discussing trade liberalisation in services, foremost the level of development of services sectors is decisive, much more than the general economic situation of a country.

In order to follow the inner logic of SDT, and in consideration of the legal position of developing countries in WTO law, this work follows the concept of graduation in evaluating the legal scope of flexibility for South-South PTAs in services, which would require deeper country- and sector-specific evaluations when implemented: it is submitted

[92] See, e.g. Ibid., p. 789. [93] Ibid., pp. 789–790.

that the scope of flexibility will decrease as the level of development increases.

The categories of 'developing country' and 'LDC' are frequently referred to in WTO law. The term LDC refers to the UN list of LDCs, and the composition of this category is generally undisputed. In addition to the favourable treatment and preferences granted to developing countries in general, LDCs also benefit from individual preferences tailored exclusively to the group of LDCs. It is, however, questionable whether the measures addressing the special needs of LDCs deliver the intended results: most LDCs are, or are becoming, members of the WTO. Yet, despite WTO membership and manifold preferences in the world trading system, the number of LDCs keeps growing and only very few LDCs have managed to graduate from the list.

The composition of the group of 'developing countries' is based on self-declaration by WTO members. The group is quite heterogeneous and large. Arguably, the composition of the group, which includes some countries that may qualify as industrialised, is part of the reason why developed countries are reluctant towards granting substantial preferences to the whole group of developing countries. Nonetheless, the principle of self-declaration is broadly accepted and well embedded in WTO law. While the composition of the group may limit the willingness of developed countries to grant substantial concessions, it cannot be excluded that the measures taken to date further fail to develop the intended developmental effect. In particular, striking the right balance between commitment and flexibility seems to be a major challenge.

Thus, with respect to SDT of LDCs and developing countries, it has been suggested that following the principle of graduation in determining the scope of flexibility and the depth of preferences granted to poor countries could improve developmental outcomes. Graduation can be achieved by taking into account the individual level of development of a country, as well as the individual level of development of a particular economic sector in individual trade rules. Graduation may encourage developed countries to commit to more substantial preferences for developing countries, which in turn might render special and differential treatment more effective.

On the other hand, it remains disputed whether preferences and flexibilities in trade regulation are indeed in the best interest of developing countries and LDCs. SDT as currently established in WTO law has not delivered the intended results. Countries that have successfully managed to escape poverty have indeed done so through trade, but without relying on SDT.

The current multilateral negotiations are primarily concerned with development aspects of trade regulation. Developing countries and LDCs, who have a majority of votes in the WTO, have successfully established a high level of pressure to ensure that their concerns are seriously discussed. This may have slowed down multilateralism in the past ten years, but may potentially ensure that development-oriented trade regulation can no longer have a contrary impact, as observed in some cases in the past. There is widespread consensus concerning the need to adjust the SDT regime, as well as the nature or the composition of the group of developing countries in the WTO.

2

The Rationale for South-South Services Trade

Trade in its various forms is a motor of welfare promotion. Advances in trade have promoted economic growth, which, in turn, has enabled poverty alleviation all around the world.[1] However, for many years, the focus of trade policy in developing countries has been on trade in goods rather than services. With the rapid technological development observed during the last two centuries, the importance of cross-border trade in services for the global economy has risen continually. Hence, trading with services is increasingly being seen as an interesting opportunity for economic development.

While the economic literature has for centuries advocated the importance of trade liberalisation for economic growth,[2] governments tend to remain reluctant to liberalise substantially all of their trade flows.[3] There

[1] Adlung, Rudolf (2007) *The Contribution of Services Liberalisation to Poverty Reduction: What Role for the GATS?*, Economic Research and Statistics Division, WTO, Geneva.

[2] See, e.g. Krueger, Anne O. (1998) 'Why Trade Liberalisation Is Good for Growth', *The Economic Journal*, vol. 108, pp. 1513–1522; Krugman, Paul R. (1979) 'Increasing Returns, Monopolistic Competition, and International Trade', *Journal of International Economics*, vol. 9, no. 4, pp. 469–479; Rodrik, Dani, Subramanian, Arvind and Trebbi, Francesco (2004) 'Institutions Rule: The Primacy of Institutions over Geography and Integration in Economic Development', *Journal of Economic Growth*, vol. 9, pp. 131–165, p. 132; Thrasher, Rachel D. and Gallagher, Kevin P. (2009) '21st Century Trade Agreements: Implications for Development Sovereignty', *Denver Journal of International Law and Policy*, vol. 38, no. 2, pp. 313–350; but also George, Clive and Kirkpatrick, Colin (2004) 'Trade and Development: Assessing the Impact of Trade Liberalisation on Sustainable Development', *Journal of World Trade*, vol. 38, no. 3, pp. 441–469.

[3] See, e.g. Yang, Yongzheng and Gupta, Sanjeev (2005) Regional Trade Arrangements in Africa: Past Performances and the Way Forward, Working Paper, International Monetary Fund, Washington DC; on the history of protectionism in developing countries, see Dornbusch, Rudiger (1992) 'The Case for Trade Liberalisation in Developing Countries', *The Journal of Economic Perspectives*, vol. 6, no. 1, pp. 69–85, pp. 70–73; McGuire, Greg (2002) *Trade in Services – Market Access Opportunities and the Benefits of Liberalisation for Developing Economies*, UNCTAD, Policy Issues in International Trade and Commodities, Study Series No. 19, New York/Geneva, pp. 16–19; Roy et al. (2007).

are several reasons for this observation: the negative impact of trade liberalisation on tariff revenues and on the ability to shape economic policy, as well as the need for structural change that can potentially lead to an increase in unemployment, inequality and poverty.[4] Consequently, keeping the costs of liberalisation to socially and politically acceptable levels is the greatest worry for both developing and industrialised countries. These concerns are rather grounded in the distributional consequences of liberalisation than in net effects, and there are powerful political interests driven by the fear of losses in income for parts of the society.[5]

Tariff revenues are of higher relative importance to low-income countries, since a narrow tax base typically constrains their ability to finance public expenditure. Furthermore, raising tariffs is more practicable for governments than raising taxes.[6] Maintaining the effectiveness of economic policy is also of higher subjective importance for low-income countries, as the prevalence of interventionist trade policies, which tends to strengthen the relative power of the state and the ruling elite, is far higher in less developed (and less democratic) countries. As evidenced by Zahrnt (2009), there is a tendency among developing countries to believe that intervening in the economy is an appropriate job for the government (framing error).[7] Moreover, developing countries tend to lack social security institutions, which would be capable of quickly counterbalancing the effects of trade liberalisation.[8]

Given the aforementioned observations, it is of little surprise that trade liberalisation in the South is accompanied by greater reluctance than in the North. In consequence, developing countries tend to hold overly pessimistic views on the effects of trade liberalisation, which may cause

[4] Zahrnt, Valentin (2009) 'How States Perceive the Costs of Trade Liberalisation in the WTO', *Aussenwirtschaft*, 64; Wolf, Martin (2001) 'Will the Nation-State Survive Globalisation?', *Foreign Affairs*, vol. 80, no. 1, pp. 178–190; Rodrik, Dani (2000) 'How Far Will International Economic Intergration Go?', *The Journal of Economic Perspectives*, vol. 14, no. 1, pp. 177–186.

[5] Zahrnt (2009); Winters, Alan L. (2002) 'Trade Liberalisation and Poverty: What Are the Links?', *The World Economy*, vol. 25, no. 9, pp. 1339–1367; Geddes, Barbara (1995) 'The Politics of Economic Liberalisation', *Latin American Research Review*, vol. 30, no. 2, pp. 195–214; but also Rodrik, Dani (1997) 'Has Globalisation Gone Too Far?', *California Management Review*, vol. 39, no. 3, pp. 29–53.

[6] Aizenmann, Joshua and Jinjarak, Yothin (2009) 'Globalisation and Developing Countries – a Shrinking Tax Base?', *The Journal of Development Studies*, vol. 45, no. 5, pp. 653–671; Konan, Denise E. and Maskus, Keith E. (2006) 'Quantifying the Impact of Services Liberalisation in a Developing Country', *Journal of Development Economics*, vol. 81, pp. 142–162, pp. 143–144.

[7] Zahrnt (2009).

[8] Munin (2010, p. 334).

them to miss out on certain trade-related opportunities for their economic development.[9]

The literature seems to indicate that multilateral trade liberalisation along with unilateral trade liberalisation is the most effective basis for economic development in developing economies.[10] However, with a particular focus on services trade, as opposed to trade in goods, and in consideration of developing countries' reluctance towards trade liberalisation, regional and bilateral approaches may be the more adequate than multilateral or unilateral liberalisation. For example, PTAs in services can take advantage of economies of scale in infrastructure provision and address bilateral or regional issues related to border crossings.[11] Loss of tariff revenue is less of an issue for services trade liberalisation, as from little to no tariffs on services exports are currently in place. While increased competition on infant services industries and related social costs may be considerable in the case of multilateral and unilateral trade liberalisation, services trade liberalisation within a more homogeneous regional or bilateral framework may be more suitable for developing countries.[12]

I. Trade in Services

In a way, trade in services is the most human form of trade. It typically requires direct, personal interaction between human beings, the service provider and the client. The quality of human relationships is a direct attribute of the service provided. Services render our life easier, more comfortable and are part of our daily routine. For example, experiencing true hospitality makes us feel welcome and at ease and actually makes the food taste better.[13] The interaction between people – sometimes even

[9] Zahrnt (2009).

[10] See, e.g. Krueger, Anne (1999) 'The Developing Countries and the Next Round of Multilateral Trade Negotiations', *The World Economy*, vol. 22, no. 7, pp. 909–932, p. 917; Trebilcock, Michael, Howse, Robert and Eliason, Antonia (2012) *The Regulation of International Trade*, 4th edition, Routledge, New York, p. 3.

[11] Newfarmer, Richard (2006) 'Regional Trade Agreements: Designs for Development', In: R. Newfarmer (ed.), *Trade, Doha, and Development: A Window into the Issues*, The World Bank, Washington DC, pp. 243–253, pp. 251–252.

[12] Mattoo, Aaditya and Fink, Carsten (2002) Regional Agreements and Trade in Services: Policy Issues, Policy Research Paper, World Bank, Washington DC, p. 5.

[13] See, e.g. Lashley, Conrad and Morrison, Alison (2011) *In Search of Hospitality: Theoretical Perspectives and Debates*, 2nd edition, Routledge, New York; NZZ (2011) *Der grosse Trumpf des Restaurants ist die Gastfreundschaft*: 'Das Einzige, was in Zukunft wirklich zählen wird, ist die Definition von Gastfreundschaft. Das ist der grosse Trumpf der Gastronomie.'

across continents – is what makes studying trade in services particularly interesting.

On the other hand, trade regulation today is shaping more and more aspects of our life. In a globalised world, services are a key ingredient of successful global value-added chains, enable high-quality production and are required for markets to converge. In an increasingly specialised and globalised economy, know-how is often transferred through services, and hence services lie at the heart of economic performance. Due to their intangibility – and oftentimes their invisibility – they can be depicted as a silent motor that is required for sustainable economic growth. To what extent services continue to shape economic integration worldwide and in which direction depends in large parts on the basic rules of trade regulation.

Trade in services is neither a straightforward nor a uniform concept. For instance, the difficulties in drawing a clear line between the human contribution to a product and a service,[14] as well as in distinguishing between public service and services trade, are key drivers of the subject matter's complexity.[15] Services trade regulation is a relatively recent phenomenon, not only at the global level.[16] Services trade regulation has not yet reached the same level of coherence and comprehensiveness as the regulation of trade in goods, and it is still in the process of development.[17]

Nevertheless, services have been moving into the focus of trade policy, particularly with the emergence of global value-added chains. For integrated global production, cross-border service provision is of essential importance or, so to say, the condition *sine qua non*: managing production as well as sharing information and know-how across borders,

[14] E.g. Is the contribution on an engineer to the product a service or part of the product? Is the transportation of semi-finished products from on site of production to the next a service?

[15] E.g. Is a public–private partnership in telecommunication a service or is it part of public services, and therewith outside of GATS regulation?

[16] The first PTAs mentioning services were the *EC Treaty of Rome* in 1957 and the European economic partnership agreements with developing countries in the 1960s and 1970s. Presumably the first PTA with substantial commitments in trade in services was *ANZCERTA* in 1988, followed by *Canada – US* in the same year. See also Cottier, Thomas, Sieber-Gasser, Charlotte, and Wermelinger, Gabriela (2015) 'The Dialectical Relationship of Preferentialism and Multilateralism', In: M. Elsig and A. Dür (eds.), *Trade Cooperation: The Purpose, Design and Effects of Preferential Trade Agreements*, Cambridge University Press, Cambridge.

[17] See for instance the on-going negotiations on GATS regulation and liberalisation at the WTO based on the Doha mandate, or the European initiative to consider the inclusion of a GATS mode 5 to general service trade regulation (see Cernat and Kutlina-Dimitrova (2014)).

logistics and financial services are central determinants of a global production chain's competitiveness. Without a global net of services, global production would be hard to think of.[18]

Today, there is consensus in defining trade in services as spanning across four modes of supply: cross-border (mode 1), such as consultancy services provided through the delivery of a report from a foreign consultant by e-mail; consumption abroad (mode 2), for instance, hospitality services consumed by tourists during their stay abroad; commercial presence abroad (mode 3), as in financial services provided by local subsidiaries of a foreign bank; and presence of natural persons (mode 4), for example, when a construction company is awarded a contract in a neighbouring country and sends its employees on site to work on the construction site.[19]

Of the four modes of supply, mode 1 and mode 3 account for roughly 35 and 50 per cent, respectively, of world commercial services trade. They are the most common ways to trade services. Mode 2 accounts only for 10–15 per cent and mode 4, the most controversially negotiated mode, accounts for not more than 1–2 per cent of world commercial services trade.[20]

The aforementioned complexities of services do not only affect their tradability, but also complicate their unambiguous definition in legal texts, hence making the regulation of services trade a challenging task: (1) their intangibility makes it difficult to measure and tax services, (2) their non-storability and their need for proximity between customer and producer make it difficult to establish universal rules and (3) the *de facto* joint production together with the customer and the need for customers to participate in the process in some cases make it impossible

[18] See, e.g. Lusch, Robert F. (2011) 'Reframing Supply Chain Management: A Service-Dominant Logic Perspective', *Journal of Supply Chain Management* vol. 47, no. 1, pp. 14–18.

[19] Hoekman, Bernard and Mattoo, Aaditya (2008) 'Services Trade and Growth', In: J. A. Marchetti and M. Roy (eds.) *Opening Markets for Trade in Services*, Cambridge University Press, Cambridge, pp. 21–57, p. 27; Cottier, Thomas, and Oesch, Matthias (2005) *International Trade Regulation*, Staempfli Publishers and Cameron May, Bern and London, p. 827; Diebold, Nicolas F. (2013) *Non-discrimination in International Trade in Services: 'Likeness' in WTO/GATS*, paperback ed., Cambridge University Press, Cambridge, pp. 23–28; WTO Secretariat (2001) *Guide to the GATS*, Kluwer Law International, The Hague, pp. 591–638.

[20] Chaudhuri, Sumanta and Karmakar, Suparna (2008) 'The Liberalisation of Cross-Border Trade in Services: A Developing Country Perspective', In: J. A. Marchetti and M. Roy (eds.), *Opening Markets for Trade in Services*, Cambridge University Press, Cambridge, pp. 184–223.

to distinguish between service provision and consumption.[21] Thus, it doesn't come as a surprise that regulation remains somewhat vague and is difficult to enforce. This is particularly true at the global level.

In the case of services trade regulation, the global benchmark is the General Agreement on Trade in Services, the GATS. The GATS was meant to be a stepping-stone to deeper integration and regulation of global trade in services. It was meant as a first step of many.[22] However, since it came into force in 1995, WTO members have not agreed to another major step towards multilateral trade liberalisation in services. Hence, the degree of global regulation and liberalisation has remained rather basic.

Preferential trade agreements (PTAs) in theory have the advantage of going beyond the limited scope of global consensus. Since the WTO as multilateral forum for trade regulation has, to date, failed to provide additional comprehensive regulation of trade in services, PTAs in services have become an attractive instrument to further develop and broaden the regulation of services trade. Therefore, academics and practitioners around the world are increasingly interested in studying the effects of PTAs in services. To date, however, their primary focus remained on the PTAs among developed countries (North-North), as well as PTAs between developed and developing countries (North-South).[23] Presumably, the interest in PTAs in services among developing countries (South-South) remained low, because they were not considered to be of high priority for developing countries' integration and for deepening their nascent and narrow services markets.[24]

This assumption can only be justified to a limited extent: developing countries acknowledge the potential and importance of a well-functioning

21 Hoekman and Mattoo (2008, p. 27).

22 GATS Art. XIX. See, e.g. Sauvé, Pierre (2008) 'Been There, Not yet Done That: Lessons and Challenges in Services Trade', In: M. Panizzon, N. Pohl and P. Sauvé (eds.), *GATS and the Regulation of International Trade in Services*, Cambridge University Press, Cambridge, pp. 599–631.

23 See, e.g. Fink, Carsten and Jansen, Marion (2008) 'Services Provisions in Regional Trade Agreements: Stumbling Block or Building Blocks for Multilateral Liberalisation?', In: R. Baldwin and P. Low (eds.), *Multilateralising Regionalism: Challenges for the Global Trading System*, Cambridge University Press, New York, pp. 221–261; Roy, Martin, Marchetti, Juan and Lim, Hoe (2007) 'Services Liberalisation in the New Generation of Preferential Trade Agreements (PTAs): How Much Further than the GATS?', *World Trade Review*, vol. 6, no. 2, pp. 155–192; Adlung, Rudolf and Morrison, Peter (2010) 'Less than the GATS: "Negative Preferences" in Regional Services Agreements', *Journal of International Economic Law*, vol. 13, no. 4, pp. 1103–1143.

24 Cernat, Lucian (2003) *Assessing South-South Regional Integration: Same Issues, Many Metrics*, Study Series No. 21, UNCTAD, Geneva, p. 6.

services market for economic development and for the productivity of the entire economy.[25] Furthermore, the level of frustration with the global negotiations, in which developed countries refuse to give up their advantages in services trade, is growing.[26] This has fostered developing countries' interest in further strengthening their services sectors. Not all but some have teamed up with other developing countries in the past fifteen years, and more and more innovative regulation in services trade emerges in these non-traditional services markets.

In addition, the GATS provides flexibility for establishing South-South PTAs in services. This should allow developing countries to better tailor South-South PTAs in services to their individual needs. The exact scope of flexibility has, however, not yet been studied in detail. Taken together with the emergence of ever more South-South PTAs in services, it therefore seems timely to study the interdependence of GATS regulation with preferential services trade liberalisation among developing countries.

While this study primarily sets out to analyse South-South PTAs in services from a legal perspective, it is firmly embedded in a body of economic and political science research on the subject. The following section seeks to provide a short overview of this literature.

A. The GATS

Following long and difficult negotiations, more than 100 members of the General Agreement on Tariffs and Trade (GATT) signed the Final Act of the Uruguay Round in Marrakesh on 15 April 1994. One of the most important achievements of the negotiations was the GATS. It forms an integral part of the Agreement Establishing the WTO, which was established by the Uruguay Round.[27] Due to the principle of 'single-undertaking', all members of the WTO are also members of the GATS.[28]

[25] Fugazza, Marco and Vanzetti, David (2006) *A South-South Survival Strategy: The Potential for Trade among Developing Countries* Study Series No. 33, UNCTAD, Geneva.

[26] See e.g. Adlung, Rudolf (2006a) 'Services Negotiations in the Doha Round: Lost in Flexibility?', *Journal of International Economic Law*, vol. 9, no. 4, pp. 865–893.

[27] Barth, Dietrich (1999) *The Prospects of International Services Trade*, Friedrich Ebert Stiftung, Bonn, p. 45.

[28] Wolfe, Robert (2009) 'The WTO Single Undertaking as Negotiating Technique and Constitutive Metaphor', *Journal of International Economic Law*, vol. 12, no. 4, pp. 835–858, p. 843: 'No Member can pick and choose among the elements of the system, and "reservations" are not allowed for existing or new Members. The Single Undertaking, in other words, reinforces the general nondiscrimination norm by requiring all Members to apply all the agreements with respect to all other Members.'

The GATS is the first legally enforceable multilateral agreement on trade in services. Contrary to the GATT and other agreements relating to trade in goods, little bilateral or plurilateral regulation of trade in services existed before the emergence of the GATS. Thus, the GATS is not only the first multilateral agreement on trade in services, it can also be considered a pioneer for the regulation of trade in services.[29]

The pressure to negotiate a multilateral agreement on trade in services came mostly from industrialised countries, such as the US and Europe. These countries had a strong interest in opening the world's markets for services, as their services sectors were steadily growing and international trade in services had become a substantial source of foreign income for them. Initially, developing countries strongly opposed to the idea of multilateral services trade liberalisation, but they finally joined the negotiations. Among other reasons, this decision was driven by the realisation that a coherent regulation of trade liberalisation in services was necessary.[30]

In general, the GATS covers all services except for air transport and services supplied under government authority. In order to organise services trade, the GATS includes a list of twelve major services sectors,[31] divided in further subsectors. The GATS was also a key driver in establishing the aforementioned modes of supply of services. The regulation of trade in services along these four modes of supply has become generally accepted and is reflected in all subsequently negotiated PTAs in services. In order to best meet the needs of modern trade in services, the GATS furthermore reaches beyond the traditional concept of trade and touches upon behind-the-border or domestic regulation, labour migration and investment issues.[32]

The GATS is built on two pillars of liberalisation, the Most-Favoured Nation (MFN) treatment and the individual schedules of commitments

[29] Cottier et al. (2015). [30] Barth (1999, p. 45).

[31] GATS Art. XX: Business Services, Communication Services, Construction and Other Engineering Services, Distribution Services, Educational Services, Environmental Services, Financial Services, Health-related and Social Services, Tourism and Travel-related Services, Recreational, Cultural and Sporting Services, Transport Services, and Other Services.

[32] This is primarily linked to GATS mode 3 and mode 4 supply of services and has sparked controversies on the remaining regulatory freedom of WTO members. See also Natens, Bregt and Wouters, Jan (2013) The Scope of GATS and of Its Obligations, Working Paper, Leuven Centre for Global Governance Studies, Leuven; Krajewski, Markus (2003) *National Regulation and Trade Liberalisation in Services*, Kluwer Law International, The Hague.

in liberalisation. The MFN treatment obliges members of the GATS to automatically and unconditionally grant all trade preferences, which they provide to any other country, to all other members of the GATS. The individual list of liberalisation commitments, called Schedules, fix the legally binding individual level of liberalisation per sector and subsector for each member of the GATS. Listed commitments in market access and national treatment in general cannot be reversed once a country has joined the GATS.[33]

As of March 2016, the WTO has 162 members, with a number of countries waiting to join. For all member countries, the provisions and obligations of the GATS apply. The concessions made by any WTO member in its PTAs in services are thus automatically extended to all members of the WTO, unless they are exempted from MFN. GATS Art. V establishes an exemption from MFN for PTAs, which meet certain requirements. Any preferential trade agreement involving one member of the WTO must, thus, fulfil the requirements established in GATS Art. V for justifying an exemption from MFN treatment. This is equally true for South-South PTAs in services, as for any other PTA. Therefore any discussion of South-South preferential services trade regulation has to include a discussion of the MFN obligation and exemption as established by the GATS. In other words, the GATS – and in particular the provisions of GATS Art. V – constitutes the regulatory framework for any preferential services trade regulation.

B. *Preferential Trade Agreements in Services and Developing Countries*

There are, of course, multiple avenues for developing countries and LDCs to take advantage of the economic potential that arguably lies within services trade liberalisation. The largest body of literature on PTAs in services involving developing countries has, thus far, focused on the economic potential embedded in North-South services trade integration.[34]

[33] Deconsolidation according to the process established by GATS Art. XXI is a possibility, however, a costly one.

[34] See e.g. Roy, Marchetti and Lim (2007); Horn, Henrik, Mavroidis, Petros C. and Sapir, André (2010) 'Beyond the WTO? An Anatomy of EU and US Preferential Trade Agreements', *The World Economy*, vol. 33, no. 11, pp. 1565–1588; Manger, Mark S. (2009) *Investing in Protection: The Politics of Preferential Trade Agreements between North and South*, Cambridge University Press, Cambridge; but also De Melo, Jaime (2007) 'Regionalism and Developing Countries: A Primer', *Journal of World Trade*, vol. 41, no. 2, pp. 351–369.

Another body of literature looks at the potential of unilateral trade liberalisation in services for developing countries and LDCs.[35] Both these avenues are more profoundly researched than the case of South-South PTAs in services.

The disinterest in South-South PTAs in services shown by the research community to date has a number of reasons. Generally, services exports continue to account for only a fraction of overall exports from developing countries.[36] Services trade integration among weaker economies also remains relatively rare and constitutes a recent phenomenon. Furthermore, reliable and coherent data on services trade is rare, particularly in developing countries.[37] Economists and political scientists have, thus, rather focused on the areas of services trade in which data exist and where economic relevance is proven.

However, it seems important and timely to deepen the understanding of South-South services trade integration. This should enable policymakers in developing countries to adjust their trade policies in the most sustainable and productive manner. For some developing countries, South-South services trade integration might be more suitable than for others.

That there is an increasing interest of developing countries and LDCs to be involved in South-South PTAs in services is, however, proved by the increasing number of South-South PTAs, which include also services trade integration. The advantage of a legal study on South-South PTAs in services is that the existing agreements can be analysed and studied, even though their actual impact on trade relations and trade volumes in the South may be disputed in certain cases.

From a literature review, in terms of their contribution to economic development for the countries involved, three major aspects of a South-South PTA in services stand out: the comparative economic strength of the parties, the geographic proximity of the parties, as well as the interdependency of their economies.

Services trade integration among countries with comparative strengths in the services sector has a potential to create potent market access for infant services industries, while at the same time increasing the quality of services and infrastructure in the PTA overall.[38] Since economic development in LDCs tends to be hampered by weak infrastructure and

35 See, e.g. Krueger (1999, p. 917); Trebilcock, Howse and Eliason (2012).

36 See e.g. Gabriele, Alberto (2004) Exports of Services and Economic Growth in Developing Countries, Report, UNCTAD; see for specific data World Bank Databank on Trade in Services.

37 See e.g. WTO (2012) *International Trade Statistics 2012*, WTO, Geneva, p. 4.

38 Mattoo and Fink (2002).

a low level of services quality, and as LDCs tend to benefit disproportionally from integrating their services markets with other developing countries, South-South PTAs in services could be of particular developmental attractiveness for LDCs.[39]

Geographic proximity is furthermore seen as crucial for the establishment of a well-functioning PTA in services. As mentioned before, services trade requires close interaction between people. Geographic and cultural proximity would hence support the effectiveness of services trade. Furthermore, it has been shown that some of the services subsectors with the highest relevance for economic development, such as business services and education, along with mode 4 supply of services better support economic growth when integrated at a regional, rather than at the global level.[40] Consequently, South-South PTAs in services can be expected to have a stronger developmental effect if they are restricted to one continent.

A South-South PTA in services will also have a greater developmental impact for the countries involved, the stronger and more integrated industrial production is between these countries. Services trade integration will in this case increase value-added production in said industries, as competition and quality increase, and the industries have the opportunity to locate and position their production sites where it is economically most sensible. While value-added production increases, trade in services and goods also naturally follow because of the closer integration of the economies involved.[41]

II. Development Effect of Services Trade

For a long time, services have been seen as a by-product of economic development through trade liberalisation in goods. More recently,

[39] See, e.g. Simo, Regis Y. (2013) 'Integrating African Markets into the Global Exchange of Services: A Central African Perspective', *The Law and Development Review*, vol. 6, no. 2, pp. S255–S297.

[40] See, e.g. Park, Innwon and Park, Soonchan (2011) 'Regional Liberalisation of Trade in Services', *The World Economy*, vol. 34, no. 5, pp. 725–740.

[41] Clancy, Michael (1998) 'Commodity Chains, Services and Development: Theory and Preliminary Evidence from the Tourism Industry', *Review of International Political Economy*, vol. 5, no. 1, pp. 122–148; Langhammer, Rolf J. (2006) Service Trade Liberalisation as a Handmaiden of Competitiveness in Manufacturing: An Industrialised or Developing Country Issue?, Kiel Working Paper, The Kiel Institute for the World Economy, Kiel; Whalley, John (2003) Assessing the Benefits to Developing Countries of Liberalisation in Services Trade, NBER Working Paper, OECD, Paris; related is also the role of GATS mode 4 supply in fostering value-added production, see Saxenian, AnnaLee (2002) *Local and Global Networks of Immigrant Professionals in Silicon Valley*, Public Policy Institute of California, San Francisco.

scholars have also started focusing on the impact of the services industry on economic growth, proving that efficient services are important determinants for economic growth.[42] Furthermore, with technological advancements, many products traditionally understood as non-tradable have become tradable not only across the borders of neighbouring countries, but across the globe. Data entry was the first service activity to be internationally outsourced, followed by software programming. While these particular services remain highly sensitive to technological change – as human input can increasingly be replaced by new software[43] – services exports in general continue to grow strongly worldwide.[44]

The relative contribution of services to GDP and employment tends to rise as per capita income increases. As of 2004, services accounted for as little as 35 per cent of GDP in numerous LDCs, compared to around 45 per cent of GDP in low-income, 60 per cent in upper-middle-income countries and values over 70 per cent in some OECD countries.[45] The competitiveness of firms is increasing based on access to low-cost and high-quality producer services (such as telecommunication, transportation or finance), in addition to efficient and effective public governance institutions.[46] Thus, strong economies tend to rely more heavily on strong services industries, while economic growth is also related more closely to the accessibility of low-cost and high-quality services. It is not surprising that, according to more recent numbers dating from 2008, the global share of services in GDP has further risen to approximately 50 per cent.[47]

Since developing countries generally tend to suffer from a weak services infrastructure and a heavily constrained access to high-quality services, trade liberalisation in services may be a substantial contributor to poverty reduction: (1) most of trade in one way or another depends on the availability of services, (2) the positive effects of liberalisation of services trade are greater and more immediate because goods trade is already quite liberalised globally, (3) services as intermediates can boost many related sectors and (4) services trade liberalisation will cause small losses of government revenue as there are usually no tariffs on services trade.[48]

[42] See, e.g. Whalley (2003) and Langhammer (2006).

[43] Primo Braga, Carlos A. (1996), 'The Impact of the Internationalisation of Services on Developing Countries', *Finance & Development*, March 1996, pp. 34–37, p. 36.

[44] E.g. UNCTAD (2015) News Release, 14 April 2015: "In 2014, world merchandise exports grew by 0.6%, while trade in services recorded a 4.2% global increase".

[45] Australian Government (2004) *South-South Trade: Winning from Liberalisation*, Department of Foreign Affairs and Trade, Barton, p. 14.

[46] Hoekman and Mattoo (2008).

[47] Chaudhuri and Karmakar (2008). [48] Adlung (2007).

The level of regulation and liberalisation in services trade is marked by great heterogeneity among different segments of the services sector: while markets for certain services tend to be substantially open (e.g. tourism), others are typically closed (e.g. education). Some restrictions apply not only to foreigners, but also to domestic suppliers. This is particularly true in the case of the wider infrastructure space, which was for a long time perceived as belonging in the remit of the government, and tended to be monopolistically organised.

Competition in certain segments of the services sectors is typically kept low despite empirical research indicating a clear positive link between trade liberalisation in services and economic growth. For example, it has been shown that countries with partially open telecommunications and financial services sectors grow on average about 1 per cent faster than other countries. Even more, full liberalisation of these two sectors is associated with 1.5 per cent faster growth. The strong productivity-enhancing role of other services suggests that these findings can be extrapolated to other segments of the services sector. Consequently, better productivity performance in the services sector should bring about overall economic growth.[49]

As shown in this section, trade openness stimulates services performance, which in turn stimulates overall productivity of the economy. Growth and diversification of the services sector are both preconditions and consequences of economic growth. Because the gains from services and goods trade liberalisation appear to be additive, combining both goods and services trade liberalisation seems to be the most promising road to economic growth.[50]

Hence, for developing countries, services trade liberalisation is attributed with lower adjustment costs and more evenly distributed welfare gains than liberalisation of goods trade. Prohibitions in services trade are rarely revenue generating, but rather constitute technical barriers to trade, and can hence be abolished at a lower opportunity cost.[51] Trade liberalisation in services is expected to boost their exports of both services and goods, while also contributing to the diversification of the local service offering and attracting additional foreign direct investment.[52]

49 Hoekman and Mattoo (2008). 50 Konan and Maskus (2006, pp. 18–19).

51 Mattoo and Carsten (2002, p. 26).

52 Dihel, Nora, Eschenbach, Felix, and Shepherd, Ben (2008) 'South-South Services Trade', In: M. Panizzon, N. Pohl and P. Sauvé (eds.), *GATS and the Regulation of International Trade in Services*, Cambridge University Press, New York, pp. 23–76, p. 72.

III. Controversies of Preferential Services Trade

Multilateralism and preferentialism have grown in parallel over the years. In the case of services trade regulation, multilateralism set the initial stage for services trade regulation through the GATS, with increasing preferentialism following thereafter.[53] While other multilateral trade agreements, such as the GATT or the TRIPS, were based on experiences of a regulatory evolution in preferential agreements over the years, the GATS came into force at a time when only a handful of preferential agreements had attempted to regulate services trade. What is often called the 'spaghetti-bow effect' – the effect that too many PTAs may have a negative impact on the regulation – was, thus, not an issue globally when the GATS was negotiated. In the meantime, the number of PTAs in services has grown exponentially, and many authors now talk of a 'spaghetti-bowl effect' in services trade regulation as well.[54]

Increasing preferentialism can also be seen as a positive force for multilateral liberalisation, as the number of PTAs in services is an indicator for the general interest in further liberalisation, including at the multilateral level. Generally, liberalisation is expected to continue expanding ('domino regionalism'). However, it is posited that multilateralism in trade regulation in services will increasingly turn to behind-the-border regulatory issues and will be less focused on liberalisation. As high preferences degrees in PTAs may in general reduce the interest in multilateralism,[55] and as substantial multilateral trade liberalisation in services currently seems less realistically achievable, given the rapidly increasing number of WTO members involved in PTAs in services, commitments in trade liberalisation in services may in the long term shift from the multilateral to the preferential level.[56]

Items typically exported by developing countries, such as low-tech manufactured products, globally tend to face higher tariffs, whereas low-tariff products, such as capital goods, generally come from developed countries.[57] Furthermore, the flexibility in terms of commitments to trade liberalisation granted to developing countries by WTO regulation has mostly been used to protect their infant industries rather than to liberalise trade.[58] Around 70 per cent of the tariffs faced by developing

[53] Cottier et al. (2015). [54] E.g. Fink and Jansen (2008, p. 237).

[55] Agu, Chukwuma (2009) 'Multilateralism, Regionalism and the Paradox of the "Spaghetti Bowl" in Developing Countries', *Aussenwirtschaft*, 64, pp. 293–316.

[56] See also Cottier et al. (2015). [57] Australian Government (2004, p. 4).

[58] Adlung (2006a).

country exporters are applied by other developing countries.[59] According to economic literature, lowering these trade barriers would enable the South to participate more fully in global production chains and would create opportunities to engage in higher value-added activities.

In addition, even though the number of South-South PTAs is constantly growing, intra-regional trade in the South is in relative decline. South-South trade was growing until 1995, the year of the establishment of the WTO, and has since been declining. This decline of intra-regional trade in the South is unlikely to have been caused by geographical or infrastructural hindrances to trade, as these have hardly changed since 1995. Hence, it seems more likely that economic integration treaties in the South have been signed with political, rather than economic, motives.[60]

Nonetheless, PTAs are expected to constitute an appropriate tool for liberalising trade among developing countries: in PTAs, more efficient bargaining should be possible, and regulatory cooperation should be more easily achievable.[61] Furthermore, PTAs are generally faster to negotiate due to the lower number of parties involved, and they provide for more policy space than multilateralism.[62]

For most developing countries, meeting the requirements for PTAs in services as established by GATS Art. V (to qualify for the so-called GATS-plus status), while at the same time ensuring that their PTAs meet their economic needs, seems to be a challenge. This may be due to the lack of capacity, knowledge and experience in dealing with such conflicting constraints in trade negotiations. The complex WTO-plus arrangements seem to be challenging for developing countries and are thus not abided by. The comparatively high level of lack of compliance with the law in general in these countries may also play its role in shaping this finding.[63] In consequence, PTAs in services among developing countries tend to either suffer from weak structural design or to be of limited economic relevance.

Some argue that South-South PTAs can serve as a training ground to prepare local industries for broad-based liberalisation in the future, while at the same time strengthening the local industries through increased competition. Others, however, point to the low complementarities of natural endowments, small markets, as well as administrative capacity constraints in many developing countries. They argue that South-South PTAs should be rendered more open to the rest of the world through

[59] Australian Government (2004, p. ix). [60] Agu (2009).
[61] Mattoo and Fink (2002, p. 5). [62] Agu (2009). [63] Ibid.

non-discriminatory liberalisation.[64] Mattoo and Fink (2002) argue in the same direction by highlighting that multilateral liberalisation is always in the best interest of economic growth in developing countries. In their view, global competition ensures that the best supplier worldwide provides the required services.[65] With respect to PTAs in services involving a developing country or an LDC, however, Mattoo and Fink (2002) support the view that South-South PTAs tend to be even more productive than North-South: they view the greatest benefits from regional economic integration as being achievable when countries with comparable regulations join forces in the liberalisation process, as this should maximise both competition and diversity.[66]

Turning to the policy preferences of developing countries, it is obvious that they prefer seeking access to developed country markets through the establishment of North-South PTAs, as opposed to South-South economic integration. This is particularly true on the African continent. Foreign partners from the North are seen as more interesting, because aid, FDI or other advantages tend to be tied to their North-South PTAs. In general, when regional and multilateral economic integration stand in competition with each other, the allegiance of developing countries usually goes with multilateralism, as the latter is perceived as promising greater gains and has a powerful international lobby.[67] To date, North-South trade agreements also seem to be economically more beneficial to developing countries than South-South trade agreements – at least in the short run.[68] This may, however, also be a reflection of the state of South-South PTAs. They typically develop little to no effect on trade, while member countries nevertheless suffer from an overall reduction of welfare due to a limited loss of tariff revenue.[69]

As argued above, political considerations may sometimes outweigh economic interests for the conclusion of a PTA. In the case of South-South PTAs in services, some argue that 'broadening the area of influence' ranks as among the top incentives for a developing country or an LDC to join a South-South PTA.[70] While this is very difficult to measure, it is generally acknowledged that PTAs comprise political goals such as 'bolstering democracy', 'strengthening the negotiating position on an international level' and 'dealing with outside threats and regional hegemons'. Political aspects of PTAs seem to be the main reason for their

[64] Yang and Gupta (2005, pp. 37–38). [65] Mattoo and Fink (2002, p. 26).
[66] Mattoo and Fink (2002, p. 13). [67] Agu (2009).
[68] De Melo (2007, pp. 357–358). [69] De Melo (2007). [70] Agu (2009).

popularity, while economic efficiency considerations suggest that PTAs are inferior to multilateral trade liberalisation.[71] What remains unclear is whether PTAs indeed deliver on the political side. For instance, for PTAs to develop a true 'conflict-preventing' effect, they would typically have to increase interdependency by strengthening intra-regional trade. Similarly, 'increasing the bargaining power' at the international level through PTAs would require member countries to focus on common interests, which has not been the case for African countries in recent negotiations.[72]

To summarise, there are good reasons for promoting the conclusion of South-South PTAs in services, but these can also be seen as unnecessary as long as multilateralism advances and unilateral liberalisation is undertaken. Developing countries and LDCs themselves seem to be less interested in South-South trade integration than in accessing industrialised country markets. Arguably, this policy orientation misses some valuable opportunities to support economic growth and poverty alleviation in these countries.

[71] De Melo (2007, p. 355). [72] Yang and Gupta (2005), p. 25.

3

The Quest of this Study

While economists and political scientists have devoted quite some attention to South-South PTAs in services, these agreements have to date largely remained outside of the scope of attention of legal scientists. Hence, as a starting point, this book sets out to take stock of the existing South-South PTAs in services.

Trade regulation in services well illustrates the challenges and difficulties faced by the legal system when the subject of regulation remains vague and complex. By studying how the GATS, the WTO in general and the PTAs in particular meet this challenge, this study also intends to create a better understanding of the dynamics between regulation and regulator in international trade law.

The legal analysis of South-South trade integration in services presented in this book also aims to provide a basis for further political and economic research on the subject. On the one hand, trade liberalisation in services tends to be closely tied to the deepening of political integration, as opposed to the liberalisation of trade in goods. Hence, the analysis of compliance provided by this study should be of value for political scientists who want to further study the subject. On the other hand, economists have shown that South-South trade liberalisation in services should support sustainable economic development in developing countries. Therefore, the comparison between theory and reality performed by this book will hopefully enable economists to further study the linkages between South-South services trade and development.

Finally, international law is often challenged by a lack of compliance and therewith a lack of significance – particularly in the global South. As some have argued, PTAs may provide the necessary policy space to render international law enforceable. This study seeks to derive some insights for the institutional setting of the multilateral trading system from the study of a number of South-South PTAs.

I. South-South in this Study

With respect to their services markets, developing countries and LDCs form a very heterogeneous group: compared to developed countries, the share of developing countries in global services trade is minor. While some developing countries export substantially less services than goods, others 'rely on the profits gained from international trade in services, to offset the deficits caused by their international trade in goods.'[1] In recent years, the available economic data show a more rapid growth in services trade in Asia compared to other developing countries.[2]

Services exports of developing countries are traditionally concentrated in tourism and other labour-intensive services,[3] which reflects their comparative advantage profile. As discussed above, developed countries tend to have much stronger services sectors in comparison with developing countries. Therefore, LDCs and developing countries have been more reluctant towards opening their services sectors unilaterally or in the context of North-South trade liberalisation.

On a South-South basis, the risk for domestic services providers of being forced out of the market by increased competition is more limited, given the similarities in the participating countries' level of economic development. In addition, the economic potential of South-South trade in services is not primarily located in high numbers of exported services, but rather in the positive side effects of trade liberalisation in services for the participating countries: better quality of services and infrastructure are expected to foster value-added production.

To date, only few LDCs have participated in services trade liberalisation among developing countries. Hence, in order to render any analysis of preferential services trade in a South-South context meaningful, it seems important to include all developing countries in such analysis. However, for the reasons mentioned in the preceding sections, it seems inappropriate to include all 'developing countries' simply based on their self-declaration under the WTO.

[1] Munin (2010, p. 319).

[2] See for specific data World Bank Databank on Trade in Services; more generally see Park, Donghyun and Noland, Marcus (2013) *Developing the Service Sector as an Engine of Growth for Asia*, Asian Development Bank, Manila.

[3] Hodge, James (2002) 'Liberalisation of Trade in Services in Developing Countries', In: B. M. Hoeckman, A. Mattoo and P. English (eds.), *Development, Trade and the WTO: A Handbook*, The World Bank, Washington DC, pp. 221–234, p. 223.

The ideal dataset for a study on South-South PTAs in services would comprise sectorial information on the different levels of regulation and economic performance beyond the boundaries of nation states. Given that research and the global community continue to divide the world into nation states, and nation states into developed and developing countries, and given that sectorial data of the required granularity is not available, substantiating the term 'South-South' based on information on the performance and regulation of individual services sectors does not seem like a realistic approach.[4]

The next best basis for substantiating 'South-South' was the OECD-list of Official Development Assistance (ODA) recipients.[5] This list is regularly updated and consists of a more sophisticated measurement than GDP per capita. However, it does not reflect the level of development of the services industries in these countries. Yet, it seems to provide an appropriate basis for the analysis, as it constitutes a generally acknowledged, well-established classification system of countries that struggle with providing the most essential public functions.

While the list of developing countries and therewith the basis for establishing whether a country belongs to the South or not is taken as such, later in the evaluation and discussion of the flexibilities of WTO law for South-South PTAs in services, a distinction is suggested of the scope of flexibility relative to the economic development of the services sectors in question. This seemed an elegant way of focusing on the poorest countries while acknowledging that even poor countries may possess strong services industries.

A. *South Status: A Substantiated List of Developing Countries*

As elaborated above, this study takes the OECD DAC list of ODA recipients, effective for reporting on 2014, 2015 and 2016 flows,[6] as the basis for the qualification of a PTA under South-South. The list shows the countries and territories, which are eligible to receive ODA. Besides the LDCs as defined by the UN, it includes low- and middle-income countries

[4] It is likely that, even if such data had been accessible, it would have required a thorough substantiation of why this data was used for this thesis instead of the classic idea of 'South' being equal to a developing country. The general idea of a global divide into North as the rich and South as the poor is still dominant in our inner global atlases.

[5] OECD (2015) DAC List of ODA Recipients: Effective for reporting on 2014, 2015 and 2016 flows.

[6] Ibid.

based on GNI as published by the World Bank. It does not include the members of the G8,[7] the EU[8] and countries with a firm date for the entry into the EU.[9] The list is revised by the DAC every three years. Countries that have exceeded the high-income threshold for three consecutive years are removed from the list.

The list in Table 2 well illustrates that, although a considerable number of LDCs and developing countries have concluded substantial PTAs in services, they are still a minority: of the 148 countries and territories listed, just a third (54) have done so. Considering that well-established regional preferential services trade integration requires more than just one agreement, it is likely that, overall, South-South services trade remains a limited phenomenon.

Table 2 also well illustrates that substantial South-South services trade integration is not restricted to emerging economies alone: at least fifteen LDCs have already concluded a substantial South-South PTA in services. This is remarkable, since services industries in LDCs tend to be particularly weak.[10] Governments of LDCs therefore tend to fear the social costs of additional competition and are reluctant vis-à-vis particular South-South trade integration.[11] At the same time, as discussed above, LDCs could potentially benefit disproportionally from South-South PTAs in services.

Furthermore, Table 2 shows that, without exception, all developing countries and LDCs that are members of a South-South PTA in services are also members of the WTO. Consequently, the general minimum level of liberalisation as provided under the GATS is in any case already established among the members of South-South PTAs. Two-thirds (104) of the countries listed above are WTO members. While it is remarkable that no

[7] Group of Eight (G8) consists of eight of the world's largest economies. Members are Canada, France, Germany, Italy, Japan, Russia, United Kingdom and the United States.

[8] In 2015, members of the EU were Austria, Belgium, Bulgaria, Croatia, Cyprus, Czech Republic, Denmark, Estonia, Finland, France, Germany, Greece, Hungary, Ireland, Italy, Latvia, Lithuania, Luxembourg, Malta, Netherlands, Poland, Portugal, Romania, Slovakia, Slovenia, Spain, Sweden and the United Kingdom.

[9] There are currently no candidate countries with a firm date for accession to the EU. See European Commission (2015) *Enlargement: Countries preparing to join* [Online], available at: http://ec.europa.eu/enlargement/countries/check-current-status/index_en.htm.

[10] South-South PTAs in services involving LDCs are the West African Economic and Monetary Union (WAEMU), the agreement between the Association of Southeast Asian Nations (ASEAN) and China, the Caribbean Community (CARICOM), and the East African Community (EAC).

[11] See, e.g. Winters, Alan L. (2002) 'Trade Liberalisation and Poverty: What Are the Links?', *The World Economy*, vol. 25, no. 9, pp. 1339–1367.

Table 2 *DAC list of ODA recipients*[a]

Least Developed Countries	Other Low-Income Countries	Lower Middle-Income Countries	Upper Middle-Income Countries
Afghanistan	**Kenya***	Armenia*	Albania*
Angola*	Korea, Dem. Rep.	**Bolivia***	Algeria
Bangladesh*	Tajikistan*	Cameroon*	**Antigua and Barbuda***
Benin*	Zimbabwe*	Cape Verde*	**Argentina***
Bhutan		Congo, Rep.*	Azerbaijan
Burkina Faso*		**Côte d'Ivoire***	Belarus
Burundi*		Egypt*	**Belize***
Cambodia*		**El Salvador***	Bosnia and Herzegovina
Central African Rep.*		Georgia*	Botswana*
Chad*		Ghana*	**Brazil***
Comoros		**Guatemala***	**Chile***
Congo, Dem. Rep.*		**Guyana***	**China***
Djibouti*		**Honduras***	**Colombia***
Equatorial Guinea		**India***	Cook Islands
Eritrea		**Indonesia***	**Costa Rica***
Ethiopia		Kosovo	**Cuba***
Gambia*		Kyrgyzstan*	**Dominica***
Guinea*		Micronesia	**Dominican Republic***
Guinea-Bissau*		Moldova*	Ecuador*
Haiti*		Mongolia*	Fiji*
Kiribati		Morocco*	Former Yugoslav Republic of Macedonia*
Laos*		**Nicaragua***	Gabon*
Lesotho		Nigeria*	**Grenada***
Liberia		**Pakistan***	Iran
Madagascar*		Papua New Guinea*	Iraq
Malawi*		**Paraguay***	**Jamaica***
Mali*		**Philippines***	Jordan*
Mauritania*		Samoa*	Kazakhstan
Mozambique*		Sri Lanka*	Lebanon
Myanmar*		Swaziland*	Libya
Nepal*		Syria	**Malaysia***
Niger*		Tokelau	Maldives*
Rwanda*		Ukraine*	Marshall Islands
São Tomé and Príncipe **Senegal***		Uzbekistan	Mauritius*
Sierra Leone*		**Vietnam***	**Mexico***
Solomon Islands*		West Bank and Gaza Strip	Montenegro*
Somalia			**Montserrat**
South Sudan			Namibia*
Sudan			Nauru
Tanzania*			Niue
Timor-Leste			Palau
Togo*			**Panama***
			Peru*

Table 2 (*cont.*)

Least Developed Countries	Other Low-Income Countries	Lower Middle-Income Countries	Upper Middle-Income Countries
Tuvalu			Serbia
Uganda*			Seychelles*
Vanuatu*			South Africa*
Yemen*			St. Helena
Zambia*			**St. Kitts-Nevis***
			St. Lucia*
			St. Vincent and Grenadines*
			Suriname*
			Thailand*
			Tonga*
			Tunisia*
			Turkey*
			Turkmenistan
			Uruguay*
			Venezuela*
			Wallis and Futuna

Sources: Derived from OECD (2015); WTO (2013); and DESTA (2013).
The countries marked with a * are WTO members. Countries in bold script have concluded a substantial PTA (A substantial PTA means here a PTA, which establishes substantial commitments in preferential trade liberalisation in services) in services with another country featuring on the list.
[a] OECD (2015) DAC list of ODA recipients: effective for reporting on 2014, 2015 and 2016 flows.

country in the list has entered into a South-South PTA in services with a non-member of the WTO, it is also interesting to note that only half of the developing country members of the WTO have engaged in South-South PTAs in services. This may be understood as an indicator that membership in the WTO alone is not decisive for the general openness of an economy.

Finally, Table 2 above shows that the group of countries involved in South-South PTAs in services is very diverse, with only a limited degree of comparability. For instance, the services industry of Mali most definitely is facing different challenges than the services industries in Brazil and China. This may, however, also simply be a reflection of the heterogeneity of countries featured on the OECD DAC list. This diversity is not only a challenge for the analysis, it is also an advantage – this list, given that there are South-South PTAs in services in all different subgroups of LDCs and developing countries, allows to link preferences in services trade integration to the country level of economic development. It also allows testing the validity of economic and political theory with respect to services trade policy for developing countries: did countries that engaged early in South-South PTAs in services indeed fare better economically than those who did not? In order to enable performing such analyses, the set of South-South PTAs in services used in this study has not been further narrowed.

II. Gap in Literature and Why Understanding South-South Services Trade Matters

The dynamics of PTAs in services among developing countries and LDCs has not yet been studied empirically. This may have been understandable until a few years back, as the developments in services trade regulation in the global South remained punctual and limited to a few countries. However, in recent years, developing countries engage more and more in preferential services trade regulation, not only with developed countries, but also with partners from other developing economies. Putting the legal development in services trade regulation stemming from South-South PTAs in services on the map of International Economic Law (IEL) and raising awareness for the growing body of South-South services trade regulation are therefore timely. Given how multilateralism struggles with trade negotiations in services – and the related conflicts of interest between developed and developing countries – understanding the regional dynamics in this particular area of trade regulation should also be of value with a global perspective.

Furthermore, a number of political scientists and economists[12] write about the potential positive impact of South-South preferential trade in services. While there seems to be consensus on the desirability of economic integration in services trade among developing countries, just a handful of legal scholars have taken up the issue and studied the related legal aspects. Further deepening this legal analysis seems important, since any attempts at implementing the economic and political theories will face a certain number of legal constraints and considerations. Even though this book cannot comprehensively assess the level of compliance with and enforcement of the South-South PTAs in question, it will analyse the content of these agreements and, among other considerations, benchmark

[12] See, e.g. Cernat (2003); Dissou, Yazid (1998) *Dynamic Effects in Senegal of the Regional Trade Agreement among UEMOA Countries*, CREFA, Québec; Fugazza and Vanzetti (2006); Whalley (2003); and Langhammer (2006); Adlung (2007); Keet (2006).

them against the suggestions made by economic and political scientists for fuelling economic growth through services trade integration.

Recent years have also seen a growth in general literature on South-South cooperation and integration. Several global initiatives – by the UN, the World Bank and others[13] – have aimed at strengthening South-South cooperation in basically all areas of policy. Little has, however, been done to date in terms of studying how South-South cooperation and integration has actually taken shape. This study, thus, also contributes to the general literature on South-South cooperation and integration. It studies the developments in the area of services trade integration and aims to shed some light on the viability of claims made by the international community about the relevance and desirability of South-South cooperation and integration.

GATS Art. V explicitly attributes more flexibility with respect to the requirements of a South-South PTA in services. However, the scope of flexibility has not yet been studied in detail. An analysis of South-South PTAs in services in light of the legal framework and requirements, as presented in this book, should provide a better understanding of the importance of WTO regulation for South-South economic integration, as well as the dynamics between the two. It also illustrates the influence of GATS regulation in developing countries. In addition, this analysis aims to show how the relatively vague language in the GATS agreement affects compliance with GATS requirements, as well as legal certainty and overall coherence of the body of IEL.

In order to establish the scope for flexibility for South-South PTAs in services, this study discusses GATS Art. V in quite some detail. This has not yet been undertaken in an equally comprehensive way and will enrich not only the discussion on flexibilities in WTO law for developing countries, but also impact on a better understanding of the general compliance with GATS Art. V in the global landscape of preferential trade in services and

[13] E.g. South-South cooperation is currently discussed with respect to the post-Millennium Goals agenda of the UN [Online], available at: www.post2015hlp.org; The 'Marrakech Declaration on South-South Cooperation' by the G77 [Online], available at: www.g77.org/marrakech/Marrakech-Declaration.htm; the International Labour Organisation (ILO) also launched a South-South Cooperation Initiative in 2012 [Online], available at: www.social-protection.org/gimi/gess/ShowProject.action?id=1695; the UN Office for South-South Cooperation by the UNDP and their cooperation framework was introduced already in 2005 [Online], available at: http://ssc.undp.org/content/ssc/about.html; and the World Bank launched the 'South-South Knowledge Exchange' in 2012 [Online], available at: http://wbi.worldbank.org/sske/.

of the general system of regulating exemptions from MFN treatment in WTO law.

This discussion is of particular importance with respect to the legal architecture of IEL, because PTAs have generally seen a boom in the last ten years as a consequence of the non-development on the multilateral level. As a result of the unspecific language in and the low level of compliance with GATS Art. V (which is mirrored in GATT Art. XXIV), the overall coherence of regulation in IEL is questioned, as PTAs contribute to contradictions in IEL, resulting in an obscure web of overlapping trade rules and commitments for most countries.[14] Overall, legal certainty has suffered considerably. This may even result in undertakings in IEL missing their common objective – the promotion of positive growth in trade – if the set of applicable rules becomes too complex to take advantage of. This book contributes to the discussion by providing detailed information on the particular case of South-South preferential trade regulation and its relationship with the GATS.

In summary, this book addresses a literature gap by studying preferential services trade regulation among developing countries and its relationship with GATS Art. V. Thereby, it relates to many other areas of interest, such as the legal architecture of IEL, the role of developing countries in IEL, the challenges of regulating services trade, as well as the case made by economists and political scientists for South-South economic integration.

III. Methodology

The core of the study consists of an empirical legal analysis of PTAs in services. For this analysis, the thesis uses data derived from the dataset called Design of Trade Agreements (DESTA) compiled by a team of researchers from the universities of Bern, Salzburg, London and Oxford.[15] Since the DESTA dataset was compiled by political scientists with the aim of providing data for the political analysis of preferentialism, the raw data was cross-checked along the initial coding scheme of the DESTA team and

[14] See, e.g. Bhagwati, Jagdish, Greenaway, David and Panagariya, Arvind (1998) 'Trading Preferentially: Theory and Policy', *The Economic Journal*, vol. 108, no. 449, pp. 1128–1148; Crawford, Jo-Ann and Laird, Sam (2001) 'Regional Trade Agreements and the WTO', *North American Journal of Economics and Finance*, vol. 12, pp. 193–211; and Baldwin, Richard E. (2006) 'Multilateralising Regionalism: Spaghetti Bowls as Building Blocs on the Path to Global Free Trade', *The World Economy*, vol. 29, no. 11, pp. 1451–1518.

[15] For more and general information on the dataset see [Online], available at: www.designoftradeagreements.org.

complemented by the author to allow for a substantial legal analysis. Each agreement was studied, and the core elements in the commitments in the services chapters were taken stock of. This enables substantiating the theoretical discussion on trade regulation in services with a meaningful empirical legal analysis. The general discussion on GATS Art. V regulation is illustrated with descriptive statistics derived from the DESTA dataset, while the discussion of South-South PTAs in services goes into a deeper level of detail and discusses the individual commitments in services trade liberalisation among developing countries.

The empirical approach was chosen with the objective of studying the entire landscape of PTAs in services and deriving all key aspects and common denominators. The quantitative approach allows covering the essence of more than 298 agreements, thereby providing new insights into how preferential services trade has evolved around the world. For the first time, a comprehensive list of South-South PTAs in services has been established and studied. Furthermore, the descriptive empirical analysis presented in this study aims to shed light into the quality and extent of South-South PTAs in services, as well as the level of compliance with them.

The empirical parts of the book are complemented by a review of the relevant literature, interpretation of treaties and comparative analysis. In addition to the relevant legal literature, this thesis also aims to link its analysis to the main trends and arguments presented in economic and political science literature on the subject. Since literature on South-South services trade is relatively scarce across all disciplines, it seems particularly important to embed any legal analysis in the lines of thinking proposed by other disciplines. The author is convinced that the law cannot be analysed in isolation from political, economic and social considerations, given the close interactions that connect them with the evolution and implementation of the law.

Finally, the issue of flexibility for PTAs among developing countries in the GATS cannot be conclusively discussed by simple treaty interpretation: in order to understand the issue, one has to look at the general debate on flexibility for developing countries in IEL. Here, the most suitable methodology is a comparative analysis, which allows considering the law and developments in related areas of regulation. The degrees of flexibility for developing countries provided in the GATT and in IEL in general need to be considered, in order to avoid contradictions between these related regimes. Because the language in GATS Art. V remains relatively vague and has not yet been further elaborated by the Dispute Settlement Body (DSB) of the WTO, comparing the GATS Art. V provision with related provisions in IEL is mandatory in order to grasp the logic of the entire system of flexibilities and in order to describe the specific task and scope of the flexibilities in GATS.

IV. Mapping Preferential Trade Agreements in Services

With the proliferation of bilateral and regional preferential trade liberalisation, PTAs both in goods and in services have been studied by political scientists, by economists and by legal scholars. Legal literature on PTAs is nevertheless relatively scarce compared with the literature in political science or the economic literature. As discussed, the focus of the existing studies of PTAs has been primarily on North-South, and North-North, and was either based on case studies or on empirical studies of the PTAs which are notified to the WTO.[16]

Restricting empirical studies to PTAs that are notified to the WTO risks missing an important part of the picture of trade liberalisation at the regional and bilateral level, because by far not all PTAs are notified to the WTO. Furthermore, not all countries are members of the WTO, but they may nevertheless be involved in trade liberalisation at the bilateral and regional level.[17] Finally, to understand the dynamics in the regulation of preferential trade liberalisation, it is important to take into consideration the historical evolution of PTAs. Given that PTAs already existed before the GATT was introduced in 1947,[18] and given that services trade agreements also existed before the GATS entered into force in 1995,[19] a sample of PTAs that have been notified to the WTO would also be incomplete with respect to the historical dimension of PTAs.

In order to provide a more complete dataset of PTAs, a team of researchers in Berne, Salzburg, London and Oxford[20] launched a project

16 For a good overview, see: Dür, Andreas, Baccini, Leonardo, Elsig, Manfred and Milewicz, Karolina (2011) The Design of Preferential Trade Agreements: A New Dataset in the Making, Staff Working Paper ERSD-2011–10, World Trade Organisation, Geneva, p. 5.

17 For a discussion of the issue, see Pomfret, Richard (2007) 'Is Regionalism an Increasing Feature of the World Economy?', *The World Economy*, vol. 30, no. 6, pp. 923–947, p. 926.

18 For information on the PTAs pre-GATT 1947, see, e.g. Bayer, Frank (2004) *Das System der deutschen Handelsverträge von 1853 und 1914*, Berliner Wissenschafts-Verlag, Berlin, pp. 57ff.; Cottier et al. (2015).

19 E.g. *ANZCERTA Protocol on Services (1988)*, *Canada – US (1988)*, or *NAFTA (1992)*.

20 Dür, Andreas, Baccini, Leonardo, Elsig, Manfred and Milewicz, Karolina; this research is conducted with the framework of the National Centre for Competence in Research (NCCR) trade regulation, University of Bern [Online], available at: www.nccr-trade.org/wps/wp2/211/.

aiming to collect all treaty texts worldwide, which would include provisions in preferential trade.[21] The group collected substantially more agreements than are notified to the WTO and is therefore able to provide a better – and much more complete – dataset for the analysis of PTAs. For the purpose of this study, all agreements recorded in the dataset as of 2011, which cover services trade, were studied and coded. A number of PTAs were added to the list, for example, those that have only recently been notified to the WTO. Using this comprehensive dataset as a basis, this book can provide the largest empirical study of South-South PTAs in services performed to date. At the same time, this thesis also provides the first comprehensive legal study of South-South PTAs in services.

A. *The Dataset*

The Design of Trade Agreements (DESTA) dataset was launched in 2008. It consists of more than 970 agreements to date, which were collected online and in libraries by students.[22] The dataset also covers annexes to treaties, treaties, which are not in force anymore, and treaties, which were not yet electronically accessible. The DESTA includes negotiated agreements between 1945 and 2009. It also covers treaties, which have not been written in Latin script, such as non-translated Arabic, Chinese, or Thai treaties.[23] The data collection continues until 2017, and the dataset will be made publicly available online.[24]

The core research team consists of political scientists, as did the majority of the students, who collected the PTAs. For indexing and research purposes, the PTAs were not only collected, but documented through code: the commitments in the PTAs were recorded in a list, based on a coding scheme developed by the core research team. This allowed a unique overview of the content and structure of the PTAs and will provide the basis for several upcoming studies in political science.

For the purposes of this book, the author was kindly granted access to all the PTAs in the dataset as of 2011, which in one way or another mention services in the treaty text. A number of treaties were added to the list by the author, such as treaties recently notified to the WTO, as well

[21] See also Dür et al. (2011).

[22] Among others, sources include the WTO, the Tuck Trade Agreements and McGill Faculty of Law Preferential Trade Agreements databases and the list of Gary C. Hufbauer, see Dür et al. (2011, p. 10).

[23] E.g. *Jordan – Sudan (2003), Egypt – Syria (1991).*

[24] See DESTA database [Online], available at: www.designoftradeagreements.org.

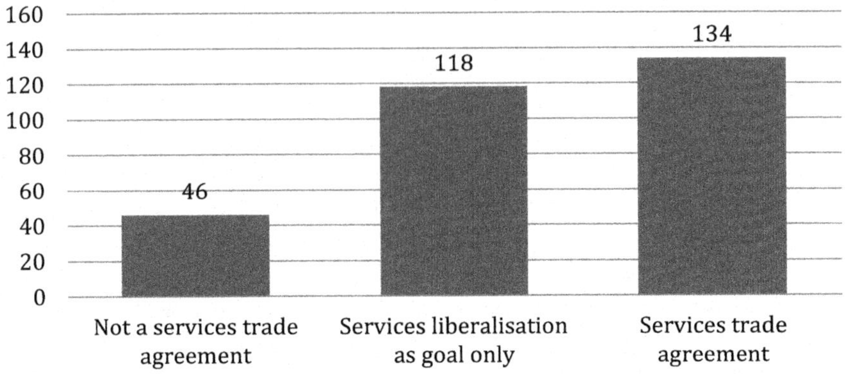

Figure 1 Services agreements in the dataset
Derived from DESTA and WTO.

as erroneous omissions in the initial data collection. The author coded all these agreements in accordance with the coding scheme developed by the DESTA core research team[25] and performed some additional analyses specifically tailored to the preparation of this study. These 298 agreements were in parallel coded by the DESTA team, and results from this exercise of double-coding were compared in order to guarantee a minimal error rate in the final dataset presented below.

B. Methodology

As mentioned above, the 298 agreements were first coded using the coding scheme of DESTA: this coding scheme uses binary code to record a number of key aspects of each PTA, such as whether there are commitments in services trade liberalisation, whether there is an MFN clause in the agreement, whether mode 4 supply of services is excluded from the agreement and so forth.

The analysis of the dataset showed that of the initial 298 agreements, the reference to services in 46 agreements was not related to services trade liberalisation, but to different issues, such as military services or aspects of goods trade. Furthermore, in 118 agreements, services trade liberalisation was only mentioned as a goal for the future, without establishing commitments. This left 134 agreements, which indeed liberalise trade in services on a preferential basis.

[25] The initial coding scheme was developed by Andreas Dür and his team at the University of Salzburg in 2008.

This study is, thus, based mainly on the analysis of the 134 PTAs, which indeed establish liberalising commitments in services trade. The dataset is taken as such and does not differ between PTAs that are in force and PTAs that are no longer in force. The reasoning for including PTAs that are no longer in force is the interest of this study in showing the evolution of South-South commitments in services trade liberalisation, in the legal language, and in the scope of the commitments. For such a legal analysis, it is not of prime relevance whether such commitments are in force or not. Irrespective of their current status, they are part of a legal evolution, which this book describes and investigates.

For the general discussion of preferential services trade, this book relies and refers to the DESTA coding. Thus, the general discussion is purely empirical. By providing an overview of the regulatory practice, it allows putting the theoretical discussions provided in other parts of this thesis in perspective. For the list of treaties see Table of Agreements at the end of this book.[26]

For the more detailed discussion of South-South services trade liberalisation, this study empirically analyses the scope of commitments, using a further refined coding scheme. This coding scheme was developed specifically for the purpose of preparing this study and also includes the schedules of commitments.[27] The empirical study of South-South commitments in preferential services trade identifies departures from the standard agreements, i.e. the more interesting cases, as well as unique characteristics and innovative regulatory approaches chosen in individual agreements. It serves as a background for a qualitative legal analysis of the treaty texts.

V. Structure of the Study

Having elaborated the foundations of the study on developing countries and preferential services trade, subsequently, this book endeavours in the assessment and discussion of the regulatory framework of South-South PTAs in services and its implementation in practice.

The first part of the book is based on the empirical legal study of the Design of Trade Agreements Database (DESTA) on PTAs in services

[26] Please note that both the EU accession treaties and the protocols to PTAs that establish commitments in services trade liberalisation appear individually in the dataset, as per the rules specified by DESTA.

[27] See Annex Table of Agreements, at the end of this study.

worldwide. It discusses the results from the quantitative analysis of the 297 agreements in the database (Chapters 1, 2 and 3). Chapter 4 of Part I offers detailed insights into the structure, spread and scope of South-South PTAs in services. Part I sets the stage for the subsequent discussion of the legal scope of flexibilities for South-South PTAs and their compatibility with WTO law. The empirical study in this part provides for new and comprehensive insights into the structure and spread of preferential services trade regulation across the globe, since the DESTA Database is larger than other databases on PTAs in services.

The main part of this book, which lays down the most important basics for the subsequent suggestion for a new approach, discusses the legal regime for preferential services trade regulation. It starts with an assessment of the history of services trade regulation and of the GATS. It then provides insights into the concept of the MFN exception for PTAs in the GATS and explains the regulatory hierarchy between preferentialism and multilateralism (Chapter 1). It analyses the regulatory purpose, content and scope of GATS Article V in great detail, since this is the key provision for the discussion of the legal regime for PTAs in services (Chapter 2). The regulatory flexibilities linked with special and differential treatment in the GATS are discussed in Chapter 3 while continuing with the legal interpretation of the scope and content of GATS Article V. The assessment of the general level of compliance with GATS regulation of the PTAs in the dataset furthermore helps to illustrate the regulatory complexity of preferential services trade regulation (Chapter 4). Against the background of the relatively weak compliance worldwide with GATS Article V, problems in legal practice and loopholes of the GATS are discussed in Chapter 5. The final chapter (Chapter 6) of Part II returns to South-South PTAs: given the regulatory shortfalls and inadequacies of the GATS, perhaps South-South PTAs are compensating through new regulatory innovations? As the empirical study of the DESTA dataset shows, South-South PTAs are generally not particularly innovative. Part II concludes by providing an assessment of the regulatory status of services trade regulation, taking into consideration the stalling of the Doha Round and recent developments in preferentialism.

The final part of this book offers a new approach to the legal scope of flexibilities for preferentialism between developing countries and LDCs in the GATS. Chapter 1 explains why the scope of flexibility is relative and why developing countries and LDCs have so far been cautious with respect to using and exploring the scope of such flexibilities. Chapter 2 aims at depicting the value of special and differential treatment if used in combination with economic and political indicators. The suggested new approach for a legal regime governing preferentialism in services trade between developing countries and LDCs is elaborated in Chapter 3 through a step-by-step legal analysis of the relevant provisions in the GATS. The author argues in favour of substantial flexibilities with respect to the requirement of covering all sectors and modes of supply while following a strict rule with respect to the level of liberalisation in covered sectors and modes of supply: not all sectors have to be covered, but the covered sectors need to be fully liberalised. This broad interpretation of the scope of flexibilities raises a number of systemic questions. The book ends by answering some of them in Chapter 4 while returning to the initial discussion of the introduction: the assessment of the efficiency and adequacy of the current concept of special and differential treatment in the WTO.

In the conclusion of the book, the most important findings of the study are reiterated with respect to the future of the regulatory interaction between preferentialism and multilateralism, and it is demonstrated why more research on special and differential treatment along with the role of developing countries in WTO law is essential and timely.

PART I

Preferential Services Trade

"I know what I have given you . . .
I do not know what you have received."

Antonio Porchia

Services trade regulation is the exception to the general rule: while new regulation most of the times is first developed in a preferential forum and subsequently moves to the multilateral forum, services trade regulation has most of its roots in multilateralism.[1] As will be shown in the following section, little experience with services trade regulation was collected before GATS. Consequently, services trade regulation has been more or less uniform across fora and adhering to the minimum standards and regulatory structure of the GATS from the start.

While GATS was a major breakthrough for global trade regulation given the share of services in global trade today, it is also a multilateral compromise and therewith limited in its regulatory and liberalising scope. Because of its highly complex structure, which allows WTO members to individually define the level of liberalising commitments in services trade, GATS did not yet achieve major services trade liberalisation worldwide. However, GATS remains the regulatory authority in services trade regulation and establishes the basic rules of services trade liberalisation today.

In consequence, PTAs in services have the capacity to increase services trade liberalisation beyond GATS levels, while at the same time, they have the capacity to advance and enhance services trade regulation in general. Given that GATS did not derive from years of regulatory experience, the regulatory scope and structure of services trade regulation in the GATS is limited, and services trade regulation is generally still in its infancy. PTAs in services also have the capacity to enhance GATS in return: should a

[1] See also Cottier, Sieber-Gasser and Wermelinger (2015, pp. 465–496).

new consensus on the scope of liberalisation and structure of regulation emerge in preferential fora, this may increase pressure in the multilateral forum to return to services trade negotiations. It has to be kept in mind that the GATS was initially thought to be a process and that the initial agreement was never intended to remain untouched for such a long period of time. Thus, while the GATS has its shortcomings, which are widely acknowledged but are unlikely to adapt in the near future, it is through preferentialism that services trade regulation is moved forward today.

This part provides an empirical overview of the current landscape of PTAs in services worldwide. It discusses their most prominent features with regard to their interaction with the multilateral forum, as well as it illustrates the most common nature of these agreements. In the second half of this part, the focus lies on preferential services trade among developing countries alone. The South-South PTAs in services in the dataset are thoroughly analysed with respect to their history, their interdependence and their geographical spread.

In this part, it is shown that WTO members generally are hesitant with respect to innovation in services trade regulation and to substantial services trade liberalisation. PTAs in services are not yet used as the laboratory for the enhancement of services trade regulation and liberalisation, as the shortcomings of GATS and the significance of the services share in global trade would suggest.

1

History and Geography of Preferential Services Trade

General rules of services trade, which are multilaterally acknowledged, only exist since the establishment of the GATS in 1995. However, the need to regulate trade in services arose before 1995. Given that finding a consensus on how to regulate services trade at the multilateral level is more difficult than agreeing on services trade regulation at the bilateral or regional level, it is not surprising that the first attempts to regulate services trade are to be found in PTAs.

In the DESTA dataset, the first agreement mentioning services trade liberalisation as a goal is the *EC (1957)*,[1] while the first agreement, which actually includes commitments in services trade liberalisation is *Yaoundé I (1969)*,[2] more than ten years later. While in the first ten to twenty years after *EC (1957)* services trade was an issue mainly in North-South[3] and South-South[4] agreements, the 1980s were marked by the conclusion of the first North-North[5] agreements. The trend towards including services trade liberalisation in North-North PTAs continued in the early 1990s,[6] when the GATS negotiations were already underway. Especially the parallel bilateral and regional services trade negotiations of the EU and the US had an impact on the final design of services trade regulation in the GATS. This is less of a surprise, given that the main drivers of services trade liberalisation before 1990 were – with a few exceptions of Caribbean and Latin American countries – the European and North American countries.

In parallel with the GATS negotiations and right after the conclusion of the GATS negotiations, the number of PTAs in services started to increase considerably. The exponential trend towards preferential liberalisation of

[1] *EC (1957)*, Title III, Chapter 3. [2] *Yaoundé (1969)*, Title III.

[3] E.g. *Yaoundé I (1963)*, *Arusha Agreement II (1969)*, *Lomé I (1975)* and *Lomé II (1979)*.

[4] E.g. *Andean Group Cartagena Agreement (1969)* and *CARICOM (1973)*.

[5] E.g. *Israel – US (1985)*, *ANZCERTA (1988)* and *Canada – US (1988)*.

[6] E.g. *EC – Hungary (1991)*, *Czech Republic – Slovakia (1992)*, *EC Maastricht (1992)*, *European Economic Area (1992)* and *NAFTA (1992)*.

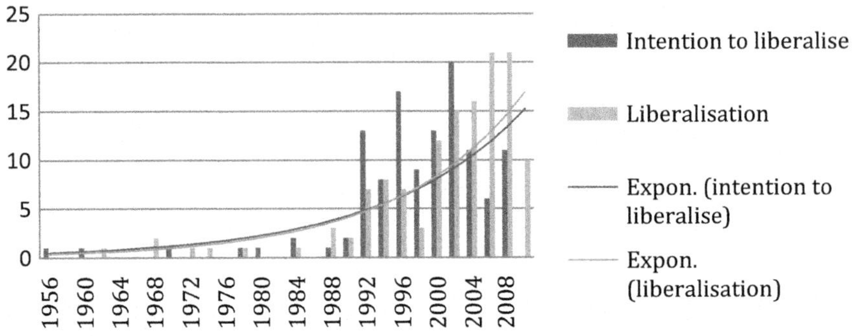

Figure 2 PTAs concluded 1956–2011, liberalisation vs. goal to liberalise
Derived from dataset.

trade in services, which gathered pace in the 1990s, has not been broken to date, see Figure 2.

When looking exclusively at the PTAs with actual commitments in preferential services trade liberalisation in the dataset, the dataset is dominated by North-South agreements (mainly Europe and African countries) until the 1980s. Only then did the first substantial commitments in North-North agreements emerge (mainly US), while the first South-South agreements with substantial commitments in services trade liberalisation only appeared in the 1990s.

The pioneer for South-South PTAs establishing substantial commitments in trade liberalisation services is Mexico, which concluded three South-South PTAs in services in 1994.[7] In 1994, the West African Economic and Monetary Union (WAEMU) was also concluded, introducing substantial commitments in South-South services trade liberalisation to the African continent. While South-South preferential trade in services continued to spread in Latin America and the Caribbean, it is only in 2003 when the first Arab developing countries established preferential services trade commitments.[8] And it took another two years until the first South-South PTAs in services involving an Asian country were concluded.[9] While the Asian countries – particularly South East Asia – quickly caught up with the rest of the world after 2005, the conclusion of South-South PTAs on the African continent and in Arab countries has slowed dramatically.

[7] *Bolivia – Mexico (1994)*, *Colombia – Mexico (1994)* and *Costa Rica – Mexico (1994).*
[8] *Jordan – Sudan (2003).* [9] E.g. *India – Malaysia (2005).*

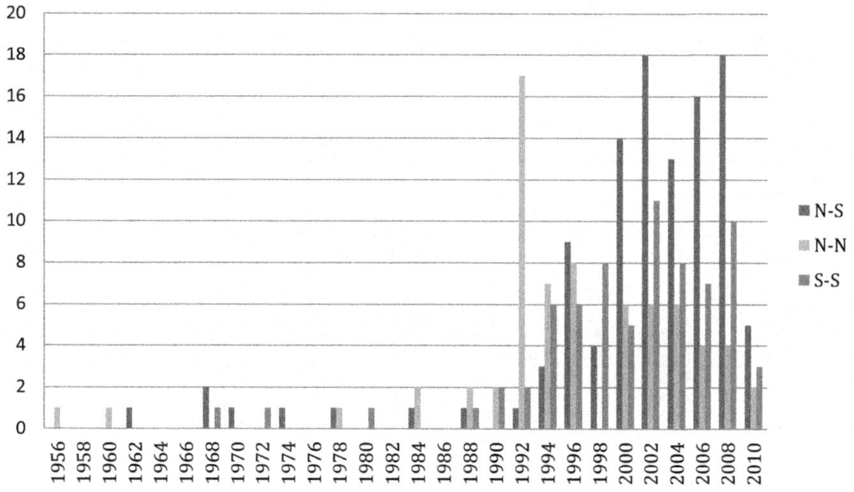

Figure 3 PTAs with reference to preferential services trade per region of the parties
Derived from dataset.

This is in stark contrast to Latin America, the Caribbean and South East Asia, where many countries continue to conclude South-South PTAs to complement their North-South services trade commitments.

Meanwhile, North-South PTAs in services continue to be concluded in high numbers, but the number of new North-North PTAs in services has been in decline for a few years.

Finally, the dataset of PTAs in services indicates that preferential services trade liberalisation is mainly promoted by a few countries. Figure 4 shows the countries, which are most involved in services PTAs.

Developed countries in Europe and in North America are particularly active in preferential services trade. However, even though the European countries and the North American countries are parties to a large number of PTAs in services, they are by far not the only countries involved in preferential services trade. Also in Asia, with Japan and Singapore,[10] preferential services trade ranks high among the preferences in foreign trade policy of developed countries. On the other hand, some of the most active countries in concluding preferential services trade agreements

[10] Please note that, as previously mentioned, Singapore has declared itself to the WTO as being a developing country. However, following the methodology described in the previous chapter, for the purpose of this study, Singapore is considered to be a developed country.

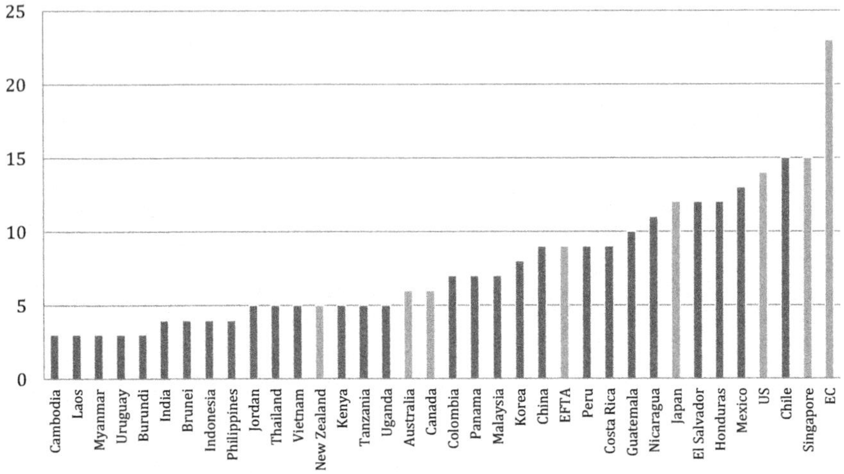

Figure 4 Countries most involved in preferential services trade liberalisation
Derived from dataset.
Notes: dark = developing countries, bright = developed countries.

are Latin American countries, such as Chile, Mexico, Central American countries, Colombia and Peru. India, China and Jordan show increasing interest in preferential services trade and have become more active recently. The observation that Latin American and Asian countries are increasingly pursuing trade policies covering preferential services trade – not only North-South, but also South-South – is an indicator for the economic relevance of regional services trade integration, and for the economic potential that is expected from South-South services trade.

In conclusion, while preferentialism was historically of little relevance before the GATS, it has been growing exponentially ever since the conclusion of the Uruguay Round. Subsequently, the most active countries in services trade preferentialism were mainly industrialised countries, with strong services industries. However, a few developing countries were involved already in the very first attempts to regulate services trade, and services trade liberalisation has never been a policy concern exclusive to industrialised countries. In particular, in the past fifteen years, developing countries are rapidly catching up and are now engaging in services trade preferentialism just as much as industrialised countries. In view of the historical development of preferentialism in services trade, nothing indicates an imminent end to the exponential growth of PTAs in services worldwide in the recent years. On the contrary, it is likely that preferentialism in services trade will increase, especially once the existing trade agreements, which establish services trade liberalisation as a goal, launch negotiations on services trade.

I. Influence of Early PTAs on GATS

With respect to the interaction between PTAs and the GATS, it is interesting to investigate the influence of the early PTAs on the initial scope and structure of services trade regulation in the GATS. The *EC Treaty of Rome*, presumably the first trade agreement with a separate chapter on services trade, provided a relatively comprehensive definition of services trade. This definition is still quite far from the definition of trade in services in the GATS; however, its reference to today's mode 4 of supply of services (temporary movement of service suppliers) is particularly interesting:[11]

> Services [. . .] shall be deemed to be services normally supplied for remuneration [. . .]. Services shall include [. . .]: (a) activities of an industrial character; (b) activities of a commercial character; (c) artisan activities; and (d) activities of the liberal professions. Without prejudice to the [. . .] right of establishment, a person supplying a service may, in order to carry out that service, temporarily exercise his activity in the State where the service is supplied, under the same conditions as are imposed by that State on its own nationals.

This initial definition and structure of services trade regulation was later introduced the EC Economic Partnership Agreements (EPAs) across the globe. The chapter on services in *Yaoundé I*, e.g. provides the following definition:[12]

> Services within the meaning of this Convention shall be deemed to be services normally provided against remuneration [. . .]. Services shall include in particular activities of an industrial character, activities of a commercial character, artisan activities and activities of the liberal professions, excluding wage-earning activities.

The same basic definition is used in the *Arusha Agreement II*, with some clarifications, such as the term 'employed persons' (instead of 'wage-earning activities').[13] The parties to the *Lomé* agreements included services provisions, without, however relying on a definition of services trade. In *Lomé III* and *Lomé IV*, a separate chapter refers to the role of services

[11] *EC Treaty of Rome (1957)*, Art. 60. [12] *Yaoundé I (1964)*, Art. 32.
[13] *Arusha Agreement II (1969)*, Art. 19.

in economic development and outlines the most development-effective services sectors.

EC – Turkey, on the other hand, also refrains from defining trade in services while introducing the first stand-still obligation in services trade:[14]

> The Contracting Parties shall refrain from introducing as between themselves new restrictions on the freedom of establishment and the free supply of services.

It is, thus, interesting that it appeared at the time that including services in a PTA did not necessarily require a definition of the term 'service'. *CARICOM*, presumably worldwide the first agreement covering services trade regulation in which the EC is not a party to, relies on a definition of services again. It establishes its own definition, which appears to be building upon the EC definition of services:[15]

> 1. Each Member State agrees [. . .] to extend [. . .] preferential treatment [. . .] with regard to the provision of services. 2. For the purposes of this Article the term "services" shall be considered as services for remuneration provided that they are not governed by provisions relating to trade, the right of establishment or movement of capital and includes [. . .] activities of an industrial or commercial character, artisan activities and activities of the professions, excluding activities of employed persons.

The *Organisation of East Caribbean States* takes yet another approach to services trade by introducing 'the abolition [. . .] of the obstacles to the free movement of persons, services and capital'[16] as a principle of the common market. However, later in the treaty it refers only specifically to the free movement of persons[17] and to transportation.[18] Partial services trade liberalisation is thus established, with a specific focus on one sector and one mode of supply.

The first agreement establishing comprehensive and encompassing regulation of services trade is *Israel – US*. At first, services were added to the main treaty in a separate – legally not binding – declaration. The declaration provides in general for National Treatment (NT),[19] for a detailed

[14] *EC – Turkey (1970)*, Additional Protocol, Art. 41. [15] *CARICOM (1973)*, Art. 36.

[16] *Organisation of Eastern Caribbean States (1981)*, Agreement establishing the East Caribbean Common Market, Art. 3(c).

[17] Ibid., Art. 12. [18] Ibid., Art. 16.

[19] *Israel – US (1985)*, Declaration on Trade in Services, Art. 3: 'Each Party will endeavor to assure that trade in services with the other nation is governed by the principle of national treatment.'

definition of services and services sectors, for transparency provisions and it sets a date for the review of the effectiveness of its measures.[20] *Israel – US* introduces a first version of the negative list approach in its transparency provision: notification on non-conforming measures is required.[21] While the different modes of supply are missing in the definition of services, *Israel – US* defines services by reference to a number of services sectors, all of which were later also covered by GATS. It refrains, however, from defining the actual term 'service':[22]

> Definition: Trade in services takes place when a service is exported from the supplier nation and is imported into the other nation. Services encompass, but are not limited to, transportation; travel and tourism services; communications; banking services, insurance; other financial activities; professional services, such as consulting in construction, engineering, accounting, medicine, education, and law, and the providing of other professional services such as management consulting; computer services; motion pictures; advertising.

Yet another approach was pursued in the protocol on trade in services of the *Australia New Zealand Closer Economic Relations Agreement (ANZCERTA)*. The protocol was adopted in 1988 and establishes legally binding, far reaching, detailed liberalisation of trade in services, based on a negative list approach. It defines the provision of services as follows:[23]

> Provision of services includes: (a) the production, distribution, marketing, sale and delivery of a service; and (b) [. . .]: (i) access to and use of domestic distribution systems; and (ii) rights of establishment.

The protocol basically liberalises the entire services market, providing for non-restricted market access, NT and MFN.[24] With the exception of a few exemptions to liberalisation listed in a separate annex to the protocol, *ANZCERTA* is liberalising services trade to an extent which was unique in 1988. The key to this substantial liberalisation differs, however, from the GATS. *ANZCERTA* fully opens services markets and refrains largely from establishing any further regulation or limitation other than the limited list of exemptions. It furthermore refrains from defining the term 'services'.

20 Ibid., Art. 9: 'The parties will review the effectiveness of this Declaration not later than eighteen months from the date that this Declaration is signed.'

21 Ibid., Art. 7: 'Each Party will make public its domestic laws and regulations affecting trade in services and notify the other Party of laws and regulations which discriminate against a service exported from the other nation.'

22 Ibid., Art. 1.

23 *ANZCERTA (1988)*, Protocol on Trade in Services, Art. 3.

24 Ibid., Art. 4–6.

Such an approach is possible between interested partners in a PTA, but certainly less adequate in a multilateral context.

The *Canada – US* agreement is based on a similar regulatory scope as *ANZCERTA* and introduces a positive list approach for the first time. This results here in an overall smaller scope of liberalisation, since liberalising commitments are limited in number and scope. Services trade regulation in *Canada – US* is, however, quite advanced and sophisticated. In addition to the chapter on services in the main treaty, some individual services sectors are also listed with a separate annex in the agreement. Trade in services is defined by a combination of the covered service provision in Art. 1402 and the covered services in Art. 1408 and Annex 1408. In particular, the term 'services' is for the first time defined by reference to a classification list, here the Standard Industrial Classification (SIC). The positive list approach, the consideration of individual services sectors and the reference to a classification list were later introduced in GATS as well.

Finally, during the final phase of the Uruguay Round, two new European agreements were concluded, also covering services trade: the *EC Maastricht Treaty* and the *EEA*. Both were, however, more or less aligned with the European agreements preceding them and did, thus, not introduce new approaches to services trade regulation. Arguably the most influential PTA for the GATS with respect to the definition of its scope was the *NAFTA* treaty. *NAFTA* uses a more or less identical definition of the modes of services supply as does the GATS:[25]

> cross-border provision of a service or cross-border trade in services means the provision of a service: (a) from the territory of a Party into the territory of another Party, (b) in the territory of a Party by a person of that Party to a person of another Party, or (c) by a national of a Party in the territory of another Party, [. . .];

However, contrary to *Canada – US*, the *NAFTA* re-introduces the negative list approach. Since GATS is based on a positive list approach, *NAFTA* was, thus, less influential in this regard. The GATS now defines the supply of services as follows:[26]

> 2. [. . .] trade in services is defined as the supply of a service: (a) from the territory of one Member into the territory of any other Member; (b) in the territory of one Member to the service consumer of any other Member; (c) by a service supplier of one Member, through commercial presence in the

[25] *NAFTA (1992)*, Art. 1213. [26] GATS Art. I:2.

> territory of any other Member; (d) by a service supplier of one Member, through presence of natural persons of a Member in the territory of any other Member.

With regard to the definition of the term 'service', GATS – similar to *Canada – US* – refers to the services listed in the individual schedules of commitments.[27] The sectors and services listed in the schedules of commitments are then linked with the Services Sectoral Classification list,[28] which in turn relies on the provisional Central Product Classification (CPC) list of the UN.[29] The GATS, thus, refrains from specifically defining the term 'service', just like most of the PTAs did before.[30]

Judging from this overview of the first provisions regulating services trade in PTAs, it appears that not a single PTA served as the basis of GATS. Rather, GATS seems to be based on a number of different PTAs, each of them influencing GATS in its own way. However, it also becomes clear that the few early PTAs in services heavily influenced the regulatory structure and scope of GATS. While experiences with services trade regulation must have been limited to say the least at the time that services were added to the *Uruguay Round*, GATS nevertheless did not introduce an entirely new approach to services trade regulation. The main achievement of the GATS is the establishment of coherent and specific regulation of services trade by combining the – arguably – best regulatory approaches already existing in PTAs at the time. Thus, the early history of the interdependence between preferential and multilateral services trade regulation illustrates well how important the evolution of preferentialism in services might prove to be for the future of GATS.[31]

In the beginning of the 1990s, the number of PTAs mentioning services trade liberalisation as a goal for the future outnumbered the PTAs with commitments in services trade liberalisation. This changed in the early 2000s, when more PTAs with substantial commitments in trade liberalisation in services were closed, compared to the agreements that only mention services trade liberalisation as a goal. Thus, in general, PTAs

[27] GATS Art. I:3(b).

[28] WTO, *Services Sectoral Classification List*, Note by the Secretariat, 10 July 1991, MTN.GNS/W/120.

[29] Diebold (2013, pp. 23–24).

[30] Abu-Akeel, Aly K. (1999) 'Definition of Trade in Services under the GATS: Legal Implications', *George Washington Journal of International Law and Economics*, vol. 32, no. 2, pp. 189–210, p. 191.

[31] See also Cottier et al. (2015, pp. 475–483).

with commitments in substantial liberalisation in services are a relatively recent phenomenon, and even though the number of 134 PTAs with commitments in services trade liberalisation may suggest that services trade liberalisation is a well-established aspect of preferential trade, compared with a total of 792 PTAs found by DESTA, preferential services trade can still be considered to be in its infancy.[32]

[32] List of Treaties, DESTA [Online], available at: www.designoftradeagreements.org.

2

Stock-taking of Preferential Services Trade Agreements

The vast majority of agreements providing for commitments in services trade liberalisation are bilateral trade agreements between countries or between an organised group of countries and a third country. Adding the number of agreements related to the establishment of some form of organised group of countries (this group can be called a union, an association, a community aso.), only Economic Partnership Agreements (EPAs) and PTAs between two different groups of countries are left. Thus, it can safely be said that commitments in trade liberalisation in services are mainly to be found either in bilateral PTAs or in PTAs establishing some form of an organised group of countries. Figure 5 illustrates the numbers of different types of agreements liberalising trade in services in the dataset.

Nevertheless, commitments in trade liberalisation in services vary in language and structure considerably. While some PTAs basically copy the schedules and structure of the GATS,[1] others have their own logic and structure[2] or copy the NAFTA structure.[3] Some agreements provide for detailed and sophisticated regulation of services trade,[4] and others manage to liberalise substantially all services trade with two or three paragraphs only.[5] Interestingly, however, of all the agreements in the dataset, only three are actually establishing a common market for trade in services.[6]

I. Lack of Notifications to the WTO

GATS Art. V:7 stipulates the requirement to promptly notify any PTA to the Council of Trade in Services (CTS) as well as the enlargement or any

[1] E.g. Chinese PTAs, African PTAs. [2] E.g. late EU PTAs, *ASEAN-China (2007)*.
[3] E.g. Mexican PTAs. [4] E.g. *MERCOSUR Services (1997)*.
[5] E.g. *WAEMU (1994)*.
[6] *Czech Republic – Slovakia (1992)*, *EC Amsterdam (1997)*, and *Faroe Islands – Iceland (2005)*.

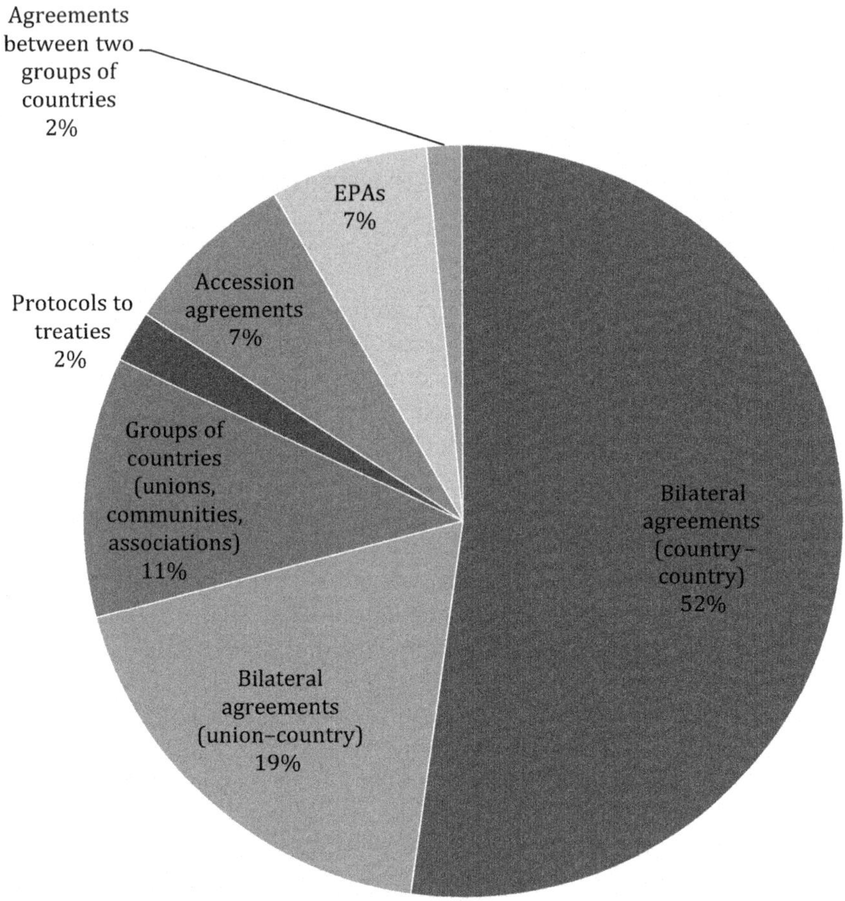

Figure 5 Types of PTAs in services
Derived from dataset.

significant modification of a services PTA. It is unclear what 'promptly notify' means. It has been suggested that notification has to take place before the implementation of the PTA, right after the ratification of the PTA.[7] State practice, however, shows that members do not always follow this rule.[8] The CTS is allowed (but not required) to examine the PTA.

[7] WTO, Transparency Mechanism for Regional Trade Agreements, WT/L671, para. 3.

[8] Quite regularly, PTAs are notified quite some time after the entry into force, see WTO Regional Trade Agreements Information System [Online], available at: http://rtais.wto.org/UI/PublicAllRTAList.aspx.

Generally, the CTS does routinely examine every PTA that is notified. The working party examining the PTA (normally the Committee on Regional Trade Agreements) is to report on the consistency of the PTA with GATS Art. V.

To date, no such report has yet been filed. Based on such a report, the CTS has the right to make appropriate recommendations to the members of the PTA. This right has so far not been used due to the requirement of consensus. Cottier and Molinuevo (2008) therefore submit that issues related to the consistency of the PTA with GATS Art. V are more likely to be raised under the DSU.[9]

In addition, the WTO Secretariat is required to prepare a 'factual presentation' of the PTA and circulate it among the members.[10] In this report, the consistency with GATS Art. V is discussed and offers an important basis for the overall assessment of compatibility.[11]

PTAs in services have to be notified to the CTS – irrespective of whether among developed or developing countries. The CTS can decide to pass the PTA to the Committee on Regional Trade Agreements (CRTA) for examination. However, unlike the case of PTAs notified under GATT Art. XXIV, such examination is only optional.[12]

Since 2006, a new WTO Transparency Mechanism for Regional Trade Agreements is formally established and executed on a provisional basis. Under this new transparency mechanism, notification has to be made as soon as possible (at least directly following the ratification) and before the application of the PTA. The examination process by the WTO should be concluded within one year after notification. In order to facilitate the factual examination, the Secretariat in its own responsibility and in consultation with the parties prepares a factual presentation of the PTA.[13] This factual presentation, however, 'shall not be used as a basis for dispute settlement procedures nor create new rights and obligations for members'.[14]

[9] Cottier, Thomas and Molinuevo, Martin (2008), 'Article V GATS', In: Wolfrum, R., Stoll, P-T. and Feinäugle, C. (eds.), *WTO – Trade in Services*, Max Planck Institute, Martinus Nijhoff Publishers, Leiden, pp. 125–151, pp. 149–150.

[10] WTO, Transparency Mechanism for Regional Trade Agreements, WT/L/671.

[11] Cottier and Molinuevo (2008, p. 151).

[12] WTO, Work of the Committee on Regional Trade Agreements (CRTA) [Online], available at: www.wto.org/english/tratop_e/region_e/regcom_e.htm.

[13] WTO, Transparency Mechanism for Regional Trade Agreements, Decision of 14 December 2006, WTO Doc. WT/L/671 (18 December 2006) (Decision on Transparency Mechanism).

[14] Transparency Mechanism, *supra* n. 162, para. 10; see also Islam, Md. Rizwanul and Alam, Shawkat (2009) 'Preferential Trade Agreements and the Scope of GATT

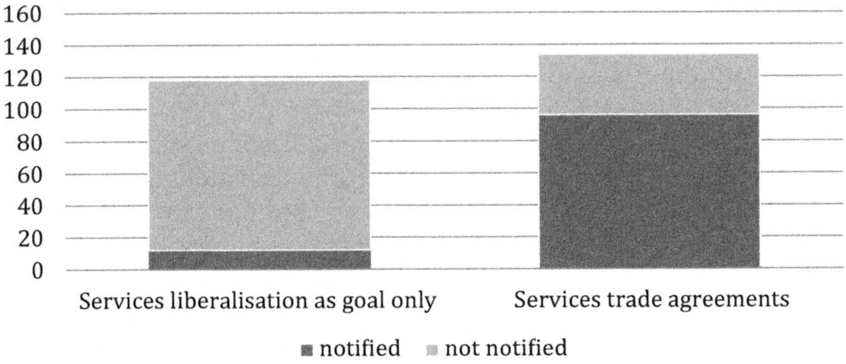

Figure 6 Level of notification of PTAs
Derived from dataset.

In addition to the relatively low level of notifications of PTAs in services, the analysis of the level of notifications of the PTAs in the dataset also suggests that there is uncertainty when a PTA has to be notified under GATS Art. V. Figure 6 illustrates the low level of notifications with respect to both PTAs aiming at liberalising trade in services and PTAs in services (Source: Dataset and WTO):

As Figure 6 well illustrates, almost a third of the PTAs in services are not notified to the WTO, and interestingly, even though they are not liberalising trade in services, twelve PTAs are nonetheless notified to the WTO under GATS Art. V. Given that both GATS Art. V:7[15] and the transparency mechanism for PTAs[16] clearly only refer to PTAs establishing commitments in trade liberalisation, the notification of the twelve PTAs which do not establish commitments in services trade liberalisation is likely to have political reasons or to be a simple mistake.

Article XXIV, GATS Article V and the Enabling Clause: An Appraisal of GATT/WTO Jurisprudence', *Netherlands International Law Review*, vol. 56, no. 1, pp. 1–34, p. 28.

15 GATS Art. V:7 lit. a states: 'Members which are parties to any agreement referred to in paragraph 1 shall promptly notify any such agreement and any enlargement or any significant modification of that agreement to the Council for Trade in Services.' GATS Art. V:1 refers only to PTAs providing commitments in services trade liberalisation. It says: 'This Agreement shall not prevent any of its members from being a party to or entering into an agreement liberalising trade in services between or among the parties to such an agreement'.

16 The Transparency Mechanism refers to GATS Art. V in A:1: 'Without prejudging the substance and the timing of the notification required under [. . .] Article V of the GATS [. . .], nor affecting Members' rights and obligations under the WTO agreements in any way'.

In the attempt to tackle the non-notification of PTAs, the transparency mechanism allows and encourages members to bring to the attention of the relevant WTO body information concerning PTAs that should have been notified. This provisional mechanism will be reviewed, modified and eventually replaced by a permanent mechanism as part of the overall results of the Doha Round.[17]

The fact that not all PTAs are notified to the WTO renders holistic surveillance of regionalism impossible to achieve for the WTO. Consequently the data gathered by the WTO remain incoherent and incomplete.[18] This turned out to be a critical issue already in the Doha Round: the surveillance of PTAs involving developing countries was perceived as inadequate.[19] Thus, important information in the process of negotiations was missing.

Prior to the establishment of the WTO, PTAs were examined by ad hoc working parties. Since the establishment of the WTO, the Committee on Regional Trade Agreements (CRTA) is mandated to review the legality of PTAs under the GATT and the GATS, as well as under the Enabling Clause. Neither the working parties nor the CRTA reached consensus on the legality of any PTA notified to the WTO. Thus, the process proved to be unsatisfactory.[20]

The WTO General Council attempted to overcome the problem by adopting a Decision on a Transparency Mechanism for Regional Trade Agreements.[21] The decision – in addition to clarifying the process – enhanced the role of the WTO Secretariat and diminished the role of the CRTA: the CRTA no longer produces a report, but holds a single meeting per PTA to consider written questions that were submitted earlier. The transparency mechanism was expected to be reviewed as part of the Doha Round, which has, however, not yet been the case. As a result, the legality of a PTA can today only be assessed through dispute settlement proceedings.[22]

[17] Transparency Mechanism, *supra* n. 162, para. 22; see also Islam and Alam (2009, p. 29).

[18] Walsh, Stephen (2004) 'Addressing the Abuse of the WTO's Exemption for Regional Trade Agreements', *ELSA Selected Papers on European Law*, no. 1, pp. 62–106, p. 79.

[19] WTO Secretariat, Compendium of issues related to Regional Trade Agreements, TN/RL/W/8/Rev.1 (02–4246), 1 August 2002, p. 7, para. II.1.

[20] Bartels, Lorand (2012) 'Regional Trade Agreements', In: R. Wolfrum (ed.), *The Max Planck Encyclopedia of Public International Law*, Vol. VIII, Oxford University Press, Oxford, pp. 853–863, p. 859.

[21] Transparency Mechanism for Regional Trade Agreements, WT/L/671 (18 December 2006).

[22] Bartels (2012, pp. 859–860).

The reason for the impotence of the CRTA is seen in the consensus rule: members are unable to agree. Critical in this may also be that the exact scope of the relevant WTO-provisions, GATT Art. XXIV, GATS Art. V and the Enabling Clause is not yet unequivocally established.[23] Multilateral surveillance may, thus, only have a limited impact on the design and content of PTAs. The potential for strengthening the WTO disciplines may be too low to justify the effort.[24] Furthermore, it has been argued that a trade policy, which would ensure that PTAs are welfare improving for both the members and the rest of the world, is doomed to fail.[25]

The surveillance of regionalism is essential for the current multilateral trade negotiations, but also for the overall functioning of the WTO system: particularly now, with the multilateral negotiations perceived as stuck and an increasing pressure to find solutions for emanating new problems, PTAs become a hub for new forms of regulation and for new areas of regulation. Insights from this dynamic process could and should feed into the multilateral negotiations.

Furthermore, as is demonstrated by this study, a considerable number of PTAs is not perfectly in line with WTO requirements. This is even more so, as the exact requirements which a PTA has to meet in order to be in line with WTO regulation are still unclear, among others as a consequence of the low level of notification of PTAs to the WTO and the more or less inexistent review of the PTAs. Given that the so-called spaghetti bowl already complicates understanding the respective rules which apply to a specific good or service, some scholars even fear that too many rules and regulations – potentially also incoherent and contradicting each other – will finally overthrow the world trade system.[26]

Since the world trade system, including the WTO remains well established, the lack of notifications will hardly develop such a devastating impact. Rather it could also be seen as a consensus on the importance of the right to conclude bilateral and regional PTAs despite being a member of the WTO. The relevant new areas of regulation and the most successful

23 For a more extensive discussion, see e.g. Kim, Bongchul (2009) 'Development and Prospect of the CRTA in WTO System', *International Area Studies Review*, vol. 12, no. 1, pp. 3–15.

24 Hoekman, Bernard and Kostecki, M. M. (2009) *The Political Economy of the World Trading System: From GATT to WTO*, Oxford University Press, Oxford, pp. 490–492.

25 See, e.g. Winters, Alan L. (1999) 'Regionalism vs. Multilateralism', In: R. Baldwin et al. (eds.), *Market Integration, Regionalism and the Global Economy*, CEPR, London.

26 See, e.g. Avila, John L. (2003) 'EU Enlargement and the Rise of Asian FTAs: Implications for Asia-Europe Relations', *Asia Europe Journal*, vol. 1, no. 2, pp. 213–222, p. 214.

new forms of regulation which have been tested in PTAs will most certainly sooner or later feed into the multilateral regulation, irrespective of the level of notification.[27]

Nevertheless, the WTO generally needs to address the issue of low compliance of its members with undisputed duties and obligations. This problem is not restricted to the notification of PTAs; it can also be observed in other areas of WTO law, such as, e.g. TRIPS Art. 66:2.[28]

[27] See Cottier et al. (2015).

[28] The obligation of developed countries to provide incentives for private companies to engage in knowledge transfer to LDCs is widely disrespected: See also Hoekman, Bernard (2005b) 'Transfer of Technology to Developing Countries: Unilateral and Multilateral Policy Options', *World Development*, vol. 33, no. 10, pp. 1587–1602.

3

The Current Level of Liberalisation

Notwithstanding the interpretation of whether or not a PTA in services has to offer National Treatment and MFN treatment to its members to be in line with WTO law, of the 134 PTAs in the dataset, the considerable number of 42 PTAs do not provide for MFN treatment. The fact that almost a third of the PTAs in services are not providing MFN treatment to its members, could be interpreted as an indicator of disagreement among WTO members on the requirement of providing MFN treatment to members of a PTA. Given that GATS Art. V does not explicitly require National Treatment and MFN treatment among members of a PTA in services, the fact that a third of the PTAs in the dataset are not providing MFN treatment could also inform a future interpretation of GATS Art. V:1. Thus, whether a PTA has to provide for both MFN treatment and National Treatment remains a matter of treaty interpretation.

In addition to the high number of PTAs, which are not providing for MFN treatment, 17 PTAs of the 134 PTAs do not provide for National Treatment. Figure 7 illustrates the relatively high number of PTAs in services, which do not provide for MFN treatment or National Treatment.

I. Low Level of Liberalisation

Introducing the GATS in 1995 certainly was a major achievement: beginning to liberalise such a complex issue as services trade meant introducing new forms of regulation, it meant that consensus had to be established on the definitions of what was to be traded and it meant to overcome the challenge of resistance towards multilateral regulation with yet unknown implications for the national economies. But this major achievement of creating a new set of rules, of establishing general principles and definitions in multinational services trade, came at the cost of a generally low level of *de facto* trade liberalisation in services.[1]

[1] See, e.g. Sauvé (2008).

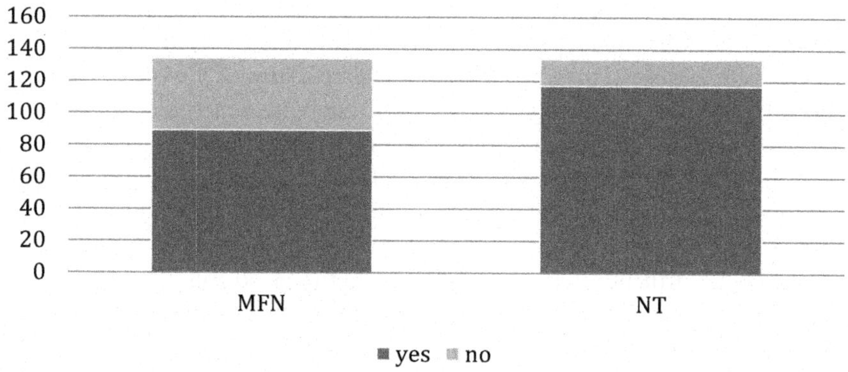

Figure 7 Services PTAs not providing for MFN or National Treatment
Derived from dataset.

From the beginning, it was agreed to continue negotiations in order to further liberalise trade in services, also at the multilateral level. Services then quickly became one of the major challenges in the Doha Round negotiations and, to date, at the multilateral level, no noteworthy progress with respect to services trade liberalisation has been achieved. At the present, offers in the Doha Round are actually lower than the average policies in place. This observation led Gootiiz and Mattoo (2009) to state:[2]

> At present, Doha offers not greater access to markets but a weak assurance that access will not get worse.

Given that the negotiations following the introduction of the GATS did not lead to the envisaged enlargement of commitments in multilateral trade liberalisation in services, the GATS can be considered to be inherently incomplete, to be left unfinished.[3]

[2] Gootiiz, Batshur and Mattoo, Aaditya (2009) Services in Doha: What's on the Table?, Policy Research Working Paper No. 4903, The World Bank, Washington DC, p. 2.

[3] See, e.g. Nielson, Julia and Taglioni, Daria (2003) A Quick Guide to the GATS and Mode 4, Paper prepared for the OCED/World Bank/IOM Seminar on Trade and Migration, 12–14 November 2003, p. 19: 'In addition to the negotiations on specific commitments, there are also negotiations related to some of the main rules, or disciplines, under the GATS which were left unfinished when the agreement was first developed in 1994. The key areas left outstanding mainly concern general disciplines, or rules and include four main areas: a possible emergency safeguard (Article X); government procurement (Article XIII); possible disciplines on trade distorting subsidies (Article XV)and possible disciplines on certain types of domestic regulation (Article VI:4)'.

While to some extent reasons for the low level of liberalisation originate from political and economic considerations – which have also been discussed widely in literature[4] – the legal structure of the GATS itself may also have contributed to the rather modest achievements of the GATS in terms of liberalising multilateral trade in services.

The positive list approach was essential for establishing a consensus and a commitment to services trade liberalisation in the first place. However, because of the complete freedom of WTO members to enter – or not to enter – commitments in their schedules, the good intentions led to the opposite outcome – i.e. commitments at the multilateral level that are oftentimes lower than the actual policies in effect.[5]

In retrospective, it may therefore be regrettable that the drafters of the GATS did not include a mechanism, which progressively leads to more liberalisation. Would there have been such a mechanism or understanding, the problems now arising in the area of services trade regulation because of the regulatory vacuum could have been prevented to some degree. Furthermore, given that the WTO members were aware of the limited impact on overall trade liberalisation in services as a consequence of the positive list approach, an understanding until when the positive list approach would be abandoned and replaced by a negative list approach would certainly have helped countries to commit more meaningfully, given the prospect of having to commit anyway within a certain period of time.[6]

Despite developed countries' interest in services trade liberalisation, they did not agree to provide for additional flexibility for developing countries in the GATS. Now that multilateral services trade negotiations are stalling, there are fears that history may repeat itself: in services trade, developing countries and developed countries are showing little willingness to meet halfway. Would the flexibilities in the GATS – and also the application of the flexibilities – for developing countries have been more

[4] See, e.g. Low, Patrick and Mattoo, Aaditya (2000) 'Is There a Better Way? Alternative Approaches to Liberalisation under the GATS', In: P. Sauvé and R. M. Stern (eds.), *GATS 2000: New Directions in Services Trade Liberalisation*, The Brookings Institution, Washington DC, pp. 449–472.

[5] See also Mattoo, Aaditya and Wunsch-Vincent, Sacha (2004) 'Pre-Empting Protectionism in Services: The GATS and Outsourcing', *Journal of International Economic Law*, vol. 7, no. 4, pp. 765–800, p. 775.

[6] See, e.g. Mattoo and Wunsch-Vincent (2004).

outspoken and effective from the start, some of the current challenges would probably not have arisen in the first place.[7]

Finally, and most importantly, the GATS is considered to be a dynamic treaty which should allow the inclusion of new developments in the area of services trade regulation. However, because it was thought to be amended within a short period of time – and because WTO members probably still wait in order to see whether there will be any progress in multilateral trade negotiations in services after all, which clarifies things – this dynamic character turned into a stumbling stone for the effectiveness of GATS: predictability, stability and certainty of the scope of commitments and the outcome of disputes have suffered considerably, and as a consequence of the scarce case law in GATS, no reliable rules for treaty interpretation have yet been established, which could compensate for the lack of clarity in the language of the GATS.[8] Reliable rules for the interpretation of the scope of GATS commitments given their dynamic character would be most welcome. The fact that the services industry has rapidly changed since the establishment of the GATS renders the need for reliable regulation of multilateral services trade all the more relevant for the global economy:[9] even if the multilateral level of liberalisation in trade in services remained low, at least the current level of liberalisation could be better enforced and established.

It has to be said, however, that of the PTAs not providing for either MFN treatment or National Treatment, the majority are EC accession agreements and EPAs. Cleaning the list of PTAs from the special cases of EC accession agreements, EPAs and similar agreements, leaves the following list of PTAs, which do not provide for either MFN treatment or National Treatment and are likely to contradict the conditions set out by GATS Art. V:1 lit. b.

It may come as a surprise that National Treatment is more or less unequivocally granted in PTAs in services, while a considerable number

[7] See also Hoekman, Bernard, Mattoo, Aaditya and Sapir, André (2007) 'The Political Economy of Services Trade Liberalisation: A Case for International Regulatory Cooperation?', *Oxford Review of Economic Policy*, vol. 23, no. 3, pp. 367–391.

[8] See, e.g. on the lack of transparency: Stephenson, Sherry (2001) Services Liberalisation by Developing Countries: Is More Progress Possible Regionally Than Under the GATS?, PSIO Occasional Paper, WTO Series No. 08, Geneva, pp. 15–16.

[9] See also Miles, Ian (2005) 'Innovation in Services', In: J. Fagerberg, D. C. Mowery and R. R. Nelson (eds.), *The Oxford Handbook of Innovation*, Oxford University Press, Oxford, pp. 433–457.

Table 3 *PTAs without provisions in MFN or National Treatment*[a]

Name of PTA	No MFN	No NT	Neg.List
CARICOM (1973)	X	X	X
China – Hong Kong (2003)	X	X	
China – Macao (2003)	X	X	
CARICOM – Cuba (2000)		X	
Canada – US (1988)	X		
Chile – China (2008)	X		
Chile – Korea (2003)	X		X
China – Costa Rica (2010)	X		
China – Pakistan (2009)	X		
China – Peru (2009)	X		
China – Singapore (2008)	X		
Jordan – Kuwait (2001)	X		
Jordan – Singapore (2004)	X		
Jordan – Sudan (2003)	X		
Jordan – US (2000)	X		
Korea – Singapore (2005)	X		
New Zealand – Singapore (2000)	X		
ASEAN – China (2007)	X		
ASEAN – Korea (2007)	X		
Chile – EC (2002)	X		X
Colombia and Peru – EC (2012)	X		
Gulf Cooperation Council – Singapore (2008)	X		
Morocco – UAE (2001)	X		
WAEMU (1994)	X		
Chile – MERCOSUR (2009)	X		

[a] Derived from dataset.

of PTAs in the dataset have no provision in MFN treatment. But, does MFN still matter, if National Treatment is already granted? This question is justified, given that it is rather unlikely that any other PTA with a third country is granting more than National Treatment – that would legally and practically not be feasible to achieve. Thus, from a practical point of view, as long as National Treatment is granted, a provision in MFN might not be required, since MFN would not be expected to have an impact on the trade relations among the members of the PTA.

Nevertheless, if MFN is expected to have no impact on the trade relations, why has it been excluded from the PTA? Here it is important to take into consideration the individual schedules of commitments. While National Treatment may be granted generally, this commitment may be restricted *de facto* to a very limited number of sectors and services. Thus, MFN is of relevance even when National Treatment is granted in a PTA, because the individual commitments in the schedules of a PTA with a third country may be more far reaching: MFN would require the members of the PTA to extend the more far-reaching commitments in a PTA with third countries to the members of the PTA with fewer commitments.

Therefore, it is not surprising that all PTAs in Table 3 but three[10] are based on a positive list approach. The positive list approach leaves more room for individual levels of commitments in liberalisation, compared to the negative list approach. The commitments are undertaken in a considerate way in every single sector, subsector and mode of supply. This complex web of individual commitments can well be adjusted to the individual trade relations among the members of a PTA. Thus, schedules in PTAs of one country will look different from one PTA to another, and MFN treatment turns out to be critical for GATS Art. V compliance.

10 *CARICOM (1973)*, *Chile – Korea (2003)* and *Chile – EC (2002)*.

4

The Special Case of South-South Preferential Services Trade

Among others, the advantages of Preferential Trade Agreements (PTAs) include the possibility to integrate different areas of trade regulation in one coherent document, which allows for a legal structure that is corresponding more closely to actual trading conditions.[1] Furthermore, PTAs allow for a different approach to the regulation of services trade liberalisation than the one of the GATS, e.g. through a negative list approach. At least in theory, developing countries would have the legal flexibility to regulate South-South trade liberalisation in services in a tailor-made, individual manner.[2] Theory furthermore suggests that smart trade liberalisation in services in developing countries would contribute to economic growth in the region and strengthen economic integration not only regionally, but also multilaterally.[3]

Generally, little is known of how the design of a PTA affects its outcome in practice. As a consequence of a relatively weak quality of services trade data, only a handful of causal links between the design of a PTA and the economic outcome have been proven to date. For instance, classic PTAs, which are restricted to goods trade are 'least likely to be beneficial to developing countries, unless concluded with major industrialised partners'.[4] Next to these few proven links between PTAs in services and economic performance, theory tends to indicate that the economic impact of a PTA finally – and mainly – depends on the willingness of the parties to the PTA to implement the agreement and on the depth of their commitments.

The following paragraphs contribute to the literature on cause and effect of PTAs in services by empirically analysing the structure of commitments in South-South PTAs in services. This allows linking the existing

[1] Stephenson (2001, p. 19). [2] See Part III of this study.

[3] See Foundations of this study.

[4] Hoekman, Bernard (2001) Strengthening the Global Trade Architecture for Development: The Post Doha Agenda, PSIO Occasional Paper, WTO Series No. 11, Geneva, p. 35.

framework of commitments in preferential trade liberalisation in services among developing countries with the general literature on the theory of South-South preferential services trade. The current structure of commitments in South-South PTAs in services is primarily linked to the literature on the potential impact of a number of services sectors on economic development in developing countries, when substantially liberalised also in a South-South context.

In the dataset and based on the OECD list of ODI recipients,[5] thirty PTAs with substantial commitments in services trade liberalisation are South-South, meaning, members of them are only developing countries. They are all relatively young agreements, the oldest dating back to 1994. In terms of geographic spread, most of them are Latin American or Asian, with a few Central American and Caribbean agreements and even fewer African and Arab countries involved in South-South preferential services trade. Table 4 illustrates the timeline and the geographic spread of the thirty South-South PTAs in services in the dataset, which substantially liberalise services trade.

As stated previously, the focus in literature was until recently on North-North and North-South PTAs in the area of preferential services trade regulation. In addition, there are quite a number of case studies on South-South PTAs, which usually look at the structure and economic impact of a single agreement or of a small number of South-South PTAs.[6] So far, the general tendencies in South-South PTAs, the history of South-South preferential trade in services and the general geographic spread of South-South PTAs were not looked into in detail.

Even though the number of agreements may seem small at first, South-South PTAs are rapidly catching up with the number of North-North agreements, exceeding them by two agreements, which mention services trade liberalisation, in 2010.

In terms of numbers, the group of North-South PTAs in services is the largest, followed by – until recently in 2009 – North-North PTAs. Given that the largest services markets worldwide are to be found in industrialised countries, the initial focus on accessing the services markets in the North follows simple economic logic. However, the number of PTAs, of course, is not an indicator for the level of economic integration: (1) the dataset includes all agreements ever negotiated, meaning that it

[5] See previously, Foundations of this study and OECD (2015) DAC List of ODA Recipients: Effective for reporting on 2014, 2015 and 2016 flows.

[6] Case studies on MERCOSUR, ASEAN, COMESA, EAC, etc.

Table 4 *PTAs in services substantially liberalising services trade*[a]

1994	**2005**
Bolivia – Mexico	*India – Malaysia*
Colombia – Mexico	**2006**
Costa Rica – Mexico	*Chile – Colombia*
West African Monetary Union	*Chile – Panama*
1997	*Chile – Peru*
CARICOM Services	**2007**
MERCOSUR Services	*ASEAN – China*
Mexico – Nicaragua	*Colombia – Northern Triangle*
1998	*Malaysia – Pakistan*
Central America – Dominican Republic	**2008**
Chile – Mexico	*Chile – China*
1999	**2009**
Central America – Chile	*Chile – MERCOSUR*
2000	*China – Pakistan*
CARICOM – Cuba	*China – Peru*
Mexico – Northern Triangle	*East African Community*
2001	**2010**
CARICOM revised	*China – Costa Rica*
2002	**2011**
Central America – Panama	*Mexico – Peru*
2003	*Panama – Peru*
Mexico – Uruguay	

[a] Derived from dataset.

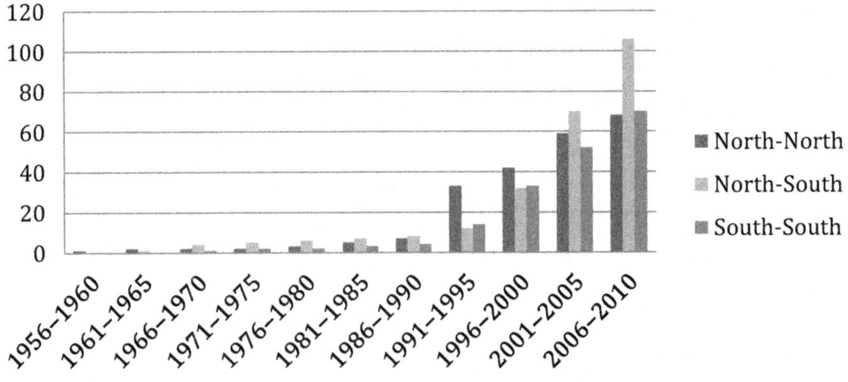

Figure 8 Number of PTAs in services by types of countries involved
Derived from dataset.

also includes agreements, which are not in force;[7] (2) some PTAs have not yet been properly implemented, even after decades;[8] (3) the dataset furthermore includes all agreements, which mention services trade at some point – in most of the cases, services trade is a more or less binding goal for future rounds of negotiations.[9]

When analysing the number of agreements, one also needs to keep in mind the number of countries belonging to the group of developed countries or developing countries. There are worldwide 196 countries. According to the OECD, 147 of them are LDCs or developing countries, with 54 countries belonging to the group of higher-middle-income countries, and the relatively small number of 49 countries being in the group of developed countries.[10] It is, thus, not surprising that even though the number of South-South agreements mentioning services trade at some point equals the number of North-North agreements and still South-South services market integration remains limited: given the large number of possible candidates in a South-South PTA in services, services market integration in the South is still in its infancy. North-North services market integration, arguably, has already reached a level at which further integration occurs through deeper commitments in existing PTAs and no longer through the conclusion of new agreements.

From a legal perspective, taking into consideration all the agreements, which were ever concluded, with the stated intention to preferentially liberalise trade in services at some point – irrespective of the economic impact of these agreements – is nonetheless relevant because it allows following the evolution and spread of preferential services trade regulation through history and geography. The following paragraphs, thus, include the entire dataset and are primarily concerned with describing and illustrating the evolution and spread of provisions governing South-South preferential services trade over time and places.

I. The History of South-South PTAs

The first mention of services trade liberalisation worldwide presumably is to be found in the *EC Treaty of Rome (1957)*, followed by a number of EPAs between Europe and African countries. The *EC Treaty of Rome (1957)* defines services basically as activities of commercial character,

[7] For instance *Bolivia – Mexico (1994)*.
[8] E.g. *Mexico – Nicaragua (1997)*.
[9] E.g. *Chile – Ecuador (1994)*.
[10] OECD (2015) DAC List of ODA Recipients: Effective for reporting on 2014, 2015 and 2016 flows.

which are not covered by the regulation of the movement of goods, capital or persons.[11] The commitments in this earliest provision on trade regulation in services can be characterised as a stand-still obligation with an obligation to negotiate further commitments in future rounds of negotiations.[12] The EU further refines its definition of trade in services in a number of subsequent EPAs with primarily African countries and Turkey.[13]

A. *South-South Services Trade Regulation Pre-Uruguay Round*

The history of South-South preferential services trade provisions dates back to as early as 1973.

The first PTA mentioning services trade regulation, which the EU is not involved in, is actually at the same time the first South-South PTA, including services trade regulation. In *CARICOM (1973)* preferentialism in services trade liberalisation is established as a general principle:[14]

> 1. Each Member State agrees as far as practicable to extend to persons belonging to other Member States' preferential treatment over persons belonging to States outside the common market with regard to the provision of services.
> 2. For the purposes of this Article the term 'services' shall be considered as services for remuneration provided that they are not governed by provisions relating to trade, the right of establishment or movement of capital and includes, in particular, activities of an industrial or commercial character, artisan activities and activities of the professions, excluding activities of employed persons.

The definition of trade in services in *CARICOM (1973)* is closely related to the definition as used by the EU at the time: services are defined

[11] See Art. 60 *EC Treaty of Rome (1957)*: 'Services shall be considered to be "services" within the meaning of this Treaty where they are normally provided for remuneration, in so far as they are not governed by the provisions relating to freedom of movement for goods, capital and persons. "Services" shall in particular include: (a) activities of an industrial character; (b) activities of a commercial character; (c) activities of craftsmen; (d) activities of the professions'.

[12] See Art. 59 *EC Treaty of Rome (1957)*: 'Within the framework of the provisions set out below, restrictions on freedom to provide services within the Community shall be progressively abolished [. . .]'; and Art. 62 *EC Treaty of Rome (1957)*: '[. . .] Member States shall not introduce any new restrictions on the freedom to provide services [. . .]'.

[13] *Yaoundé I (1961), Arusha Agreement II (1969), Yaoundé II (1969), EC Turkey Additional Protocol (1970).*

[14] *CARICOM (1973)*, Art. 36.

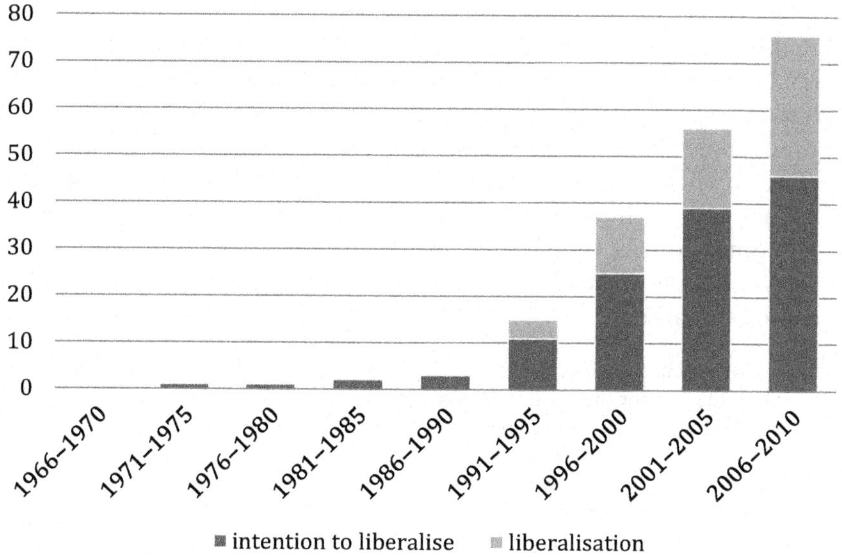

Figure 9 South-South PTAs in services from 1973 to 2010
Derived from dataset.

through falling outside of the regulation of trade, establishment and capital. With the limitation of 'as far as practicable', *CARICOM (1973)* furthermore establishes a commitment to grant preferential treatment of service providers of a member of CARICOM over third-party service providers. However, the nature of preferential treatment in this context is not further elaborated, and considering the limitation of practicability, this commitment is to be understood as a commitment to the idea of preferential services trade integration without yet establishing specific measures of liberalisation.

The use of a definition of services trade that is similar to the one used by the EU at the time is not a coincidence: the CARICOM was – next to being the result of a common struggle to emancipate from colonial rule – the attempt to replicate the success of the EU economic integration process. While initially similarities in the structure of the agreement with the European integration treaties were considerable, CARICOM later developed into a different direction, as it turned out that political integration was not a primary goal of the integration process.[15]

[15] For more information on the history of CARICOM, see, e.g. O'Brien, Derek (2011) 'CARICOM: Regional Integration in a Post-Colonial World', *European Law Journal*, vol. 17, no. 5, pp. 630–648.

The next South-South effort in services trade regulation was initiated by Caribbean countries as well: in 1981, the Organisation of Eastern Caribbean States (OECS) introduced provisions establishing services trade liberalisation as an official goal of economic integration, next to goods trade liberalisation and the movement of capital and persons. The objectives of the common market established in 1981 were, among others, 'to facilitate the interchange of goods and services by approximating the economic policies of Member States'.[16] Furthermore, free trade in services was to be considered a principle for achieving the objectives of the common market:[17]

> To achieve the objectives [. . .], the activities of the Member States shall include under the conditions and timing set out in this Agreement [. . .] the abolition, as between Member States, of the obstacles to the free movement of persons, services and capital.

However, while more specific provisions follow on the free movement of persons[18] and capital,[19] services provisions are missing in the subsequent treaty text. Thus, the *OECS (1981)* establishes a commitment to future preferential services trade liberalisation without a binding time frame or a stand-still obligation with regard to services trade among members. Furthermore, neither services nor the provision of services is defined. As such, *OECS (1981)* is more independent from other regulatory developments of services trade occurring at the time, in particular in European EPAs. However, given that all members of the OECS were also members of CARICOM, arguably, the basis for regulation of trade in service was already provided by the definition and scope in the *CARICOM (1973)*. It is in any case unlikely that members of the OECS would – at that time – engage in an inherently different approach to services trade regulation than CARICOM.

The OECS was formed by almost all of the LDC members of CARICOM. More than just economic integration, the underlying impetus for the formation of the OECS was that its members perceived a 'hostile world environment insensitive to the needs of small states'.[20] They felt that cooperation was necessary to strengthen their bargaining power vis-à-vis other states. Insofar, the OECS was not meant to be limited to economic integration only, but its main purpose also consisted in political integration.

[16] *OECS (1981)*, Annex I, Art. 2.
[17] *OECS (1981)*, Annex I, Art. 3.
[18] *OECS (1981)*, Annex I, Art. 13.
[19] *OECS (1981)*, Annex I, Art. 14 and Art. 15.
[20] Lewis, Patsy (2002) *Surviving Small Size: Regional Integration in Caribbean Ministates*, University of the West Indies Press, Kingston, p. 40.

OECS countries were successful in representing their development needs at the regional and global level. The process initiated by *OECS (1981)*, thus, delivered the results it was aiming for. However, internally, political integration is faced with obstacles already due to missing communication links among the OECS countries.[21]

Following the Caribbean integration process, Latin American countries began to extend their economic integration policies to services trade regulation. In 1988, Argentina and Brazil concluded a PTA with the objective of creating a common market between the two countries. All barriers to trade – both in tariffs and non-tariffs – were to be abandoned within ten years subsequent to the signatory of the agreement:[22]

> La remoción de todos los obstáculos tarifarios y no tarifarios al comercio de bienes y servicios en los territorios de los dos Estados Partes serán alcanzados, gradualmente, en un plazo máximo de diez años, a través de la negociación de protocolos adicionales [. . .]

Argentina – Brazil (1988) furthermore makes reference to the sectors of communication, education and transportation.[23] It does, however, only establish full preferential liberalisation of trade in services within ten years as a goal and leaves the details of services trade regulation open for subsequent negotiations. Subsequent negotiations led to the conclusion of *MERCOSUR (1991)*, with Paraguay and Uruguay joining Argentina and Brazil.[24]

Interestingly, around the same time, the first North-North PTAs in services with substantial commitments in services trade liberalisation were concluded.[25] These then new approaches to services trade regulation did, however, not impact on South-South services trade regulation.

B. *South-South Services Trade Regulation 1991–2000*

Around the time of the conclusion of the Uruguay Round, arguably also under the influence of multilateral trade negotiations in services, South-South services trade regulation took off. Between 1991 and 2000, twenty-two South-South PTAs in services covering services trade regulation as a goal, and twelve South-South PTAs in services covering

21 For more information on the Caribbean integration process, see Lewis (2002).

22 *Argentina – Brazil (1988)*, Art. 3. 23 *Argentina – Brazil (1988)*, Art. 4.

24 See also Levy Yeyati, Eduardo and Sturzenegger, Federico (2000) 'Is EMU a Blueprint for Mercosur?', *Cuadernos de Economia*, vol. 37, no. 110, pp. 63–99.

25 *Israel – US (1985)*, *ANZCERTA (1988)* and *Canada – US (1988)*.

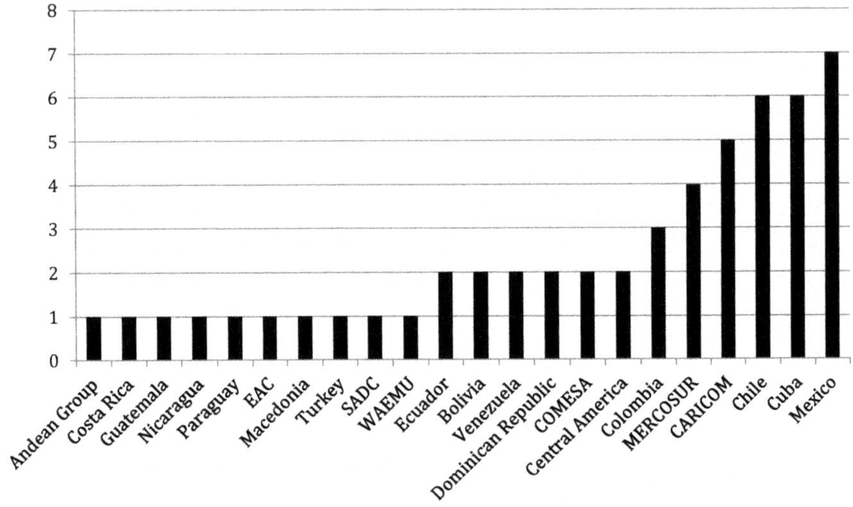

Figure 10 Number of PTAs by country of the South, 1991–2000
Derived from dataset.

substantial commitments in trade liberalisation in services were concluded. Primary drivers behind South-South preferentialism in services were the Latin American, followed by Caribbean countries and Central American countries.

The most active developing countries in the early wake of South-South preferentialism in services were Mexico, Cuba, Chile and the members of CARICOM. Most PTAs concluded at the beginning of the 1990s established a commitment to future trade liberalisation in services.[26] A few of them indeed turned into PTAs in services with substantial liberalising commitments in the meantime.[27] Mexico furthermore was among the first developing countries to introduce binding commitments in services trade liberalisation in the context of a South-South PTA.[28] Together with the West African Economic and Monetary Union,[29] Mexico and its partners undertook binding and substantial commitments in preferential services trade before the GATS went into force in 1995.

[26] *Chile – Mexico (1991), MERCOSUR (1991), CARICOM – Venezuela (1992), COMESA (1993), Chile – Colombia (1993), COMESA (1994), Chile – Ecuador (1994)* and *CARICOM – Colombia (1994).*

[27] *Chile – Mexico (1998), MERCOSUR Services (1997)* and *Chile – Colombia (2006).*

[28] *Costa Rica – Mexico (1994), Bolivia – Mexico (1994)* and *Colombia – Mexico (1994).*

[29] *WAEMU (1994).*

Chile – Mexico (1991) is the first South-South PTA, which makes a reference to multilateral regulation in the area of services trade.[30] The language used in *Chile – Mexico (1991)* became a template for trade negotiations led by Chile.[31] Another standardised reference to preferential services trade regulation appears for the first time in *CARICOM – Venezuela (1992)*. This choice phrasing is also found before and thereafter in other PTAs in services around the world:[32]

> 1. The Parties recognise the importance of trade in services for the development of their economies.
> 2. The Parties further recognise that it will be opportune and necessary to develop cooperation in this sector when the outcome of the Uruguay Round of Multilateral Trade Negotiations in the GATT is known. To this end, the Parties will negotiate amendments or further elaboration of this Agreement to take account of and to take advantage of the outcome of these negotiations.

Thus, the early 1990s see a steep increase in interest of developing countries in South-South PTAs in services, which results in the spread of two main models of services trade-related provisions in South-South PTAs, the Caribbean and the Chilean model. After entry into force of the GATS, standardised language in South-South PTAs changed again. Most likely, this is owed to the GATS and the establishment of multilateral regulation in trade in services as the basis for South-South preferential services trade regulation.

Not surprisingly, the structure and language of the three early substantial South-South PTAs in services, in which Mexico is a member, are quite similar. They all include a relatively extensive chapter on the regulation of trade liberalisation in services, as well as similar definitions and scope of application, which are closely related to the definition and scope in the GATS. Quite striking is, however, that two of the three agreements are based on a negative list approach,[33] while one is based on a positive list approach.[34] These three early South-South PTAs do, thus, not follow one single model agreement, like the NAFTA or the GATS. They are, however, following along the general structure already established by NAFTA and

[30] *Chile – Mexico (1991)*, Capitulo XII: '[. . .] considerando las negociaciones que se lleven a cabo en el ambito del GATT [. . .]'.

[31] Practically the same language is to be found in *Chile – Colombia (1993)*, Capitulo XIII; and in *Chile – Ecuador (1994)*, Capitulo XIII.

[32] *CARICOM – Venezuela (1992)*, Art. 13; the same language is to be found in *CARICOM – Columbia (1994)*, Art. 14.

[33] *Costa Rica – Mexico (1994)* and *Bolivia – Mexico (1994)*.

[34] *Colombia – Mexico (1994)*.

about to be established at the time by the GATS. In that respect, they do not differ from North-North PTAs in services.

Parallel to the first South-South preferentialism in Latin and Central America and in Caribbean countries, African developing countries started to engage in South-South services trade.

COMESA (1993), the pioneer agreement on the African continent, established in Art. 164 an individual commitment to adopt appropriate measures which would lead eventually to achieving free movement of services:[35]

> 1. The Member States agree to adopt, individually, at bilateral or regional levels the necessary measures in order to achieve progressively the free movement of persons, labour and services and to ensure the enjoyment of the right of establishment and residence by their citizens within the Common Market.
> 2. The Member States agree to conclude a Protocol on the Free Movement of Persons, Labour, Services, Right of Establishment and Right of Residence.

It is interesting to note that *COMESA (1993)* introduces entirely new language as to how the commitment to future trade liberalisation in services could be phrased. The commitment remained unchanged in the subsequent agreement of *COMESA (1994)* and the council of ministers adopted in 2009 the protocol on service trade. The protocol is closely related to the structure and scope of the GATS, and commitments are generally substantial.

While also relying heavily on the GATS (e.g. by limiting trade liberalisation under the PTA to the obligations under GATS), *SADC (1996)* introduces a slightly new definition of 'service':[36]

> "Services" means intangible activities and those enumerated in Annex 1B to the World Trade Organisation's General Agreement on Trade in Services (GATS);

In other words, the SADC introduces a definition of 'service', which includes on top of the definition by the GATS, also 'intangible activities'. While it would remain to analyse in detail what this differentiation in the definition of 'service' implicates in practice, obviously, the general scope of regulation based on this definition would be larger than that of the GATS. As an additional protocol on trade liberalisation in services

[35] *COMESA (1993)*, Art. 164. [36] *SADC (1996)*, Art. 1.

among the SADC countries yet has to be implemented, it remains unclear to what extent this larger scope of definition of 'services' was intentional and whether it will be kept.

Finally, the West African Economic and Monetary Union (WAEMU) introduced the first binding and substantial South-South commitments in preferential services trade on the African continent in 1994. It pursues an interesting avenue for trade liberalisation in services: by abolishing all discrimination among the nationals of the WAEMU members on the territory of the WAEMU, in fact services markets are fully integrated. Again, it is striking how *WAEMU (1994)* acts in relative independence from all other developments in the area of services trade regulation. It is quite likely, thus, that the timing of the *WAEMU (1994)* was less linked to the conclusion of the Uruguay Round, but rather linked to the commitment to achieving economic growth through regional economic integration.

In the second half of the 1990s, South-South preferentialism is already quite marked by the GATS as the underlying basis of services trade regulation and by the proliferation of services trade regulation in other PTAs.[37] Furthermore, with the two exceptions of the PTA between Turkey and Macedonia and the East African Community (EAC), South-South preferentialism related to services trade is limited to countries in Latin and Central America and the Caribbean.

What is new is that even PTAs, which only establish a commitment to future negotiations on trade liberalisation in services, provide for a rudimentary definition of services trade. This definition tends to be a more or less exact copy of the definition in the GATS.[38] Furthermore, with the exception of two PTAs involving the CARICOM,[39] in the second half of the 1990s, all South-South PTAs in services make a reference to GATS regulation or to multilateralism.

With differences in the language, generally, South-South PTAs, which establish services trade liberalisation as a goal for the future,[40] follow

[37] E.g. *Mexico – Nicaragua (1997)* and *Central America – Dominican Republic (1998)* are based on the GATS model, while *Chile – Mexico (1998)* and *Central America – Chile (1999)* both are based on the NAFTA model.

[38] E.g. *Chile – MERCOSUR (1996)*, Art. 35; *Andean Group (1997)*, Art. 80.

[39] *CARICOM Services (1997)* and *CARICOM – Dominican Republic (1998)*. *CARICOM – Cuba (2000)* and *CARICOM revised (2000)*, however, make a reference to the GATS again.

[40] *Bolivia – MERCOSUR (1996)*, *Chile – MERCOSUR (1996)*, *Chile – Peru (1998)*, *CARICOM – Dominican Republic (1998)*, *EAC (1999)*, *Cuba – Guatemala (1999)*, *Cuba –*

the following structure in the second half of the 1990s: (1) they make an explicit reference to the liberalisation of services trade in the future, usually in a separate – short – chapter or a separate article; (2) they do not go into further detail on the regulation and commitments in services trade aimed for; and (3) while the majority already provides for basic commitments in transportation,[41] with one exception,[42] movement of persons is not yet included in the commitments at this stage.

With a few differences, e.g. in the depth of commitments with respect to the movement of persons,[43] or the structure of financial services trade regulation,[44] the South-South PTAs with substantial services trade commitments involving either Chile, Central America or Mexico are more or less identical: (1) they all are based on a negative list approach, (2) the chapters on services trade regulation are relatively large and detailed and (3) business services, communication, financial services and the movement of persons are explicitly mentioned in the main treaty text in the majority of the PTAs. These agreements all tend to lean toward the NAFTA model of preferential services regulation.[45]

In 1997, two regional organisations, the MERCOSUR and CARICOM, adopted a protocol on preferential trade liberalisation in services. While *CARICOM Services (1997)* is essentially establishing stand-still obligations in the area of services trade regulation, *MERCOSUR Services (1997)* provides for extensive and detailed regulation of preferential services trade, limited however to a number of sectors of special interest. MERCOSUR is more closely related to GATS regulation than the other PTAs in services in the region, pursuing a positive list approach.[46]

Macedonia – Turkey (1999) re-introduces similar language to the South-South level to the one used in the CARICOM agreements in 1992:[47]

Venezula (1999), *Macedonia – Turkey (1999)*, *Columbia – Cuba (2000)*, *Cuba – Ecuador (2000)* and *Cuba – Paraguay (2000)*.

41 All except for *Bolivia – MERCOSUR (1996)*, *Chile – Peru (1998)*, *Macedonia – Turkey (1999)*. In addition to transportation, *CARICOM – Dominican Republic (1998)* furthermore explicitly includes business services, communication services, financial services and tourism in the PTA. *EAC (1999)* explicitly includes communication, energy, environment and tourism in addition to transportation.

42 *EAC (1999)*.

43 Less commitments in *Chile – Mexico (1998)*.

44 Financial services are regulated separately from services trade regulation in *Chile – Mexico (1998)*.

45 Derived from dataset.

46 Derived from dataset.

47 *Macedonia – Turkey (1999)*, Art. 13.

1. The Parties to this Agreement recognise the growing importance of certain areas, such as services and investments. In their efforts to gradually develop and broaden their cooperation, in particular in the context of the European integration, they will cooperate with the aim of achieving a progressive liberalisation and mutual opening of their markets for investments and trade in services, taking into account relevant provisions of the General Agreement on Trade and Services.
2. The Parties will discuss in the Joint Committee this cooperation with the aim of developing and deepening of their relations governed in this Article.

This phrasing is used more or less identically in EFTA PTAs.[48] The European influence on trade regulation in services and on the structure of PTAs in *Macedonia – Turkey (1999)*, similar to the European influence on CARICOM, thus, is reflected in the treaty language as well.

The EAC on the other hand pursues a different approach to trade liberalisation in services: the *EAC (1999)* establishes detailed and extensive regulation, first on the cooperation in the field of services-related aspects of trade. While *EAC (1999)* does not yet establish commitments in trade liberalisation in services, arguably, it paves the way for relatively substantial and quick regulation of services trade liberalisation by already establishing far-reaching cooperation among the members.[49]

C. South-South Services Trade Regulation 2001–2011

After 2000, the growth of the number of South-South PTAs related to services trade regulation further accelerates. Beginning in 2001, forty-one South-South PTAs in services were concluded within ten years. About half of them established substantial commitments in services trade liberalisation.[50] While South-South preferentialism in services now also

48 See, e.g. *EFTA – Estonia (1995)*, Art. 29: 'The States Parties to this Agreement recognize the growing importance of certain areas, such as services and investments. In their efforts to gradually develop and broaden their co-operation, in particular in the context of European integration, they will co-operate with the aim of achieving a gradual liberalization and mutual opening of markets for investments and trade in services, taking into account the results of the Uruguay Round as well as any relevant work under the auspices of the WTO'.

49 *EAC (1999)*, Chapter 15. Substantial commitments in trade liberalisation in services were adopted by EAC members in 2009.

50 Between 2001 and 2011, nineteen substantial South-South PTAs in services were concluded (Source: Derived from dataset).

spread to Asia, North Africa and South-East Europe, substantial preferential trade liberalisation in services on a South-South basis remained centred on Central and Latin American countries and the Caribbean: South-South PTAs in services establishing substantial trade liberalisation involved at least one member of said regions between 2001 and 2011.[51]

Notable exceptions to this rule are Asian South-South PTAs in services either involving Malaysia[52] or China.[53] While Malaysia's only two South-South PTAs in services are both concluded with Asian partners, China in fact also engaged in cross-continental South-South preferentialism in services. The Asian South-South PTAs with substantial commitments all take a positive list approach and tend to resemble the GATS model. While the PTAs involving China tend to go a bit further in depth of commitments, the Malaysian PTAs nevertheless establish commitments in all sectors, with the notable exception of financial services.[54]

Finally, the only other South-South PTA in services establishing substantial liberalising commitments is the protocol of the EAC in 2009. Given that the protocol is the result of the previous establishment of EAC in 1999, and considering that no other African countries did substantially commit to preferential South-South services trade liberalisation during this period of time, the conclusion of the *EAC Services (2009)* cannot be understood as representative. Rather, the fact that next to *EAC Services (2009)* no other African countries committed to substantial services trade liberalisation on a South-South basis could be interpreted as a sign for decreasing interest in South-South preferential services trade liberalisation on the African continent.[55] Since African countries were among the first developing countries to enter into South-South trade negotiations over trade liberalisation in services in the early 1990s, this finding comes as a surprise to a certain extent.[56]

Despite the still prevalent focus of substantial South-South preferential trade liberalisation in services on Central and Latin American countries

[51] *CARICOM revised (2001), Central America – Panama (2002), Mexico – Uruguay (2003), China – Panama (2003), Chile – Colombia (2006), Chile – Peru (2006), Chile – Panama (2006), Colombia – Northern Triangle (2007), Chile – China (2008), Chile – MERCOSUR (2009), China – Peru (2009), China – Costa Rica (2010), Mexico – Peru (2011)* and *Panama – Peru (2011).*

[52] *India – Malaysia (2005)* and *Malaysia – Pakistan (2007).*

[53] *ASEAN – China (2007)* and *China – Pakistan (2009).*

[54] Derived from dataset.

[55] Maybe with the exception of North African countries, which started to engage on a non-binding level in South-South PTAs in services during 2001 until 2011.

[56] See *WAEMU (1994).*

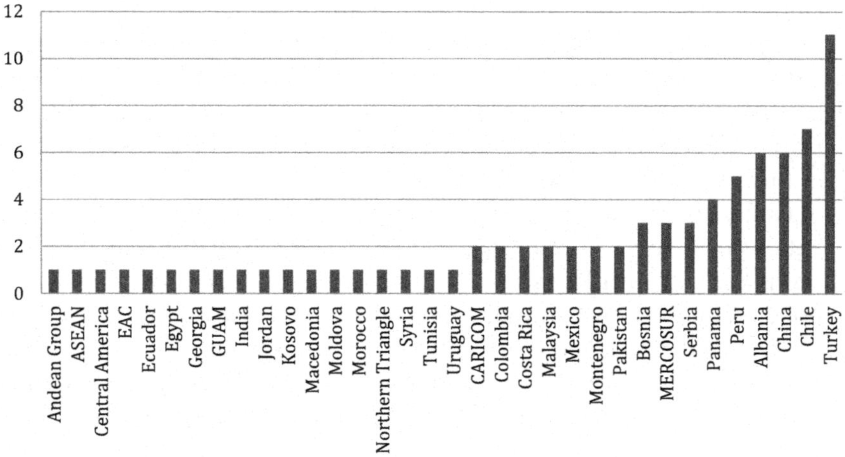

Figure 11 Number of PTAs by country of the South, 2001–2011
Derived from dataset.

and the Caribbean, Figure 11 illustrates well the breadth and scope of the increasing interest in South-South PTAs in services beginning in 2001.

Given that a number of developing countries, in the 2000s, began to negotiate South-South PTAs and established a commitment to future preferential services trade liberalisation, it is likely that the 2010s will see an increase in substantial South-South services trade commitments involving the countries, which established commitments to future South-South trade liberalisation in the 2000s.

Notably, Turkey was particularly active, concluding no less than eleven South-South PTAs, which established a commitment to future services trade liberalisation.[57] Most of Turkey's South-South PTAs related to services trade regulation are concluded with neighbouring countries. The South-South economic integration in the region corresponds with Turkey's policy on international trade, which was meant to increase regional economic integration in the Black Sea region in order to foster economic growth in Turkey.[58] The provision establishing the Turkish

[57] *Bosnia and Herzegovina – Turkey (2002), Syria – Turkey (2004), Morocco – Turkey (2004), Tunisia – Turkey (2004), Egypt – Turkey (2005), Albania – Turkey (2006), Georgia – Turkey (2007), Montenegro – Turkey (2008), Jordan – Turkey (2009), Serbia – Turkey (2009)* and *Chile – Turkey (2009).*

[58] See 'The Effect of New Turkish Foreign Policy on International Trade', *Insight Turkey*, vol. 15, no. 3.

commitment to preferential services trade in the future is based on the same structure and language as in *Macedonia – Turkey (1999)*. Thus, although there arguably is sincere interest in substantial economic integration among the countries involved in Turkish South-South PTAs, the provision does not establish a specific time frame, nor did the members of these PTAs commit to specific liberalising measures.[59]

Chile, although previously strongly engaged in South-South preferentialism in services trade between 2001 and 2011 concluded another seven South-South PTAs in services.[60] The main focus of Chile's trade policy remained on Latin and Central America. However, with *Chile – China (2008)* and *Chile – Turkey (2009)*, Chile is among the first developing countries to engage in cross-continental South-South preferentialism. Notably, with the exception of *Chile – Ecuador (2008)* and *Chile – Turkey (2009)*, all of the Chilean South-South PTAs in services established substantial liberalising commitments.

China, finally, another major driver behind South-South preferentialism in services trade in the years 2001–2011, interestingly engaged in cross-continental South-South preferentialism in services right after the conclusion of its first South-South PTA in services: *ASEAN – China (2007)* is China's first South-South PTA in services, followed by *Chile – China (2008)* just one year later. China, thus, to the contrary of other developing countries, did not begin to liberalise services trade first primarily with neighbouring developing countries, but immediately entered into cross-continental economic integration. In 2011, China is already relatively well integrated with Central and Latin American services markets, with a total of three South-South PTAs establishing substantial commitments in trade liberalisation in services.[61]

In general, Asian countries are late starters with reference to South-South preferentialism in services. *India – Malaysia (2005)* was the first South-South PTA in services in Asia, being concluded almost fifteen years after Caribbean, Latin and Central American countries, as well as African countries started to engage in South-South preferentialism in services. In 2011, only four intra-Asian South-South PTAs in services existed.[62]

[59] E.g. *Jordan – Turkey (2009)*, Art. 36: The title of the article is, for instance 'Co-operation in Services', which does not necessarily imply trade liberalisation.

[60] *Chile – Colombia (2006)*, *Chile – Peru (2006)*, *Chile – Panama (2006)*, *Chile – Ecuador (2008)*, *Chile – China (2008)*, *Chile – Turkey (2009)* and *Chile – MERCOSUR (2009)*.

[61] *Chile – China (2008)*, *China – Peru (2009)* and *China – Costa Rica (2009)*.

[62] *India – Malaysia (2005)*, *ASEAN – China (2007)*, *Malaysia – Pakistan (2007)* and *China – Pakistan (2009)*.

Compared to the vast number of South-South PTAs in Latin and Central America, thus, Asia definitely lags behind with respect to South-South economic integration in services.

Moreover, it is interesting that, besides the members of ASEAN, only three Asian countries have engaged in an Asian South-South PTA until 2011: China, India and Pakistan. The limited number of Asian South-South PTAs should, however, not deceive: all of the four Asian South-South PTAs in services establish substantial liberalising commitments, encompassing in general all services sectors.[63] Compared to the large number of South-South PTAs established in the Black Sea region that, however, do not establish binding commitments just yet, Asia is arguably more integrated on a regulatory basis with respect to services trade.

Finally, with respect to the South-East and Eastern European engagement in South-South PTAs related to services, it has to be noted that despite the high number, none of the PTAs establishes binding and substantial commitments in trade in services.[64] The next decade will most likely show to what extent the intention to liberalise services trade among developing countries in South-East Europe and in Eastern Europe and their neighbouring developing countries indeed translates into economic and regulatory integration in services trade.

To summarise, South-South preferential services trade regulation first appeared in the Caribbean in 1973. It was taken up by Brazil and Argentina in 1988 and subsequently spread to whole Central and Latin America in the 1990s. In parallel to the Central and Latin American proliferation of South-South preferentialism in services, African countries, too, were among the first developing countries worldwide to engage in South-South services trade integration. However, African countries' interest in substantially committing to South-South preferential services trade rapidly decreased after the conclusion of *WAEMU (1994)*, leading only to one other substantial African South-South PTA by the EAC in 2009. South-Eastern Europe, North Africa and Asia started to engage in South-South preferentialism in services as late as of beginning of 2000.

Substantial commitments in South-South services trade liberalisation are mainly established in Central and Latin America. In addition, substantial services trade integration continues to progress in the Caribbean. All of the rather young Asian South-South PTAs in services establish substantial commitments in trade liberalisation, while South-Eastern and Eastern Europe, as well as the Black Sea region, although beginning to

[63] Derived from dataset. [64] Derived from dataset.

engage in South-South preferentialism, have not yet established substantial commitments in services trade integration.

Finally, the first cross-continental South-South PTAs in services were concluded between China and Central and Latin American countries in the late 2000s. All in all, particularly in the Black Sea region, in Asia and on the African continent, the level of South-South trade integration in services remains relatively low. Thus, the bulk of the alleged economic potential of South-South PTAs in services remains untapped in 2011, with the notable exception of Central and Latin America.

II. The Geography of South-South PTAs

The historical analysis already showed that South-South preferentialism in services roots in the Caribbean and is most proliferated in Central and Latin America today. Asia may be beginning to catch up, with the first substantial South-South PTAs in services concluded within the past eight years. On the African continent, South-South preferentialism is still limited to a few regional economic unions, with only WAEMU and EAC establishing substantial commitments. The Black Sea region started to endeavour into South-South preferentialism in services in the past ten years, without, however, yet establishing substantial liberalising commitments. Finally South-Eastern and Eastern Europe, too, started to endeavour to establish South-South PTAs in services in the past ten years; however, no binding commitments have yet resulted from these efforts.

While in the 1990s South-South preferentialism in services was dominated by Latin and Central America and the Caribbean, this has changed in the past ten years.

While in the years 2001–2011 Latin American countries continue to be the most active developing countries with establishing South-South PTAs in services, regions subsequently absent in South-South preferentialism start to engage in South-South PTAs in services as well. In particular, Asia, Europe and the African countries near the Black Sea region are most actively engaging in South-South preferentialism.

Part of the reason why Latin American countries continue to be so strong in South-South services trade integration may also be that a few Latin and Central American countries have started to engage in cross-continental preferentialism in the past ten years. However, South-South preferentialism is generally limited to regional economic integration. Cross-regional or even cross-continental South-South preferentialism in services trade remains limited in 2011.

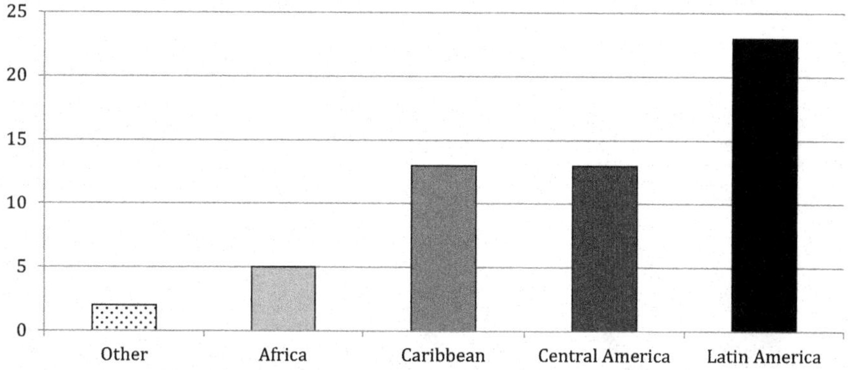

Figure 12 Number of countries involved in PTA by region of the South, 1991–2000
Derived from dataset.

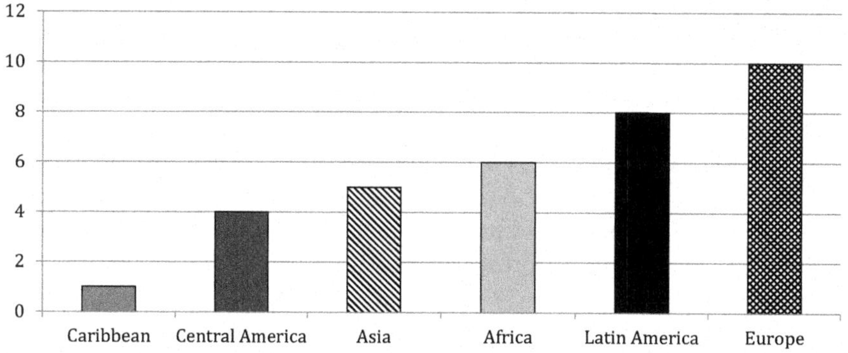

Figure 13 Number of countries involved in PTA by region of the South, 2001–2010
Derived from dataset.

The fact that the majority of the South-South PTAs in services are regional – meaning, they are concluded among countries which are geographically not located too far away from each other – contradicts the theory that from an economic point of view trade liberalisation in services would be more suitable for cross-continental liberalisation than goods trade, because transportation costs are limited.[65] It may indicate that services trade liberalisation is in tendency incorporated into regional PTAs,[66] meaning also into existing agreements. It may also be understood

[65] Dihel, Eschenbach and Sheperd (2008, p. 54).
[66] See also Dihel et al. (2008, p. 71).

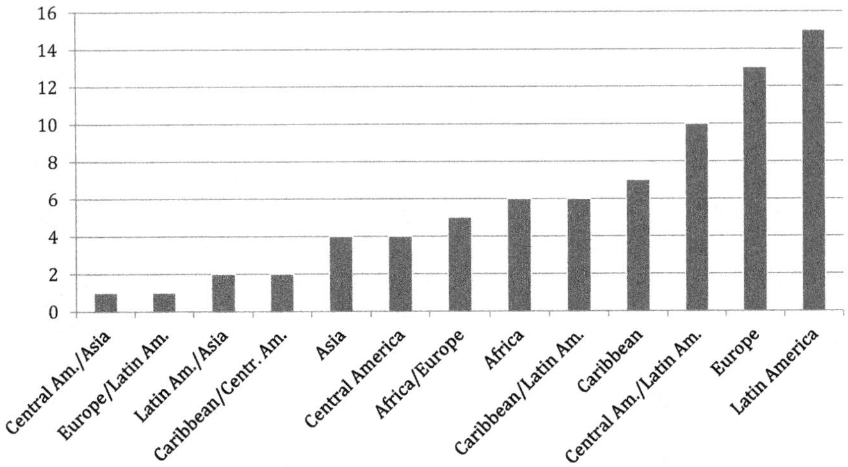

Figure 14 Regional distribution of South-South PTAs in services.
Derived from dataset.

as an indicator that services trade liberalisation itself is not incentive enough to launch negotiations on free trade with another country.

In conclusion, the analysis shows that the majority of South-South PTAs in services are regional. Cross-regional South-South preferentialism in services is most prevalent between Central and Latin America and the Caribbean. Cross-continental South-South PTAs are a more recent phenomenon, limited to PTAs between Asia and Latin and Central America, and Europe and Latin America in 2011.

While South-South PTAs in services continue to proliferate in Latin and Central America, developing countries in Asia, Europe and the Black Sea region recently started to engage on a larger scale in South-South preferentialism in services. African countries – with the exception of North African countries – have not engaged on a larger scale in South-South preferentialism in services in recent years.

PART II

Legal Regime for Preferential Services Trade

> "Laws are not made like lime-twigs or nets, to catch everything that toucheth them; but rather like sea-marks, to guide from shipwreck the ignorant passenger."
>
> *Philip Sidney, The Countess of Pembroke's Arcadia*

All international economic law is linked one way or another to WTO law. Even though WTO law has no *de jure* supremacy over regional or bilateral trade agreements, it is nevertheless the benchmark for the establishment and implementation of preferential trade agreements.[1] This is important because WTO law constitutes the multilateral framework for all international economic law, therewith establishing a common ground of shared principles, dispute settlement and the basic logic of international economic law.

WTO law embraces the option of other means and *fora* for the establishment of trade law and provides for a couple of basic rules and requirements governing the global structure of international economic law. It aims at securing the underlying logic of trade law and at ensuring that trade law in its various forms contributes to global equality and economic growth.[2] By introducing commitments on the multilateral level and a well-working dispute settlement system in the case of disregard of multilateral commitments, at least with respect to WTO members, WTO law develops a potentially constitutional character: multilateral commitments in WTO law, which impact on trade policy also beyond the strict sense of world

1 See, e.g. Cottier, Thomas and Oesch, Matthias (2001) 'WTO Law, Precedents and Legal Change', *Turku Law Journal*, vol. 3, no. 1, pp. 27–41, pp. 36–8.

2 See, e.g. Cottier, Thomas (1993) 'Constitutional Trade Regulation in National and International Law: Structure-Substance Pairings in the EFTA Experience', In: M. Hilf and E-U. Petersmann (eds.), *National Constitutions and International Economic Law*, Kluwer Law and Taxation Publishers, Boston, pp. 409–442, pp. 410–411; Cottier, Thomas and Nadakavukaren Schefer, Krista (1998) 'The Relationship between World Trade Organisation Law, National and Regional Law', *Journal of International Economic Law*, vol. 1, no. 1, pp. 83–122.

trade policy, can be enforced through WTO dispute settlement and therefore need to be respected.

GATS Art. V, which establishes the requirements that a PTA in services needs to meet in order to justify an MFN exemption, is an example of such a commitment under WTO law, which impacts relatively widely on trade policy of WTO members. Disregarding GATS Art. V may potentially trigger a dispute settlement, which is costly, not only financially, but also with respect to legal certainty and economic stability. Thus, members are generally expected to fulfil their commitments under GATS Art. V at their best.

With trade negotiations at the multilateral level being stuck for the moment, many members of the WTO have turned to regional and bilateral trade in order to compensate for the vacuum left by incomplete WTO law.[3] Thus, the regulation and guidance of PTAs (primarily through GATT Art. XXIV and GATS Art. V) is of utmost importance for the global structure of international economic law,[4] especially until meaningful progress is made at the multilateral level: the idea behind those two provisions is to avoid that preferentialism introduces regulatory contradictions to multilateral trade regulation or compromises the overall coherence and enforceability of IEL.

This issue of the legal hierarchy between multilateralism and preferentialism has occupied legal scholars for more than a decade. In his essay on the reform of GATT Art. XXIV, Picker (2005) suggests that, most importantly, WTO supremacy needed to be established.[5] Devuyst and Serdarevic (2007) also suggest that the supremacy of WTO regulation be established. They consider the constitutional approach of Jackson (1997)[6] and Cottier and Foltea (2006)[7] to be stretching the concept too far and

[3] See, e.g. Marchetti, Juan A. and Roy, Martin (2008) 'Services Liberalisation in the WTO and in PTAs', In: J. A. Marchetti and M. Roy (eds.), *Opening Markets for Trade in Services*, World Trade Organisation, Cambridge University Press, Cambridge, pp. 61–112, pp. 71–72.

[4] E.g. Stephenson, Sherry (2000a) 'Regional Agreements on Services in Multilateral Disciplines: Interpreting and Applying GATS Article V', In: S. Stephenson (ed.), *Services Trade in the Western Hemisphere*, Brookings Institution Press, Washington DC, pp. 86–104.

[5] Picker, Colin B. (2005) 'Regional Trade Agreements v. the WTO: A Proposal for Reform of Article XXIV to Counter this Institutional Threat', *Journal of International Economic Law*, vol. 26, no. 2, pp. 267–319, p. 268.

[6] Jackson, John H. (1997) *The World Trading System: Law and Policy of International Economic Relations*, 2nd edition, The MIT Press, London.

[7] Cottier, Thomas and Foltea, Marina (2006) 'Constitutional Functions of the WTO and Regional Trade Agreements', In: L. Bartels and F. Ortino (eds.), *Regional Trade Agreements and the WTO Legal System*, Oxford University Press, Oxford.

instead suggest minor changes in the language of GATS Art. V and GATT Art. XXIV, as well as some institutional changes with respect to how the PTAs should be controlled.[8]

Arguably, despite the undisputed relevance of WTO law for the regulation of trade in its various forms, GATS Art. V is, however, not the strongest provision and of limited constitutional nature: to date, no dispute over disregarding GATS Art. V has been brought before the Dispute Settlement Body (DSB). The reason for this absence of dispute settlement cases relating to GATS Art. V may even lie in the dispute settlement system itself: members will only institute legal proceedings if a substantial trade gain or trade loss is at stake. It is difficult to substantiate such a significant impact on trade volumes based on a PTA that is not completely in line with GATS Art. V requirements. And since the inherent unattractiveness of the dispute settlement route for GATS Art. V provisions is unlikely to change any time soon, a violation or infringement of GATS Art. V may possibly be of limited consequence. Thus, members may be less afraid of paying limited attention to GATS Art. V and may be prepared to risk a potential collision between GATS Art. V commitments and commitments in PTAs. Therefore, analysing the exact meaning and scope of GATS Art. V provisions is all the more relevant.

In the context of this debate, this part investigates and evaluates the legal regime for PTAs in services. It starts with a historical view on preferentialism and its regulation, followed by the history of flexibilities in services trade regulation as established by the GATS. It then continues with a legal analysis of these flexibilities, which highlights the key challenges in finding the appropriate regulatory balance with respect to the functioning of preferentialism in services trade. It highlights that the GATS provisions establishing the requirements for PTAs in services are not straightforward and do not contribute to improving legal certainty. The legal discussion of GATS Art. V further shows that the relative vagueness of multilateral regulation of preferentialism in services trade does not only have implications with respect to the protection of the systemic logic of IEL but also affects the content and structure of PTAs in services, as well as the work of WTO bodies. This part concludes by outlining possible amendments that could re-establish a functioning system of checks and balances with respect to preferentialism in services trade.

[8] Devuyst, Youri and Serdarevic, Asja (2007) 'The World Trade Organisation and Regional Trade Agreements: Bridging the Constitutional Credibility Gap', *Duke Journal of Comparative & International Law*, vol. 18, no. 1, pp. 1–75.

1

Historical Background of Preferentialism in Services Trade and its Regulation

The regulation of preferentialism in services trade at the multilateral level began with the adoption of the GATS, which entered into force on 1 January 1995. Before the GATS, PTAs were primarily regulated through GATT Art. XXIV, which, however, does not refer to the regulation of preferential services trade. As preferentialism in services trade usually is one aspect of preferentialism in other areas of trade – mainly goods, but also investment and intellectual property – the preferential regulation of services trade was indirectly limited through GATT XXIV before the existence of the GATS. Theoretically, however, countries were entirely free to invent and commit to any form of preferential services trade regulation until the entry into force of the GATS in 1995.

Multilateral services trade regulation was negotiated in a fifteen-year-long process that had started in the 1980s. As argued above, the GATS can be considered as a major innovation for the global trading system since it was negotiated before preferential services trade flows reached a critical mass. Prior to that, attempts to include services trade regulation in the early GATT had failed, mainly because services were to a large extent considered non-tradable.[1] Therefore, it is less surprising that prior to the GATS, only a handful of PTAs included a reference to services trade regulation. Thus, the introduction of GATS Art. V in 1995 did not pose a general threat or a problem for PTAs in services which had been established prior to GATS regulation.

At the international level, 'The OECD codes of liberalisation of capital movements and of current invisible transactions', which were adopted in 1961, represented a first step towards liberalising movements of services and capital. Even though the codes were not legally enforceable, they provided the first international framework for liberalising trade in

[1] Hoekman, Bernard and Mattoo, Aaditya (2007a), 'International Trade: Trade in Services', In: A. T. Guzman and A. O. Sykes (eds.), *Research Handbook in International Economic Law*, Edward Elgar Publishing Limited, Cheltenham, pp. 113–150, p. 113.

services.[2] One of the first people to recognise the importance of trade in services was Hugh Corbet,[3] an Australian who in 1968 established the Trade Policy Research Centre in London. He commissioned Brian Griffiths from the London School of Economics to undertake a study of international flows of services and restriction on transactions in the services sector. The resulting book called *Invisible Barriers to Invisible Trade* (published in 1975)[4] became the starting point for much of the subsequent work in the field of services trade liberalisation.[5]

More or less in parallel to the work on said book, the OECD countries identified the need for action in order to ensure liberalisation and non-discrimination in the services sector, and the US government adopted the strategy to include services in international trade liberalisation negotiations. Consequently, the Tokyo Round resulted in a few references to services, however, only insofar as they affected trade in goods.[6]

The following years were marked by the international community's efforts to collect meaningful background information on services trade. In the 1980s, the United States conducted bilateral consultations and negotiations over services trade liberalisation with both Canada and Israel, resulting in the conclusion of the first binding bilateral US trade agreement in services with Canada. These negotiations were considered to serve as a 'dress rehearsal' for the following multilateral negotiations.[7]

Most interestingly, while literature on multilateral trade negotiations usually focuses on the role of the United States, the EU and developing countries, it tends to be forgotten that in parallel to the US American efforts to bring trade regulation in services forward, Australia and New Zealand signed an exceptionally far-reaching and comprehensive

[2] Barth (1999, p. 40).

[3] See, e.g. Corbet, Hugh (1977) 'Prospect of Negotiations on Barriers to International Trade in Services', *Pacific Community*, vol. 8, no. 3, pp. 454–469.

[4] Griffiths, Brian (1975) *Invisible Barriers to Invisible Trade*, Trade Policy Research Centre, Macmillan, London.

[5] Feketekuty, Geza (1988), *International Trade in Services: An Overview and Blueprint for Negotiations*, Ballinger Publishing Company, Cambridge, p. 296.

[6] Feketekuty (1988, pp. 298–304); Malmgren, Harald B. (1985) 'Negotiating International Rules for Trade in Services', *The World Economy*, vol. 8, no. 1, pp. 11–26.

[7] Feketekuty (1988, pp. 305–313); Bhagwati, Jagdish N. (1987) 'Trade in Services and the Multilateral Trade Negotiations', *The World Bank Economic Review*, vol. 1, no. 4, pp. 549–569, p. 566–567: 'My suspicion is that, while this multilateral "constitution making" on the principles of a services Agreement will go on, the United States will continue to use bilateral approaches [. . .] to pry open selected service sectors in selected countries".

agreement on preferential trade liberalisation in services, the *ANZCERTA (1987)*.[8] This agreement is based on a negative list approach and encompasses all trade in services while abstaining from defining services sectors or modes of supply. It is a binding commitment to the status quo as a minimum standard and to liberalising trade in services entirely in the future. It provides for full market access as the general principle, along with National Treatment. Furthermore, it provides for the free movement of natural and legal persons.[9] Arguably, the approach to services trade regulation in *ANZCERTA (1987)* was too much focused on trade liberalisation instead of trade regulation to serve as a blueprint for multilateral services trade regulation. While the agreement provided an ideal basis for the services market integration in the region, its implementation depended on the strong commitment to services trade liberalisation of its members. Such a commitment and such regulatory bravery were not given at the multilateral level at the time.

During the process of collecting information on trade regulation of services, all the industrialised countries came to the conclusion that services trade is in their interest. Thus, they aimed at putting services trade regulation on the agenda of the GATT for new multilateral trade negotiations. However, in 1984 this attempt failed because no consensus could be reached between developed and developing countries over services. Finally, and after many meetings with developing countries, the agenda for the Uruguay Round of multilateral trade negotiations, including negotiations over services trade liberalisation, was approved, and subsequently led to the establishment – separate from the GATT – of the multilateral treaty for trade in services, the GATS.[10]

However, negotiations over trade liberalisation in services were difficult for a multitude of reasons, and consensus of the GATS treaty is not understood as the final goal for multilateral trade liberalisation and regulation in services, but rather as a first step in the right direction. The GATS was meant as a stepping-stone for subsequent rounds of multilateral trade negotiations, which would aim at further differentiating the regulatory principles of trade in services and deepening the level of liberalisation. However, to date, offers for further liberalisation suffer from a lack of

[8] See also Shingal, Anirudh and Sauvé, Pierre (2011) Reflections on the Preferential Liberalisation of Services Trade, MPRA Paper No. 32816, Munich, p. 6.

[9] See *ANZCERTA (1987)* and Holmes, Frank (1990) 'ANZCERTA, Trade in Services, and ASEAN', *ASEAN Economic Bulletin*, vol. 7, no. 1, pp. 1–10, p. 4.

[10] Feketekuty (1988, p. 321); for the reasons why developing countries finally joined the negotiations, see Bhagwati (1987, pp. 567–568).

ambition, and multilateral regulation has not substantially evolved since the establishment of the GATS.[11]

There are numerous reasons why multilateral liberalisation of trade in services has not further advanced since 1995.[12] Next to the fact that industrialised countries and developing countries do not yet agree on a specific agenda for multilateral trade negotiations in services, today services trade liberalisation in general is constrained by powerful, vested interests of governments, labour unions and the constituency (access to services, demand for cheap services, safe workplaces). Furthermore, because services are more difficult and complex to trade, export interests in services are generally weaker than in manufacturing/goods.[13] Finally, trade barriers to services are hard to quantify. Notwithstanding the measurement difficulties, empirical estimates suggest that barriers to services trade tend to be higher than those applying to goods trade.[14] Tariff equivalent estimates of barriers to services trade suggest that maritime cabotage, air transport, postal services, telecommunications and life insurance are the 'most restricted sectors in both developing and developed countries, with reported rates of 200% for most countries'.[15]

Thus, to date, the overall level of trade liberalisation in services through the GATS is limited, since most of the liberalising commitments in the country schedules remain unimportant in their scope. True trade liberalisation in services has mainly been achieved through the negotiating process of WTO accession and through PTAs.[16] The fact that the liberalisation and regulation of services trade in PTAs is more animated than in the multilateral forum raises the question how preferential services trade regulation interacts – and impacts – with multilateral regulation. GATS Art. V is the most prominent link between the two regulatory levels.

To discuss the implications of GATS Art. V provisions for the interaction between preferential and multilateral services trade regulation, one has to keep in mind the current state of the legal basis for services trade regulation. Despite the emphasis on transparency at the beginning of the GATS treaty, this is, however, a challenge: the GATS is inherently a non-transparent agreement. As a consequence of the adopted scheduling

[11] Marchetti and Roy (2008, p. 70).

[12] For a discussion, see, e.g. Schwab, Susan C. (2011) 'After Doha: Why the Negotiations Are Doomed and What We Should Do about It', *Foreign Affairs*, vol. 90, no. 3, pp. 104–117.

[13] Hoekman, Bernard (2000) 'The Next Round of Services Negotiations: Identifying Priorities and Options', Review, Federal Reserve Bank of St. Louis, p. 32.

[14] Australian Government (2004, p. 7). [15] Ibid.

[16] Adlung (2007, p. 10).

of voluntary commitments in trade liberalisation in services, the structure of multilateral services trade regulation is particularly complex and it requires a high level of expertise to understand the scope of commitments and the regulatory implications in individual cases. Furthermore, the GATS cannot be used as a source of information for any service sector, which is not included in a national schedule. Even on the scheduled sectors, the GATS contains little information, because it is restricted to the regulation of liberalising commitments and provides no information on the regulation with respect to areas of trade in services, in which no commitments have been entered in the schedule.[17]

Thus, GATS regulation is primarily viewed as securing the 'status quo' and consists mainly in 'stand-still bindings': in essence, Member States are only committed to maintain the current level of liberalisation.[18] The level and depth of liberalisation, as well as the regulatory environment of trade in services, therefore, differs substantially from one country to another. In order to discuss the link between multilateral and preferential services trade regulation, the legal discussion needs to be split into different layers: (1) the general principles and provisions in multilateral services trade regulation as provided by the main treaty text of the GATS; (2) the general principles and provisions in preferential services trade regulation as provided by the main treaty text of PTAs (here, already a minimum level of empirical estimation is required in order to embrace the main issues) and finally (3) the commitments in services trade liberalisation as scheduled in services sectors and subsectors, either on a case-by-case basis, or on the basis of empirical evidence. As the GATS includes a list of 12 services sectors divided into an additional approximately 160 subsectors, conclusive regulatory information on preferential versus multilateral trade in services can only be provided by including all the different regulatory layers.[19]

Given that the GATS was initially meant as a stepping-stone for further liberalisation and new regulation of services trade, the resulting low level of liberalisation is less of a surprise: GATS is the first – and so far the only – pluri- or multilateral agreement in trade in services, and the regulation

[17] Stephenson, Sherry (2002) 'Regional versus Multilateral Liberalisation of Services', *World Trade Review*, vol. 1, no. 2, pp. 187–209, p. 190.

[18] Stephenson (2002, p. 192).

[19] For an overview and general discussion of the different regulatory layers in the GATS, see Adlung, Rudolf and Roy, Martin (2005) Turning Hills into Mountains? Current Commitments under the GATS and Prospects for Change, Staff Working Paper, Economic Research and Statistics Division, WTO, Geneva.

of services trade at the time of the implementation of the GATS in 1995 was a new phenomenon. Thus, countries were cautious with respect to entering liberalising commitments in their schedules. The following paragraphs outline the regulatory basis of multilateral trade in services as established by the main treaty text of the GATS. A particular focus lies on the regulatory flexibilities: flexibilities are important, as they may enable multilateral consensus and are thus central for the conclusion of multilateral negotiations. Flexibilities, however, may also erode multilateral commitments if they are too far reaching in scope. Given that the levels of commitments under the GATS differ from one country to another already as a consequence of the positive list approach, flexibilities under the GATS are at a particularly high risk of eroding overall commitments in multilateral liberalisation and regulation of services trade.

In principle, the GATS regulation would cover more aspects of trade than the GATT, particularly by covering also certain behind-the-border regulation of services trade, like, e.g. how foreign service suppliers have to be treated by the institutions of a member (non-discrimination). However, this breadth came at a cost: the theoretical depth of commitments under GATS was structurally balanced through flexibility. Flexibility was foremost provided through the positive list approach, the system of entering liberalising commitments individually in the schedules. This structure allows exempting a measure from the GATS disciplines and enables countries to tailor their liberalising commitments under the GATS to a minimum.[20]

The discussions on these flexibilities started back in 1986 when developing countries tried to prevent multilateral trade negotiations on services. Although they did not succeed, their opposition allowed for a separate agreement, which was not part of the GATT.[21] During the negotiations it was agreed that governments needed to be able to impose conditions on inward Foreign Direct Investment (FDI) and to support domestic

[20] Das, Kasturi (2006) *GATS Negotiations and India: Evolution and State of Play* Centre for Trade and Development (Centad), New Delhi, p. 10.

[21] The primary proponent of multilateral trade liberalisation in services was the United States because of pressure from private actors. They threatened to abandon the GATT if trade in services was not placed on the table. The final compromise was put forward by Switzerland and Colombia, suggesting to include services in the negotiations with letting it open whether or not to include services in the GATT. For more information, see Reyna, Jimmie V. (1993) 'Services', In: T. P. Stewart (ed.), *The GATT Uruguay Round: A Negotiating History (1986–1992)*, vol. II, Kluwer Law and Taxation Publishers, Deventer, pp. 2335–2425.

industries. Consequently, National Treatment[22] as a general principle in the GATS was considered to be unacceptable. Thus, the general level of liberalisation was already reduced to Most-Favoured Nation (MFN)[23] treatment, which in turn was softened through individual commitments under MFN, and the possibility to even exempt certain measures from MFN.[24]

Flexibility could also have been provided through a negative list approach. In general, both approaches – depending on how carefully commitments are scheduled – can provide for the same general level of openness. The positive list approach emerged partly because developing countries did not feel they had the administrative resources to decide upon all the measures, which they wanted to exempt from MFN. Thus, developing countries along with the EU did not intend to commit to substantial trade liberalisation in services in the first place and preferred the positive list approach, because they felt that it would cost them less administrative work to schedule only the commitments and not all exemptions.[25] The general idea of the positive list approach,[26] however, could be understood as more liberal in essence than the negative list approach[27] in the GATT:[28] countries are free to open their services markets entirely and even beyond the scope of the general regulatory principles in the main treaty text. In addition, the positive list approach provides – at least in theory – for a powerful tool in negotiations, because offers are made more visibly than under the negative list approach, and arguably it is more flexible than the negative list approach, given that any liberalising measure can be scheduled.

So-called Dunkel-Draft (the treaty-draft which had the most impact on the GATS)[29] finally included several additional regulatory flexibilities

[22] The principle of National Treatment commits members to treat foreign nationals/products/companies in the same way as nationals. This principle essentially guarantees equal treatment and complete access to the respective domestic market.

[23] The principle of Most Favoured Nation Treatment commits members to treat foreign nationals/products/companies of another member in the same way as the foreign nationals/products/companies of the member, which receives the most-favourable treatment. This principle essentially secures progressive multilateral liberalisation through granting the same level of access to the domestic market to any member, even without additional trade negotiations.

[24] Hoekman and Kostecki (2009, p. 334).

[25] Hoekman and Kostecki (2009, p. 335).

[26] Under the positive list approach, members declare in an individual list their commitments to liberalisation.

[27] Under the negative list approach, members declare in an individual list their exemptions from liberalisation.

[28] Das (2006, p. 11).

[29] See, e.g. Stephenson, Sherry (2000a) 'Regional Agreements on Services in Multilateral Disciplines: Interpreting and Applying GATS Article V', In: S. M. Stephenson (ed.), *Services*

in order to overcome contradicting positions in the final phase of multilateral negotiations: exemptions from MFN, as well as the possibility to include exceptions in the individual schedules on commitments under the GATS.[30] Thus, in its final form, GATS offers more 'allowances for departures from [MFN] treatment, one of the few horizontal obligations that apply across virtually all services, than is the case under relevant GATT Articles'.[31]

Adlung (2006a) distinguishes three different types of flexibilities in the GATS, which all lead to the result that being a member of GATS is not particularly difficult, because there are few binding provisions, and obligations can be altered and changed according to individual needs and requirements: (1) horizontal flexibilities: discrimination between members through MFN exemptions and other permissible departments from MFN, (2) vertical flexibilities: variations in market access and National Treatment across sectors and modes of supply and (3) diagonal flexibilities: divergences in trading conditions because of non-harmonised regulatory approaches.[32]

Thus, given that Market Access and National Treatment are not established as a general commitment in all services sectors for all members, the core principle applying to all services trade involving a WTO member is MFN treatment. However, even this universally valid principle is provided with a certain level of regulatory flexibility: among others, most prominently, GATS Art. V and the possibility to enter into discriminatory, preferential trade relations over services constitutes such an element of flexibility. Thus, GATS Art. V, which establishes the rules for treating some members more preferential than others, is one aspect of many in the general prevalence of regulatory flexibility in GATS disciplines.

I. Regulatory Flexibilities for Preferential Trade

Until a single global market becomes reality, if ever, members may want to liberalise at different speed, e.g. by opening their markets on the regional level when liberalisation on the global level is slow or politically more challenging. Provisions governing such preferential trade agreements were already established in the GATT and have a relatively long history. These

Trade in the Western Hemisphere, Brookings Institution Press, Washington DC, pp. 86–104, p. 88; for a more detailed discussion, see Part IV.

30 Krancke, Jan (1999) Liberalisierung des internationalen Dienstleistungshandels: Analyse des GATS und Perspektiven für die zukünftige Handelsliberalisierung, Kieler Working Paper No. 954, Institut für Weltwirtschaft, Kiel, p. 18.

31 Adlung, Rudolf (2006a, p. 867).

32 Adlung (2006a, pp. 867–868).

provisions are based on the logic that an international agreement can only last if it provides for the regulated possibility to derogate from its commitments.[33] Provisions such as GATS Art. V or GATT Art. XXIV are seen as a pre-condition for state participation. Therefore, in order to keep Member States involved, multilateral agreements at the same time provide for flexibility and regulatory stability.

The core task of GATS Art. V is to allow for regional and bilateral preferential trade that contributes to further trade liberalisation at the global level (trade creation), while at the same time preventing preferential trade that renders global free trade more difficult or impossible to achieve (trade diversion). The provisions regulating preferentialism have, thus, two objectives: (1) providing the necessary flexibility for country-level trade policy and (2) securing the coherence of the global regulatory system through regulatory stability.

Consequently, GATS Art. V:1 explicitly recognises PTAs in services and states that it 'shall not prevent any of its Members from being a party or entering into' such an agreement. With reference to GATT Art. XXIV, GATS Art. V may 'justify the adoption of a measure which is inconsistent with certain other [WTO] provisions and may be invoked as a possible "defence" to a finding of inconsistency'.[34] Even though it is debated whether or not GATS Art. V may also justify deviations from other WTO obligations than MFN,[35] the scope of flexibility of GATS Art. V is rather broad.

PTAs infringe upon the MFN principle, which is among the core concepts of free trade in general, and WTO law in particular.[36] The reason for this overarching importance attributed to the MFN principle has to be found in the logic of the world trade system: global competition in a single and global market is the ultimate goal of members to the WTO. With the introduction of MFN, further and continuing trade liberalisation was made certain of. Every single endeavour of any member of the WTO towards further liberalising trade or towards more open markets would automatically have an effect on the global level and therewith accelerate the process of achieving a single global market. Consequently, any deviation from the MFN principle lies at the heart of the world trade system

[33] Zleptnig, Stefan (2010) *Non-Economic Objectives in WTO Law*, Martinus Nijhoff Publishers, Leiden, pp. 88–89.
[34] *Turkey – Textiles*, WT/DS34/AB/R (22 October 1999), Report of the Appellate Body, para 45.
[35] See Cottier and Molinuevo (2008, p. 129).
[36] E.g. Cottier and Oesch (2005, p. 346).

and requires special consideration by the legislator. This is even more so the case for GATS regulation, as the MFN principle is basically the only and most prominent binding commitment in the sphere of multilateral trade liberalisation in services.

The main treaties of the WTO all have special provisions regulating the conditions for a deviation from the MFN principle. Next to the provisions related to preferentialism, such as GATS Art. V and GATT Art. XXIV, a number of additional provisions regulate deviations from MFN.[37] Although the number of provisions creating a suspension from MFN might seem paradox at first, such provisions are crucial for the functioning of the world trade system: trade negotiations on the global level always risk to fail or they may last for years without noteworthy achievements.[38] Provisions creating meaningful flexibility for individual trade policies can, thus, become a key for achieving multilateral consensus.

An additional reason why MFN suspending provisions play an important role in the trade system is linked to developing countries: some provisions agreed to at the global level might prove to be counterproductive for economic development – in the short term – in the poorest areas of the world. Thus, by introducing exemptions from the general provisions of WTO law, members have created a loophole for including a more development-friendly stance to free trade. Therefore, GATS Art. V does not only have the task of ensuring that preferentialism is 'trade creating' as opposed to 'trade diverting', but it is also meant to create opportunities for economic development in the poorer countries.

The following paragraphs first provide an overview over MFN treatment in the GATS, since GATS Art. V provides for an MFN exemption under the GATS. In a second step, the main and general requirements as established by GATS Art. V are explained, interpreted and analysed. This section does not yet specifically refer to flexibilities provided to developing countries and LDCs under the GATS, but discusses the general flexibilities as established for and applied to all members of the WTO. The particular additional flexibilities for South-South PTAs in services are discussed in the next part. The final paragraph of this section discusses parallels and

[37] See Adlung, Rudolf and Carzaniga, Antonia (2009) 'MFN Exemptions under the General Agreement on Trade in Services: Grandfathers striving for Immortality?', *Journal of International Economic Law*, vol. 12, no. 2, pp. 357–392.

[38] For failed trade negotiations, see the failure to establish the International Trade Organisation (Havana Charter) in 1947, for seemingly endless negotiations see the Doha Round, lasting in 2014 for more than ten years with no end in sight.

differences to GATT Art. XXIV and explains how the GATT regulation of preferentialism informs the legal scope and interpretation of GATS Art. V.

II. Most-Favoured Nation Treatment (GATS Art. II)

The MFN principle is among the core concepts of WTO law and secures that, under the rule of WTO Agreements, countries cannot normally discriminate against one another. The principle's essential role is also reflected in its prominent place in the regulatory framework of IEL: it is established in the very first article of the GATT. With slight differences, MFN treatment is also embedded in GATS Art. II and TRIPS Art. IV. Together, all major trade areas of the WTO are governed by MFN treatment as the basic principle of trade relations.

A. The Scope and History of Most-Favoured Nation Treatment

As MFN has a history of more than 800 years in preferentialism, arguably the major innovation of the GATT 1947 was to incorporate unconditional MFN into a multilateral treaty.[39] Not surprisingly, the MFN principle – being so well established – is incorporated in GATS likewise. Being the basic principle of free trade, the clause has great significance for the entire GATS, and therewith for services trade liberalisation in general.[40]

MFN treatment has two consequences for the international trading system: (1) existing bilateral relations are being multilateralised and (2) the fragmentation of trade relations into bilateral ones, at least in principle, is becoming less likely. As the objective of the MFN clause is to abolish differences, this process of equalisation can either go through the adoption of a lower or a higher level for all. This holds true for the GATS as well: GATS Art. II (MFN) does not provide a guarantee that the higher level in question is being preserved. But MFN treatment is, of course, not restricted to the multilateral level: most PTAs in services include an MFN clause and therewith contribute to the overall acceleration of the globalisation of commitments in trade liberalisation.

[39] See Snape, R. H. (1993) 'History and Economics of GATT's Article XXIV', In: K. Anderson and R. Blackhurst (eds.), *Regional Integration in the Global Trading System*, Harvester Wheatseaf and St. Martin's Press, London and New York, pp. 273–291.

[40] Wolfrum, Rüdiger (2008), 'Article II GATS', In: Wolfrum, R., Stoll, P-T. and Feinäugle, C. (eds.), *WTO – Trade in Services*, Max Planck Institute, Martinus Nijhoff Publishers, Leiden, pp. 71–91, p. 72.

The economic rationale for applying the MFN clause also on preferential trade relations is that discrimination may lead to wasteful trade diversion, as the most efficient provider may not have access to the market because of discriminatory trade preferences. The idea of applying MFN to PTAs is, therefore, in the first place to guarantee the most efficient service providers market access to foreign markets and therewith support the best allocation of resources. MFN also facilitates trade negotiations, as it provides the members of a trade agreement with a guarantee that whatever favourable trade agreement other members will negotiate with third-party countries, they will not be denied the benefits from it.[41]

Interestingly, the United States initially did not intend to agree to include MFN exceptions in the GATT during the post-war period,[42] because preferentialism during the inter-war period was considered to be a contributing cause to falling back to war.[43] It was then only due to political pressure from the rest of the GATT members that the United States agreed to an exception for custom unions first and later to an additional exception for non-custom unions as well, as they 'erroneously believed that serious [PTA] technical difficulties would quickly lead participants to embrace customs unions instead'.[44] Thus, MFN was seen as instrumental to gradual global trade liberalisation, but also to securing peace through ever-deepening trade relations.

The effect of MFN is further consolidated through the principle of reciprocity, which is considered an appropriate standard of behaviour, and which is theoretically attached to every legal norm in international law.[45] In the trade negotiations over the GATT, reciprocity has helped to achieve a high level of liberalisation: every measure taken to reduce the level of protection in a country will automatically lead to reciprocal reduction of protection by its trading partners. Thus, providing advantages to others will also bring along the same benefits to oneself.

The principle of reciprocity, however, is only applied to a limited extent to the provisions and the logic of GATS. This is mainly so as a consequence

[41] Wolfrum (2008, pp. 73–75).

[42] See Atlantic Joint Declaration, Joint Statement by President Roosevelt and Prime Minister Churchill, 14 August 1941 [Online], available at: http://avalon.law.yale.edu/wwii/at10.asp: 'Fourth, they will endeavor, with due respect for their existing obligations, to further the enjoyment by all States, great or small, victor or vanquished, of access, on equal terms, to the trade and to the raw materials of the world which are needed for their economic prosperity' (emphasis added).

[43] Picker (2005, pp. 279–280).

[44] Picker (2005, p. 281).

[45] Keohane, Robert. O. (1986) 'Reciprocity in International Relations', *International Organisation*, vol. 40, no. 1, pp. 1–27, p. 1.

of the positive list approach that the GATS is built on: by giving each member the right to open the services sectors on an individual basis to an explicitly defined degree, the power of collective action and peer-pressure through reciprocity is lost. Mattoo (2000b) notes in this context:[46]

> While reciprocity-based negotiations are widely credited with the substantial reduction in levels of protection achieved in goods trade, it is surprising that the limited application of the principle has not conversely been seen as the reason for the disappointing results in services trade.

With respect to preferentialism in services, not only the lack of reciprocity in the framework of the GATS is slowing liberalisation, but also insufficient reciprocal treatment as it is inherent in the MFN principle: members to a PTA will all benefit from any favourable treatment of third countries by another member of the PTA, which can work as facilitator, because they are not denied the benefits. But it can also work as a hindrance to negotiations as it may not seem enough profitable to negotiate with third countries any longer (time and negotiations of other governments may bring about the benefits for free). This perceived lack of reciprocity may, thus, make it increasingly difficult for governments to commit to trade liberalisation at all.[47]

B. *Most-Favoured Nation Treatment in the GATS*

The MFN clause of GATS Art. II applies to all measures covered by the GATS and is closely linked to Market Access in GATS Art. XVI and to National Treatment in GATS Art. XVII: advantages in Market Access and National Treatment have to be provided to WTO members on an MFN basis. GATS Art. II:1 reads as follows:[48]

> With respect to any measure covered by this Agreement, each Member shall accord immediately and unconditionally to services and service suppliers of any other Member treatment no less favourable than that it accords to like services and service suppliers of any other country.

Thus, like services and like service suppliers have to be treated in a non-discriminatory manner, meaning that like service suppliers have the right to the same treatment as service suppliers. Whether a service or service

[46] Mattoo (2000b, p. 22).

[47] Collier, Paul (2006) 'Why the WTO Is Deadlocked: And What Can Be Done about It', *The World Economy*, vol. 29, no. 10, pp. 1423–1449, p. 1428.

[48] GATS Art. II:1.

supplier is 'like' – and consequently whether or not a measure is discriminatory – should be established by the necessity test.[49] However, it is not yet consolidated among WTO members how to establish when a service or service supplier is to be considered 'like'.[50] Given that it is agreed that like services and like service suppliers equally fall under the scope of application of MFN and therewith of Market Access and National Treatment, the scope of MFN with multilateral services trade regulation can be considered broad. It will, in other words, generally be difficult to discriminate on a preferential basis with respect to the provision of services without infringing GATS and the MFN principle, since in general all services are covered by the GATS.

MFN treatment in GATS Art. II more specifically applies to 'all measures affecting trade in services', while 'affecting trade' is understood broadly (see *EC – Bananas III*). It encompasses any measure affecting the supply of services, regardless of whether such a measure directly governs the supply of a service or regulates other matters but nevertheless affects trade in services. Thus, no measures were a priori excluded from the scope of GATS Art. II.[51] Measures exclusively affecting trade in goods would be excluded from GATS Art. II, whereas measures affecting both trade in goods and trade in services would fall under the scope of GATT and of GATS Art. II.[52]

Thus, GATS Art. II with its broad scope comprises not only measures concerning services, but also all measures concerning service suppliers. Furthermore, the broad wording results in broad coverage of national laws and regulations and is to be understood broader than in the MFN treatment under GATT Art I:1,[53] which states:[54]

> With respect to customs duties and charges of any kind imposed on or in connection with importation or exportation or imposed on the international transfer of payments for imports or exports, and with respect to the method of levying such duties and charges, and with respect to all rules and formalities in connection with importation and exportation, [. . .] any

49 Mattoo, Aaditya (2000b) Shaping Future Rules for Trade in Services: Lessons from the GATS, NBER Conference in Trade in Services, World Bank, Washington DC, p. 13.

50 See also Diebold, Nicolas F. (2010), *Non-discrimination in International Trade in Services: 'Likeness' in WTO/GATS*, Cambridge University Press, Cambridge.

51 Mattoo, Aaditya (2000a) 'MFN and the GATS', In: T. Cottier and C. Mavroidis (eds.), P. Blatter (asst. ed.), *Regulatory Barriers and the Principle of Non-discrimination in World Trade Law*, SIE The World Trade Forum, vol. 2, The University of Michigan Press, Michigan, pp. 51–100, p. 53ff.

52 Wolfrum (2008, p. 79). 53 Ibid., p. 82. 54 GATT Art. I.1.

> advantage, favour, privilege or immunity granted by any contracting party to any product originating in or destined for any other country shall be accorded immediately and unconditionally to the like product originating in or destined for the territories of all other contracting parties.

Whereas the GATT only includes measures affecting goods and does not apply to the supply of goods, the MFN provision in the GATS encompasses measures affecting services and service suppliers. With respect to the scope of such measures, the Panel introduced in *EC – Bananas* a broad interpretation of 'measures by Members', and of 'affecting'.[55] It stated furthermore that treatment 'no less favourable' should include both *de facto* and *de jure* discrimination. This was upheld by the Appellate Body (AB). However, the AB based its interpretation on an analogy to GATT Art. I, instead of GATS Art. XVII.[56] Arguably, the limited level of achieved liberalisation under the GATS is to a certain extent balanced through a broad interpretation of the scope of MFN treatment under the GATS: by including measures which at first may not be exclusively concerned with the regulation of services trade, the GATS suddenly develops a broad scope of application and increases regulatory influence.

As the GATS entered into force before members were willing to open their services sectors entirely, the agreement had to 'strike a difficult balance between creating meaningful multilateral disciplines and accommodating discriminatory trade practices'.[57] Therefore, the Annex on GATS Art. II Exemptions was introduced, which allowed every member of the GATS to maintain measures inconsistent with MFN treatment as established by GATS Art. II, provided that such measures are listed in the Annex.[58] The Annex covers only measures in existence before the entry into force of the GATS. Original members and new members have a once-and-for-all opportunity to exempt themselves from a number of MFN obligations when accessing the GATS.[59] To a later moment in time, no new MFN exemptions can be granted using this route. Mattoo (2000b)

55 Mattoo (2000a, p. 53); *EC – Bananas*, WT/DS27/R/ECU (22 May 1997), Report of the Panel, para. 7.281.

56 See *EC – Bananas*, WT/DS27/AB/R (9 September 1997), Report of the Appellate Body, para. 234.

57 Mattoo (2000b, p. 16).

58 By the time the GATS went into force, the three services sectors that were still negotiated were excluded from the rule that no new exemptions could be listed. These were the telecommunication services, the financial services and the maritime transport sectors. In the meantime, only maritime transportation is still under negotiations and may be subject to additional self-declared exemptions to MFN; see Mattoo (2000a, pp. 55–56).

59 Wolfrum (2008, p. 89).

describes the scope and significance of these explicit departures from MFN as follows:[60]

> Around 380 MFN exemptions have been listed by some 70 Members, with many Members listing several exemptions in the same sector. Nearly two-thirds of the exempted measures are to be found in communication services and in transport services.

Thus, members did use the possibility of exempting measures from the application of MFN treatment quite vividly. This behaviour contributed to the rather low level of trade liberalisation in the services sectors.[61] However, considering the overall low level of liberalisation as achieved by the GATS, the limitations on liberalising commitments based on MFN exemption in said Annex play an inferior role: even without the Annex on Exemptions to GATS Art. II, the overall level of liberalising commitments in trade liberalisation in services would most likely have remained limited, while without the possibility to exempt certain measures from the application of MFN treatment, members would have had to overcome even greater difficulties in crafting a consensus on the multilateral regulation of trade in services.[62]

As a means to pursue the overarching goal of liberalisation in trade in services nevertheless, time limits were attributed to the different exemptions: some of them are subject to an explicit limit, while all the other listed exemptions are subject to a general time frame of ten years. Thus, most exemptions should have been revoked in 2005, which is ten years after the entry into force of the GATS. However, the state of the exemptions has not been controlled by the WTO and, as far as is known today, members have done little to fulfil the given time frame for abandoning the exemptions to GATS II.[63]

In addition to the exemptions as listed in the Annex on GATS Art. II Exemptions, there are additional and – as has been pointed out earlier – numerous avenues to further soften the strict application of MFN treatment in multilateral services trade regulation. For instance, MFN treatment as established by GATS Art. II can also be limited through

[60] Mattoo (2000b, p. 16).

[61] It is important to note that the scheduling is relevant to all MFN exemptions: Exemptions apply only to the commitments that are scheduled. Consequently, if a member has not scheduled any commitment in a sector or in a mode of supply of services, the possibility of complete discrimination on the vertical level with an exemption from MFN exists and would be fully in line with IEL provisions; see Wolfrum (2008, p. 91).

[62] See also Mattoo (2000b, p. 16ff.).

[63] Adlung and Carzaniga (2009, pp. 390–391).

invoking WTO Agreement XIII[64] and declaring the non-application of the GATS Art. XX[65] vis-à-vis a particular member of the WTO: through the non-application of the schedules of specific commitments vis-à-vis a particular member of the WTO, MFN treatment with respect to this particular member is exempted. However, this can only happen in very specific cases and requires the observation of a strict procedure.[66] While in theory, this avenue provides for an interesting additional flexibility softening the application of MFN treatment under GATS, in practice this avenue of limiting MFN treatment is of limited relevance to date.

A number of additional provisions provide for limitations to MFN treatment under GATS or to partial exemptions from the principle of MFN. Besides the prominent provisions of GATS Art. V, these include: GATS Art. II:3, which exempts advantages for services in frontier zones from MFN, if the services are both locally produced and consumed. GATS Art. IV:3 allows for more favourable treatment of least-developed countries, and GATS Art. V:3 lit. b of legal persons owned or controlled by natural persons of developing countries. Further exceptions from MFN are possible under GATS Art. XIV and GATS Art. XIVbis (Exceptions) and in accordance with GATS Art. XIII (government procurement). Another related exception from the MFN rule is permitted by GATS Art. Vbis (Labour Markets Integration Agreements), which provides members with the right to participate in agreements that establish full integration of labour markets. More or less the same holds true for the right to enter into a mutual recognition agreement, based on GATS Art. VII (Recognition).[67]

Thus, in conclusion, since the MFN principle is the basic binding commitment in the area of multilateral services trade regulation, it is attributed with considerable systemic and regulatory weight for the regulation of services trade in general. The scope of MFN treatment under GATS is broader than, for example, the scope of MFN treatment under GATT: it extends to behind-the-border barriers to trade, to like services and like service suppliers and, most importantly, to all measures affecting trade in services. MFN treatment under the GATS may, therefore, also include the regulation of goods trade.

Given the broad scope of application of MFN treatment under the GATS, it comes with no surprise, that flexibilities are manifold: when

[64] Agreement Establishing the World Trade Organisation (WTO Agreement), Art. XIII on the 'Non-Application of Multilateral Trade Agreements between Particular Members'.

[65] GATS Art. XX on schedules of specific commitments.

[66] See WTO Agreement Art. XIII.

[67] Mattoo (2000a), p. 58.

joining the GATS, members have a once-and-for-all opportunity to list MFN incompatible measures in the Annex on Exemptions from GATS Art. II: the Annex provides members with an MFN exemption on these measures. A number of additional avenues for limiting MFN treatment under GATS exist, the most prominent being GATS Art. V, which is discussed further.

2

GATS Art. V

Because many countries are reluctant to make substantial commitments multilaterally, a growing number of countries seek to include services trade liberalisation in PTAs. However, the proliferation of PTAs entails a number of challenges, not only for the respective trading partners, but also for the regional and multilateral trading system. Particularly, preferential trade agreements are generally in conflict with MFN. There is no clear answer to the impact of PTAs on trade diversion: trade diversion can occur even without a PTA, and a PTA does not necessarily have to have a trade-diverting impact.[1] Thus, GATS Art. V sets out to establish the rules and pertinent requirements that PTAs have to meet in order to be legally compatible with the multilateral trading system.[2]

As stated previously, the objective of GATS Art. V is to allow for regional and bilateral preferential trade, which is contributing to further trade liberalisation on a global level (trade creation), and to prevent preferential trading which is inherently rendering global free trade more difficult or impossible to achieve (trade diversion). This sensitive issue has links to several underlying principles of the trade system, such as the MFN clause, National Treatment, the principle of reciprocity or the development goals embedded in the WTO agreements. To strike a balance between the protection of the idea of global free trade and the individual interests of both developing and other countries is, thus, challenging.

The difficulties in balancing preferential versus multilateral trade liberalisation have already been known through the GATT: the experienced regulatory weaknesses of GATT Art. XXIV were, thus, meant to be amended by GATS Art. V. However, in the particular case of services trade, the very nature of services trade renders clear regulation of the

[1] Horn, Henrik and Mavroidis, Petros C. (2001) 'Economic and Legal Aspects of the Most-favoured-Nation Clause', *European Journal of Political Economy*, vol. 17, no. 2, pp. 233–279, p. 267.

[2] Cottier and Molinuevo (2008, p. 127).

conditions for a regional or bilateral PTA a challenging task. But also, lacking the knowledge of how services trade will develop in the future, the drafters of GATS Art. V did not think of all the necessary benchmarks that would be required in order to guarantee for a trade creating effect of services PTAs.

Several aspects of GATS Art. V intend to stimulate and promote free trade not only on the regional but also on the global level. However, due to shortfalls in the definition of terms and a general lack of consensus on the scope of the relevant percentages of trade affected by the PTA, the provisions of GATS Art. V develop limited impact on the content and structure of PTAs in services.

The chapeau of GATS Art. V refers broadly to all agreements 'liberalising trade in services'. Thus, all measures that define market access and conditions of competition in the services sector become relevant for the requirements established by GATS Art. V. And meeting these requirements is mandatory in nature, as mad clear by the language of GATS Art. V: PTAs are admitted 'provided that' the conditions set out in GATS Art. V are met.[3]

It is important to keep in mind that the requirements of GATS Art. V apply only to members of the WTO. Non-members 'remain free, under the principle of sovereign equality, to enter into discriminatory agreements'.[4] PTAs between members and non-members are insofar subject to GATS Art. V as the member's obligations are concerned.[5]

I. Positioning GATS Art. V in International Economic Law

Public international law is not organised in a hierarchical way (except for the supremacy of the Charter of the United Nations over any other international agreement[6]). This means that, from a strictly formal point of view, a bilateral or regional PTA is standing on an equal footing with the GATS: both are international treaties in nature. Consequently, some

[3] Qureshi, Asif H. and Wittayawarakul, Chotika (2010) 'International Development Law and Preferential Trade Agreements involving Developing Countries', In: Y. Ngangjoh-Hodu and F. Matambalya (eds.), Trade Relations Between the EU and Africa, *Routledge*, London, pp. 115–150, p. 131.

[4] Cottier and Molinuevo (2008, p. 130).

[5] Choi, Won-Mog (2005) 'Legal Problems of Making Regional Trade Agreements with Non-WTO-Member States', *Journal of International Economic Law*, vol. 4, no. 8, pp. 825–860, pp. 843–847.

[6] See Art. 103 of the Charter of the United Nations and Art. 30 of the Vienna Convention on the Law of Treaties (VCLT).

argue that WTO rules do not formally have the legal supremacy to control the content of a PTA.

Nonetheless, and in contradiction with general opinion, Islam and Alam (2009) argue for *de jure* supremacy of the GATS over PTAs:[7]

> As [. . .] Article V of the GATS plainly allow[s] the execution of international treaties [. . .], by virtue of Article 41(1)[8] of the Vienna Convention, the latter kind of treaties could modify the provisions in the former only if it is allowed by the former. Therefore the argument is tenable that Article 41(1) implies the WTO rules are inherently of a higher rank than PTAs.[9]

In addition, inconsistencies of PTAs with WTO agreements and requirements have implications within the WTO legal framework (third-party objection, dispute settlement). Therefore, there is also *de facto* supremacy of the GATS over PTAs, and when negotiating a PTA in services, governments are well advised to take the requirements for PTAs in GATS Art. V into consideration. However, until now members have been reluctant to challenge PTAs, and GATS Art. V did not yet develop into a reliable guarantee for coherence and compatibility of PTAs and the disciplines of WTO law.[10]

The general discussion of the hierarchy of legal norms in IEL is, however, slightly different in the case of the GATS: only a handful of PTAs established provisions on services trade regulation prior to the GATS. The vast majority of PTAs in services worldwide were concluded after the entry into force of the GATS. Thus, the basic regulatory framework guiding preferentialism in services trade already existed at the time when most PTAs in services were concluded.[11] Ignoring this regulatory framework would put the existence of a PTA at risk: thanks to the well-established dispute settlement system of the WTO, violating GATS Art. V with material economic repercussions for other WTO members could be expensive for the parties to the PTA and fatal for the PTA itself.

[7] Islam and Alam (2009, p. 4).

[8] Art. 41(1) VCLT states: 'Two or more of the parties to a multilateral treaty may conclude an agreement to modify the treaty as between themselves alone if:
(a) the possibility of such a modification is provided for by the treaty; or
(b) the modification in question is not prohibited by the treaty and:
  (i) does not affect the enjoyment by the other parties of their rights under the treaty or the performance of their obligations;
  (ii) does not relate to a provision, derogation from which is incompatible with the effective execution of the object and purpose of the treaty as a whole.'

[9] See also Cottier and Foltea (2006).

[10] Cottier and Molinuevo (2008, p. 128).

[11] Of the 252 PTAs in services, 50 were concluded before 1995 (Source: Derived from DESTA).

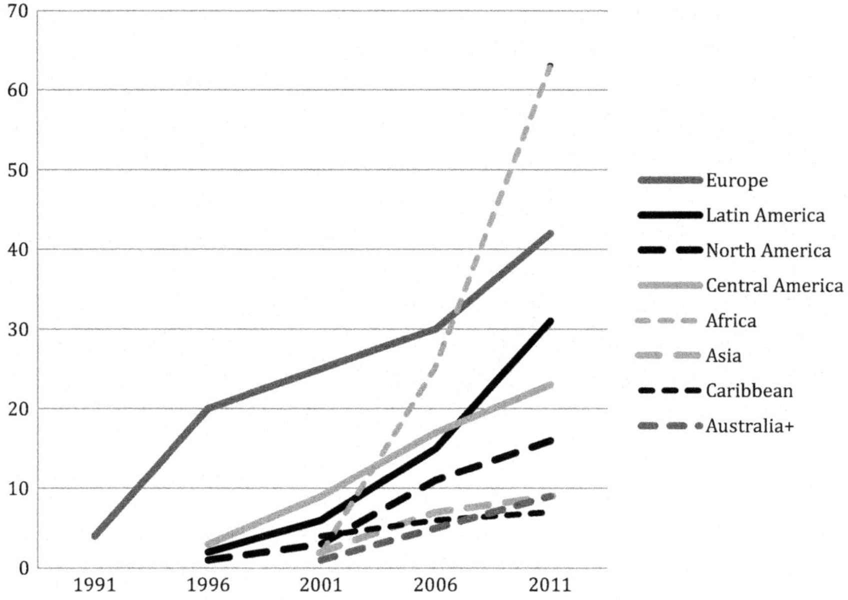

Figure 15 Services PTAs referring to GATS or multilateral services trade regulation
Derived from dataset.
Explanation: Basis = 234 PTAs either liberalising services trade or planning to liberalise services trade since the first reference to multilateral services trade regulation as regulatory basis in 1991. Cumulative illustration: All parties to PTA considered for regional count. Economic communities and unions are counted as one.

Interestingly, of the 234 PTAs in services concluded since the first reference to multilateral services trade regulation in 1991, 194 mention the GATS or multilateral services trade regulation as a regulatory framework.

In these cases, the PTA itself establishes a hierarchy of legal norms in favour of prevailing GATS regulation over preferential provisions. Disregarding GATS regulation would, thus, not only infringe upon the commitments under the GATS, but also be in contradiction to the PTA.[12] Arguably, by establishing GATS regulation as the basic regulatory framework in a PTA ensures that the members of the PTA all agree on the substance and on the basic principles and structure of regulation.

[12] See also VCLT Art. 30.

In addition to the widespread references to GATS regulation in PTAs in services, some PTAs incorporate GATS regulation without adding anything to it: it is often the case that an entire article of the GATS is incorporated into a PTA *tel-quel.* The standard treaty language in these cases is:[13]

> For the purposes of Chapters 6 and 8, Articles XIV and XIV bis of the GATS are incorporated into and form part of this Agreement, mutatis mutandis.

While it may come as a surprise that countries do not attempt to adjust GATS regulation to the specific context of a PTA in some cases, incorporating GATS regulation into the services chapter of a PTA has the advantage that the content of the regulation has been previously approved by the countries involved through their membership in the WTO, and in addition, it increases overall regulatory coherence by extending the multilateral regulation without adjustment to the preferential level.

The influence and wide acceptance of the GATS is furthermore reflected in the structure of the services trade chapters in PTAs: with just a very few exceptions, all PTAs in services follow the basic regulatory structure of dividing liberalising commitments into the four different modes of supply, along with commitments in services sectors and subsectors in a separate annex or schedule. Differences exist with respect to a positive or negative list approach (NAFTA model) and with respect to the separation of the different modes of supply from the main services chapter (NAFTA and EU model). However, these differences have a rather formal character and do not lead to a significantly different regulatory scope and character than the GATS.

This basic rule of incorporating the GATS structure and scope of services trade regulation may, however, see changes in the near future, since the United States and the EU are currently negotiating the so-called mega-regionals, the Transpacific Trade Partnership (TPP) and the Transatlantic Trade and Investment Partnership (T-TIP). Furthermore, a plurilateral agreement, called Trade in Services Agreement (TiSA), is in preparation by a group of WTO members. All of these agreements involve major economies and cover large shares of global services trade. Thus, de facto their members arguably would not necessarily have to follow GATS rules and regulatory structure, given their economic and political power. They could establish new rules and regulatory structure for trade regulation in

[13] *India – Japan (2011)*, Art. 11:2 (Exceptions).

services, which other countries would be expected to adopt quickly, since they would not want to be left outside entirely.

However, there are no indications to date that either the United States or the EU (or any other member) attempts to establish an entirely new regulatory framework for services trade regulation. Most recent PTAs of the EU and the US divide services trade regulation in the main treaty text into different chapters, separating the different modes of supply. Mode 4 supply of services is covered in a separate chapter on temporay movement of persons, and mode 3 supply is covered in the chapters on investment and financial services. Depending on the PTA, there might also be amendments in the schedules of commitments. Most recent EU and US PTAs are based on a negative list approach, with the possibility to exempt a number of services entirely from the application of the PTA.[14] Furthermore, new types of tradable services emerging after the ratification of the PTA are explicitly and fully covered. While there are new – provocative – ideas put forward for instance by the Europeans,[15] regulatory innovation in services trade in PTAs to date is not substantially deviating from the basic structure of GATS. Furthermore, the level of services trade liberalisation remains relatively low even in the most recent PTAs. It will therefore be interesting to see the outcome of the negotiations within the plurilateral forum of the TiSA: it is the declared objective of the TiSA negotiations to further develop services trade regulation and to deepen liberalising commitments. Regulatory innovation in the TISA is nevertheless expected to be of limited impact on the GATS, since the objective of the TiSA is to broaden and further develop trade regulation in services and not to replace the GATS.[16]

Thus, in conclusion, in the past, the GATS was deeply embedded in PTAs in services through the incorporation of GATS provisions, references, and through establishing superiority of GATS regulation over PTA provisions. Even considering the newest developments in preferentialism – the so-called mega-regionals and the plurilateral TiSA – it is

[14] See e.g. Trans-pacific Partnership (TPP) [Online], available at: https://ustr.gov/trade-agreements/free-trade-agreements/trans-pacific-partnership/tpp-full-text

[15] See most recently, Cernat, Lucian and Kutlina-Dimitrova, Zornitsa (2014) *Thinking in a Box: A 'Mode 5' Approach to Service Trade*, Chief Economist Note, European Commission, Brussels. Available at: http://trade.ec.europa.eu/doclib/docs/2014/march/tradoc_152237.pdf

[16] For more information, see Coalition of Services Industries [Online], available at: https://servicescoalition.org/negotiations/trade-in-services-agreement; Sauvé, Pierre (2013) A Plurilateral Agenda for Services? Assessing the Case for a Trade in Services Agreement *(TISA)*, Working Paper No. 2013/29, NCCR trade regulation, Bern.

unlikely that the basic regulatory scope and structure of the GATS as the basis for all subsequent services trade regulation is contested in the near future.

II. Chapeau of GATS Art. V

Generally, GATS Art. V allows members to be a party to an agreement liberalising trade in services on a preferential basis, given that the agreement has 'substantial sectorial coverage' and provides 'for the absence or elimination of substantially all discrimination'.[17] Thus, apart from services specified in individual MFN exemption lists, permitted departure from MFN treatment under the GATS covers preferential treatment among countries that are members of regional trading arrangements.[18]

GATS Art. V:1 explicitly recognises the possibility of preferential agreements in services and states that it 'shall not prevent any of its Members from being a party or entering into' such an agreement. With reference to GATT Art. XXIV and its wording of 'shall not prevent', GATS Art. V may 'justify the adoption of a measure which is inconsistent with certain other [WTO] provisions and may be invoked as a possible "defence" to a finding of inconsistency'.[19]

It is controversial whether or not GATS Art. V may also justify deviations from other WTO obligations than MFN. Generally, there seems little reason for such other deviations; however, in some individual cases such other deviations may be adopted nevertheless. Cottier and Molinuevo (2008) point out:[20]

> While the likelihood of such constellations is limited, the wording, context and object of the provision do not rule out the possibility of deviating from provisions other than [MFN] [. . .] In dispute settlement, it would be for the defending party to demonstrate that such deviations are necessary in order for the [PTA] to work.

The chapeau of GATS Art. V refers broadly to all agreements 'liberalising trade in services'. Consequently, all measures which essentially define market access and conditions of competition in the services sector become relevant for the requirements imposed by GATS Art. V. And meeting these requirements is mandatory in nature, as makes the language of GATS

[17] GATS Art. V:1. [18] Mattoo (2000a, p. 57).

[19] *Turkey – Textiles*, WT/DS34/AB/R (22 October 1999), Report of the Appellate Body, para 45.

[20] Cottier and Molinuevo (2008, p. 129).

Art. V clear: PTAs are admitted 'provided that' the conditions set out in GATS Art. V are met.[21]

Liberalisation in services trade has not yet reached a level where commitments look alike across the majority of the countries involved in services trade liberalisation. Therefore, taking the broad scope of the chapeau of GATS Art. V into consideration is relevant, because preferentialism in services may appear in various forms.

It is important to keep in mind that the requirements of GATS Art. V apply only to members of the WTO. Non-members 'remain free, under the principle of sovereign equality, to enter into discriminatory agreements'.[22] However, preferential agreements between members and non-members are insofar subject to GATS Art. V requirements as the member's obligations are concerned: members must ensure that their own obligations stemming from their membership in the WTO are met by the PTA with a non-member.[23]

III. Quantitative Requirements: GATS Art. V:1 lit. a and lit. b

It is agreed that the conditions set out in GATS Art. V consist of quantitative and qualitative requirements. The first is embedded in the term 'substantial sectorial coverage' in GATS Art. V:1 lit. a and in the corresponding footnote, which requires the liberalisation of those services that amount to substantial trade volumes between the parties, currently and potentially. Thus, the sectors or particular services where limitations are maintained 'cannot be those where significant trade between the parties occurs or would occur in the absence of restrictions'.[24]

The meaning of 'significant trade' has not yet been substantiated with respect to trade volumes affected by a PTA. And since it is agreed that also potential trade flows have to be included in the calculation of 'significant trade', the interpretation of the quantitative requirements of GATS Art. V is even more a challenging task.

Even if the legal side of the quantitative requirement was clear, a particular difficulty in assessing the volumes of international trade in services relates to statistical data: statistical data on services trade currently falls short of providing coherent basis for such calculations both in amount and quality (compared to the data available for goods trade). Cottier and Molinuevo (2008), thus, suggest – recalling that 'WTO law essentially

[21] Ibid., p. 130. [22] Ibid., p. 130. [23] Choi (2005, pp. 843–847).

[24] Cottier and Molinuevo (2008, pp. 132–133).

relates to conditions of competition and *per se* is less concerned with the impact on particular trade flows' – that the qualitative requirements established by GATS Art. V are 'of paramount importance'.[25]

However, considering the different services sectors that differ greatly in terms of trade volumes, number of employees, amount of FDI, and so forth, the quantitative requirement may nevertheless be of importance for ensuring that a PTA contributes to substantial liberalisation in services trade: if the quantitative requirement was left aside, a PTA could focus liberalisation on the economically less relevant sectors of services trade and would develop little to no impact on economic integration among the parties to the PTA. This should normally contradict the requirement to deepen economic integration in services trade of GATS Art. V:2 in particular, and the overall logic of GATS Art. V in general.

From the analysis of main treaty texts of the PTAs of the dataset (not taking into account the individual commitments in the schedules), it becomes clear that the quantitative requirement is likely to be complied with in most cases. Out of 134 PTAs in services, only 9 agreements have excluded an entire services sector in the main treaty text, and 21 agreements have excluded one mode of supply. Table 5 provides a list of PTAs in the dataset, which exclude an entire sector or a priori a mode of supply from the PTA already on the level of the main treaty text.[26]

Possibly, the excluded sectors and modes of supply are relevant in terms of quantity of affected trade volumes in services. However, with the exception of *Guatemala – Taiwan (2005)*, the PTAs do either exclude a sector or a mode of supply. It is, thus, rather unlikely that indeed substantial trade volumes are affected.

Mode 3 supply of services can be covered by the regulation of FDI and is possibly included elsewhere (chapter on Investment, BIT or IIA), especially in PTAs which copy the structure of the NAFTA agreement. Mode 4 is generally of limited relevance in terms of trade volumes affected, as the movement of services suppliers is very restricted in most countries (few commitments in the GATS schedules, immigration policies). Financial services, similar to mode 3 supply of services, are oftentimes partially regulated in a separate chapter on investment, in a BIT or an IIA. Finally, a quick look on the remaining exclusions of sectors (transportation and communication) suggests that these may not be the most important sectors for services trade among the countries concerned.

[25] Ibid., p. 133.

[26] It is likely that additional services sectors are exempted from the scope of the PTA in the country schedules, which have not been taken into consideration in this analysis.

Table 5 *PTAs excluding entire sectors or 'a priori' modes of supply in treaty text*[a]

Name of PTA	Sector	Mode of supply
Brunei – Japan (2007)	Transportation	–
Bahrain – US (2004)	Transportation	–
Canada – Chile (1996)	Transportation	–
Costa Rica – Mexico (1994)	Finance	–
Guatemala – Taiwan (2005)	Finance	Mode 3
Jordan – Kuwait (2001)	–	Mode 4
Jordan – Sudan (2003)	–	Mode 4
Korea – Singapore (2005)	Transportation	–
Mexico – Uruguay (2003)	Finance	–
Colombia – Northern Triangle (2007)	Finance	–
EC – Estonia (1995)	–	Mode 4
El Salvador – Honduras – Taiwan (2007)	Communication	–
CARICOM (1973)	–	Mode 4
EFTA (2001)	–	Mode 3
EC – Jordan (1997)	–	Mode 4
CARIFORUM – EC (2008)	–	Mode 3
Lomé I-IV	–	Mode 4
Japan – Peru (2011)	–	Mode 3
Yaoundé I-II	–	Mode 4
Chile – Panama (2006)	–	Mode 3

[a] Derived from dataset.

Even when considering the individual schedules of the countries in a PTA in services and the trade flow of services between the countries involved in a PTA, substantiating whether the critical volume of trade has been liberalised in the PTA will be extraordinarily challenging and has so far not yet been undertaken. Such a test is, however, likely to be of no greater relevance, given that PTAs in services tend to include all the sectors and all the modes of supply, and therefore, presumably major volumes of services trade are indeed covered by the PTAs.

IV. Qualitative Requirements: GATS Art. V:1 lit. b

The exact interpretation of the qualitative conditions set out in GATS Art. V is highly controversial. However, despite the imprecision in the wording of GATS Art. V and the divergent opinions of the members, there is general agreement that GATS Art. V does not authorise the exclusion of essential services, which are of eminent importance for the economic activity – such as transportation – from the coverage of a PTA.[27]

As is discussed in the following paragraphs, the legal content of this basic consensus is difficult to grasp nevertheless. Consequently, as long as we do not have case law, which further elaborates the legal interpretation of GATS Art. V, these qualitative requirements will remain relatively uncertain and may be subject to change.

A. *Substantial Sectorial Coverage: GATS Art. V:1 lit. a and Footnote*

The wording of the footnote to GATS Art. V ('in terms of numbers of sectors') suggests that the sectorial coverage is based primarily on the concept of entire sectors and that substantially all sectors should be included in the agreement in order to comply with GATS Art. V.[28]

In *Turkey – Textiles* the AB discussed the meaning and the flexibility inherent in GATT Art. XXIV's 'substantially all trade' and came to the following conclusion:[29]

> Neither the GATT CONTRACTING PARTIES nor the WTO Members have ever reached an agreement on the interpretation of the term "substantially" in this provision. It is clear, though, that "substantially all the trade" is not the same as all the trade, and also that "substantially all the trade" is something considerably more than merely some of the trade.

Since GATS Art. V is based on the same logic as GATT Art. XXIV and has references to the provision of 'substantially all trade' by requiring 'substantial sectorial coverage',[30] it is generally agreed that *Turkey – Textiles* also holds true for the interpretation and evaluation of GATS Art. V. This means that GATS Art. V does not require complete opening of the services market in a PTA, but will not allow for a pick-and-choose-agreement, which only liberalises services trade to a limited degree and only in specific sectors and services industries.

During the history of drafting GATS Art. V, the question arose whether the comprehensiveness of an agreement's scope should be examined based only with respect to services trade or rather in the wider context of trade in goods and services. The emerging compromise allows taking into account

[27] Islam and Alam (2009, p. 25). [28] Cottier and Molinuevo (2008, p. 131).
[29] *Turkey – Textiles* WT/DS34/AB/R (22 October 1999), Report of the Appellate Body, para. 48.
[30] GATS Art. V:1.

whether the economic integration process in question also covers trade in goods when evaluating the sectorial coverage of a PTA.[31] As a consequence, some scholars argue that it seems possible that a partial PTA in services when combined with a partial PTA in goods satisfies the requirement of 'substantial sectorial coverage'.[32] This view is, however, a minority interpretation. Generally, it is agreed that the provision should be read separately from the context of trade in goods and applied only to services trade liberalisation.

In GATS Art. V, 'substantial sectorial coverage' is further defined in the footnote as:

> This condition is understood in terms of number of sectors, volume of trade affected and modes of supply. In order to meet this condition, agreements should not provide for the a priori exclusion of any mode of supply.

It is still disputed whether or not and under what circumstances a services sector can be excluded from a PTA under GATS Art. V. Some members argue that the wording in the footnote would have been clarifying that 'all' the sectors had to be covered, instead of 'number of sectors' if GATS Art. V did not want to allow for single exclusion of sectors.[33] Additionally, some members support the view that a priori exclusion of sectors is permitted, given that the footnote specifies that a priori exclusion of modes of supply is not permissible while the same is not extended to sectors or volumes of trade.[34] However, others argue that single sectors cannot be excluded from a PTA, because the word 'substantial' does already restrict such flexibility.[35]

A middle way and therewith less unequivocal view in this context is that services, which are essential for economic activity, may not be excluded from the coverage of a PTA[36] and that in the case of an exclusion of major services sectors, such an exclusion may have to be evaluated together with the commitments in modes of supply and the volume of trade affected.[37]

[31] WT/REG/W/21/Rev.1 Committee on Regional Trade Agreements, Systemic Issues Related to Substantially All Trade – Background Note by the Secretariat, 5 February 1998.

[32] Munin (2010, p. 226); Zdouc, Werner (2002) Legal Problems Arising under the General Agreement on Trade in Services – Comparative Analysis of GATS and GATT, Dissertation, University of St. Gallen, p. 221.

[33] EC, WT/REG50–52/M/2, para. 16; New Zealand, WT/REG/M/22, para. 17.

[34] EC, WT/REG/W/35, para. 4.

[35] WTO, Committee on Regional Trade Agreements, Note by the Secretariat, *Synopsis of 'Systemic' Issues related to Regional Trade Agreements*, WT/REG/W/37, para. 72.

[36] Japan and Korea, WT/REG/M/22, paras. 18 and 20.

[37] Argentina, WT/REG/M/22, para. 16.

In other words, excluding more than two out of the twelve current services sectors identified by the Services Sectorial Classification List, most likely fails to meet the requirements. It is important, however, to take into account the economic importance of the excluded sector in terms of international exchange.[38] Therefore, it is suggested that the exclusion of a major sector would in itself prevent GATS Art. V compatibility.[39]

As mentioned above, it has been suggested that the excluded sectors should not be 'essential' services sectors that serve as the infrastructure for economic activity.[40] Following this line of thinking, arguably only the exclusion of a limited number of sensitive services (such as *service public*), and tourism and recreational services may possibly be defended on the basis of GATS Art. V. Every other service sector directly or indirectly relates to the establishment and maintenance of infrastructure for further economic activity. However, nothing in the language of GATS Art. V seems to enshrine such an interpretation.

The resulting requirement to include all sectors directly or at least indirectly in a PTA serves as a barrier to the creation of PTAs, as it renders their conclusion more difficult. At the same time, the requirement of 'substantial sectorial coverage' also serves as a means to promote trade creation as opposed to trade diversion by rendering PTAs in services more substantial and comprehensive in coverage.[41]

Exclusion of sectors and/or subsectors in PTAs is common practice, but it remains unclear how this should be computed. The Secretariat (2000) writes in its 'Synopsis of Systemic Issues related to Regional Trade Agreements':[42]

> Still in this context, the degree of detail of the examination, i.e. whether it should [. . .] take place on a sector-by-sector, subsector-by-subsector or on a completely disaggregated basis, has been briefly addressed. Some Members have favoured examination on a sector-by-sector basis, given the lack of detailed data on services trade and the fact that footnote 1 to subparagraph 1(a) lists the number of sectors covered by an [PTA] as one of the three separate factors to be examined in evaluating sectorial coverage.

38 As the GATS does not provide for a definition of 'service sector', calculation of the economic importance of a particular sector may be based on the Services Sectorial Classification List.

39 Argentina, WT/REG/M/22, para. 16.

40 Japan and Korea, WT/REG/M/22, paras 18 and 20.

41 Cottier and Molinuevo (2008, p. 132).

42 WTO, Committee on Regional Trade Agreements, Note by the Secretariat, *Synopsis of 'Systemic' Issues related to Regional Trade Agreements*, WT/REG/W/37 (2 March 2000), para. 74.

The Secretariat (2000) does, however, not provide the required answers to how the coverage of all sectors is determined, how the volume of trade is calculated if a sector is less than fully liberalised and if a percentage target would be feasible to determine 'substantial coverage'. Thus, even though GATS Art. V provides basic information on the extent of liberalisation, which is required from a PTA, it is not specific enough to apply the requirements to cases where compliance with GATS is uncertain.

The PTAs in the Table 5 excluding an entire sector from the PTA are likely to not meet the qualitative requirement of sectorial coverage as it is established by GATS Art. V. The sectors excluded from liberalisation (communication, finance and transportation) are of particular relevance to economic activity. While it has been discussed earlier that services trade liberalisation in financial services is often partially included in investment regulation (PTA chapter on investment, BIT, IIA), this is not regularly the case for other services sectors, such as communication and transportation.

Starting from a more practical point of view, considering the relevance of the different services sectors for economic integration among the members of the PTA may prove to be helpful: transportation services between Bahrain and the United States,[43] between Brunei and Japan[44] or between Canada and Chile[45] may be of limited relevance. On the other hand, transportation services between Korea and Singapore[46] seem to be more crucial for economic integration in services, given the geographic proximity and the hub character of Singapore for South-East Asia.

Such a test of relevance to the economic integration in services trade would be in line with the view that sectors, which are essential for economic activity, may not be excluded from the PTA. Other than attributing a set of sectors with the *de facto* tag 'non-excludable' – independently of individual economies involved in services trade liberalisation – a look at the landscape of exclusions of sectors in the dataset suggests that the individual trade relations of the members of a PTA ought to be taken into account with a view on the relevance of the different sectors for achieving economic integration in services trade.

B. No a Priori Exclusion of Mode of Supply: Footnote to GATS Art. V:1 lit. a

The footnote to GATS Art. V:1 clarifies that none of the four modes of supply should be a priori excluded from the PTA. This additional

[43] *Bahrain – US (2004).* [44] *Brunei – Japan (2007).*
[45] *Canada – Chile (1996).* [46] *Korea – Singapore (2005).*

Table 6 *PTAs excluding 'a priori' mode 3 supply of services*[a]

EFTA (2001)	*CARIFORUM – EC (2008)*
Guatemala – Taiwan (2005)	*Japan – Peru (2011)*
Chile – Panama (2006)	

[a] Derived from dataset.

information on the interpretation and scope of GATS Art. V leads to a better understanding of the scope of 'substantial' than in the GATT.[47]

However, the wording 'a priori' implies that the PTA may provide for differential degrees of liberalisation for different modes of supply as long as none of them is entirely excluded. Furthermore, the footnote is indicating that the requirement of 'substantial volume of trade' is not limited to the number of sectors, but is also relevant for the commitments within the modes of supply. Consequently, (1) no mode of supply should be excluded from the PTA, while (2) the commitments in trade liberalisation in services may differ among the different modes of supply, as long as (3) the different levels of commitments do not impair the overall liberalisation of a substantial volume of trade.[48]

Generally, PTAs should particularly not a priori exclude investment and labour mobility in the sense of mode 3 and mode 4 of supply of services. To what extent PTAs in services need to include aspects related to mode 4 supply, which are exempted from the GATS through the *Annex on the Movement of Natural Persons*, remains controversial.[49]

Interestingly, particularly mode 3 and mode 4 of supply in services are in fact excluded a priori in a number of PTAs in the dataset (see Tables 6 and 7). Additionally, mode 3 supply is often excluded from the chapter on services trade with reference to the chapter on investment. In addition, newer PTAs between the EC and third countries limit the services chapter to mode 1 and mode 2 supply of services only. These PTAs feature separate (partial) regulation of mode 3 and mode 4 supply in the chapters on investment and on labour movement.

As the lists in Tables 6 and 7 illustrate well, there have been a number of PTAs in services concluded over time, which clearly do not meet the requirement of GATS Art. V of not excluding a priori any of the modes of

[47] Matoo (2000a, p. 57). [48] Cottier and Molinuevo (2008, pp. 133–134).
[49] WTO, Committee on Regional Trade Agreements, Note by the Secretariat, *Synopsis of 'Systemic' Issues related to Regional Trade Agreements*, WT/REG/W/37, para. 73.

Table 7 *PTAs excluding 'a priori' mode 4 supply of services*[a]

CARICOM (1973)	*EC – Jordan (1997)*
Lomé I-IV	*Jordan – Kuwait (2001)*
Yaoundé I-II	*Jordan – Sudan (2003)*
EC – Estonia (1995)	

[a] Derived from dataset.

supply. However, caution is required: a number of the agreements on the lists are in fact Economic Partnership Agreements (EPAs) and fall under the Enabling Clause in addition to GATS Art. V, and some are older than the GATS, and, thus, did not have the chance to include the GATS model of services trade regulation with its four modes of supply.[50]

The EPAs which exclude a priori a mode of supply raise an important legal question: to what extent does an EPA, which is notified under the Enabling Clause with respect to goods trade, have to fulfil the requirements of GATS Art. V? As the Enabling Clause is restricted to goods trade, and as the respective agreements are in fact notified to the WTO under GATS Art. V, at first sight, there is no obvious reason for an exemption from the requirements set out by GATS Art. V.

The first agreement in the dataset a priori excluding mode 3 supply of services is *EFTA (2001)*. The relevant paragraph reads:[51]

> For the purposes of this Chapter, services shall be considered to be "services" within the meaning of this Convention where they are normally supplied for remuneration (a) from the territory of one Member State into the territory of another Member State; (b) in the territory of a Member State to the service consumer of another Member State [. . .]; (c) by service supplier of a Member State, through presence of natural persons of that Member State in the territory of another Member State [. . .].

In *EFTA (2001)* there is no reference to mode 3 supply of services and, thus, mode 3 is excluded. *Japan – Peru (2011)*, on the other hand, introduces a more complex language by defining cross-border supply as restricted to modes 1, 2 and 4 of supply:[52]

50 *CARIFORUM – EC (2008)*, *Lomé I-IV*, *Yaoundé I-II* and *CARICOM (1973)*. In addition, the EU accession agreement *EC – Estonia (1995)* likewise qualifies as a special case.

51 *EFTA (2001)*, Art. 29:2.

52 *Japan – Peru (2011)*, Art. 102:1(d).

> [. . .] the term "cross-border trade in services" or "cross-border supply of services" means the supply of a service: (i) from the Area of a Party into the Area of the other Party; (ii) in the Area of a Party by a person of that Party to a person of the other Party; or (iii) by a national of a Party in the Area of the other Party; [. . .]

In the same article of *Japan – Peru (2011)*, however, a 'service supplier' is defined in a way, which allows a regulation of supply of services similar to the one in GATS mode 3 supply:[53]

> [. . .] the term "service supplier" means a person that supplies or seeks to supply a service; Note: Where the service is not supplied or sought to be supplied directly by an enterprise but through its covered investments such as a branch or a representative office, the service supplier (i.e. the enterprise) shall, nonetheless, through such covered investments be accorded the treatment provided for service suppliers under this Chapter. Such treatment shall be extended to the covered investments through which the service is supplied or sought to be supplied and need not be extended to any other parts of the service supplier located outside the Area of a Party where the service is supplied or sought to be supplied. [. . .]

Whether mode 3 supply is a priori excluded in *Japan – Peru (2011)* requires treaty interpretation: to what extent is the definition of cross-border supply (which does not use the term 'service supplier') exhaustive? And what are the implications of this note on the supply of cross-border services? The fact that *Japan – Peru (2011)* does not directly refer to mode 3 supply of services constitutes an additional challenge. Therefore, it remains unclear to what extent the definition in the note above complies with the definition of mode 3 supply in GATS,[54] particularly with respect to ownership and control of the 'covered investments'.[55]

The outcome of such treaty interpretation is not evident at first sight. However, it is more likely that *Japan – Peru (2011)* indeed intended to exclude mode 3 supply of service from its services chapter, given that mode 3 is not listed under the different ways of cross-border trade in services, and given that, in the rest of the agreement, *Japan – Peru (2011)* extensively incorporates provisions from and refers to the GATS. In addition, because *Japan – Peru (2011)* does not include a chapter on investment, there is no partial, indirect mode 3 regulation, at least through the regulation

[53] *Japan – Peru (2011)*, Art. 102:1(j). [54] See GATS Art. XXVIII.

[55] Karsenty, Guy (2000) 'Assessing Trade in Services by Mode of Supply', In: P. Sauvé and R. M. Stern (eds.), *GATS 2000: New Directions in Services Trade Liberalisation*, The Brookings Institution, Washington DC, pp. 33–56, p. 45.

of investment, which renders the restriction of the services chapter on primarily modes 1, 2 and 4 all the more restrictive.

A third version of the language of a priori exclusion of mode 3 supply of services can be found in the agreements *Guatemala – Taiwan (2005)* and *Chile – Panama (2006)*. They both explicitly exclude mode 3 supply:[56]

> comercio transfronterizo de servicios o suministro transfronterizo de un servicio significa el suministro de un servicio: (a) del territorio de una Parte al territorio de la otra Parte; (b) en el territorio de una Parte, por una persona de esa Parte, a una persona de la otra Parte; o (c) por un nacional de una Parte en el territorio de la otra Parte; pero no incluye el suministro de un servicio en el territorio de una Parte mediante una inversión, en ese territorio;

However, both agreements have a chapter on investment,[57] and therefore indirectly include – at least partially – mode 3 supply of services in the agreement. As will be discussed later in this section, including mode 3 supply in services indirectly in the investment chapter is, however, not exactly what GATS Art. V establishes as minimal requirements for PTAs in services. Since GATT Art. XXIV is restricted to the chapter on goods trade only, GATS Art. V presumably applies primarily to the services chapter of a PTA. The question of where to find the relevant provisions in a PTA with respect to the evaluation of compliance with GATS Art. V is more complex for services than for goods. As has been shown, services trade provisions may be found in different parts and chapters of a PTA in services, while goods provisions tend to be more concisely located in one distinct chapter.

Mode 4 supply of services, on the other hand, surprisingly is less often a priori excluded from PTAs. Mode 4 supply is generally the least committed mode of supply, as it involves the cross-border movement – and therewith the entry into the country – of foreign labour.[58] However, even if mode 4 supply of services is included in the services chapter of a PTA that does not necessarily mean that natural persons are more or less free to enter the member countries of a PTA in order to supply services: countries may restrict entrance for natural persons supplying

[56] *Chile – Panama (2006)*, Art. 10.11.

[57] *Chile – Panama (2006)*, Ch. 9; *Guatemala – Taiwan (2005)*, Ch. 10.

[58] Panizzon, Marion (2010) Trade and Labour Migration: GATS Mode 4 and Migration Agreements, Occasional Papers No. 47/January2010, Friedrich Ebert Stiftung, Geneva, p. 9.

services through visa requirements and other professional certification requirements.[59]

Nevertheless, of the PTAs that exclude mode 4 supply altogether, only the two PTAs *Jordan – Kuwait (2001)* and *Jordan – Sudan (2003)* do not fall within the scope of an exemption from the GATS Art. V requirement to include all four modes of supply. These two agreements, thus, do not fulfil the GATS Art. V requirements entirely.

As mentioned previously, another relatively common feature of commitments in modes of supply in PTAs in services is the regulation of mode 3 supply of services outside of the services chapter, in the investment chapter (see Table 8). This model of treaty language derives from the NAFTA agreement and is spreading from North America to Central and Latin America, and more recently also to other parts of the world, as is illustrated in Table 8.[60] The result differs from the usual commitment in mode 3 to the extent that mode 3 supply of services is excluded from the services chapter and is regulated exclusively in the investment chapter through the regulation of FDI. This also means that the multilateral rules and regulations of GATS to a limited degree may apply to both the services and the investment chapter. If they were only limited to apply to the services chapter, then the NAFTA model of PTAs in services would in fact not fulfil the minimal requirement of GATS Art. V to not a priori exclude any mode of supply from the PTA. In consequence, GATS Art. V may not only apply to the services chapter but also to the investment chapter with respect to the regulation of commercial presence (mode 3 supply).

As the investment chapter – because it is only concerned with mode 3 supply and does not refer to other modes of supply – is bound to fail to meet the GATS Art. V requirements,[61] the scope and number of modes of supply included in a NAFTA type of PTA can only be established through inclusion of the regulation in both the services and the investment chapters. This not only means that in the area of services trade liberalisation in a PTA, two different systems of dispute settlement may apply (the

[59] Dawson, Laura Ritchie (2012) 'Labour Mobility and the WTO: The Limits of GATS Mode 4', *International Migration*, vol. 51, no. 1, pp. 1–23.

[60] On the implications of the NAFTA, or the GATS model for mode 3 supply of services, see OECD (2008) 'The Interaction Between Investment and Services Chapters in Selected Regional Trade Agreements', In: *International Investment Law: Understanding Concepts and Tracking Innovations*, OECD Trade Working Paper No. 55, Paris, pp. 241–340.

[61] Ortino, Federico and Sheppard, Audley (2006) 'International Agreements Covering Foreign Investment in Services; Patterns and Linkages', In: L. Bartels and F. Ortino (eds.), *Regional Trade Agreements and the WTO Legal System*, Oxford University Press, Oxford, pp. 201–214, p. 210ff.

WTO system and investment arbitration);[62] it also extends the regulation of services trade to other chapters, in which different multilateral rules apply. Unless compliance with GATS Art. V in such an agreement is not an issue in a dispute, it remains open to what extent the NAFTA model of mode 3 supply regulation meets the requirements of GATS Art. V, and which multilateral rules and dispute settlement procedures apply to mode 3 supply in that case.

It is disputed whether the NAFTA or the GATS model of mode 3 supply regulation is better for commerce: while some highlight the advantage of protection against expropriation through the inclusion in the investment chapter of a PTA, others point out that mode 3 supply applies both to pre-establishment and to establishment, while investment protection normally only applies to already established investments.[63] Certain NAFTA-type agreements,[64] however, extend the protection in their investment chapter already to the pre-establishment, which results in an overall stronger position of mode 3 supply of services, than in the GATS model.

The structure of the following PTAs in Table 8 is similar to the NAFTA model, which excludes mode 3 supply of services in the services chapter but includes commercial presence in the investment chapter.

In the case of the NAFTA model of exclusion of mode 3 supply from the services chapter, the standard language (linked to North American countries) is the following:[65]

> 1. cross-border trade in services or cross-border supply of services means the supply of a service: (a) from the territory of one Party into the territory of the other Party; (b) in the territory of one Party by a person of that Party to a person of the other Party; or (c) by a national of a Party in the territory of the other Party; but does not include the supply of a service in the territory of a Party by a covered investment.

A 'covered investment' is generally understood as an investment, which is protected one way or another through a legal instrument. Thus, a covered investment can also be protected through another agreement than

[62] Khor, Martin (2008) *Bilateral and Regional Free Trade Agreements: Some Critical Elements and Development Implications*, Third World Network, Penang, p. 13.

[63] Steger, Debra (2013) 'International Trade and Investment: Towards a Common Regime?', In: R. Echandi and P. Sauvé (eds.), *Prospects for International Investment Law and Policy*, Cambridge University Press, Cambridge, pp. 156–165.

[64] *NAFTA (1993)* and the US and Canada PTAs, see also: Steger (2013).

[65] *Australia – US (2004)*, Art. 10.14; similar or the same in *Canada – Colombia (2008), Bahrain – US (2004), Colombia – US (2006)* and *Canada – Peru (2008), aso.*

Table 8 *PTA with separate regulation of mode 3 supply*[a]

NAFTA (1993)	*Korea – US (2007)*
Chile – Mexico (1998)	*Colombia – Northern Triangle (2007)*
Central America – Panama (2002)	*El Salvador – Honduras – Taiwan (2007)*
Chile – Korea (2003)	*Canada – Colombia (2008)*
Mexico – Uruguay (2003)	*Canada – Peru (2008)*
Australia – US (2004)	*Canada – Panama (2010)*
Bahrain – US (2004)	*Chile – Japan (2010)*
Japan – Mexico (2004)	*Korea – Peru (2011)*
Korea – Singapore (2005)	*Mexico – Peru (2011)*
Colombia – US (2006)	*Panama – Peru (2011)*

[a] Derived from dataset.

the PTA in services. It may also be covered through the general commitment in mode 3 under GATS (e.g. concerning pre-establishment). Thus the term 'covered investment' would have to be interpreted according to the respective treaty and according to the legal situation between the parties involved. As has been mentioned earlier, it is unclear to what extent the regulation of mode 3 (commercial presence) in the investment chapter is covering the scope of the definition of mode 3 supply of services in GATS.[66] Furthermore, as there are different multilateral rules applicable to the investment chapter – aside from GATS regulation with respect to mode 3 supply of services – it is unclear whether the regulations concerning expropriation, arbitration, and so forth, which are characteristic for investment regulation, really apply to mode 3 supply of services. Thus, in conclusion, these PTAs do not exclude mode 3 supply of services if the entire treaty text is taken into consideration. Establishing if *de facto* mode 3 supply is nevertheless more restricted – or even better protected – than required by GATS Art. V requires detailed analysis of the individual agreements.

Finally, very recent agreements by the EC have introduced an entirely new structure of commitments in modes of supply: the horizontal commitments in the services chapter are restricted to mode 1 and mode 2 supply of services only. But the PTAs have both a separate chapter on investment, including regulation of mode 3, and a chapter on labour migration, including regulation of mode 4.

[66] E.g. with reference to ownership and control of an investment.

Table 9 *PTAs restricting the services chapter on mode 1 and mode 2 supply*[a]

EC – Korea (2010)
Colombia and Peru – EC (2012)
Central America – EC (2012)

[a] Derived from dataset.

Possibly the tendency to split the regulation of services trade into several parts is also a consequence of the nature of services trade: as it is so closely related to investment and labour migration, the regulation of services trade liberalisation may indeed be more meaningful when linked to and included into the larger context of services trade (see Table 9). As many argue that the separation of services trade from goods trade was artificial and did not meet the needs of businesses,[67] the development of splitting services trade regulation into different parts and including it into the larger context may be seen as a sign that PTAs are trying to overcome this artificial separation.

In *EC – Korea (2010)*, the first time in the dataset that the services chapter was restricted to mode 1 and mode 2 supply of services, the language was the following:[68]

> 3. For the purposes of this Section: (a) cross-border supply of services is defined as the supply of a service: (i) from the territory of a Party into the territory of the other Party; and (ii) in the territory of a Party to the service consumer of the other Party.

In the more recent agreements, the language has only changed insofar as the two modes of supply are indicated explicitly (see Table 9).[69] As these agreements are still very recent, and as it is not quite clear whether this model of services trade regulation will spread to other PTAs, it is too early to tell whether this model is an indicator of combining the regulation of closely related areas of trade into more comprehensive and overarching chapters in the future. Given, however, that many PTAs already include

67 E.g. Baldwin, Richard (2011) Trade and Industrialisation after Globalisation's 2nd Unbundling: How Building and Joining a Supply Chain Are Different and Why It Matters, Working Paper 17716, NBER, Cambridge.

68 *EC – Korea (2010)*, Art. 7.4.

69 *Colombia and Peru – EC (2012)*, Art. 117; *Central America – EC (2012)*, Art. 169.

both services, an investment and a labour migration chapter, in which naturally regulation is overlapping to a certain degree, the tendency to embed the regulation of modes of supply of services into the larger context in which they belong seems reasonable and helpful in terms of transparency and comprehensiveness.

Others argue that the more recent design of the European PTAs in services is rather linked to a change in the EC trade policy, in which services and investment have been identified as key drivers for preferential trade liberalisation. Thus, the new design is not primarily based on a strategy to conclude more comprehensive agreements and contribute to enforceability of the commitments, but rather on strengthening of investment and services vis-à-vis other areas of preferential trade liberalisation.[70]

If the focus on global value-added chains and the movement of semi-finished products continues to grow as it did in recent years, it also seems possible that services trade regulation could in the future be embedded into chapters on value-added production and goods trade.[71] After all, and particularly with respect of global value-added chains and the processing of semi-finished products, services are so closely linked to aspects of modern trade in goods that separate regulation may start to fail to meet the regulatory goals in the nearer future.

C. *Absence or Elimination of Substantially all Discrimination: GATS Art. V:1 lit. b*

GATS Art. V:1 lit. b requires PTAs to provide for 'the absence or elimination of substantially all discrimination' in the services sectors covered by the PTA and by the means of granting National Treatment to the service suppliers of the other member(s) of the PTA. Due to the nature of services trade, market opening is essentially brought about by granting National Treatment 'to avoid legal or *de facto* discrimination against imported services in accordance with the disciplines set out in GATS Art. XVII:2 and 3, to which the provision explicitly refers'.[72] Additionally, the case *Canada –*

[70] See, e.g. Heron, Tony and Siles-Brügge, Gabriel (2012) 'Competitive Liberalisation and the "Global Europe" Services and Investment Agenda: Locating the Commercial Drivers of the EU-ACP Economic Partnership Agreements*', *Journal of Common Market Studies*, vol. 50, no. 2, pp. 250–266; Erixon, Fredrik and Lee-Makiyama, Hosuk (2010) Stepping into Asia's Growth Markets: Dispelling Myths about the EU-Korea Free Trade Agreement, Policy Brief No. 03/2010, ECIPE, Brussels.

[71] Cernat and Kutlina-Dimitrova (2014).

[72] Cottier and Molinuevo (2008, p. 135).

Autos[73] (the only case to date in which the WTO jurisprudence dealt with GATS Art. V) arguably imposes MFN treatment among members to a PTA.[74]

In order to establish the level of discrimination and to eliminate 'substantially all discrimination', level playing fields have to be established on the basis of reciprocity. However, in cases where one party commits to much more than the other party (which can already derive from the GATS schedules that differ greatly among members), evaluating the degree of discrimination and finding level playing fields become particularly difficult if not impossible.

In *EC – Bananas III*[75] the commitments of the EU under the GATS schedules were used as the reference for the evaluation of potentially discriminatory measures. Thus, starting point of any evaluation of level playing fields must be the individual commitments of members to a PTA under the GATS schedules.

When level playing fields have been established, another difficulty arises: it is unknown how 'substantially all discrimination' can be quantitatively measured. It has been suggested that each PTA be examined on its own merit, without further clarifying how 'substantial elimination of all discrimination' may be quantified.[76]

However, it is agreed that not 'all' discrimination has to be eliminated – a substantial part of it will suffice to comply with GATS Art. V. Considering the type of restriction, it has to be mentioned that horizontal restrictions are not formally ruled out by GATS Art. V, but may violate the law given the high level of restriction they entail.[77]

The wording of 'and/or' has led to some disagreement in the interpretation of GATS Art. V:1 lit. b. The main question is whether members can choose between either 'eliminating substantially all discrimination' or 'prohibiting new or more discriminatory measures' (stand-still obligation).[78]

[73] The finding of the Panel may, however, be disputable, see *Canada – Autos*, WT/DS 139 (11 February 2000), Report of the Panel, para. 10.270.

[74] Islam and Alam (2009, p. 26).

[75] *EC – Bananas III*, WT/DS27/RW2/ECU and WT/DS27/RW/USA (26 November 2008), Reports of the Appellate Body.

[76] WTO, Committee on Regional Trade Agreements, Note by the Secretariat, *Synopsis of 'Systemic' Issues related to Regional Trade Agreements*, WT/REG/W/37, para. 84.

[77] Cottier and Molinuevo (2008, p. 137).

[78] Different positions of WTO members: WTO, Committee on Regional Trade Agreements, Note by the Secretariat, Synopsis of 'Systemic' Issues related to Regional Trade Agreements, WT/REG/W/37, para. 82.

Considering that GATS Art. V:1 lit. b deals with 'substantially all discrimination' in the sense of GATS Art. XVII (National Treatment), the less unequivocal view is that both paragraphs are applicable. Cottier and Molinuevo (2008) support the view of not perceiving the two channels as independent alternatives: rather, the members are bound to adopt one and/or another in the process of bringing about non-discrimination. Thus, it depends on the domestic regulatory framework, which channel(s) serve the cause the best.[79]

In *Canada – Autos* the question was whether GATS Art. V:1 lit. b allows for a PTA in which certain service suppliers are treated more favourably than others. The panel found that GATS Art. V:1 lit. b requires not only National Treatment but also MFN treatment among the parties to a PTA in services, and thus, refuted Canada's argument that GATS Art. V:1 lit. b allowed for more or less favourable treatment of service suppliers:[80]

> Although the requirement of [GATS] V:1(b) is to provide non-discrimination in the sense of [GATS] XVII (National Treatment), we consider that once it is fulfilled it would also ensure non-discrimination between all service suppliers of other parties to the economic integration agreement. It is our view that the object and purpose of this provision is to eliminate all discrimination among services and service suppliers of parties to an economic integration agreement, including discrimination between suppliers of other parties to an economic integration agreement. In other words, it would be inconsistent with this provision if a party to an economic integration agreement were to extend more favourable treatment to service suppliers of one party than that which it extended to service suppliers of another party to that agreement.

The panel further elaborated the minimum level of liberalisation required by GATS Art. V:1 and stated that a PTA based on GATS Art. V typically had to establish higher levels of liberalisation among the members of a PTA than the level achieved among WTO members:[81]

> [. . .] the purpose of [GATS Art. V] is to allow for ambitious liberalisation to take place at a regional level, while at the same time guarding against undermining the MFN obligation by engaging in minor preferential arrangements. [. . .] in our view, it is not within the object and purpose of [GATS Art. V] to provide legal coverage for the extension of more favourable treatment only to a few service suppliers of parties to an

[79] Cottier and Molinuevo (2008, pp. 136–137).

[80] *Canada – Autos*, WT/DS139/R and WT/DS142/R (11 February 2000), Report of the Panel, para. 10.270.

[81] Ibid., para. 10.271.

> economic integration agreement on a selective basis, even in situations where the maintenance of such measures may explicitly be provided for in the agreement itself.

However, this particularly broad understanding of the scope and applicability of GATS was reversed and heavily criticised by the AB. Primarily, the AB criticised that the panel had failed to establish whether the GATS was applicable to the measures at dispute at all.[82] With reference to the interpretation of the scope of GATS Art. II (MFN), the AB expressed its dismay about the fact that the panel did not substantiate its conclusions:[83]

> We consider these "findings" of the Panel to be pure speculation. As we stated above, the Panel did not provide an interpretation of [GATS] II:1; nor did it apply its interpretation to findings of fact.

The AB did not elaborate on the findings and interpretation of GATS Art. V:1 lit. b of the panel. Therefore, it remains unknown whether the panel's interpretation of the requirements in GATS Art. V:1 lit. b, namely National Treatment and MFN treatment among the members of a PTA in services and the requirement of establishing a higher level of liberalisation in a PTA compared to the level at the WTO, would be upheld by the AB or in a different dispute. However, it is likely, given that the panel did not further substantiate its findings on the scope of GATS Art. V either, that the findings of the interpretation and application of GATS Art. V:1 lit. b in a different dispute would not entirely uphold the decision of the panel in *Canada – Autos.*

D. Trade Creation: GATS Art. V:2, 4, 5, 6, 8

GATS Art. V:2 allows for taking into account the relationship of the PTA in services with a 'wider process of economic integration'. This 'wider process of economic integration' refers to the liberalisation – within the PTA[84] – not only of trade in services, but also of trade in goods.[85] GATS Art. V:2 may lead to a lower threshold for allowing remaining discriminatory

[82] *Canada – Autos*, WT/DS139/AB/R and WT/DS142/AB/R (31 May 2000), Report of the Appellate Body, para. 172.
[83] Ibid., para. 174.
[84] WTO, Committee on Regional Trade Agreements, Note by the Secretariat, Synopsis of 'Systemic' Issues related to Regional Trade Agreements, WT/REG/W/37, para. 86.
[85] WT/REG/W/34, para. 11; Japan, WT/REG/M/23, para. 31; EC, WT/REG/W/35, para. 11.

measures if the overall evaluation under the consideration of the impact on the 'wider process of economic integration' is more positive.[86]

However, GATS Art. V:2 could as well be used to be more rigorous about GATS Art. V:1 or to be more specific about the measures affecting services trade. The provision has so far not developed much impact on the evaluation of PTAs in services, because it is not imperative to take into account the overall economic integration, and GATS Art. V:2 does not apply to the sectorial coverage.[87] In the case of South-South PTAs in service, taking into account the impact of a PTA on the 'wider process of economic integration' might provide for additional reason to allow for differential treatment where the potentially remaining discriminatory measure serves the cause of economic development in the South and brings the world closer to global free trade.

GATS Art. V:4, furthermore, provides that the PTA shall not raise the overall level of barriers to trade in services with respect to third parties. The aim of this provision is to prevent so-called fortress economic integration, with PTAs liberalising services trade among the members, but raising barriers to outsiders. It is, however, not specified, what the term 'barriers' in this context may mean: does it cover all measures related to the GATS or just the measures related to the specific commitments? A similar problem relates to GATS Art. V:5, which regulates the issue of compensation, if measures are adopted, which increase the barriers to trade compared to the levels applicable prior to the PTA. Cottier and Molinuevo (2008) suggest that both GATS Art. V:4 and 5 refer to the specific commitments rather than to the general disciplines of the GATS. Thus, the levelling rule is the level of the multilaterally agreed commitments.[88]

Identifying the appropriate method for determining a change in the level of barriers to trade with respect to third parties remains a main concern for the members. In the case of GATS Art. V:4, it has been suggested to require that a PTA is not allowed to reduce either the level or growth of trade with third parties in any sector or subsector below a historical trend.[89] To avoid the problems with the lack of data on services trade, changes in the volume of trade could also be judged on the basis of data on domestic economic activity.[90] However, despite some additional suggestions on how to measure PTA-related changes in the level of barriers

[86] HKC, WT/REG/W/34, para. 11. [87] Cottier and Molinuevo (2008, p. 139).
[88] Ibid., pp. 143–145. [89] HKC, WT/REG/W/34, para. 13.
[90] Japan and HKC, WT/REG/M/22, paras. 18 and 27.

to trade with respect to third parties,[91] to date, no general rule exists on how to determine such changes.

Yet unsolved as well is the question on how to deal with MFN exemptions which are extended to the new members of a particular form of PTA, a Customs Union. These MFN exemptions are seen as a change in the barriers to trade with third parties (GATS Art. V:4) and may also provide the basis for claims for compensation (GATS Art. V:5). Both views are, however, disputed.[92]

A special feature of the free trade spirit embedded in GATS is GATS Art. V:6. This provision is granting the benefits of a PTA to any service supplier of any other WTO member, given that the service supplier is a legal person and engages in substantive business operations on the territory of the PTA. The main concern for the interpretation is the meaning of 'substantive', while with respect to the legal personality of the services supplier, GATS adopts a broad notion in this context.

GATS Art. V:6 is generally understood in the way that only branches and representative offices from services suppliers with regular commercial activity on the territory of either member of the PTA (more disputed) or on the territory of the member in which the supplier is established (less disputed) are to benefit from the PTA.[93] In this context, GATS Art. V:8 becomes relevant: members to a PTA are not entitled for compensation for any benefit that non-members may accrue through the PTA.[94]

V. Related Provision: GATT Art. XXIV

The possibility to enter into additional trade agreements, which infringe upon commitments under WTO law, has always existed. Because of many reasons elaborated earlier, it did not seem viable and sustainable to forbid the advancement of economic integration outside the multilateral forum.

Thus, regulation alike GATS Art. V has existed even before the first GATT treaty was signed in 1947 and has evolved ever since. The most prominent relative of GATS Art. V is GATT Art. XXIV, which also served as a prototype for GATS Art. V. The following paragraphs illustrate how

[91] E.g. to utilise data from balance of payments, or stocks of FDI; WTO, Committee on Regional Trade Agreements, Note by the Secretariat, Synopsis of 'Systemic' Issues related to Regional Trade Agreements, WT/REG/W/37, para. 93.

[92] WTO, Committee on Regional Trade Agreements, Note by the Secretariat, Synopsis of 'Systemic' Issues related to Regional Trade Agreements, WT/REG/W/37, paras. 94, 95 and 99.

[93] Cottier and Molinuevo (2008, pp. 146–148).

[94] Ibid., p. 151.

the GATT provision on the regulation of preferentialism impacts on the scope and the interpretation on GATS V. According to the Vienna Convention on the Law of Treaties,[95] related regulation and practice can be taken into account. Thus, even though GATT XXIV does not apply directly to services trade regulation, its provisions nevertheless inform the interpretation of GATS Art. V.

GATT Art. XXIV has divided scholarly opinions for a long time and continues to do so. The observations range from 'extremely elastic', over 'full of holes' to 'a failure, if not a fiasco'.[96] There is general agreement, however, that GATT Art. XXIV has failed to function in practice. The WTO Committee on Regional Trade Agreements, which is entrusted with verifying whether PTAs comply with the GATS and the GATT, for instance, does not seem to be effective in securing the compliance of PTAs with WTO rules.[97]

Considering the experiences with the provision of GATT Art. XXIV, the drafters of GATS attempted to amend some of the weaknesses of GATT Art. XXIV while at the same time adjusting the provisions to the specific nature of services trade. The outcome is a similar regulation of economic integration agreements, with some – even remarkable – differences to the model-article GATT Art. XXIV.

Contrary to GATT Art. XXIV, GATS Art. V makes no distinction between a Customs Union and a Free Trade Area. Under GATS Art. V, all preferential services trade, whatever form it may take, is possible. Arguably, this difference between the provisions of GATT Art. XXIV and GATS Art. V was introduced in order to reflect the nature of services trade, in which tariffs and quotas on imports have a very limited role.[98]

The provision of GATT Art. XXIV:5, 'shall not prevent, *as between the territories of contracting parties*, the formation of a customs union or of a free trade area or the adoption of an interim agreement necessary for the formation of a customs union or a free trade area' [emphasis added], has led to the legal opinion that the conclusion of PTAs under the provisions of GATT Art. XXIV is limited to WTO members only.[99] However, through GATT Art. XXIV:10, which stipulates an exception of GATT Art. XXIV:5–9, the violation of GATT Art. XXIV by executing a

95 VCLT, Art. 31. 96 Cited in Islam and Alam (2009, p. 4).
97 Ibid., p. 5. 98 Ibid., p. 24.
99 For in-depth analysis of the question, see Choi (2005).

PTA with a non-member can be legalised by an approval granted by a two-thirds majority of the entire WTO. It is important to note that this is not a waiver: GATT Art. XXIV:10 requires that the PTA in question should eventually 'lead to the formation of a Customs Union or a Free Trade Area in the sense of this Article'.[100] Thus, the non-members of such a PTA must eventually become members to the WTO.

GATS Art. V takes a different stance in this question by providing that the GATS 'shall not prevent any of its Members from being a party to or entering into an agreement liberalising trade in services between or among the parties to such an agreement'. Thus, GATS Art. V allows for PTAs that engage non-members, given that all other requirements are met.

Unfortunately, no direct materials explain this difference between GATT Art. XXIV and GATS Art. V. Following the drafting process it is, however, clear that the drafters of GATS Art. V intended to allow for PTAs in services with non-members. Choi (2005) suggests three possible explanations: (1) the approach of 'progressive liberalisation' by the GATS should allow for more flexibility in the issue of integration in services trade; (2) as some members had already concluded PTAs in services by the time the GATS was negotiated, allowing for PTAs with non-members made it more likely to conclude the negotiations and (3) the fact that the non-member status of parties to a PTA in services has never been brought up in the evaluation procedure of such PTAs also confirms that there is consensus among the WTO members that GATS Art. V may justify the conclusion of a PTA in services with non-members.[101]

Both articles underline the purpose of PTAs to facilitate trade rather than to raise additional or new barriers to trade. Thus, PTAs have to create more trade liberalisation than *status quo* and may not raise barriers to trade inside or outside the agreement. Both provisions establish a minimum level of liberalisation required for PTAs: substantially all trade and National Treatment, with adjustments to the particular nature of services trade. And both provisions require that the intentions to commit to a PTA and finalised PTAs have to be notified to the WTO. Since the establishment of the Committee on Regional Trade Agreements in 1996, the same body examines both PTAs in goods and services.

GATT Art. XXIV refers throughout to customs territories, which has historical reasons: the exception from unconditional MFN was given

[100] Ibid., *supra* n. 173, p. 839. [101] Ibid., pp. 844–847.

mainly to customs unions. Thus, the focus on customs territories has historically grown.[102] One possible explanation for the prominence of customs union in GATT Art. XXIV is that free trade areas were not known prior to GATT 1947. The exception was extended to free trade areas during negotiations because of pressure from developing countries, which were interested in regional economic integration without fully establishing a customs union.[103]

GATT Art. XXIV seeks to prevent the exceptions from entirely subverting MFN through a compromise: GATT Art. XXIV:5 provides for neutrality for third countries as far as formal barriers to trade are concerned. GATT Art. XXIV:8 distinguishes 'true' preferential agreements from only partial agreements through the requirement of eliminating barriers to trade for 'substantially all the trade'. One problem is that the requirement of eliminating barriers to 'substantially all the trade' is not a guarantee to prevent trade diversion. Thus, GATT Art. XXIV did not live up to its task with this respect.

There are some additional aspects of GATT Art. XXIV, which led to the conclusion that the regulation did not fulfil its task. In particular, the fact that there is no general agreement on the volume of 'substantially all the trade' – just like in GATS Art. V – poses a real challenge to the implementation and enforcement of GATT Art. XXIV. Furthermore, it has been criticised that the figures about trade are biased, because they are based on pre-liberalisation levels. GATT Art. XXIV, thus, does not take into account the potential trade flows, which may in fact matter even more for the evaluation of the liberalisation impact of a PTA than the current figures. In addition, it remains unclear whether and to what extent GATT Art. XXIV permits asymmetrical agreements. This limitation of GATT Art. XXIV should be avoided in GATS Art. V by the qualitative requirements. And finally, more problems with the language of GATT Art. XXIV persist in terms of internal (definition of 'other restrictive regulations of commerce') and external conditions (reverse compensation, difficulties with calculating the effects of 'other regulations of commerce', violation of other WTO provisions in PTA).[104]

Overall, GATS Art. V reflects the general logic of GATT Art. XXIV and carries more sophisticated and better regulation with respect to MFN exemption for PTAs. Nonetheless, both GATS Art. V and GATT

[102] Snape (1993, p. 380).
[103] Bartels, Lorand (2012, p. 855).
[104] Bartels (2012, pp. 856–858).

Art. XXIV suffer from weak language and inadequate regulation which is not capable of avoiding trade diversion and ensuring regulatory coherence in IEL. GATS Art. V may be the ameliorated version of GATT Art. XXIV, but it cannot be considered the final and winning regulation of MFN exemption for PTAs it was supposed to be.

3

Regulatory Flexibilities in the GATS

Special and Differential Treatment

As described in the Foundations of this book, GATS – as well as all other WTO agreements – provides for a number of Special and Differential Treatment (SDT) provisions. While the provisions were previously listed and discussed in some detail at the beginning of this book, the following paragraphs will focus on their implications for services trade regulation in developing countries in general. First it is, however, important to take a closer look at the implications of the general regulatory flexibility already embedded in the regulatory structure of GATS.

Generally, the GATS establishes a great amount of regulatory flexibilities to all of its members and limited legally binding obligations. The result of the Uruguay Round led to an agreement, which for the first time establishes multilateral rules of trade in services, but consists, however, mainly of a compromise. Arguably, it was the intent of the driving forces behind the GATS to multilaterally codify the then largely prevalent move away from the public services tradition. GATS was then meant to capture this development rather than initiating it. In consequence, regulatory flexibilities for all of the GATS members are particularly distinct in comparison also with other WTO agreements.[1]

The only binding commitment of GATS, MFN, is limited by the nature of services trade and by the possibility to list individual MFN exemptions, a right used frequently. It lies in the nature of services trade that mutual recognition of equivalence is a pre-condition for successful trade in services. This, however, requires complex assessment and regulatory procedures and is a hindrance to MFN therefore. Furthermore, WTO members can both define the level of binding commitments under GATS, but also the timing of the commitments. Thus, while MFN applies in

[1] Delimatsis, Panagiotis (2015) Trade in Services and Regulatory Flexibility – 20 Years of GATS, 20 Years of Critique, TILEC Discussion Paper, DP 2015–016, August 2015, Tilburg, p. 4.

theory, it is hard to investigate in practice whether the MFN obligation under GATS is always complied with.[2]

One additional aspect of regulatory flexibility in GATS is its reference to the static list of classification. This list was established in the 1990s and has since not evolved, while technological development and advances have led to a number of important new types of services, which are, thus, not covered by GATS or individual schedules of commitments. This leaves considerable regulatory flexibility to GATS members in those services, which are not covered by their schedule of commitments – basically they do not have to comply with any of the GATS obligations.[3]

These flexibilities – as they apply to all of the GATS members equally – are intrinsic in the structure of GATS and, thus, allow regulatory diversity. An aspect, Delimatsis points out, which is not necessarily biased towards developed countries, but rather the opposite.[4] On the other hand, regulatory flexibility can also limit legal certainty, which in turn diminishes the impact of the law in question. Krajweski, however, also agrees that the flexibilities generally provided by GATS are not necessarily negative. He suggests that contrary to limiting regulatory flexibility, increasing transparency on relevant domestic regulation would be one way to balance the potential shortcoming of GATS in this regard.[5]

Thus, the GATS generally allows individual liberalisation at individual pace already by definition. Therefore, SDT provisions granting more flexibility to developing countries and LDCs – while present in GATS – are less prominent in GATS than under other WTO agreements. The general assessment of the limited contribution of GATS to sustainable economic growth in the global South so far[6] also did not lead to a demand for more flexibility, but to a demand for more preferential market access to industrialised countries of service suppliers and services from developing countries and LDCs.[7] The demand resulted in the LDC services waiver in 2011.[8]

[2] See also Delimatsis (2015, p. 5). [3] Ibid., p. 6. [4] Ibid., p. 12.

[5] Krajewski, Markus (2013) *Balancing Legal Certainty with Regulatory Flexibility*, 1 March 2013 [Online], available at SSRN: http://ssrn.com/abstract=2419885, p. 10.

[6] Delimatsis argues on the contrary, Delimatsis (2015, p. 2): 'Even if not all regions have benefited from trade in services, the gains from trade in services still have been more substantial and equally distributed globally when compared to merchandise trade in the last two years'.

[7] Manrique Carpio, Claudia and Comas Mir, Jaume (2014) 'The Least-Developed Countries Services Waiver: Any Alternative under the GATS?', *Goettingen Journal of International Law*, vol. 6, pp. 115–143, p. 122.

[8] Ministerial Conference, Preferential Treatment to Services and Service Suppliers of Least-Developed Countries, Decision of 17 December 2011, WT/L/847, Geneva.

As is discussed later in this study in Legal Regime for South-South Preferential Services Trade, waivers in theory provide for an opportunity to more preferential market access to industrialised countries for LDCs while preventing free riding. Granting such preferential market access is, however, not mandatory for industrialised countries. Therefore, LDCs depend on the willingness of developed country WTO members to use a waiver, which has proven difficult to achieve in the past and appears to be no different here.[9]

The concept of SDT, as elaborated in more detail in the Foundations of this study, has its institutional roots in the creation of the UNCTAD in 1964, and the formation of a political bloc of developing countries in the UN called the Group of 77 (G77).[10] In 1965 the demands of developing countries for a special status in the world trading system led to the drafting of a new part IV in the GATT, which formalised the concept of SDT. SDT originally means that developing countries are not required to grant reciprocal tariff concessions and to bind tariffs.

This initial concept of SDT is only to a limited degree transferable to services trade regulation, since tariff concessions in services trade are less relevant. According to senior WTO staff, the drafters of the GATS therefore attempted to develop a new model of regulation providing flexibility for developing countries. The SDT in GATS is, thus, to be found in the general flexible structure of the agreement and in the provisions explicitly granting additional flexibilities to developing members without exempting them from general GATS obligations.[11]

The GATS system of SDT can, however, be considered to be of mixed success. For instance, developing countries and LDCs are particularly interested in more preferential market access to industrialised countries in GATS mode 4. Industrialised countries up until today refuse to grant such substantial preferential market access, particularly because of labour migration considerations. The GATS fails to provide LDCs and developing countries with the necessary instruments to achieve better access in this regard, since industrialised countries are not obliged to engage in such measures. Thus, the inherent flexibility of GATS may, after all, have proven to be in parts a disadvantage for developing countries and LDCs.

[9] Delimatsis (2015, p. 14); Manrique Carpio and Comas Mir (2014, p. 126).

[10] Hoekman and Kostecki (2009, p. 536).

[11] Manrique Carpio and Comas Mir (2014, pp. 118–119).

4

Compliance with GATS Worldwide

Because of the nature of services trade regulation in general, and the flexible regulatory structure of GATS in particular, it remains challenging to assess compliance with GATS. In order to conduct such an assessment, each individual schedule of commitments would have to be analysed and compared with domestic laws and actual services trade in practice. Since most of the barriers to services trade are hidden in laws and regulations, an assessment of compliance with GATS requires a high level of transparency and a good understanding of the regulatory context in each GATS member.

There are, however, several indicators, which suggest that compliance is generally good: first, there are only very few GATS cases brought to the dispute settlement bodies of the WTO.[1] Assuming that interest in access to services markets is as large as economic literature suggests,[2] it appears as a legitimate conclusion that major breaches of GATS commitments would indeed be spotted and raised. Thus, given the limited number of GATS disputes, relatively good compliance with GATS is likely. Second, GATS commitments are multilateral minimum standards. Most countries have bound their commitments at a relatively low level under GATS[3] but are considerably more open in practice.[4] Commitments under GATS are, therefore, a fall-back option and GATS members appear to use the instrument of voluntary unilateral liberalisation in services quite regularly. Given this, it is generally unlikely that GATS members would go below their liberalising commitments under GATS.

[1] Between 1995 and 2015, twenty-three cases were submitted *inter alia* on the basis of GATS complaints, compared to 404 cases on the basis of GATT 1994 complaints. Source: WTO.

[2] E.g. Francois, Joseph and Hoekman, Bernhard (2010) 'Services Trade and Policy', *Journal of Economic Literature*, vol. 48, September, pp. 642–692.

[3] Adlung and Roy (2005).

[4] E.g. Van der Marel, Erik and Miroudot, Sébastien (2014) 'The economics and political economy of going beyond the GATS', *The Review of International Organisations*, vol. 9, no. 2, pp. 205–239; Francois and Hoekman (2010).

And finally, the logic argument would suggest that compliance is high, given that GATS members are allowed to design their commitments individually. Because of the flexible structure of GATS, countries were not forced to make substantial commitments in areas of services trade policy, in which they were not prepared to do so. In particular, the initial GATS members were substantially free in their scope of commitments under GATS. Therefore, it appears counterintuitive for GATS members to breach their individually tailored commitments. However, the more recent WTO members had to make more substantial commitments under GATS in their accession to the WTO.[5] Some argue that GATS achieves trade liberalisation in services only through the accession procedures in recent years.[6] Not surprisingly, a substantial share of the recent GATS cases before the WTO dispute settlement bodies concerned breaches of GATS obligations by a more recent GATS member.[7]

In conclusion, general compliance with GATS commitments and obligations appears to be relatively good worldwide. Less than an indicator of the strict implementation of GATS, this might much rather be resulting from the large scope of flexibility inherent in GATS regulation of services: due to the overall limited achievement of services trade liberalisation in the GATS, there are generally only limited GATS commitments, which could be breached.[8]

[5] E.g. Adlung, Rudolf (2009) Services Liberalisation From a WTO/GATS Perspective: In Search of Volunteers, Staff Working Paper ERSD-2009-05, WTO, Geneva, pp. 6–7.

[6] E.g. Roy, Martin (2008) 'Out of Stock or Just in Time? Doha and the Liberalisation of Distribution Services', In: J. A. Marchetti and M. Roy (eds.), *Opening Markets for Trade in Services: Countries and Sectors in Bilateral and WTO Negotiations*, Cambridge University Press, Cambridge, pp. 224–263, p. 237.

[7] In 2015, in six of the twenty-three GATS cases before the WTO, China was the respondent.

[8] See also Adlung, Rudolf and Mamdouh, Hamid (2014) How to Design Trade Agreements in Services: Top Down or Bottom Up?, Staff Working Paper ERSD-2013-08, WTO, Geneva: They show that the limited commitments are not necessarily linked with the flexible structure of GATS, but much more with the political reluctance of WTO members to liberalise trade in services.

5

Loopholes in the GATS

Problems in Practice

With regard to the implementation of GATS provisions, Islam and Alam (2009) write the following:[1]

> Scholarly works show that treaty obligations that are imposed by general and equivocal wordings, and provide ample scope for interpretation, are always likely to be less complied with by states than those obligations that are imposed by precise and unequivocal wording. If non-compliance of treaty provision is commonplace, then it could well be the treaty provision itself might have been defective to some extent.

As it is not commonplace that members to the WTO ignore the obligations of WTO law, the reason for the relatively weak compliance with the provisions of GATS Art. V is likely to be found in the fact that the provisions can be interpreted in a variety of ways. Thus, if the WTO rules relating to PTAs in services were clarified, they might be implemented and complied with to a greater degree.

Given that the required level of clarification is unlikely to be reached within the next couple of years, some additional angles for the interpretation of the scope of GATS Art. V might prove to be helpful, particularly in the case of economic integration in the South.

GATS Art. V intends to stimulate and promote free trade not only at the regional but also at the global level. Several shortfalls in the definition of terms and a general lack of agreement among members on the relevant quantitative thresholds, however, restrict the real impact of GATS Art. V on the content of PTAs.

It has been observed that compliance with GATS Art. V is low[2] and that PTAs in services are not all readily notified to the WTO. Both aspects

[1] Islam and Alam (2009, pp. 32–33).

[2] E.g. Roy, Martin, Marchetti, Juan and Lim, Hoe, A. (2008) 'The Race towards Preferential Trade Agreements in Services: How Much Market Access Is Really Achieved?', In: M. Panizzon, N. Pohl and P. Sauvé (eds.), *GATS and the Regulation of International Trade in Services*, Cambridge University Press, Cambridge, pp. 77–110, p. 105.

weaken the protection of the systemic logic of the world trade system: if Member States do not comply with WTO law, the latter may lose credibility and the power to govern world trade. If PTAs are not notified to the WTO, it no longer has control over the numerous different trade agreements and their interaction among each other and with the WTO. The reason for weak compliance and low level of notification is possibly the variety of ways how GATS Art. V can be interpreted and the resulting uncertainty of whether or not a PTA is in compliance with GATS.[3]

This general difficulty is exacerbated in the case of South-South PTAs. Compliance with the law and implementation of legal provisions is generally an institutional weakness of developing countries. Furthermore, developing countries tend to have difficulties with finding specialists advising them in WTO law when entering trade agreements, be it on the regional or on the multilateral level.[4] The language of GATS Art. V and the resulting legal uncertainty of how to interpret the provision constitute a real obstacle to compliance of South-South PTAs with GATS: first, members do not know how to deal with GATS Art. V, and second, they do not use the potential scope provided by GATS for establishing useful, secure and economically fruitful PTAs.

And finally, there is also a considerable risk of overlapping provisions in different PTAs if the stock of individual PTAs is not governed consistently through clear-cut requirements. This – and the sheer number of PTAs – can render trade liberalisation at a multilateral level more difficult, and thus, develop a trade diverting and not creating effect.[5]

The following paragraphs outline the different limitations of GATS Art. V and discuss how these limitations impact on the overall coherence of services trade regulation. Three aspects particularly stand out: the difficulties with the language of GATS Art. V, the consequences of the lack of notifications of PTAs to the WTO and, finally, the overall low level that has been achieved through PTAs in services.

[3] Roy et al. (2008, pp. 106–107).

[4] For a discussion of the problem see: Evans, D., Gasiorek, M., Ghoneim, A., Haynes-Prempeh, M., Holmes, P., Iacovone, L., Jackson, K., Iwanow, T., Robinson, S. and Rollo, J. (2006) Assessing Regional Trade Agreements with Developing Countries: Shallow and Deep Integration, Trade, Productivity, and Economic Performance, DFID Project Number 04 5881, University of Sussex.

[5] Roy et al. (2008, p. 107).

I. Language of GATS Art. V

The language of GATS Art. V allows for a number of loopholes for PTAs, which do not fully comply with GATS disciplines: GATS Art. V:2 allows taking into consideration the wider process of economic integration, GATS Art. V:3 gives additional flexibility to developing countries in terms of internal requirements, and it allows for discrimination against firms originating in non-members. These special and differential treatment type of provisions 'are unlikely to be very effective in achieving their presumed objective: attracting FDI'.[6] Rather, they weaken the multilateral trading system and allow governments to conclude PTAs that are more detrimental to non-members.

A number of technical terms, which lack guidelines on how to assess them (e.g. 'the overall level of barriers' or 'the overall level of development'), further weaken the impact of GATS Art. V: technical terms, which point towards a quantitative evaluation of the situation, but do not provide guidelines on how to assess them, are difficult to implement. Members have to come up with their own interpretation of what the terms encompass, and a generally acknowledged interpretation will either emerge through practice, which requires time, or through treaty interpretation in a dispute settlement process. The latter would be the easiest way to gain a better understanding of the scope of GATS Art. V; however, it is rather unlikely that within the next years, a dispute involving GATS Art. V is brought to the DSB.[7]

Table 10 illustrates the different terms in GATS Art. V, which require interpretation and contribute to the impression that GATS Art. V inherently is built on weak treaty language.

As discussed earlier, there is a general minimal consensus and agreement among members of the WTO on what GATS Art. V means. Nevertheless, when drafting a new PTA in services, which is not entirely liberalising services sectors among members to the PTA, the legal uncertainty with respect the exact scope of GATS Art. V suddenly becomes relevant: even if a country did its best to respect and fulfil the requirements of GATS Art. V, it remains unclear if this is even possible. Given that the scope of interpretation of GATS Art. V is broad, meeting the requirements inevitably requires picking one possible interpretation of the scope. Thus, a PTA in services that does not entirely liberalise all trade in services among its members can possibly be challenged on the basis of

[6] Hoekman and Kostecki (2009, p. 489). [7] See, e.g. Islam and Alam (2009).

Table 10 *GATS Art. V terms requiring interpretation*[a]

GATS Art. V	Treaty language	Problem
GATS Art. V:1(a)	'substantial sectorial coverage'	What is considered to be 'substantial', based on what numbers?
Footnote 1	'volume of trade affected'	What is volume of trade, to what extent may it be affected?
	'not provide for the a priori exclusion of any mode of supply'	Under what circumstances – if – is it then possible to exclude a mode of supply?
	'in terms of number of sectors'	Does the choice of language mean that a limited number of sectors can be excluded?
GATS Art. V:1 lit. b	'substantially all discrimination'	Does it require National Treatment or just the elimination of more barriers to trade than the GATS does?
	'and/or'	Does a PTA have to have both or only one?
	'reasonable time-frame'	What is a reasonable time-frame?
GATS Art. V:2	'wider process of economic integration'	On the bilateral, regional or global level, goods- and services-trade?
GATS Art. V:3 lit. a	'level of development of the countries concerned'	How should the level of development be assessed?
GATS Art. V:4	'shall not [. . .] raise the overall level of barriers to trade'	What is the overall level of barriers to trade and how should it be established?
GATS Art. V:6	'engages in substantive business operations'	When are business operations 'substantive'?

[a] Derived from GATS Art. V.

a different interpretation of the scope of GATS Art. V as long as the scope is not further defined by treaty language or the DSB.

It is likely that, as a consequence of the weak language of GATS Art. V, not all PTAs in services are notified to the WTO. The potential harms and consequences of review may be too high to be risked.[8] Furthermore, the prevalent low level of liberalisation and language in PTAs in services may also be a consequence of the weak language of GATS Art. V, since the GATS fails to serve as a strong 'role-model' for coherent, comprehensive and meaningful regulation of services trade liberalisation. Interestingly, many – if not most – PTAs in services copy the structure of the GATS and sometimes even the language of the individual GATS provisions:[9] in order to avoid potential claims based on a different interpretation of the scope of GATS Art. V, countries are on the safer side if PTAs are also based on weak language. This leaves enough scope for various interpretations of the commitments taken under the PTA, just like it is the case with the commitments under GATS.

Finally, it is regrettable that GATS Art. V remains ill equipped to ensure substantial liberalisation of trade in services on the bilateral and regional level. Given that many PTAs in services are more or less copying the commitments already taken under GATS, had GATS Art. V been more precise, it had had the power to render unlikely the conclusion of PTAs, which essentially have no intent to and no impact on further liberalising trade in services.

II. Missing Case Law

Even though the GATS Agreement has been in force for quite some time, the number of dispute settlement cases is limited.[10] Only in seven cases the DSB has had the opportunity to elaborate on the GATS commitments.[11] As there is a growing tendency to rely on the interpretation in former case law, the limited number of cases affects the comprehensive legal approach to the GATS, which in the GATT is based on a systematic, well-established reasoning for the interpretation of GATT commitments in the vast body of case law.[12]

[8] Arguments are still valid: Stephenson (2000a).

[9] Latrille, Pierre and Lee, Juneyoung (2012) Services Rules in Regional Trade Agreements: How Diverse and How Creative as Compared to the GATS Multilateral Rules?, Staff Working Paper ERSD-2012-19, World Trade Organisation, Geneva.

[10] The WTO currently counts twenty-three cases related to GATS.

[11] Of the twenty-three cases related to GATS, fifteen were settled before a panel was established. One request for consultations is pending. The main GATS cases to date are *EC – Bananas III*, *Canada – Autos*, *Mexico – Telecoms*, *US – Gambling*, *China – Publications and Audiovisual Products* and *China – Electronic Payment Services* [Online]. Available at: www.wto.org/english/tratop_e/dispu_e/dispu_status_e.htm.

[12] Munin (2010, p. 43).

The systemic approach to the interpretation of WTO provisions established by the AB in *US – Gasoline*[13], which relied among others on dictionary definitions, was criticised heavily in literature. Davey (2005) even jokes:[14]

> Nonetheless, the Appellate Body's particular focus on individual words and very extensive use of dictionary meanings was new and caused some to joke that The New Oxford Shorter English Dictionary – the Appellate Body's favorite dictionary – had become a 'covered agreement' under the DSU.

In *US – Gambling*, one of the few GATS cases, the AB attempted to move away from the extensive use of dictionary meanings, in order to minimise their relevance:[15]

> In order to identify the ordinary meaning, a Panel may start with the dictionary definitions of the terms to be interpreted. But dictionaries, alone, are not necessarily capable of resolving complex questions of interpretation, as they typically aim to catalogue all meanings of words – be those meanings common or rare, universal or specialized.

However, the AB in *US – Gambling* was equally criticised in literature for undermining predictability, certainty, stability and security of GATS provisions, as was the AB earlier when it relied more on dictionary definitions. Ortino (2006) states:[16]

> It is not really altogether clear whether the Appellate Body is discarding simply dictionary definitions or more broadly the value of a pure textual interpretation. How else would an interpreter carry out an examination of the text if not principally through dictionary definitions?

With respect to the revival of the intentionalist[17] approach Ortino (2006) and Horn and Weiler (2005) criticise that the AB is not considering all the relevant elements of treaty interpretation as established by VCLT Art. 31:1, such as text, context, teleology and good faith. Both papers raise the

[13] E.g. *US – Gasoline*, WT/DS2/AB/R (29 April 1996) Report of the Appellate Body, p. 20.

[14] Davey, William J. (2005) 'The WTO Dispute Settlement System: The First Ten Years', *Journal of International Economic Law*, vol. 8, no. 1, pp. 17–50, in footnote 22, p. 22.

[15] *US – Gambling*, WT/DS285/AB/R (7 April 2005), Report of the Appellate Body, para. 164 (footnotes and emphasis omitted).

[16] Ortino, Federico (2006) 'Treaty Interpretation and the WTO Appellate Body Report in US Gambling: A Critique', *Journal of International Economic Law*, vol. 9, no. 1, pp. 117–148, p. 123.

[17] The belief that the meaning of a text is determined primarily by the stated or implied intention of the author.

question whether arguments and elaborations on treaty interpretation are not merely used as an ex post justification for the final decision. They particularly criticise that the AB in general does not sufficiently take into consideration the context of the dispute,[18] claiming that a shift in the emphasis of treaty interpretation towards intentions would considerably harm the overall legitimacy of the WTO Dispute Settlement System.[19]

It is true that, in the GATS cases, the context as well as teleology and good faith used to play a minor role in the process of treaty interpretation. In *China – Publications and Audiovisual Products* the AB clarified the weight of dictionary definitions in treaty interpretation in line with the main arguments of previous criticism:[20]

> Dictionaries are important guides to, but not dispositive of, the meaning of words appearing in treaties. For these reasons, the Appellate Body has cautioned panels against equating the "ordinary meaning" of a term with the definition provided by dictionaries. Under Article 31 of the Vienna Convention, the "ordinary meaning" of treaty terms may be ascertained only in their context and in the light of the object and purpose of the treaty. In this respect, the Appellate Body has explained that interpretation pursuant to the customary rule codified in Article 31 of the Vienna Convention is ultimately a holistic exercise that should not be mechanically subdivided into rigid components.

Thus, it is finally acknowledged and well established that, in addition to the interpretation of the raw text, contextual and teleological elements constitute important elements of treaty interpretation.[21] In *China – Publications and Audiovisual Products*, the AB paid considerable attention to the context of the provision at dispute, as well as did the panel in *China – Electronic Payment Services*. While it is – as has been discussed earlier – questionable to what extent the provisions in the preamble of the GATS are considered to be relevant for the interpretation of a specific GATS commitment, it is now well established that the regulatory context and the teleology of the concerned GATS commitment should be taken into consideration.

[18] Ortino (2006, p. 146); Horn, Henrik and Weiler, Joseph (2005) 'European Communities – Trade Description of Sardines: Textualism and Its Discontent', In: H. Horn and P. C. Mavroidis (eds.), *The WTO Case Law of 2002*, Cambridge University Press, Cambridge, pp. XX, p. 253.

[19] Ortino (2006, pp. 146–147).

[20] *China – Publications and Audiovisual Products*, WT/DS363/AB/R (21 December 2009), Report of the Appellate Body, para. 348 (footnotes and emphasis omitted).

[21] Ortino (2006, p. 123); Munin (2010, p. 43).

With respect to flexibility for South-South PTAs in services, this clarification of the relevance of the regulatory context and the teleology for treaty interpretation is relevant: given that the overall intent to provide for flexibility for South-South PTAs in services, including the context and teleology into the interpretation of the scope of GATS Art. V should generally provide for a relatively broad understanding of the scope of flexibility for South-South PTAs.

Nevertheless, case law in GATS remains scarce and aside from the relevance of the contextual and teleological elements for the interpretation of GATS commitments, little systemic approaches to the GATS have been established. This is not only impacting in a negative way on the predictability, stability and certainty of GATS regulation – as the GATS is a dynamic treaty, well-established rules for the interpretation of the scope of commitments are essential – it may also develop a discouraging effect on WTO members who would wish to claim a violation of GATS commitments. Furthermore, the scarcity of case law also impacts on the interpretation of GATS in a dispute, as puts the AB in *Canada – Autos*:[22]

> In reaching this conclusion, we are mindful of the importance of the GATS as a new multilateral trade agreement covered by the WTO Agreement. This appeal is only the second case in which we have been asked to review a panel's findings on provisions of the GATS. Given the complexity of the subject-matter of trade in services, as well as the newness of the obligations under the GATS, we believe that claims made under the GATS deserve close attention and serious analysis. We leave interpretation of Article II of the GATS to another case and another day.

Although this decision dates back more than ten years, since then the AB only twice had again the opportunity to review a panel decision on GATS provisions, in *US – Gambling* and in *China – Publications and Audiovisual Products*. Thus, it may be too early to consider the AB's statement in *Canada – Autos* to be outdated and the urge to give close attention and serious analysis to claims under GATS remains valid and highly relevant.

[22] *Canada – Autos*, WT/DS139/AB/R and WT/DS142/AB/R (31 May 2000), Report of the Appellate Body, para. 184.

6

Innovation in South-South Agreements?

Trade in services in a developing country context is generally better known for North-South than for South-South partnerships. India's telecommunication and IT-services exports are one famous and well-known example for that.[1] However, in the case of North-South trade in services, there is a remarkable risk of brain-drain for the developing countries and a risk of social upheaval for the recipient countries in the North. Nevertheless, most developing country services trade has been with developed countries. As the services sectors in developing countries expand, so should the South-South trade in services.[2]

The overwhelming majority of PTAs in services offer at least some value-added commitments relative to countries' GATS undertakings. However, mode 4 liberalisation is still very rare. Finally, most recent trade agreements in services encompass a non-party MFN clause. This clause means that the countries will extend to each other any preferences granted to any third country.[3]

As previously discussed, the GATS' achievements in terms of trade in services liberalisation were limited. The question is, therefore, whether or not PTAs have managed to provide additional liberalisation in comparison with the GATS. At least in theory, this should be easier to achieve for PTAs for a number of reasons:[4] (1) the opportunity to cover a full set of disciplines simultaneously (goods, services, intellectual property rights, investments, etc.), which has allowed for a legal structure that is coherent and seamless with respect to the application of trade rule;

[1] Chanda, Rupa (1999) *Movement of Natural Persons and Trade in Services: Liberalising Temporary Movement of Labour under the GATS*, Indian Council for Research on International Economic Relations, New Delhi, p. 13.

[2] Australian Government (2004).

[3] Fink, Carsten and Jansen, Marion (2007) Services Provisions in Regional Trade Agreements: Stumbling or Building Blocks for Multilateral Liberalisation?, Paper presented at a Conference, World Trade Organisation, Geneva, p. 12.

[4] Stephenson (2002, pp. 187–199).

(2) the opportunity to take a 'negative list' approach to services trade liberalisation (as opposed to the 'positive list' approach embedded in the GATS), which basically liberalises all services sectors except for the ones featured on the list; (3) transparency: the 'negative list' approach enables much more transparency and gives detailed information about the market access to a particular services sector; (4) stability: the 'negative list' approach requires that all the restrictions are linked to the actual national law or regulation, which together with the 'status quo' provision provides for greater stability (accurate, bound restrictions); (5) the opportunity to target deeper integration than can an agreement at the multilateral WTO level and (6) liberalisation: PTAs are generally required to be substantially more liberal, although they rarely liberalise all services trade and keep some cross-border barriers to services trade.

Until 2002 PTAs have not achieved significantly more than the GATS, other than for certain selected sectors and in certain well-specified ways. However, if the PTAs stick to their objective as established by GATS Art. V and GATT Art. XXIV – the complete removal of all restrictions on trade in services – the margin of differential liberalisation and market openness should widen considerably over time. There are two key reasons for the more ambitious liberalisation objectives of PTAs in services: (1) the awareness of the need to comply with GATS Art. V, which requires all PTAs to be more liberalising than the GATS and (2) the greater ease and ability to arrive at consensus in a context of smaller numbers of more like-minded trading partners.[5]

As mentioned at various occasions, innovative regulation in services trade is expected to stem from PTAs.[6] This seems to be a reasonable assumption, given that countries agreeing on preferential services trade presumably have a real interest in efficient regulation, and may want to go beyond the scope of the – limited – multilateral commitments. When going substantially beyond the scope of the commitments under GATS, new regulation eventually has to be invented.

Furthermore, the evolution of IEL can be described as one that follows waves: a wave of multilateralism is followed by a wave of preferentialism.[7] Some argue that it is during the wave of preferentialism that the terrain for

[5] Ibid., pp. 202–204.

[6] On the risk and limits of regulatory innovation in PTAs, see Trachtman, Joel P. (2011) 'The Limits of PTAs: WTO Legal Restrictions on the Use of WTO-Plus Standards Regulation in PTAs', In: K. W. Bagwell and P. C. Mavroidis (eds.), *Preferential Trade Agreements: A Law and Economics Analysis*, Cambridge University Press, Cambridge, pp. 115–149.

[7] Cottier et al. (2015).

new regulation on the multilateral level is prepared, e.g. by *de facto* creating a new consensus voluntarily followed in new models of trade regulation, or through testing new models of regulation and, thus, developing good arguments for and against a certain form of regulation.[8]

With respect to services trade regulation, presumably, we are now in the phase of preferentialism, and, arguably in a phase of consolidation of a new global or multilateral consensus about where and how to proceed with respect to services trade regulation. Thus, taking a closer look at regulatory innovations with respect to services trade regulation is timely.

Since little evidence backing theories about the innovative character of PTAs in services has been provided to date, taking a look at this aspect from a fresh angle seems worthwhile.[9] There are also a number of authors claiming that services trade liberalisation – at least with respect to certain sectors – is more meaningful and promising at the regional and bilateral than at the multilateral level.[10] They argue that the evolution and extension of services trade regulation and liberalisation at the multilateral level will take a while, because the expected benefits of regional, bilateral and unilateral liberalisation still outweigh the predicted gains of further multilateral liberalisation.[11]

In South-South PTAs in services substantial liberalisation and innovative regulation would be most meaningful in the sectors that are presumably more promising for regional and bilateral economic development than others. In theory, these sectors should show the most far-reaching commitments.

I. Sectors of Interest

Services trade liberalisation requires the removal of discriminatory measures among trading partners. The required changes in national laws and regulations follow lengthy processes and necessitate developing and

[8] Critical, see Crawford and Laird (2001); for a general discussion, see Woolcock, Stephen and Sampson, Gary (2003) *Regionalism, Multilateralism and Economic Integration: The Recent Experience*, United Nations University Press, Tokyo; for the underlying theories, see Baldwin (2006).

[9] See e.g. Roy, Marchetti and Lim (2007); Adlung, Rudolf, and Miroudot, Sébastien (2012) Poison in the Wine? Tracing GATS-minus Commitments in Regional Trade Agreements, Staff Working Paper, ERSD No. 2012-04, World Trade Organisation, Geneva.

[10] Stephenson (2002); Adlung (2007); Nielson, Julia and Taglioni, Daria (2004) Services Trade Liberalisation: Identifying Opportunities and Gains, OECD Trade Policy Papers, Paris.

[11] Hufbauer and Stephenson (2007); Fink and Jansen (2008, p. 249).

obtaining a consensus among policymakers, service operators, regulators and consumers. Thus, finding the most appropriate forum for liberalising services trade and removing discrimination takes on considerable importance: on the one hand, governments may not wish to undertake this process several times, but on the other hand, combining negotiations at the regional or multilateral level reduces their ability to differentiate between different trading partners.

According to Stephenson (2002) the character of each of the twelve services sectors as established under GATS regulation determines whether it would be most beneficial to liberalise it bilaterally, regionally or multilaterally. In summary, she argues that among others, infrastructure services (cheaper infrastructure through competition) and business services (knowledge transfer, global value-added chains) should be liberalised at the multilateral level. She further points out that construction/engineering services and professional services should be liberalised at the regional or bilateral level (recognition of diplomas), as well as educational, legal and social type of services (cultural background) with some exceptions. For recreational and cultural services, she views the decision as being different from one type of service subsector to another.[12]

The argument of Stephenson (2002) is widely acknowledged. It has been validated in different ways by others, albeit oftentimes indirectly. Nielson and Taglioni (2004),[13] Adlung (2007),[14] Hoekman and Mattoo (2008b),[15] Dihel et al. (2008)[16] and Lee (2011)[17] focus on the potential of different services sectors to contribute to poverty alleviation and economic growth. They agree that, in order to promote poverty reduction, both communication and transportation services, together with financial services and infrastructure services, are of particular interest because they are conduits through which individual economies can interact.[18] The effect of interaction is outsourcing, which again results in economic growth.

This is evidenced by the fact that shipping costs constitute the most binding trade barrier.[19] Furthermore, poor infrastructure in developing countries accounts for 40 per cent of predicted transport costs in coastal countries and for 60 per cent in landlocked countries. Infrastructure is therefore not only a facilitating factor for exports, but a key determinant

[12] Stephenson (2002, pp. 206–208). [13] Nielson and Taglioni (2004).
[14] Adlung (2007). [15] Hoekman and Mattoo (2008).
[16] Dihel, Eschenbach, and Sheperd (2008). [17] Lee (2011a).
[18] Dihel et al. (2008, pp. 72–73). [19] Adlung (2007, p. 3).

and potential trade barrier. Similarly, the absence of competition in the transport/logistics services sector can constitute a barrier to trade.[20] These arguments substantiate the need for liberalisation and competition in the wider infrastructure services space.

Economic theory states that PTAs in services are particularly interesting if they can result in unlocking economies of scale or increasing competition. Transportation has been shown to be of particular importance for unlocking economies of scale, as it enables a higher degree of specialisation in production chains. Business services are of particular interest in terms of increasing competition, as they may enhance overall productivity in a region.[21] Furthermore, communication, financial services and mode 4 supply of services have been shown to be of essence, since they enable better provision of transportation and business services while also enhancing the functioning of value-added chains.[22] Developing countries could reasonably be expected to focus their efforts on trade liberalisation services in these core sectors, in order to gain most from their PTAs in services. Commitments in these sectors would, therefore, also be expected to be relatively far reaching. This should not only be the case in South-South PTAs, but it may equally apply to North-South PTAs.

In conclusion, there are a number of services sectors that are more suitable for liberalisation at the regional and bilateral level than at the multilateral level (hereinafter PTA priority sectors), while other services sectors are of key importance with respect to stimulating economic growth (hereinafter growth priority sectors).

The PTA priority sectors would be expected to exhibit more far-reaching commitments at the regional and bilateral level than at the multilateral level. Furthermore, these sectors should in theory also be the sectors in which commitments reach furthest beyond the scope of the GATS, and therewith, include the highest prevalence of new and innovative regulation. If innovative regulation was found in these sectors, this would indicate that PTAs are not mainly used as a compensation for the lack of multilateral liberalisation, but rather because they are perceived as more suitable than multilateral instruments. A spreading consensus in these sectors would not be expected to develop a great impact at the multilateral level, since they are more suitable for regional and bilateral liberalisation.

[20] Hoekman and Mattoo (2008, p. 40).

[21] Mattoo and Fink (2002, p. 16).

[22] See, e.g. Dihel et al. (2008, pp. 72–73).

Table 11 *Relevance of individual services sectors as growth and PTA priorities*

Sector	Growth priorities[a]	PTA priorities[b]
Transportation	Yes	No
Communication	Yes	No
Financial services	Yes	No
Business and professional services	Yes	Yes
Construction services	No	Yes
Educational services	No	Yes
Mode 3 supply of services	Yes	No
Mode 4 supply of services	Yes	Yes

[a] Based on Adlung (2007), Hoekman and Mattoo (2008) and Dihel et al. (2008).
[b] See Stephenson (2002), Lee (2011) and Nielson and Taglioni (2004).

Developing countries could also be expected to focus their efforts of services trade liberalisation on the growth priority sectors, in order to maximise the economic growth effect of their South-South PTAs in services. Commitments in these sectors should, therefore, also be relatively far reaching, even though this would be expected to equally apply to North-South PTAs.[23] If more innovative regulation was to be found in these growth priority sectors as opposed to the PTA priority sectors, this would indicate that the need for trade liberalisation in growth priority sectors is indeed so high that PTAs are used as a compensation for the lack of liberalisation on the multilateral level. If new models of regulation in the growth priority sectors were found to be spreading over the PTAs in the dataset, this would indicate that, indeed, a new consensus on how to proceed in multilateral liberalisation was emerging from PTAs.

For each of the services market segments of interest, Table 11 illustrates their relevance as growth priorities and PTA priorities – the two main dimensions of potential interest for the analysis of South-South PTAs in services.

The following paragraphs elaborate in more detail the reasons for the particular interest in each of the services sectors featured in Table 11. The analysis of the level of commitments and the prevalence of innovative regulation of this thesis will focus on these sectors. Other sectors, such as

[23] See, e.g. Adlung (2007).

distribution, energy, environmental services, health and social services,[24] will be left aside because of their presumably lesser relevance for economic growth in developing countries and their lesser suitability for preferential as opposed to multilateral liberalisation.

A. *Transportation*

The GATS differentiates between air, maritime, rail and road transport services. All these different transportation services are relevant for cross-border value-added chains as well as for economic productivity in general. In air transportation, currently no liberalisation is taking place under GATS.[25] The maritime sector, however, is fairly liberalised compared to other services sectors. This is not due to the integration of maritime services into the GATS, but the sector is generally more liberalised than others: bulk traffic 'faces no restrictions except for one or two countries',[26] and liner traffic is organised in conferences (cartels which fix prices and frequencies) and increasingly large independent operators. Furthermore, a framework of bilateral intergovernmental cargo-sharing agreements regulates most of the maritime traffic between countries. Thus, the GATS did not add much to the general level of liberalisation in maritime services.[27]

With respect to rail transportation, liberalisation is still relatively fragmented because of the historical background of rail transportation as being state-owned. Therefore, competition was very limited in this subsector until recently:

> In the case of mode 1, for a long time international transport of passengers and freight only consisted of joining successive national segments of transport. No single entity was responsible for an international journey, the freight or the passenger being passed on from one monopolistic network to another.[28]

[24] Even though STEPHENSON (2002) argues that health and social services are more suitable for regional and bilateral trade liberalisation than for multilateral trade liberalisation, this sector and the underlying assumption of cultural proximity is covered partially by the analysis of the level of commitment in mode 4 supply of services: Without mode 4 supply of services, trade in health and social services will in any case be very restricted.

[25] Annex on Air Transport Services; WTO SECRETARIAT (2000) *Guide to the GATS: An Overview of Issues for Further Liberalisation of Trade in Services*, World Trade Organisation, Kluwer Law International, The Hague, pp. 51–70.

[26] WTO SECRETARIAT (2000, p. 430).

[27] See ROY, MARCHETTI AND LIM (2007); DEE, P. (2005) A Compendium of Barriers to Services Trade, Paper prepared for the World Bank, Asia-Pacific School of Economics and Government, Canberra; and WTO SECRETARIAT (2000).

[28] WTO SECRETARIAT (2000, p. 488).

Cross-border trade in railway services is difficult not only because of political reasons, but also because of technical obstacles such as incompatibilities in braking systems, height of railway wagons and type of electric power. And as long as railway companies remain state-owned – which is often the case in developing countries – commercial presence (mode 3 supply) is basically excluded. Thus, as a consequence of state monopolies, the level of liberalisation in rail transport services remains low.[29]

Road transportation is more liberalised at the regional than at the multilateral level.[30] The overall level of liberalisation of passenger transportation services seems low, while level of liberalisation with respect to freight transportation depends on the type of goods that are transported. Liberalisation is higher in the transportation of economically more significant goods.[31]

A well-functioning transportation sector and good transportation services are crucial for economic development in developing countries: goods and people need to be moved from one place to another reliably and quickly. Without a good infrastructure for transportation, many businesses are doomed to fail because their products will not reach their consumers or because they will not be able to find the right people to work for them. Transportation is, in one way or another, linked with all economic activities. Thus, the entire sector is expected to have a strong impact on economic growth.[32]

Trade theory claims that more liberalisation leads to more competition, resulting in better services at a cheaper prize. Thus, the fact that multilateral trade liberalisation in transportation services is particularly restricted is seen as a problem, especially for developing countries.[33] If PTAs were found to include far-reaching commitments in transportation services, this may be an indicator for the need for further liberalisation in this sector, given that it would best be liberalised at the multilateral level according to theory.

[29] Findlay, Christopher (2008) 'Transport Services', In: A. Mattoo, R. M. Stern and G. Zanini (eds.), *A Handbook of International Trade in Services*, Oxford University Press, Oxford, pp. 356–387.

[30] WTO Secretariat (2000, p. 501).

[31] Ibid., p. 521; see also Findlay (2008).

[32] See also Lee (2011, pp. 18–19).

[33] See e.g. Francois, Joseph F. and Wooton, Ian (2002) 'Trade in International Transport Services: The Role of Competition', *Review of International Economics*, vol. 9, no. 2, pp. 249–261.

B. *Communication*

The telecommunication industry is in a process of rapid structural change. Not only are national monopolies being privatised in many countries, or are facing competition by private suppliers, but technological progress also changes the landscape of telecommunication considerably. In order to manage the regulatory challenges caused by the rapid structural change in the telecommunication industry, the definition of the subsectors was drafted in a way that should allow incorporating and classifying new forms of services that may emerge over time.[34]

In terms of the level of liberalisation, value-added services generally tend to be more liberalised than basic services, and developed countries generally have a more open telecommunication market than developing countries.[35] Despite the prediction that the amount of cross-border trade in telecommunication services and consumption abroad will increase due to new technologies, commercial presence is expected to remain important for service suppliers in the telecommunication industry. Developing countries – and emerging markets in particular – seem to acknowledge this and have aligned their trade policies accordingly.[36]

However, three types of market access restrictions typically remain in place, which are of considerable relevance for the sector: (i) limitations on the number of suppliers, (ii) restriction on type of legal entity and (iii) limitations on the participation of foreign capital. Particularly emerging markets maintain such restrictions, which impact mostly on commercial presence – the most relevant mode of supply for the industries in developing economies.[37]

Telecommunication services – just like transportation – are linked to all types of economic activity. They are seen as being of high relevance for cross-border value-added production: the different stages in the

[34] GATS Services Sectorial Classification List MTN.GNS/W/120; WTO Secretariat (2000, p. 534).

[35] WTO Secretariat (2000, p. 540).

[36] See, e.g. Garbacz, Christopher and Thompson, Herbert G. (2007) 'Demand for Telecommunication Services in Developing Countries', *Telecommunications Policy*, vol. 31, no. 5, pp. 276–289.

[37] Cowhey, Peter F. and Aronson, Jonathan D. (2008) 'Trade in Services Telecommunications', In: A. Mattoo, R. M. Stern and G. Zanini (eds.), *A Handbook of International Trade in Services*, Oxford University Press, Oxford, pp. 389–436; Adlung, Rudolf (2006b) 'Public Services and the GATS', *Journal of International Economic Law*, vol. 9, no. 2, pp. 455–485.

production process have to be supervised, and good communication between the actors in the production process is crucial.[38] Better and cheaper communication services are expected to increase productivity and enable new businesses to be started in the first place.

Emerging markets and developing countries seem to be reluctant to liberalise telecommunication services under GATS.[39] And, while the sector is fairly open on the multilateral level with respect to mode 1 supply of services, the underdevelopment of the infrastructure in developing countries constitutes an almost insurmountable *de facto* market entry barrier.

In order to strengthen the quality and availability of telecommunication services, more adequate definitions of specific services in the telecommunication sector would also be required.[40] Both an increase in competition and more adequate definition of services could be introduced in PTAs. If PTAs tend to innovate in terms of regulating trade in telecommunication services, this, too, may be an indicator of the need and the consolidation of further multilateral liberalisation.

C. *Financial Services*

Financial services are also rapidly evolving. Thus, regulation of financial services is challenging, given the revolutionary changes in this sector in recent years.[41] The technological advances render cross-border trade in financial services more common. However, commercial presence is still required for many types of financial services. At the multilateral level, liberalisation with respect to commercial presence is predominating, while cross-border supply in services remains restricted.

Generally, the financial industry is among the most heavily regulated services sectors. Regulation is so heavy, because the financial sector is of imminent importance for economic growth, but also because government intervention may be required to prevent market failure and correct systemic externalities. Liberalisation efforts at the multilateral level, thus,

[38] See, e.g. Batt, Rosemary (2002) 'Managing Customer Services: Human Resource Practices, Quit Rates, and Sales Growth', *The Academy of Management Journal*, vol. 45, no. 3, pp. 587–597, pp. 595–596.

[39] See Fink, Carsten, Mattoo, Aaditya and Rathindran, Randeep (2002) 'An Assessment of Telecommunications Reform in Developing Countries', *Information Economics and Policy*, vol. 15, no. 4, pp. 443–466, p. 444.

[40] See generally Weber, Rolf H. and Burri, Mira (2012) *Classification of Services in the Digital Economy*, Springer, Berlin and Heidelberg.

[41] WTO Secretariat (2000, p. 338).

aim at enhancing competition, while at the same time endorsing the need for regulatory interventions.[42]

With respect to liberalisation at the multilateral level, developing countries fear that the competitive advantage of globally active MNCs would displace local banking and loan institutions. Thus, most developing countries remain sceptical towards liberalisation of financial services through the GATS. However, studies point out that developing countries could benefit considerably from multi- or unilateral trade liberalisation in financial services and predicted in 2006 substantial gains, particularly in a South-South context.[43]

The financial services sector arguably is the most intertwined with economic activities and with economic performance: more or less at every stage of economic activity, financial services are in one way or another required.[44] Thus, availability, quality and price of financial services all directly affect economic performance. With respect to developing countries, mode 1 supply of financial services is of particular relevance, along with commercial presence. However, both are shallowly liberalised at the multilateral level.[45] Given that developing countries are reluctant towards multilateral trade liberalisation in financial services, regional or bilateral liberalisation may find more support among stakeholders and could provide the right instrument to introducing trade liberalisation in financial services on a small scope.

D. *Business and Professional Services*

Professional services are infrequent, technical or unique functions performed by contractors or consultants. They include legal services, architectural and engineering services, accountancy services, as well as some IT-related services.

The global level of liberalisation in professional services is fairly high. Particularly commitments in architectural services, for accounting and

[42] Roy et al. (2007); Hoekman, Bernard and Mattoo, Aaditya (2007b) Services Trade and Growth, Paper prepared for a meeting of the Commission in Growth and Development, World Bank, Washington DC.

[43] Sauvé, Pierre and Irace, Mary (2006) The Doha Development Agenda and GATS: The Benefits of Open Services Markets, Report for the National Foreign Trade Council, NFTC, Washington DC and New York, p. 15.

[44] See also Lee (2011, pp. 19–20).

[45] Dobson, Wendy (2008) 'Financial Services and International Trade Agreements: The Development Dimension', In: A. Mattoo, R. M. Stern and G. Zanini (eds.), *A Handbook of International Trade in Services*, Oxford University Press, Oxford, pp. 289–337, pp. 305–306.

engineering are relatively far reaching, providing for a high level of full market access with respect to mode 3 and mode 4 supplies. Commercial presence and presence of the natural person are obviously relevant for trade in professional services; this may explain the high level of commitments in mode 3 and mode 4 supply of services. However, mode 4 supply of services – and therewith temporary labour migration – is always limited by other measures, such as horizontal measures, Visa requirements or recognition of certificates.[46]

One relevant subsector is IT-related services, which merged from a number of other sectors and is a fast-growing, lucrative market. The industry has developed in an open and competitive environment, which is often credited with having driven its rapid growth:[47]

> As the industry has matured, however, some segments have shown a tendency to concentration in large companies. So while sector-specific regulation is nearly non-existent, competition authorities in some countries have had an influence on the development of the computer industry and related services.

There are, thus, concerns that the traditionally unregulated computer services sector could begin facing similar constraints as the telecommunications services sector.[48] Particularly, in emerging markets, the presence of natural persons is important due to prevailing shortages of skilled labour. As a consequence of these shortages, cross-border trade in IT-related services has become increasingly important, as employers seek to alleviate labour shortages by cross-border relationships with foreign IT-related services suppliers.[49]

Developing countries tend to be more reluctant with respect to trade liberalisation in professional services, than industrialised countries, and have, with a few exceptions, made few commitments under the GATS.[50]

[46] Winters, Alan L. (2008) 'The Temporary Movement of Workers to Provide Services (GATS Mode 4)', In: A. Mattoo, R. M. Stern and G. Zanini (eds.), *A Handbook of International Trade in Services*, Oxford University Press, Oxford, pp. 480–541; Carzaniga, Antonia G. (2003) 'The GATS, Mode 4 and Pattern of Commitments', In: A. Mattoo and A. Carzaniga (eds.), *Moving People to Deliver Services*, The World Bank and Oxford University Press, Oxford, pp. 21–26, p. 21; Panizzon (2010, pp. 30–34).

[47] WTO Secretariat (2000, p. 154).

[48] Cowhey and Aronson (2008); Parikh, Vaibhav (2003) 'Mode 4 and the Software Services Sector: An Indian View', In: A. Mattoo and A. Carzaniga (eds.), *Moving People to Deliver Services*, The World Bank and Oxford University Press, Oxford, pp. 163–170.

[49] Primo Braga (1996).

[50] WTO Secretariat (2000, pp. 32–33).

Thus, particularly in developing countries, the potential benefits from trade liberalisation in professional services are considered to be high.[51]

Furthermore, it is generally agreed that when people need to interact, language skills or shared values and a shared history are most welcome: working together is easier and there are less misunderstandings, as people 'speak a common language'.[52] Therefore, trade liberalisation in professional services may also be more suitable for regional and bilateral trade liberalisation, as opposed to multilateral liberalisation. Since neighbouring countries tend to have a more similar education system, professional certificates should be easier to recognise.

E. Construction Services

Construction services encompass any work that is related to the construction, the pre-erection, or the demolition of a building, as well as renting services related to the construction equipment and special trade construction work. Generally, the sector is marked by a large number of small companies, which are active locally, and a small number of large companies, which are active globally. Construction services are mainly supplied through commercial presence, which is usually limited to the duration of the construction work. Joint ventures between domestic and foreign companies are quite common in this sector.

The construction services sector is historically large in developing countries. In developing countries, according to the UNCTAD (1999), the construction services sector on average accounts for 10 per cent of total employment.[53] In the recent past, 70 per cent of international construction business opportunities were undertaken in developing countries:[54]

> In these countries, construction services are a fundamental economic activity, often constituting the largest single sector of the economy. Construction is also a key infrastructure service for all other industries and a tool for upgrading domestic welfare.

Given construction work requires that a large number of people work closely together in a single project, regional liberalisation may be more suitable than multilateral liberalisation. Furthermore, it is already the case that construction companies in developing countries start to build up

[51] See Adlung (2007); Hoekman and Mattoo (2008); Dihel et al. (2008).
[52] See Stephenson (2002); Lee (2011); Nielson and Taglioni (2004).
[53] UNCTAD (1999) *Analysis of Experiences in Selected Services Sectors*, Geneva.
[54] Nielson and Taglioni (2004, p. 40).

joint ventures in other developing countries, or they start to expand their businesses to other developing countries.

The level of multilateral liberalisation in construction services compares favourably to other sectors. Particularly in the most relevant mode of supply, commercial presence, full commitments were often made.[55] However, behind-the-border-barriers, such as limitations on FDI, requirements for permits and licences, and public procurement procedures, are of relevance in construction services. Furthermore, given the need for both high- and low-skilled labours, this sector is particularly affected by restrictions and regulations of labour migration and mode 4 supply.[56]

Thus, in a South-South PTA, trade liberalisation particularly in mode 3 and mode 4 supply of construction services should be rather extensive, given the needs of the market and given the suitability of PTAs for trade liberalisation in construction services.

F. Educational Services

Education services are defined as primary, secondary and higher education services and as adult education. However, these definitions may be outdated to a certain degree because of rapid changes taking place in the area of higher education. Basic education (up to secondary education) is understood by many countries as a basic entitlement and considered as falling within the definition of services supplied in the exercise of governmental authority, which places it outside of the scope of GATS and trade in services in general.[57] Thus, trade in educational services is limited to the services that go beyond the basic entitlement and that lie outside of the exercise of governmental authority.

It is well recognised that education plays a key role in fostering economic growth, social and personal development, as well as in lowering the level of inequality. Furthermore, education as a provider of skills and creator of employability is considered to be of crucial importance in

[55] WTO Secretariat (2000, p. 188).

[56] WTO Secretariat (2000, pp. 186–187); for a general discussion, see Wickramasekera, Piyasiri (2002) *Asian Labour Migration: Issues and Challenges in an Era of Globalisation*, International Labour Office, Geneva.

[57] Larsen, Kurt, Martin, John P. and Morris, Rosemary (2002) 'Trade in Educational Services: Trends and Emerging Issues', *The World Economy*, vol. 25, no. 6, pp. 849–868; Sauvé, Pierre (2002) 'Trade, Education and the GATS: What's In, What's Out, What's All the Fuss About?', *Higher Education Management and Policy*, vol. 14, no. 3, pp. 47–76.

facilitating economic adjustment and enabling effective participation in the global market.[58] This is particularly relevant for the ability of a country to meet the economic challenges, which inevitably accompany economic liberalisation. Nonetheless, the effect of education on economic growth is much less direct and considerably more difficult to measure than, for example, in the case of transportation.

Trade in educational services has increased, particularly with respect to tertiary education: students are going abroad to study, faculties and researchers are cooperating, and academic programmes are marketed worldwide. While the data of students studying abroad is available, data on the increasingly important subsector of corporate training is not yet available. The main mode of supply for trade in educational services seems to be consumption abroad. However, commercial presence (mode 3 supply) has become more important recently, especially since developing countries are suffering from a large outflow of students to foreign universities and have started allowing these universities to establish branches and joint ventures in-country.[59]

Given that the focus in this sector has been on the students consuming educational services abroad, the supply of educational services through temporary labour migration (mode 4 supply, e.g. by lecturers) has been neglected somewhat by literature and foreign policy.[60] Mode 4 supply of educational services would be very relevant, however, in the context of a South-South PTA, given that skills and talents may be relatively scarce, and thus, more competition and freer movement of good lecturers and professors would enrich all members of a PTA.

After energy services, the educational services sector is the sector with the lowest commitments made under GATS.[61] The key reason for this low level of multilateral liberalisation may be found in recognised differences in the quality of education worldwide. Countries may also prefer to protect the education sector in order to ensure that invested amounts benefit their own labour force. Finally, the movement of natural persons is key in educational services trade. The various restrictions on labour migration further limit the scope of trade in educational services.

Educational services may be more suitable for regional and bilateral trade liberalisation than multilateral liberalisation, possibly with the

[58] Stephenson (2002); WTO Secretariat (2000, p. 230); Nielson and Taglioni (2004).
[59] WTO Secretariat (2000, pp. 235–237).
[60] See, e.g. Larsen et al. (2002, p. 849); Sauvé (2002, pp. 53–54).
[61] WTO Secretariat (2000, p. 240).

exemption of mode 2 supply.[62] Commitments in educational services in South-South PTAs could, thus, easily exceed the scope of GATS commitments, and – except for mode 2 supply – regional and bilateral liberalisation is more likely to be complementary to multilateral liberalisation.

II. Modes of Supply

As there are many different ways how services can be traded, the commitments in the different modes of supply have an important impact on the overall economic development. For example, liberalisation of cross-border supply in services (mode 1) in many cases will not actually foster trade in services, because many types of services essentially cannot be traded like this.[63] Therefore, taking into consideration which modes of supply are liberalised and to what extent (e.g. with or without limitations) is also of importance.

In the context of South-South preferential trade in services, it has been shown that labour migration and commercial presence are of particular importance.[64]

A. *Commercial Presence: Mode 3 Supply*

Limitations to mode 3 supply of services are particularly frequent in telecommunication, financial and transportation services. Since these are growth priority sectors for developing countries (see above), these limitations are of relevance for the developing countries' growth prospects.

Commitments in mode 3 differ, and there seems not to exist a persistent pattern in the GATS schedules. Limitations refer to geographic coverage, to pre-commitments and to licensing and qualification requirements.[65] The reason behind such reluctance towards making substantial commitments in mode 3 supply of services may relate to the perceived need to protect domestic firms from competition in the domestic market (e.g. in the case of developing countries, the reluctance to commit in mode 3

[62] Stephenson (2002); Nielson and Taglioni (2004); Bloom, David E. (2004) 'Globalisation and Education', In: M. M. Suarez-Orozco and D. B. Qin-Hilliard (eds.), *Globalisation, Culture and Education in the New Millennium*, University of California Press, Berkeley and Los Angeles, pp. 56–78, pp. 72–73.

[63] E.g. waitressing or caretaking.

[64] Larsen, Kurt and Vincent-Lancrin, Stéphan (2002) 'International Trade in Educational Services: Good or Bad?', *Higher Education Management and Policy*, vol. 14, no. 3, pp. 9–46, pp. 37–39.

[65] See WTO Secretariat (2000, pp. 594–595).

supply of financial services), but it may also relate to regulatory issues and to the close linkage between commercial presence and the entry of foreign labour into the domestic market.[66] Especially for developing countries, the relative competitive advantage of services suppliers in industrialised countries vis-à-vis their local counterparts seems to be a major reason for restricting mode 3 supply of services.

The willingness of developing countries to enter into substantial mode 3 commitments may be higher in South-South services trade agreements than at the multilateral level. For one, the relative difference in competitive advantage among developing countries would be expected to be much smaller. Regulatory issues should also be easier to address in regional or bilateral agreements. Finally, the orderly (temporary) entry of juridical and natural persons into the domestic market is likely to be more manageable when there are strong geographic and cultural ties.

South-South mode 3 supply of services – and therewith South-South FDI – is considered to carry a large potential for the economic development in developing countries. Given that some of the more advanced 'developing' countries serve as a global base for a number of potent investors, who may better be able to adapt to the specificities of other developing countries than investors from developed countries, South-South FDI could potentially offer a higher 'win-win-potential' than North-South FDI.[67] Given the close link between mode 3 supply of services and FDI, PTAs sometimes include parts of the mode 3 supply regulation in their investment chapters. According to economic theory, the benefits for developing countries would be even higher if South-South FDI was liberalised across the board, and not only in relation to services, as this would be expected to strengthen competition, promote diversification and foster the creation of value-added production.[68]

B. Movement of Natural Persons: Mode 4 Supply

Labour migration, and particularly movement of high-skilled labour, is a key factor in economic development. Labour migration is required in order to ensure that the best people work at the right place in cross-border

[66] Chanda, Rupa (2004) Movement and Presence of Natural Persons and Developing Countries: Issues and Proposals for the GATS Negotiations, Working Paper 19, South Centre, Geneva, pp. 23–24.

[67] Aykut, Dilek and Ratha, Dilip (2004) 'South-South FDI Flows: How Big Are They?', *Transnational Corporations*, vol. 13, no. 1, pp. 149–176, pp. 150–151.

[68] Whalley, John (2004) 'Assessing the Benefits to Developing Countries of Liberalisation in Services Trade', *The World Economy*, vol. 27, no. 8, pp. 1223–1253, pp. 1242–1244.

value-added chains. At the same time, labour migration is expected to support the transfer of knowledge, which would bolster productivity in general.[69]

Trade liberalisation in mode 4 supply remains heavily restricted under GATS. This observation is primarily attributed to the GATS' multilateral nature, under which many countries fear making substantial mode 4 supply commitments for fear of unpredictable migration flows.[70] To date, the GATS mode 4 supply of services also has a bias towards high-skilled labour: if members enter commitments in their schedules, they usually open their markets to the highly skilled or to persons with special talents.

Labour migration is further met with a variety of additional at-the-border and behind-the-border barriers to trade. The recognition of certificates is of particular importance for high-skilled labour. This problem is further exacerbated by the fact that most developing countries are excluded from mutual recognition agreements.[71] Immigration law barriers are also excluded from the scope of GATS, i.e. at-the-border-barriers to mode 4 supply of services including visa restrictions and border securitisation programmes can legitimately be used, as they are excluded from GATS disciplines, such as transparency,[72] MFN[73] or domestic regulation.[74] Extensive authorisation requirements for the admission to work, economic need tests and quotas constitute additional limitations on services trade under mode 4 supply. With these barriers to trade in place, commitments to mode 4 supply of services are not necessarily a reliable indicator for the openness towards foreign labour.[75]

The inclusion and regulation of labour migration in PTAs is particularly important in the context of developing countries: while labour migration can accelerate economic development, it can also deplete the human resources of a migrant source country when left unregulated.[76] Therefore, inclusion and regulation of mode 4 supply in South-South PTAs in services would be expected to have a significant economic impact.

Further multilateral liberalisation of mode 4 supply of services, including for low-skilled labour, has been a concerted demand of developing

[69] See e.g. Williams, Allan M. (2007) 'Listen to Me, Learn with Me: International Migration and Knowledge Transfer', *British Journal of Industrial Relations*, vol. 45, no. 2, pp. 361–382.

[70] Winters (2008, pp. 480–481). [71] Chanda (2004, pp. 12–14). [72] GATS Art. III.

[73] GATS Art. I. [74] GATS Art. IV. [75] See Panizzon (2010).

[76] Martin, Philip and Abella, Manolo (2009) 'Migration and Development: The Elusive Link at the GFMD', *International Migration Review* vol. 43, no. 2, pp. 431–439.

countries in the Doha negotiations.[77] However, industrialised countries were not prepared to guarantee access to their labour markets through mode 4 commitments.[78] Thus, PTAs constitute one temporary alternative to introduce a more liberal regime on labour migration.[79] Some developing countries have already included labour migration provisions in their PTAs with industrialised countries, which may be considered the second-best option to multilateralism. Including labour migration provisions in South-South PTAs may nevertheless be interesting for developing countries, given the importance of labour migration for economic performance in the services sectors and given the need for regulation of labour migration in general.[80]

Commitments in mode 4 supply of services may, thus, on the one hand constitute an attempt to pave the way for further liberalisation at the multilateral level, and on the other hand, commitments in mode 4 supply of services may also be understood as an indicator of the parties' seriousness in promoting services trade liberalisation.

[77] See, e.g. Winters, Alan L. (2005) *Developing Country Proposals for the Liberalisation of Movements of Natural Service Suppliers*, Working Paper, Sussex Centre for Migration Research, Sussex; see also WTO Negotiating Mandates [Online], available at: http://www.wto.org/english/tratop_e/serv_e/nego_mandates_e.htm.

[78] On the limited success of post-Uruguay negotiations on mode 4 supply of services see WTO Movement of Natural Persons [Online], available at: http://www.wto.org/english/tratop_e/serv_e/mouvement_persons_e/mouvement_persons_e.htm.

[79] See also Winters, Alan L. (2001) Trade Policies for Poverty Alleviation: What Developing Countries Might Do, PSIO Occasional Paper, WTO Series No. 10, Geneva, p. 39.

[80] On the risks of South-South labour migration and the need for regulation, see Ratha, Dilip and Shaw, William (2007), South-South Migration and Remittances, Working Paper, World Bank, Washington DC, p. 33; on the link between labour migration and development, see De Haas, Hein (2007) 'Turning the Tide? Why Development Will Not Stop Migration', *Development and Change*, vol. 38, no. 5, pp. 819–841.

7

In Summary

The conclusion of a multilateral agreement on the regulation and liberalisation of services trade can be seen as a major stepping-stone in the convergence of regional markets into a global market. However, given that negotiations over multilateral services trade liberalisation were difficult as a consequence of the great divide in the sophistication of services industries between North and South, the GATS left some of the essential work on services trade regulation and liberalisation for future rounds of negotiations. The negotiations on multilateral trade liberalisation in services, which followed the GATS, have to the detriment of the GATS not (yet) resulted in a new consensus.

Because little was moving on the multilateral level, the regional and bilateral agreements became an ever more attractive way of regulating international services trade. Therefore, GATS Art. V, which outlines the requirements that a PTA in services has to fulfil, is gaining in relevance with each PTA that is concluded.

For many reasons, the requirements set out by GATS Art. V are relatively vague, and it is not quite clear what the scope of GATS Art. V exactly is. Furthermore, there is no working system in place, which guarantees that the PTAs in services are analysed according to their compatibility with GATS. Thus, even though the requirements established in GATS Art. V in general are meaningful, they are not really capable of developing impact on the actual design of PTAs as *de facto*, compliance is almost voluntary, or at least, non-compliance does not have any consequences: there are a number of PTAs – even PTAs that are notified to the WTO – which do not even fulfil all the requirements of GATS Art. V at the level of horizontal commitments.

At the same time, it is quite remarkable how the vast majority of PTAs in services actually is in line with the general requirements of GATS Art. V. Although the exact meaning and scope of the individual requirements are not yet well established, the general idea of GATS Art. V arguably is well respected and embedded in the design of PTAs in services. This may also be a consequence of the missing consensus on the exact meaning of GATS Art. V and the fact that the language of GATS Art. V and the general structure of the GATS leave considerable scope for interpretation. Arguably, it is relatively easy to meet the requirements of GATS Art. V.

With a view on the emerging 'mega-regionals', such as the TPP, TTIP and the plurilateral TiSA, the missing consensus on the meaning and scope of GATS Art. V may turn out to have an impact on the future of services trade regulation: if the mega-regionals or the TiSA are in substantial contradiction to the requirements of GATS Art. V, others will follow. Additionally, given the considerable weight of these (mega-) regional and plurilateral agreements in the global economy, innovation in services trade regulation – and deviation from GATS regulation – in these agreements would impact on the GATS system and pre-define the regulatory future of the GATS.

On the other hand, given the shortfalls of the current system of services trade regulation, the mega-regionals could potentially also push the trade agenda further at the multilateral level, and the services trade agenda could be revived by new approaches to regulation, such as embedding services trade regulation into the greater context of labour migration, investment, value chain production and processing of semi-finished products, instead of treating it separately and in isolation from the rest of trade regulation.[1]

According to recent economic literature, certain services sectors are of particular importance for economic development in developing countries,[2] while other sectors are particularly suitable for regional and bilateral liberalisation.[3] The same holds true for modes of supply, as not all modes of supply are equally relevant for economic development[4] and are equally suitable for regional and bilateral liberalisation.[5] The sectors identified as well as their attributes are used as the basis for the quantitative and qualitative analysis of the dataset and the discussion about the relationship between the GATS and South-South PTAs in services.

[1] Similar Horn, Mavroidis and Sapir (2010, p. 1566): '[. . .] the EC and the US are sometimes viewed as the 'regulators of the world'. It is estimated [. . .] that, together, they accound for 80 per cent of the rules that regulate the functioning world markets'.

[2] Telecommunication, Transportation, Financial Services, Professional Services.

[3] Professional Services, Construction, Education.

[4] Mode 3 and mode 4 are attributed with a positive impact on economic growth.

[5] Mode 4 is attributed with particular suitability for regional or bilateral liberalisation.

PART III

Legal Regime for South-South Preferential Services Trade

> "To give real service you must add something which cannot be bought or measured with money, and that is sincerity and integrity".
>
> *Douglas Adams*

In one of the very first documents mentioning negotiations over trade liberalisation in services (by the OECD) in 1973, the last sentence on services was addressed to the treatment of developing countries:[1]

> As in the case of goods, consideration might be given to allowing developing countries a limited time to adapt themselves before undertaking the full commitments.

On the one hand, this sentence points to future negotiations on trade in services outside the OECD framework, without saying so explicitly;[2] on the other hand, it is remarkable that in one of the very first documents on services trade liberalisation, developing countries are given a specific thought.

Given the potential impact on economic development, which is attributed to strong services sectors in developing countries, such considerations are not too much of a surprise. Furthermore, developing countries provided already at the time for an interesting market for the strong service industries in industrialised countries. The role of developing countries in a global services market therefore continued to be at the core of multilateral negotiations. During the negotiations of the GATS, discussions on the role of developing countries in the process of global trade liberalisation in services have influenced the wording and outcome of the GATS to varying degrees.

Already in the *Ministerial Declaration on the Uruguay Round* in September 1986,[3] which identified the objective of the negotiations of the

[1] OECD *Code of Liberalisation of Current Invisible Operations* (1973).
[2] Feketekuty (1988, p. 299).
[3] WTO/GATT *Ministerial Declaration on the Uruguay Round* (20 September 1986).

Uruguay Round,[4] developing countries in services trade liberalisation played a central role:[5]

> [. . .] with a view to expansion of such trade under conditions of transparency and progressive liberalisation and as a means of promoting economic growth of all trading partners and the development of developing countries.

Furthermore, the declaration already mentioned that the framework for trade liberalisation in services 'shall respect the policy objectives of national laws and regulations applying to services'.[6] Thus, both aspects of flexibility, special consideration for the economic realities in developing countries, and flexibilities for national regulation were agreed upon already at the very beginning of multilateral negotiations on trade in services.

However, before further negotiations could continue, a couple of central issues had to be agreed upon. Among those basic issues was the question on how to develop a multilateral framework for trade in services in a manner that would increase the participation of developing countries and recognise their special needs.[7]

Because of the efforts by the United States, a multilateral agreement on trade in services became realistic. Thus, even though Least-Developed Countries (LDCs) did not want to join negotiations – they argued that their services industries were culturally sensitive and that they required time to develop before they were able to face global competition[8] – the risk of not participating in negotiations and being left out was too big.

Thus, the LDCs agreed to the following strategy: the negotiations had to establish a process which actively fosters export opportunities for LDCs, which provided for transfer of technology to LDCs, and which gave the LDCs sufficient time to adjust to the changes brought by a multilateral agreement.[9]

[4] *Ministerial Declaration on the Uruguay Round* (20 September 1986), at 10; Reyna (1993, p. 2358).

[5] *Ministerial Declaration on the Uruguay Round* (20 September 1986), at 10.

[6] Ibid. [7] Reyna (1993, p. 2360).

[8] Position advanced by India in a 'statement', an informal paper.

[9] Heydon, Kenneth (1990) 'Developing Country Perspectives, in the Uruguay Round: Services in the World Economy', P. A. Messerli and K. P. Sauvant (eds.), *The Uruguay Round: Services in the World Economy*, The World Bank, Washington DC, pp. 159–165; Reyna (1993, pp. 2366–2367).

Different methods for providing special treatment to LDCs were subsequently proposed during negotiations: in October 1989, New Zealand[10] proposed safeguard-type provisions, which would allow LDCs to protect their infant industries. Additionally, the proposal would allow for acceptable forms of market access restrictions, such as limiting the number of service providers allowed entry into the market. In November 1989, Peru[11] proposed that LDCs should be permitted to provide access to their markets contingent on transfer of technology, training of national personnel, and a number of related measures. The Republic of Korea,[12] likewise, proposed that a multilateral agreement should, among others, contain provisions on technology transfer to developing countries. This was opposed by the United States, suggesting that the development of LDCs was provided through 'immediate and progressive liberalisation of trade in services with due respect to national policy objectives'.[13] Several initiatives followed, some supported by a larger group of countries,[14] some mainly led by the United States. The disagreement on the treatment of developing countries and LDCs in a multilateral agreement on trade in services continued, with no major compromise until 1990.

The so-called July-Text,[15] a draft framework provided by the chairman of the Group of Negotiations on Services on 23 July 1990 listed that most crucial principles needed for an agreement had not yet been settled, including the special treatment for LDCs. Although the July-Text did not identify specific measures or mechanisms for increased participation

[10] *Communication from New Zealand*, Structure and Mechanism for a General Agreement on Trade in Services – Key Issues, MTN.GNS/W/72 (28 September 1989), paras. 6 and 8.

[11] *Communication from Peru*, Elements of a Framework Agreement in Trade on Services, GATT Doc. No. MTN.GNS/W/84 (20 November 1989), para. 5.

[12] *Communication from the Republic of Korea*, On the Structure of General Agreement on Trade in Services (25 October 1989), informal paper.

[13] *Communication from the United States*, Agreement on Trade in Services, GATT Doc. No. MTN.GNS/W/75 (17 October 1989), Art. 1, para. 1.1.

[14] *Communication from Brazil, Chile, Colombia, Cuba, Honduras, Jamaica, Nicaragua, Mexico, Peru, Trinidad and Tobago, and Uruguay*, Structure of a Multilateral Framework for Trade in Services, GATT Doc. No. MTN.GNS/W/95 (26 February 1990), paras. 12–13; GATT, Draft Text of Services Compromise, paras. III(A)(1)(b)(i) and (ii) XX; *Declaration of the Countries of Latin America and the Caribbean*, at the V Latin American Consultation Meeting of SELA on the Uruguay Round of Multilateral Trade Negotiations, GATT Doc. No. MTN.TNC/W/22 (23 July 1990).

[15] *Draft Multilateral Framework For Trade In Services*, GATT Doc. No. MTN.GNS/35 (23 July 1990).

of LDCs, it provided for special treatment of South-South economic integration.[16]

In December 1990, the negotiations collapsed as a result of the deadlock that developed over agricultural issues. Remaining issues, particularly on the MFN provision, were not resolved. Neither had the changes to the July-Text brought the negotiations closer to an agreement. Negotiations were resumed in February 1991 with work on more technical aspects of the Agreement.[17] Negotiations advanced well, and in December 1991, Arthur Dunkel presented a draft text of an agreement for all the negotiating areas, the so-called Dunkel-Draft.[18]

The 'Dunkel-Draft' included a draft of the now known as GATS Art. V provision. The language was similar to that of GATT Art. XXIV, and the draft included the concept of 'substantially all trade'. It was agreed that further criteria were needed in order to determine what 'substantially all trade' meant. Finally, at the end of 1991, the footnote to GATS Art. V:1 was added to the 'Dunkel-Draft'. The rest of GATS Art. V, as it is established today, is more or less identical with the provision in the 'Dunkel-Draft'.[19]

However, the 'Dunkel-Draft' was quickly also criticised for crafting consensus at the cost of developing countries: it was not seen as being in the interest of developing countries to have a multilateral organisation presiding over all the different multilateral trade agreements and therewith allowing for cross-retaliation across areas of trade in dispute settlement. Furthermore, most of what developing countries had entered into previous drafts was ignored, with a major focus on the two powers, the United States and the EC.[20]

Nevertheless, given that there are quite a few flexibilities for developing countries and LDCs in the final GATS, along with the positive list approach, which was most relevant for most of the developing countries, the 'Dunkel-Draft' after all was an elaborate political compromise. Reaching that compromise was challenging and not the least also the result of the active involvement of a group of developing countries called

[16] Ibid., para. 7. [17] Reyna (1993, p. 2396).

[18] Draft Final Act Embodying the Results of the Uruguay Round of Multilateral Trade Negotiations, GATT Doc. No. MTN.TNC/W/FA (20 December 1991).

[19] Stephenson, Sherry (2000b) 'GATS and Regional Integration', In: P. Sauvé, and R. M. Stern (eds.), *GATS 2000: New Directions in Services Trade Liberalisation*, The Brookings Institution, Washington DC, pp. 509–529, p. 511.

[20] J. M. (1992) 'GATT, the Dunkel Draft and India', *Economic and Political Weekly*, vol. 27, no. 4, pp. 140–142.

café au lait, which served as a mediator between the developing nations and the United States and the EC.[21]

In the currently stalled Doha Round of multilateral trade negotiations, the developing countries play an important role, particularly also because the Round is supposed to be the 'Development Round' and therefore, developing countries are at the heart of negotiations. However, unlike in the 1980s, developing countries now have differing interests and defend their positions on their own – without relying on a leading nation or external advisers. New groups of countries have found together and, particularly in services negotiations, developing countries and LDCs are not working together.

In the current round of multilateral trade negotiations, securing additional market access through mode 4 supply of services is a top priority for LDCs. They put forward a proposal to cover semi-skilled labour under mode 4 supply of services, and an additional provision to the GATS, which would allow developed countries to grant preferential treatment to LDCs. Most likely, non-LDC countries will more or less strongly oppose to this proposal.[22]

However, aside from the many different groups of countries, which have similar interests in the various areas of trade negotiations, three major regional organisations of developing countries, which play a distinct role in the WTO, have now also started playing a prominent role: ASEAN, MERCOSUR and CARICOM. The members of all three regional organisations represent the interests of their members jointly in the WTO and can share costs, staff and competencies with respect to their participation in the world trading system.[23]

It remains open when and how multilateral trade negotiations in services will take off again: as it is currently the case, the divide in the services agenda between developed countries, LDCs and also developing countries will be difficult to overcome. However, as the GATS was meant to be further developed in successive rounds of trade negotiations, and is thus an incomplete agreement waiting to be amended, the stalling of the multilateral negotiations certainly has considerable implications on the

[21] See also Marchetti, Juan A. and Mavroidis, Petros C. (2011) 'The Genesis of the GATS (General Agreement on Trade in Services)', *The European Journal of International Law*, vol. 22, no. 3, pp. 689–721.

[22] Page, Sheila, Calì, Massimiliano and Te Velde, Dirk W. (2008) *Development Package at the WTO? What Do Developing Countries Want from the Doha Round?*, Overseas Development Institute, London, p. 9.

[23] Kennes (2000, p. 22).

overall depth of regulation and liberalisation in trade in services, along with a lack of legal certainty.

The following paragraphs first discuss the different provisions in the GATS, which provide for regulatory flexibility for South-South PTAs in services. Based on the legal analysis of the scope of flexibility for South-South PTAs in services, a structural model providing for mainly three different levels of flexibility is proposed. This part concludes by discussing the legal implications of flexibility for South-South PTAs in general and the impact of the regulatory structure of the GATS in particular on South-South preferentialism in services trade.

1

The Legal Scope of Flexibilities for South-South Preferential Services Trade

With respect to the particular case of economic integration in services trade in the South, GATS Art. V provides for a number of specific rights and allowances amounting to a form of more favourable treatment of South-South PTAs in services. From the perspective of policymakers, economists, but also lawyers, a few considerations concerning the formation of South-South PTAs in services have to be taken into account. This is particularly the case as the wording of GATS Art. V leaves considerable room for interpretation, which could also be used in a favourable way for the economic integration and the fostering of services trade among developing countries.

GATS Art. V treats South-South PTAs in services more favourably. Despite the remaining uncertainty about the exact scope of GATS Art. V, it is generally agreed that the provision is indeed aiming at promoting South-South PTAs.[1] Thus, given the broad variety of possible interpretations of the scope of flexibility of GATS Art. V, it is worthwhile investigating the different possibilities for the South.

Interestingly, Art. 15 of the Havana Charter for an International Trade Organisation (ITO, done 24 March 1948)[2] included the possibility of otherwise non-compliant PTAs among developing countries. However, such a provision was not included in the GATT 1947, and after the failure of the ITO was not transferred to GATT 1947 either.[3] Subsequently, the idea of economic integration among developing countries gained momentum again, in conjunction with the economic independence of developing countries from developed countries. In 1974, the UN General Assembly

[1] E.g. Qureshi, Asif H. and Wittayawarakul, Chotika (2010) 'International Development Law and Preferential Trade Agreements involving Developing Countries', In: Y. Ngangjoh-Hodu and F. Matambalya (eds.), *Trade Relations between the EU and Africa*, Routledge, London, pp. 115–150, p. 131ff.

[2] United Nations Conference on Trade and Employment, Final Act and Related Documents, Havana Charter for an International Trade Organisation, UN Doc E/CONF.2/78.

[3] Bartels, Lorand (2012, p. 860).

Resolution on a 'Programme of Action on the Establishment of a New International Economic Order'[4] stated that developing countries should 'ensure that no developing country accords to imports from developed countries more favourable treatment than that accorded to imports from developing countries' and that 'wherever possible, preferential treatment should be given to imports from developing countries and the exports of those countries'.[5] In the GATT, the idea was realised through the adoption of the Enabling Clause in 1979, which establishes a permanent exception from MFN for PTAs among developing countries.

More favourable treatment of developing countries and the general goal of the economic advancement of developing countries are already clearly stated in the preamble of GATS.[6] Additionally, GATS Art. V:3(a) allows for flexibility in the requirements of 'substantial sectorial coverage' and 'elimination of substantially all discrimination' in the case of South-South PTAs. It is thought to allow for the exemption of uncompetitive sectors and a lesser degree of liberalisation in certain sectors. However, due to the lack of case law and absence of concluded examinations of PTAs by the Committee on Regional Trade Agreements, it is disputed what the provision of GATS Art. V:3(a) exactly means in terms of modes of supply, the possibility and the number of sectors being excluded and the amount of trade affected by a lesser degree of liberalisation. Finally, GATS Art. V:3(b) frees the members of a South-South PTA from the requirement of equal treatment of third country nationals, even if they were engaged in substantive business.

In addition to the legal text of the GATS treaty, the principle of Special and Differential Treatment[7] could be invoked, as well as the parallels to GATT Art. XXIV and its Enabling Clause.[8] Also, taking into account the impact of a PTA on the 'wider process of economic integration' might provide for additional reason to allow for more flexibility where

[4] *United Nations*, 'Programme of Action on the Establishment of a New International Economic Order', General Assembly, A/RES/S-6/3202 (S-VI) of 1 May 1974.

[5] Ibid., para. VII (1) (e).

[6] Preamble GATS says: '[. . .] as a means of promoting the economic growth of all partners and the development if developing countries. [. . .] Recognising the right of Members to regulate, and to introduce new regulations, on the supply of services within their territories in order to meet national policy objectives and, given asymmetries existing with respect to the degree of development of services regulations in different countries, the particular need of developing countries to exercise this right; [. . .] Desiring to facilitate the increasing participation of developing countries in trade in services and the expansion of their service exports including, inter alia, through strengthening of their domestic services capacity and ist efficiency and competitiveness. [. . .]'

[7] See Hoekman (2005a).

[8] See Qureshi and Wittayawarakul (2010, p. 129).

the potentially remaining discriminatory measure serves the cause of economic development in the South while bringing the world closer to global free trade.

All these different provisions of IEL informing the scope of flexibility for South-South PTAs in services are elaborated and discussed in detail in the paragraphs below.

I. Preamble of the GATS

Unlike the GATT, the GATS does not structurally provide provisions for special and differential treatment of developing countries. It aims at achieving development via liberalisation. However, the overall objective of development is clearly stated already in the preamble of the GATS. Thus, it is somewhat surprising that there are so few concrete provisions favouring developing countries in the treaty text. There are a few particular provisions, such as wider access to information via contact points (GATS Art. IV:2), more flexibility with respect to integration agreements (GATS Art. V:3) or technical cooperation (GATS Art. XXV:2).

During the negotiating process over GATS Art. V, developing countries were making demands for special provisions for their PTAs in services. These proposals included the idea of all economic integration agreements in trade in services being unconditionally extended to developing countries[9] and of an overt recognition of PTAs in services among developing countries as a rule.[10] Their aim was to redress the asymmetry in flows of trade in services between the developed and developing countries. These demands were to a limited extent accommodated in GATS Art. V by allowing developing countries some flexibility in the application of the provisions.[11] Thus, to a limited degree, GATS Art. V is also one of the few provisions targeting the overall aim of promoting development in poorer regions of the GATS, and therewith substantiating the language of the preamble.

[9] Group of Negotiations on Services, Note on the Meeting of 18–22 July 1988, GATT Doc. MTN.GNS/16 (8 August 1988), para. 79. This paragraph erroneously contains the following words, 'the need for such arrangements should be admonished as one way of reducing the current asymmetry in flows of trade in services between the developed and developing countries'. It was later clarified that the word 'admonished' should be replaced by 'recognised' (see Group of Negotiations on Services, Note on the Meeting of 31 October – 3 November 1988, GATT Doc. MTN.GNS/16 (18 October 1988), para. 55).

[10] Group of Negotiations on Services, Note on the Meeting of 19–23 September 1988, GATT Doc. MTN.GNS/17 (18 October 1988), para. 39.

[11] Islam and Alam (2009, p. 24).

In this context, it is important to note that the WTO law 'must be situated in the wider context of the relationship between WTO law and public international law generally'.[12] This was first brought up by *US – Gasoline*, where the Appellate Body (AB) stated that GATT 'is not to be read in clinical isolation from public international law'.[13] However, the extent to which public international law should be taken into account with respect to WTO regulation remains disputed.[14] Undisputed is, however, that the preamble is an important interpretative instrument.[15] As the preamble states that the growth and development of the global economy as well as progressive liberalisation are the goals of GATS, this provides for a pro-development twist in the interpretation of the rest of the GATS provisions.

However, the two major goals of the agreement – relative to the perspective of interpretation – are the purpose of international trade liberalisation (which is favouring trade liberalisation over domestic regulatory autonomy) and the objective of preventing protectionism (which gives deference to national autonomy).[16] While the purpose of international trade liberalisation is linked to a rather broad understanding of the scope of IEL, the main objective of preventing protectionism is related to a more narrow understanding of the role of IEL, also including the approach of progressive, step-by-step liberalisation.

In practice, using the preamble for the interpretation of the scope of a particular provision proves therefore to be challenging: in *China – Publications and Audiovisual Products*,[17] the Panel used the preamble as an interpretative instrument in order to establish the content and scope of China's commitments. The panel particularly focused on the principle of progressive liberalisation and argued in several instances that the scope of a commitment should not be interpreted in a broad way, because such a broad understanding would contradict the principle of progressive liberalisation.[18] The panel particularly referred to the importance of the principle of progressive liberalisation for developing countries:[19]

[12] Zleptnig (2010, p. 56).
[13] *US – Gasoline*, WT/DS2/AB/R (29 April 1996) Report of the Appellate Body, p. 17.
[14] Zleptnig (2010, p. 56ff.).
[15] According to VCLT Art. 31:2; See also Munin (2010, pp. 39ff.).
[16] Munin (2010, p. 40).
[17] *China – Publications and Audiovisual Products*, WT/DS363/R (12 August 2009), Report of the Panel.
[18] Ibid., paras. 4.159, 4.270, 7.1166, 7.1219, and 7.1348.
[19] Ibid., para. 4.159.

> Unduly extending the scope of this contentious principle would be against the principle of progressive liberalisation as reflected in the preamble of the GATS and would preclude members, especially developing members, from making further commitments.

Thus, with reference to the preamble, the panel chose to follow a developing member-friendly interpretation of the GATS provisions. This illustrates how the preamble could be used for the interpretation of GATS provisions in favour of more flexibility for developing countries. The decision of the panel was, however, changed by the AB, who stated:[20]

> [. . .] we observe that none of the objectives listed in the GATS preamble provides specific guidance as to the correct interpretation to be given to China's GATS Schedule entry [. . .]

The issue at stake in *China – Publications and Audiovisual Products* was whether the scope of the Chinese commitment was interpreted in a broad or in a narrow way. The AB disagreed with the panel and argued that a broad interpretation of the scope of the commitment was more adequate, given also the goals defined in the preamble:[21]

> The principle of progressive liberalisation is reflected in the structure of the GATS, which contemplates that WTO members undertake specific commitments through successive round of multilateral negotiations with a view to liberalising their services markets incrementally, rather than immediately and completely [. . .] We do not consider, however, that the principle of progressive liberalisation lends support to an interpretation that would constrain the scope and coverage of specific commitments that have already been undertaken by members and by which they are bound.

Thus, because of the variety – and inconclusiveness – of different goals and purposes in the preamble of the GATS, they can only to a limited degree inform the interpretation of the scope of a specific commitment. Furthermore, the position of the AB implies a preference of the purpose of international trade liberalisation and therewith of a broad interpretation of the scope of the commitments in GATS.[22] Because it is mainly directed at the interpretation of a commitment in a member's schedule, and not of a provision in the main GATS treaty, that decision of the AB should, however, not develop too much relevance for the interpretation of the scope of GATS Art. V. The argument that the development purpose in

[20] *China – Publications and Audiovisual Products*, WT/DS363/AB/R (21 December 2009), Report of the Appellate Body, para. 393.

[21] Ibid., para. 394.

[22] See also Munin (2010, p. 41).

the preamble provides for an interpretation of the scope of GATS Art. V, which is conducive to more flexibility for developing countries, is still valid.

II. Preferential Trade in Services: GATS Art. V

It has been suggested that services trade liberalisation is easier to attain at the regional and bilateral level because of the very nature of services: a common language, a similar education system, similar certification processes, shared values and shared culture matter for the establishment of a fully integrated services market.[23] Thus, economic integration in the services sectors might be considered more feasible at a regional than at the multilateral level.

However, deeper regional integration is desired only if such integration eventually leads to deeper integration also at the global level. Thus, GATS Art. V has to strike a difficult balance between encouraging the South to open their services markets, while at the same time ensuring that the regional or bilateral PTAs do not hinder multilateral economic integration.

It can be argued that the economic potential of integrated services markets in the South is large enough to justify favourable treatment for South-South PTAs in services vis-à-vis North-South or North-North PTAs: more competition and better infrastructure in the services markets, as well as an integrated market over the boundaries of states will eventually lead to more value-added production in the entire region, to more sustainable economic growth (as a consequence of diversification) and to more capacity to compete in the global market.[24]

Such economic growth promoted by regional free trade fosters new markets for products from the North and stabilises the world economy as it relieves the North from economic support to the South. Thus, in the end all players on the global market will benefit from more favourable treatment of South-South PTAs in services.

Granting more favourable treatment to developing countries (and not only to least-developed countries, as these might not be the ideal candidates for services-led economic growth[25]) is also in line with the overall

[23] See before, Part II. [24] Ibid.

[25] See e.g. Mattoo, Aaditya and Payton, Lucy (2007) 'Services Trade For Zambia's Development: An Overview', In: A. Mattoo and L. Payton (eds.), *Services Trade and Development*, Palgrave Macmillan and World Bank, New York and Washington DC, pp. 1–60, p. 5.

aim of the WTO to promote economic development in the South, to support its weak members in their attempt to catch up with the North and with the promise to use the instruments of free trade in a way that eventually promotes equality.[26]

This line of reasoning, thus, builds the backbone of the argument for additional flexibility in meeting the requirements of GATS Art. V for South-South PTAs in services. The following paragraphs focus on the interpretation of the specific terms of GATS Art. V, which allow for more or additional flexibility in meeting the general requirements as established by GATS Art. V:1.

A. *Flexibilities in GATS Art. V:1*

A first important flexibility with respect to meeting the requirements of GATS Art. V is to be found already in GATS Art. V:1. It says that an economic integration agreement has to fulfil the requirements of GATS Art. V either when it enters into force or 'on the basis of a reasonable time-frame'.[27] This temporal dimension can also be found in GATT XXIV and is meant to accommodate development concerns. The interpretation of GATT XXIV provides that the period for adjustment to the requirements of a PTA should not exceed ten years, unless under exceptional circumstances. Qureshi and Wittayawarakal (2010) argue that 'exceptional circumstances should be interpreted to include circumstances arising from the development conditions of the RTA parties, particularly liberalisation in sensitive sectors of concern to developing countries'.[28]

Even though the GATS uses a slightly different language and allows for a 'reasonable time frame' without further clarifying its length, it is generally agreed that the considerations and interpretations of the similar provision in GATT XXIV apply to the interpretation of the length of the 'reasonable time-frame' of GATS as well.[29]

However, there are virtually no rules in WTO regulation governing 'interim' agreements up to full-fledged PTAs. Formally, WTO members may make binding recommendations to ensure that an interim agreement will eventually turn into a PTA in the sense of GATT Art. XXIV and GATS Art. V. But, to date, this option has not been used by WTO members. Instead, WTO members have developed a practice of notifying *de facto* interim agreements as *de jure* 'full' PTAs with an

[26] Preamble of the GATS. [27] GATS Art. V:1.
[28] Qureshi and Wittayawarakul (2010). [29] See Islam and Alam (2009).

implementation period. Bartels (2009) considers this practice to be one motivated by circumventing the control mechanisms for interim agreements.[30]

Nonetheless, given that the transitional period for establishing a full PTA is – in practice – currently more than ten years for developing countries, it may be even substantially longer for PTAs among developing countries or involving an LDC.[31] Thus, the temporal flexibility for establishing a PTA in services that is able to fulfil all the requirements of GATS Art. V is a powerful tool for introducing South-South PTAs on a step-by-step basis, starting with only a limited number of sectors and extending liberalisation in a gradual process to all services trade.

B. Flexibilities in GATS Art. V:2

In order to establish whether an agreement meets the requirements of GATS Art. V:1 lit. b, GATS Art. V:2 stipulates that 'consideration may be given to the relationship of the agreement to a wider process of economic integration or trade liberalisation among the countries concerned'.[32] Thus, when it is uncertain whether the requirements are met, the overall impact of the agreement on trade liberalisation among the countries and globally may provide additional guidance for the assessment.

The term 'wider process of economic integration' is of key interest here: it has been argued that it includes the existence of parallel measures, such as trade liberalisation in goods.[33] Services trade liberalisation usually follows trade liberalisation in goods or is established in addition to goods trade liberalisation. To date, there is no knowledge of a stand-alone agreement in services trade liberalisation, independent from goods trade liberalisation and other economic integration. Thus, there is a strong link between trade liberalisation in services and trade liberalisation in goods. Given that trade liberalisation in services is enabling the implementation of goods trade liberalisation, taking into consideration how a PTA in services impacts on overall economic integration may, thus, provide a good basis for additional flexibility.

This is particularly relevant in the context of South-South PTAs in services, as it provides for an additional argument for more flexibility in the

30 Bartels, Lorand (2009) 'Interim Agreements' under Article XXIV GATT', *World Trade Review*, vol. 8, no. 2, pp. 339–350, p. 349.

31 Bartels (2009, p. 350).

32 GATS V:2.

33 See e.g. Adlung and Miroudot (2012, p. 8).

interpretation of the scope of GATS Art. V with respect to South-South economic integration: oftentimes, services trade liberalisation among the countries concerned may be limited before taking up negotiations on a PTA in services. Thus, any additional commitment compared to the schedules of commitments in the GATS will be favourable for the 'wider process of economic integration', insofar as stronger services markets in the South should contribute to more value-added production in underdeveloped regions and to better implementation measures of goods trade liberalisation, to more stability in economic growth and therewith to more overall equality on the global market.

There may be instances in which a PTA would not come into existence without additional flexibility: services industries in developing countries tend to be weak and underdeveloped and oftentimes they are not yet privatised.[34] Insisting on fulfilling all the requirements of GATS Art. V:1 lit. b also in the context of South-South trade integration may render the conclusion of a services trade agreement impossible. Thus, GATS Art. V:2 is one aspect, which allows for balancing flexibility versus stand-still and opens up the application of GATS Art. V in the interest of global world trade and systemic considerations.

As a rule of thumb, one could argue, that as long as a South-South PTA overall contributes to more liberalisation among the countries concerned and as long as the PTA is set up in a way that other countries are welcome to join, GATS Art. V:2 provides for a strong argument that not all requirements of GATS Art. V:1 lit. b have to be met in all rigour. Arguably, the numbers of sectors liberalised in a South-South PTA or the number of modes of supply included in liberalisation can be limited if the overall assessment of the PTA shows that it serves the 'wider process of economic integration'.[35]

C. *Flexibilities in GATS Art. V:3 lit. a*

With a reference specifically to developing countries, additional flexibility is provided with respect to the requirements established in GATS Art. V:1, 'substantial sectorial coverage' and 'absence and elimination of substantially all discrimination'. GATS V:3 lit. a says:[36]

[34] Aykut, Dilek and Goldstein, Andrea (2006) Developing Country Multinationals: South-South Investment Comes of Age, Working Paper, OECD Development Centre, Paris.

[35] See also Qureshi and Wittayawarakul (2010).

[36] GATS Art. V:3 lit. a.

> Where developing countries are parties to an agreement of the type referred to in paragraph 1, flexibility shall be provided for regarding the conditions set out in paragraph 1, particularly with reference to subparagraph (b) thereof, in accordance with the level of development of the countries concerned, both overall and in individual sectors and subsectors.

The scope of this specific flexibility for PTAs involving at least one developing country is, however, unclear. Adlung and Miroudot (2012), thus, state that at least it would not cover the introduction of new restrictions and discriminatory elements, which would be more restrictive than the countries' commitments in their GATS schedules.[37] In general, flexibility is to be accorded in accordance with the level of development in the countries concerned (progressive regulation). Consideration should be paid to the state and prospects of the service sectors. Uncompetitive sectors may, thus, benefit from flexibility and therewith become subject of exemption or a lesser degree of liberalisation. Another means to providing flexibility would be to allow for longer transition periods.

Given that the provision of GATS Art. V:3 lit. a can be understood as an extra incentive for developing countries to enter into PTAs in services both North-South and South-South,[38] one might wonder how this flexibility would be applied in practice in a North-South PTA in services. Despite the imprecision in the language, certainly the provision was not meant to provide for additional flexibility for developed countries given their dominant position on the global services market. Generally, there are few templates for unequally balanced PTAs, and it would be challenging to establish when such a North-South PTA in services exceeds the scope of flexibility of GATS Art. V:3 lit. a.

Qureshi and Wittayawarakul (2010) interpret GATS Art. V:3 lit. a in the way that taking into account the economic development of a country would allow developing countries 'to reserve service sectors that are important for development purposes from the national treatment obligation'.[39] While this interpretation seems to be in line with the language and aim of GATS Art. V:3 lit a, it is not obvious why such flexibility would be restricted to National Treatment, when commitments in Market Access equally matter. GATS Art. V:3 lit. a does not indicate the specific commitments that may be attributed with additional flexibility. Insofar, there is no indication in the language that flexibility in Market Access would be a contradiction to GATS Art. V:3 lit. a.

There is an element of graduation in GATS Art. V:3 lit. a: by establishing that flexibility 'shall be provided [. . .] in accordance with the level

[37] Adlung and Miroudot (2012, p. 8). [38] Munin (2010, p. 330).

of development of the countries concerned, both overall and in individual sectors and subsectors',[40] GATS V:3 lit. a encourages a distinction between the different levels of development in the different services sectors and subsectors. Arguably, sectors that are competitive in the global market will, thus, be exempted from the flexibility in GATS V:3 lit. a. This may matter more in the context of a North-South PTA, in which developing countries may seek preferential access to the large markets in industrialised countries, in particular for their competitive sectors. It is, however, also relevant for South-South PTAs in services: the element of graduation in GATS V:3 lit. a may provide the basis for exempting a number of services sectors from the PTA or for establishing generous time frames for implementing commitments, and therewith introducing tailor-made, gradual liberalisation among the members of a South-South PTA in services with the argument of taking into consideration the level of development in individual sectors and subsectors.

The provision faces, however, the usual difficulties due to the fact that a generally accepted list of developing countries is still missing. Members to a PTA can choose their status of a 'developing country' under WTO themselves. While, such a status could, of course, be challenged in front of the bodies of the WTO,[41] in the case of North-South PTAs in services in particular, GATS V:3 lit. a is rather a possibility to use additional flexibilities for developing members than a right. It will finally always depend on the negotiating partner whether such flexibility is finally embedded in the PTA or not.

D. *Flexibilities in GATS Art. V:3 lit. b in Conjunction with GATS Art. V:6*

As has been illustrated above, the flexibility in applying GATS Art. V:1 requirements to a PTA is generally greater in the case of a PTA with a developing country involved. GATS Art. V:3 lit. b is explicitly dedicated to PTAs among developing countries only:[42]

> Notwithstanding paragraph 6, in the case of an agreement of the type referred to in paragraph 1 involving only developing countries, more favourable treatment may be granted to juridical persons owned or controlled by natural persons of the parties to such an agreement.

[39] Qureshi and Wittayawarakul (2010). [40] GATS V:3 lit. a.
[41] Cottier and Molinuevo (2008, pp. 140–142). [42] GATS Art. V:3 lit. b.

Thus, GATS Art. V:3 lit. b in conjunction with GATS Art. V:6 allows PTAs among developing countries to impose stricter rules of origin on legal persons, than developed countries are allowed to: South-South PTAs in services may be restricted to service suppliers owned or controlled by nationals of the members to the PTA, and exempt third country nationals, even if they previously engaged in substantive business operations. GATS V:3 lit b. basically exempts South-South PTAs in services from the obligations of GATS V:6:[43]

> A service supplier of any other Member that is a juridical person constituted under the laws of a party to an agreement referred to in paragraph 1 shall be entitled to treatment granted under such agreement, provided that it engages in substantive business operations in the territory of the parties to such agreement.

Thus, the provision allows for more preferential treatment of service suppliers of citizens of the members of the PTA, but does not allow raising overall barriers to trade against third countries.

At first, the provision and its additional flexibility seems to some extent arbitrary and the reference to third-party legal persons in the context of a PTA seems somewhat unusual. Furthermore, there are a number of questions surrounding GATS V:6 regulation, which have to date not yet been answered. The scope of 'substantive business operations', for instance, remains unclear. It also remains to be discussed whether the term intends to distinguish between services suppliers 'producing' from the ones 'selling' services, alongside with a number of questions concerning the legal status of the service supplier in question.[44]

Fink (2007) offers three explanations for GATS Art. V:6, which essentially establishes liberal rules of origin for PTAs in services: (1) governments consider domestically established non-party services suppliers as part of the domestic economy, (2) a wider set of suppliers eligible for trade preferences implies greater import competition, which may be in the interest of the importing country's government, and (3) restrictive rules of origin will make multinational services providers collectively worse off. He concludes, however:[45]

[43] GATS V:6.

[44] See *Synopsis of Systemic Issues related to Regional Trade Agreements* CRTA, WT/REG/W/37 (2 March 2000), p. 38.

[45] Fink, Carsten (2007) *Preferential Trade Agreements in Services: Friends or Foes of the Multilateral Trading System?*, GEM, Paris, pp. 11–12.

> In sum, there are plausible political economy reasons why PTAs opt for liberal rules of origin. Still, we are left with some open questions about the precise motivations and political economy influences underlying government choices – not least because selected agreements *have* opted for a more restrictive approach.

The relatively unclear implications of GATS Art. V:6, and its uncertain value for WTO members, are further illustrated and confirmed by the fact that few developing countries have actually taken advantage of the exemption of GATS Art. V:3 lit. b in conjunction with GATS Art. V:6.[46] With respect to the scope of flexibility for South-South PTAs in services, GATS V:3 lit. b seems, thus, of limited practical relevance.

Finally, it has been suggested to read GATS Art. V:6 together with the flexibility provision in GATS Art. V:3 lit. a. This view is, however, not unequivocally shared and has been challenged. Cottier and Molinuevo (2008), e.g. argue that as there seems not to be a link between the two provisions, and as they are concerned with two independent and cumulative means of granting special and differential treatment to developing countries, they should not be read together.[47]

III. Flexibilities on the Basis of the Positive List Approach

The positive list approach of GATS contributed to additional flexibility for South-South PTAs by allowing every member to maintain certain measures that are inconsistent with GATS Art. II (MFN), provided that such measures are listed in the Annex, and meet the conditions. The Annex covers only measures in existence before the entry into force of the GATS Agreement. Original members and new members have a once-and-for-all opportunity to exempt themselves from a number of MFN obligations when accessing the GATS.[48] To a later moment in time, no new MFN exemptions by this route can be granted. Mattoo (2000b) describes the scope and significance of these explicit departures from MFN like this:[49]

> Around 380 MFN exemptions have been listed by some 70 Members, with many Members listing several exemptions in the same sector. Nearly two-thirds of the exempted measures are to be found in communication services and in transport services.

[46] Ibid., p. 11. [47] Cottier and Molinuevo (2008, pp. 142–143).
[48] Wolfrum (2008, p. 89). [49] Mattoo (2000b, p. 16).

Thus, the members did use the possibility of exempting measures from the application of MFN treatment quite vividly. The result is a rather low level of trade liberalisation in the services sectors. Many developing countries in particular took advantage of the positive list approach and committed themselves only to the basic level of liberalisation while *de facto* opening their services sectors to a larger degree.[50] This gives them the opportunity to close their services sectors to the level of their commitments under GATS in case they should feel that the economy requires protection. Also, the basic level of liberalisation under GATS leads to a level playing field for the establishment of the 'elimination of all discrimination', which is so basic that it is relatively easy to conclude a PTA among developing countries that eliminates more discrimination that GATS did.

According to GATS Art. XX:1, each member is required to submit a schedule of individual commitments in Market Access (GATS Art. XVI) and National Treatment (GATS Art. XVII). The submission of a schedule of specific commitments is mandatory, however, there is no minimal threshold that would force members to offer better conditions than the prevailing ones. It is, thus, possible to become a member of GATS without substantial commitment to services trade liberalisation.[51]

The absence of particular provisions on the special treatment of developing countries can be explained by the positive list approach, which gave the members the right to liberalise to an individual extent in individually chosen sectors. Developing countries have made use of this right and have generally committed to fewer sectors than developed countries. This right to commit to fewer sectors in the process of progressive liberalisation is also embedded in GATS Art. XIX:2, providing for appropriate flexibility, depending on the respective level of development. Developing countries are, thus, not bound to the principle of reciprocity.[52]

The flexibility attributed to members with respect to their entries in their schedules has, thus, advantages for developing countries insofar as it enables them to open their services markets progressively. However, exactly this flexibility has led to numerous entries in schedules, which do not meet the minimal standards set out by the Guidelines on Scheduling,[53]

[50] On the character of a 'stand-still obligation': STEPHENSON (2002).

[51] MUNIN (2010, p. 125); CARZANIGA (2003, p. 21).

[52] HESTERMEYER, HOLGER (2008), 'Preamble General Agreement on Trade in Services', In: R. Wolfrum, P-T. Stoll, and Feinäugle, C. (eds.), *WTO – Trade in Services*, Max Planck Institute, Martinus Nijhoff Publishers, Leiden, pp. 17–29, p. 28.

[53] Guidelines for the Scheduling of Specific Commitments under the General Agreement on Trade in Services (GATS), S/L/92 (28 March 2001).

and listed commitments may even be contradictory.[54] Recent GATS cases have had to interpret the scope of the commitments in schedules and have had to deal with inconclusive entries: *China – Electronic Payment Services*[55] and *China – Publications and Audiovisual Products*,[56] as well as to a limited degree also *US – Gambling*.[57]

In the most recent case, *China – Electronic Payment Services*, the panel noted an ambiguity in China's schedule of commitments: China had entered an unbound commitment in mode 1 Market Access in the subsector 7.B(d), and a full commitment in mode 1 National Treatment in the same subsector.[58] After considering GATS Art. XX:2,[59] the panel upheld China's position that the unbound commitment under mode 1 Market Access for Electronic Payment Services was limiting the scope of the full commitment under mode 1 National Treatment.[60]

The case well illustrates how important the individual country schedules of GATS are and highlights that members ought to carefully enter commitments. It remains to be researched how well developing countries in general perform in using the flexibility in the schedules to their advantage without creating contradictory commitments.[61] In *China – Electronic Payment Services* the panel agreed with China on the narrow interpretation of its commitments. In another case of ambiguous, contradictory commitments, the decision by the DSB – which is based on treaty interpretation – could potentially go against the committed country's interpretation and intention. Thus, the flexibility in drafting the

[54] Feketekuty, Geza (2000) 'Assessing and Improving the Architecture of GATS', In: P. Sauvé and R. Stern (eds.), *GATS 2000: New Direction in Services Trade Liberalisation*, The Brookings Institution, Washington DC, pp. 85ff, p. 98.

[55] *China – Electronic Payment Services*, WT/DS413/R (16 July 2012), Report of the Panel, para. 7.148.

[56] E.g. *China – Publications and Audiovisual Products*, WT/DS363/R (12 August 2009), Report of the Panel, para. 7.1014; WT/DS363/AB/R (21 December 2009), Report of the Appellate Body, paras. 361–372.

[57] E.g. *US – Gambling*, WT/DS285/AB/R (7 April 2005), Report of the Appellate Body, para. 180.

[58] *China – Electronic Payment Services*, WT/DS413/R (16 July 2012), Report of the Panel, para. 7.655.

[59] GATS XX:2 says: Measures inconsistent with both Articles XVI [Market Access] and XVII [National Treatment] shall be inscribed in the column relating to Article XVI [Market Access].

[60] *China – Electronic Payment Services*, WT/DS413/R (16 July 2012), Report of the Panel, para. 7.663.

[61] Given the complexity of the issue and the general problem of understaffed WTO representations at the WTO, there is a certain likelihood that developing countries perform poor with respect to coherent GATS scheduling.

schedules potentially is a double-edged sword, providing for 'limited predictability and security in the interpretation of GATS Schedules'.[62] This is particularly remarkable as it was due to the pressure of developing countries and the EU that the GATS is finally based on a positive list approach and not on a negative list approach as is the GATT. Given that there have only been few disputes over GATS commitments in the WTO to date, developing countries may have fared well with the flexibility of the positive list approach.[63] This may change in the future, however, as the impact of services on global value-added production moves more and more into the focus of policymakers, governments, and multinational corporations (MNCs).

Furthermore, *China – Electronic Payment Services*, *US – Gambling* and *China – Publications and Audiovisual Products* confirmed the dynamic character of schedules by ruling that services, which fall within the scope of definition of a commitment but are not explicitly enumerated in the schedule, may still create an obligation. To a certain degree, this important interpretation of the dynamic character of the GATS Schedules is limiting the flexibility of the members in entering their own set of commitments and in choosing commitments deliberately. While it is certainly important to strengthen the dynamic character of the GATS, such a broad interpretation of the scope of commitments further weakens predictability.

Thus, in conclusion, the positive list approach certainly provides for more flexibility for developing countries with respect to speed and scope of progressive liberalisation in services trade. However, the positive list approach comes not without disadvantages to developing countries: commitments may be ambiguous and their scope remains relatively broad, which both contributes to a lack of predictability with respect to the exact scope of the commitments entered in a country schedule and limits the flexibility in a relatively arbitrary way.

IV. Flexibilities Embedded in Special and Differential Treatment

With its development focus, GATS Art. V also attempts to protect weak economies and their services sectors in the case of regional trade

[62] Delimatsis, Panagiotis (2012) 'The WTO Outlaws the Privileges of the Chinese Payment Services Giant', *American Society of International Law*, insights, 28 September 2012, vol. 16, no. 31.

[63] Except maybe for China, given that the respective Chinese measures at dispute were inconsistent with its commitments in *China – Publications and Audiovisual Products* and in *China – Electronic Payment Services*.

liberalisation. This is desirable as in many cases members are reluctant to further open their markets because they are afraid of the potentially negative effects of trade liberalisation and the increased competition, as well as the structural change in the economy that comes along with free trade.[64]

With a more favourable treatment of South-South PTAs in services, the GATS encourages economic integration and provides instruments for the protection of the services sectors against global competition. In the best case, the increased competition at the regional level and the gains from it will lead to a more positive approach towards trade liberalisation on the multilateral level in the services sectors.

The protection – and more favourable treatment – of the services sectors in developing countries that enter into a PTA in services is particularly important because these economies – with a few exceptions – tend to suffer from a relatively weak services sector that cannot easily compete with the service providers from the North. In consequence, most of the recent growth in services exports from developing countries is unrelated to PTAs.[65] Therefore, additional protection of the concessions granted in a PTA among developing countries is essential for the overall likelihood of developing countries entering into a PTA, which liberalises services trade to a relevant degree.

However, while such flexibility is widely acknowledged and accepted with respect to the implementation of GATS commitments, the flexibility granted with respect to entering into economic integration agreements at first sight is not considerably higher for developing countries than for the rest of WTO members. Thus, with respect to flexibility for South-South PTAs in services, the implicit SDT of GATS does not provide for substantial additional flexibility. GATS Art. V:3 provides for the following:

> 3. (a) Where developing countries are parties to an agreement of the type referred to in paragraph 1, flexibility shall be provided for regarding the conditions set out in paragraph 1, particularly with reference to subparagraph (b) thereof, in accordance with the level of development of the countries concerned, both overall and in individual sectors and subsectors.

[64] See before, Part II.

[65] Grover Goswami, Arti, Mattoo, Aaditya and Saez, Sebastian (2012) 'Exporting Services: a Developing-Country Perspective', In: a. Grover Goswami, A. Matto and S. Saez (eds.), *Exporting Services: A Developing Country Perspective*, The World Bank, Washington DC, pp. 1–24, p. 19; Seyoum, Belay (2007) 'Revealed comparative advantage and competitiveness in services: a study with special emphasis on developing countries', *Journal of Economic Studies*, vol. 34, no. 5, pp. 376–388, p. 385.

> (b) Notwithstanding paragraph 6, in the case of an agreement of the type referred to in paragraph 1 involving only developing countries, more favourable treatment may be granted to juridical persons owned or controlled by natural persons of the parties to such an agreement.

Thus, SDT in GATS Art. V remains relatively vague with respect to the scope of flexibility provided in GATS Art. V:3 lit. a, and with respect to South-South PTAs in particular, the flexibility provided in GATS Art. V:3 lit. b although clearly defined, appears to be of limited practical implication. Consequently, there are two strong arguments for reading a relatively large scope of flexibility for South-South PTAs in services into GATS Art. V based on the concept of SDT:

(1) The general structure of the GATS, which already provides for non-reciprocal liberalisation among its members due to the positive list approach. Since the entire agreement is built on the concept closely related to SDT, GATS Art. V has to be read under the same premises.
(2) The provision of GATS Art. V:3, which clearly attributes SDT to PTAs in services involving a developing country. Such flexibility, in particular, should be attributed to South-South PTAs in services.

Nevertheless, since the flexibility and the exact scope of SDT provided for South-South PTAs in services are not defined in GATS Art. V, the concept of SDT and the provisions of GATS Art. V:3 are primarily underlining the general systemic reason of flexibility. They are, however, not providing clarification with respect to the actual scope of flexibility.

V. Waiver

Already GATT 1947 knew an opt-out clause in the form of a waiver. Through the waiver, members could request to be exempted from any obligation of the GATT 1947 treaty. Today, WTO Agreement IX:3 regulates the competence to adopt a waiver:[66]

> In exceptional circumstances, the Ministerial Conference may decide to waive an obligation imposed on a Member by this Agreement or any of the Multilateral Trade Agreements, provided that any such decision shall be taken by three fourths of the Members unless otherwise provided for in this paragraph.

And the footnote to this provision further states:[67]

[66] WTO Agreement IX:3. [67] WTO Agreement IX:3, footnote 4.

> A decision to grant a waiver in respect of any obligation subject to a transition period or a period for staged implementation that the requesting Members has not performed by the end of the relevant period shall be taken only by consensus.

Thus, given that the GATS is one of the multilateral trade agreements which WTO Agreement IX:3 refers to, the waiver can be applied to commitments and obligations under the GATS.[68] The waiver is meant to be of limited duration,[69] although the waiver is actually frequently extended once its term has expired. The duration of waivers ranges from a few months up to ten years and more.[70] As such, the waiver has particularly strong advantages as 'an interim solution before a permanent treaty amendment is adopted and enters into force'.[71]

By allowing for trade preferences in deviation of MFN, the waiver was used in several instances to address the claims that WTO law did not sufficiently take into account the economic situation of developing countries. Consequently, the waiver has been used in 2011 to permit preferential treatment of service suppliers from LDCs[72] exactly based on the motivation to address the economic needs of LDCs more appropriately. However, as the use of a waiver in order to provide developing countries and LDCs with advantages remains voluntary, such a waiver will develop little impact. Arguably, allowing for more preferential treatment for LDCs through a waiver decision is, thus, not the most efficient way for appropriately taking into account the economic situation in the global South – and even more importantly, the waiver may not be particularly suitable for changing the inequalities on the global market.[73]

Generally, however, the waiver seems like an ideal instrument for LDCs and developing countries to bridge the regulatory gap in preferential

68 See also Feichtner (2012, p. 175).

69 WTO Agreement Art. IX:4 states: 'A decision by the Ministerial Conference granting a waiver shall state the exceptional circumstances justifying the decision, the terms and conditions governing the application of the waiver and the date on which the waiver shall terminate. Any waiver granted for a period of more than one year shall be reviewed by the Ministerial Conference not later than one year after it is granted, and thereafter annually until the waiver terminates'.

70 Feichtner (2012, p. 224). 71 Ibid., p. 324.

72 Ministerial Conference, Preferential Treatment to Services and Service Suppliers of Least-Developed Countries, Decision of 17 December 2011, WT/L/847, Geneva.

73 The waiver decision on Services and Services Suppliers of LDCs has also been criticised for not taking into account rules of origin and basically restricting the waiver to market access: South Centre (2011) *Analysis of Draft Waiver Decision on Services and Services Suppliers of LDCs*, Analytical Note, Geneva.

services trade caused by the non-movement of the Doha Round: countries interested in pushing services trade regulation forward could ask for a waiver for their individual – more far-reaching – PTAs in services, without having to fear free-riders. Such a waiver – as it can only be of limited duration – would then have to be used in negotiations in order to push services trade regulation towards more adequate and balanced levels.

Through waivers alone, the potential inadequacies in GATS with respect to LDCs and developing countries, can, however, not be solved: waivers can address issues only selectively and with limited impact. The larger and more effective changes in services trade regulation have to be addressed elsewhere. In addition, because obtaining a waiver decision is a relatively demanding procedure, it is in any case not expected that the application of the waiver will become much more frequent in the future.[74]

VI. Enabling Clause

In addition to the MFN exemption of GATT XXIV, the GATT also knows the so-called Enabling Clause, which allows for special and differential treatment (SDT) (of commitments which otherwise would violate MFN) for developing countries. GATS does not know a similar provision to date, thus, the advantage of the Enabling Clause is limited to goods trade.

The Enabling Clause derives from the 1971 Generalised System of Preferences (GSP) waiver decision,[75] which suspended GATT Art. I:1 for ten years to allow developing countries to adopt the GSP legislation. Following a debate on which countries were to benefit, the members agreed to adhere to the principle of self-declaration, with the result that GSP preferences had to be extended to all countries which declared themselves as developing countries.[76] Feichtner (2012) states:[77]

> The waiver neither legalised specific GSP legislation of individual contracting parties nor did it include a flexible reference to UNCTAD [. . .]. Thus, the waiver established a new general rule which could be formulated as follows: [GATT I:1] shall not prevent contracting parties from according generalised, non-reciprocal, and non-discriminatory preferential tariff treatment to products from developing countries.

74 See Munin (2010, p. 338).
75 Contracting Parties, Generalised System of Preferences, Decision of 25 June 1971, L/3545 (28 June 1971).
76 GATT Council, Minutes of the Meeting on 25 May 1971, C/M/69 (28 May 1971).
77 Feichtner (2012, p. 135).

A few months after the introduction of the GSP waiver, members adopted a second waiver, which suspended GATT Art. I:1 to allow developing countries to grant preferential treatment to products from each other.[78] This waiver, thus, introduced particular flexibility for South-South economic integration in goods trade and was also limited to a period of ten years.

These decisions are considered to be critical for the role of developing countries within the WTO. Hudec (1975) puts it as follows:[79]

> The two waivers of Article I in 1971 can be viewed as the end of the period of upheaval that began with the 1957 ministers resolution which called for the Haberler Report. By 1971, the GATT's new relationship with developing countries had been redefined.

The Enabling Clause is one of the results of the Tokyo Round in 1979 and was included in the framework agreement, following a demand of developing countries to make the exception from MFN for GSP preferences permanent.[80] The Enabling Clause provided for departures from MFN and other GATT rules and weakened GATT Art. XXIV by eliminating the requirement of 'substantially all the trade' and the provision prohibiting an increase of the average level of external protection. This codification was balanced by the inclusion of a graduation principle.[81] However, the graduation principle was only vaguely worded and remained a statement of principle. A possible explanation for this fuzziness was that most SDT provisions were not binding.[82]

Ismail (2011) understands the Enabling Clause as the direct consequence of the failure to accommodate the needs of developing countries in the GATT 1947 and of the failure of developed countries to address the key interests of developing countries in their markets. Furthermore, he sees 'the failure of the GATT during the first eight rounds to address the issues of the appropriate balance between the principles of reciprocity and MFN on one hand and the special development needs of

[78] Contracting Parties, Trade Negotiations among Developing Countries, Decision of 26 November 1971, L/3636 (30 November 1971).

[79] Hudec, Robert E. (1975) *The GATT Legal System and World Trade Diplomacy*, Praeger, New York, p. 65.

[80] Feichtner (2012, p. 137); Ismail (2011, p. 145).

[81] The graduation principle could be understood as an illustration of the interaction between the normative current state (developing countries may revoke reciprocity) and the political target state (equal treatment of all WTO members): Eberhard (2008).

[82] Hoekman and Kostecki (2009, p. 537).

developing countries on the other', as still haunting the WTO during the Doha Round.[83]

The Enabling Clause furthermore introduced a permanent exception from MFN for PTAs among developing countries. Such an exception is subject to any 'criteria or conditions' set out by WTO members. However, none of these criteria and conditions have ever been established. The EC has argued that the failure of establishing any such conditions or criteria meant that the waiver in para. 2 (c) Enabling Clause did not apply to non-tariff measures;[84] however, it seems to be fairly clear that the possibility of such 'criteria or conditions' is optional.[85] In any case, the Enabling Clause does not authorise any violations of WTO law other than MFN.

Two main questions persist: (1) whether PTAs among developing countries should be notified under the Enabling Clause or under GATT Art. XXIV. And (2) whether the MFN clause in a PTA between a developing country and a developed country prevents further trade liberalisation among developing countries, because based on a specific interpretation of the Enabling Clause, any more favourable treatment given under any PTA would have to be extended to other developing countries (collective self-reliance argument).[86]

Given that five PTAs in services were notified to the WTO under both the Enabling Clause and GATS Art. V,[87] and considering that the general principle and logic of the Enabling Clause should in theory also apply to services trade arguably the Enabling Clause informs the scope of flexibility in GATS with respect to developing countries. In addition, the importance of the Enabling Clause is generally acknowledged among the members of the WTO, thus, extending the regulation to services trade may not entirely be outside the scope of negotiation.

Nevertheless, the Enabling Clause is not mandatory because there is no effective sanction to non-compliance: it enables developed countries to provide advantages to developing countries, but it is not an obligation

[83] Ismail (2011, pp. 145–146).

[84] WTO Committee on Trade and Development 'Gulf Co-operation Council Customs Union – Saudi-Arabia's Notification: Communication from the European Communities', 25 November 2008, WT/COMTD/66/Add.2, para. 5.

[85] Derived from the fact that the possibility is set out in a sub-clause, see also Bartels (2012, p. 861).

[86] Bartels (2012, p. 861), p. 861.

[87] WTO (2013) Regional Trade Agreements Information System (RTA-IS) [Online], available at: http://rtais.wto.org/UI/PublicMaintainRTAHome.aspx (last visited 13 June 2013): *ASEAN – China (2007)*, the *East African Community (2009)*, *MERCOSUR (1997)*, *Pakistan – Malaysia (2007)* and *India – Malaysia (2011)*.

to do so.[88] Therefore, it is questionable whether extending the Enabling Clause to services trade is the best instrument available for creating more equal trade relations in North-South trade in services. While the Enabling Clause would certainly empower developing countries vis-à-vis the large services markets in industrialised countries, reducing non-tariff barriers to trade in services in developed countries may be much more efficient than allowing – in theory – for optional more favourable treatment of developing countries.

In the case of South-South PTAs in services, the Enabling Clause could, however, contribute to more predictability and legal security with respect to the scope of flexibilities attributed to South-South PTAs in services. The Enabling Clause carries the potential of establishing a clear set of conditions and criteria which are applied to South-South PTAs in services, and which establish a comprehensive regulation of flexibilities. The problem of non-compliance and of the voluntary character of the Enabling Clause should arise to a lesser degree, as using such flexibilities should be more equally in the interest of all parties involved: since trade and power relations are more equal, within a typical South-South PTS, not making use of the flexibilities would come as a disadvantage to all its members – which stands in contrast with North-South PTAs.

[88] LEE, YONG-SHIK (2011b) 'World Trade Organisation and Developing countries', In: Y-S. Lee, G. N. Horlick, W-M. Choi and T. Broude (eds.), *Law and Development Perspective on International Trade Law*, Cambridge University Press, New York, pp. 105–129, pp. 114–115.

2

Legal Arguments for a Large Scope of Flexibilities in the GATS

As previously discussed, the compliance with the requirements of GATS Art. V is relatively modest and PTAs in services are not all notified to the WTO. Both aspects weaken the protection of the systemic logic of the world trade system: if members do not comply with WTO law, it may lose credibility as well as the power to govern world trade. And if PTAs are not notified to the WTO, it no longer has control over the many different trade agreements and their interaction among each other and with the WTO.

However, it is possible to argue that the reason for weak compliance and low level of notification is not due to bad behaviour of WTO members, but much rather to the variety of ways how GATS Art. V can be interpreted and the resulting uncertainty of whether or not a PTA is in compliance with GATS.

This difficulty is exacerbated in the case of South-South PTAs. Compliance with the law and implementation of legal provisions tends to be generally an institutional weakness of developing countries.[1] Furthermore, developing countries tend to have difficulties with finding well-educated specialists advising them in WTO law when entering trade agreements, be it on the regional or on the multilateral level.[2] The language of GATS Art. V and the resulting legal uncertainty of how to interpret the provision constitute a real obstacle to South-South PTAs complying with GATS: first, members do not know how to deal with GATS Art. V, and second, they do not use the potential embedded in GATS-compatible PTAs, which can also be understood as help for establishing a useful, secure and economically fruitful PTA.

And finally, there is also a considerable risk of overlapping provisions in different PTAs, which might even be contradictory and render further

[1] See before, Foundations.

[2] On this, see VAN DER BORGHT, KIM (1999) 'The Advisory Center on WTO Law: Advancing Fairness Equality', *Journal of International Economic Law*, vol. 2, pp. 723–728.

trade liberalisation at the multilateral level more difficult and have a trade diverting effect. In this jungle of PTAs (the so-called Spaghetti-Bowl), the WTO as the governing institution for equal and fair trade relations is missing also in the interest of developing countries: it becomes more difficult to protect the trade interests of developing countries, when trade relations continue to increasingly move out of the multilateral forum.[3]

Given the broad scope of GATS Art. V and the many instruments that provide for more flexibility for South-South PTAs, several different options unfold: from arguing that GATS does not necessarily allow for additional flexibility for South-South PTAs to arguing that GATS can be interpreted as allowing even for partially sectorial agreements among developing countries.

Feichtner (2012) suggests considering three different perspectives with respect to the flexibility challenge: (1) a domestic perspective, (2) an intra-regime perspective, and (3) an inter-regime perspective. In the domestic perspective, flexibility in the application and interpretation of international law provides for a balance to the fact that international law usually is static and not responsive to 'changes in the balances of interests and preferences in the polity domestically'.[4] Because withdrawal from international institutions is not a practical solution due to the dependency of states on international cooperation, opt-out clauses are necessary to maintain consent, acceptance and overall compliance with international institutions.[5]

From the inter-regime perspective, flexibility is required because international law needs to adapt to a certain extent to societal needs and preferences in order to remain legitimate and effective.[6] Additionally, international legal regimes rarely take into consideration the different stages of development of state parties to a sufficient degree. In order to foster acceptance and compliance, international institutions need to be able to address such imbalances through lawmaking. Regulation of opt-outs in the law provide for more transparency and inclusion than individual negotiations do.[7]

[3] Crawford, Jo-Ann and Fiorentino, Roberto V. (2005) The Changing Landscape of Regional Trade Agreements, Discussion Paper, World Trade Organisation, Geneva.

[4] Feichtner (2012, pp. 8–12).

[5] See e.g. Pauwelyn, Joost (2008) *Optimal Protection of International Law: Navigating between European Absolutism and American Voluntarism*, Cambridge University Press.

[6] Pound, Roscoe (1923) *Interpretations of Legal History*, Cambridge University Press, p. 1XX; Feichtner (2012, p. 10).

[7] Feichtner (2012, p. 10); Cullet (2003).

With respect to the inter-regime perspective, Feichtner (2012) argues that 'legal conflict rules do not provide an adequate solution where conflicts of norms result from underlying conflicts of interest'.[8] Thus, flexible linkages between the regimes are required so that both regimes remain effective.[9]

This study argues that the GATS could provide for sufficiently clear and sufficiently broad flexibility to accommodate and regulate development interests in South-South PTAs in services. The following paragraphs are based on the legal analysis of the provisions in IEL providing for flexibility for South-South PTAs in services and referring to the principle SDT as discussed in Part I. As the scope of flexibility differs depending on how and which WTO provisions are taken into consideration, the possibilities for establishing the scope of flexibility are structured in a model based on three different interpretations: (1) the narrow interpretation, which is strictly based on GATS V and allows for limited flexibility, (2) the medium interpretation, which takes into consideration other GATS provisions providing for additional flexibility, and (3) the broad interpretation, which is based on taking into consideration also related provisions in IEL and the general principle of SDT, as well as the general objective of WTO law of contributing to economic growth around the world.

I. No Additional Flexibility: The Narrow Interpretation

Given that GATS Art. V and the GATS treaty itself do not include provisions similar to the Enabling Clause in the GATT, it can be argued that the drafters of the treaty did not necessarily intend to allow for additional flexibility for developing countries. This view could be substantiated by the wording of GATS Art. V that consists of just one clearly stated – and sufficiently substantiated – additional flexibility for PTAs among developing countries, which is to be found in GATS Art. V:3 lit. b, the equal treatment of third country nationals.

The practical consequence of such a positivist interpretation would be that with the exception of not having to provide equal treatment to legal persons of a third country engaged in substantive business, members of a South-South PTA in services would have to comply with all other requirements established in GATS V. South-South PTAs would have to

[8] Feichtner (2012, p. 12).

[9] Young, Margaret A. (2009) 'Fragmentation or Interaction: The WTO, Fisheries Subsidies and International Law', *World Trade Review*, vol. 8, no. 4, pp. 477–515, p. 477.

cover substantially all the trade, they would have to eliminate substantially all the barriers to trade and they would not be allowed to exclude major services sectors or a priori any of the four modes of supply.

Arguably, in some cases this narrow interpretation of the scope of flexibility would render it rather challenging for developing countries to conclude a South-South PTA in services. Thus, this raises the question whether such a narrow interpretation is indeed in the interest of the multilateral trading system. Furthermore, taking into consideration the general rules on the interpretation of international law, and given the strong commitment to promoting economic growth in developing countries as established in WTO law, it may be questionable if such a narrow interpretation is indeed in line with the GATS.

Nevertheless, as long as the scope of flexibility is not further elaborated and explained in case law, possibly such a positivist approach to the interpretation of the scope of flexibility for South-South PTAs in services remains a viable option.

II. Flexibility in Number of Sectors and Level of Liberalisation: The Medium Interpretation

This middle way would argue for slightly more flexibility for South-South PTAs, substantiated by GATS Art. V:3 lit. a and GATS Art. V:3 lit. b, which would allow for the exemption of more sectors than is possible in North-South or North-North PTAs, it would allow for a slightly lesser degree of liberalisation than in the case of other PTAs and, evidently, the requirement of equal treatment of third country nationals would be abolished.

Additionally, by including the impact of the PTA on the 'wider process of economic integration', the wording of the preamble and the principle of special and differential treatment, variations of this interpretation are possible (1) by allowing the exemption of the sectors which are not essential for economic activity and (2) by allowing even the exemption of substantial sectors and trade volumes.

Thus, also the medium interpretation of the scope of flexibility for South-South PTAs in services is mainly based on the interpretation of the provisions of GATS Art. V. However, the positivist approach of the narrow interpretation is abandoned, and the overall objective of GATS Art. V is taken into account. This medium interpretation arguably allows for excluding a number of services sectors from the PTA, as well as for limited horizontal commitments, while, however, not going as far as allowing the exclusion of one of the four modes of supply or major services sectors from the PTA.

From a preliminary analysis of the commitments in South-South PTAs, the medium interpretation seems to be the most likely one to be followed by developing countries. Furthermore, given that quite a number of North-South and North-North PTAs in services are not entirely complying with the requirements of GATS Art. V, the medium interpretation seems to be met with agreement among members.

The medium interpretation would already allow for including graduation in the scope of flexibilities, by providing for more flexibility in terms of numbers of sectors which can be excluded from a PTA the poorer a country is or the weaker its services industries are. However, that presumably a majority of WTO members have concluded PTAs in services, which would be in line with the medium interpretation, does not necessarily mean that this interpretation prevails in case of a dispute.

III. Sectorial Agreements: Broad Interpretation

Not all services sectors are equally important for economic growth in general and for value-added production in particular. Furthermore, not all services sectors are equally well suited for trade liberalisation at the global level or at the regional level. Thus, it has been suggested that consideration might be given to the specific needs and structure of the services sectors in a developing country: in order to support economic development to the extent possible, the different services sectors could be allowed for individual liberalisation on individual levels.[10]

Transportation and telecommunication, for instance, might be opened on the global level as experience shows that trade liberalisation in these sectors is feasible, leads to a positive impact on the economic performance in the newly opened market and stimulates the entire economy of the country. On the other hand, education and health are most likely better suited for regional trade liberalisation.

Furthermore, in a particular developing country, the need for high-quality services in the investment sector might be much more urgent than the need for good-quality transportation services. Thus, in the light of GATS Art. V, it would be desirable to use the scope for interpretation to the extent of which different levels of liberalisation can be attributed to different sectors in a South-South PTA in services. All of this, given the

[10] For more details, see Part II.

positive list approach and the few commitments that developing countries have entered under the GATS, arguably, and depending on the relative wording of the PTA, can comply with the provisions in GATS Art. V.[11]

The most far-reaching interpretation of the scope of GATS would be to argue for flexibility for partially sectorial agreements among developing countries. GATS Art. V:3 lit. a attributes more flexibility to the requirements of 'substantial sectorial coverage' and the 'elimination of substantially all discrimination'. Given that the general level of liberalisation remains low in the case of international services trade and that many sectors – particularly in developing countries – have not yet been liberalised to a substantial degree, excluding several sectors from a South-South PTA does not seem to necessarily carry the weight of a violation of GATS Art. V:3 lit. a. This interpretation is furthermore supported by the preamble of GATS, the principle of SDT and the departure from the requirement of reciprocity introduced by the positive list approach.

In addition, one has to consider the basic idea of SDT, which is meant to provide flexibility to weak economies that cannot compete on the global market otherwise. Taking into consideration the criticism voiced concerning the efficiency of SDT, and the related theories of graduation and others, there is a strong theoretical argument to be made for the non-application of GATS Art. V to South-South PTAs in services: since services industries tend to be generally underdeveloped in developing countries, these industries are not yet competitive on the global market.[12] South-South PTAs in services are, therefore, not expected to impact on global competition in trade in services.

However, this may not always be the case. Certain services sectors in certain developing countries may nevertheless already have reached a level of global competitiveness.[13] Therefore, such flexibility or non-application

[11] It is possible to read such a broad scope of flexibility into GATS Art. V, particularly when considering 'its object and purpose' (VCLT Art. 31:1): GATS Art. V was left as vague because members wanted to keep the broadest possible scope for preferential trade policies. In addition, based on VCLT Art. 31:2 and 31:3, Qureshi and Wittayawarakul (2010, p. 124), make an argument for reading a stronger development focus into WTO law, than has previously been done.

[12] See e.g. Konan and Maskus (2006).

[13] E.g. the services industries in India and China, see Bosworth, Barry and Collins, Susan M. (2007) Accounting for Growth: Comparing China and India, NBER Working Paper, National Bureau of Economic Research, Cambridge MA; Dossani, Rafiq (2007) 'The Next Wave of Globalisation: Relocating Service Provision to India', *World Development*, vol. 35, no. 5, pp. 772–791; on the health services industry in the Philippines and Indonesia, see Kanchanachitra, Chumrurtai, Lindelow, Magnus, Johnston, Timothy,

of the requirements of GATS Art. V on South-South PTAs in services may have to relate to the individual level of competitiveness in each services sector: if a service sector is globally competitive, this sector will also have to fully comply with WTO law, such as GATS Art. V. If a services sector is not yet privatised or generally under-developed, an exemption from MFN for preferential agreements in this sector will likely not develop any impact on the global market and, thus, such an under-developed sector would not have to fully comply with GATS Art. V.

The threshold for global competitiveness and therewith for full commitment to the obligations of WTO law would have to be established individually for each services sector in each member of a South-South PTA in services. Furthermore, the general contribution to economic development and the suitability for preferential liberalisation of a services sector would have to be taken into consideration. Liberalised sectors in a PTA need to be on a comparable level among the members of a PTA, in order to increase the positive spill-over effect of trade liberalisation. Thus, not only the individual sectors would have to be assessed, but the assessment would also need to take into account the competitive comparison between members of a PTA.[14] This may well lead to the conclusion that on a South-South basis, even a PTA in services encompassing just one services sector of particular interest could be justifiable under WTO rules.

On the other hand, flexibility going as far as allowing for sectorial agreements on just a single services sector would necessarily have to be balanced by a requirement to full liberalisation in this particular services sector. Otherwise, such a sectorial agreement could not be justified with the consideration of its contribution to economic development, since partial liberalisation is unlikely to actually substantially increase economic development.[15]

Hanvoravongchau, Piya, Lorenzo, Fely M., Huong, Nguyen L., Wilopo, Siswanto A. and Dela Rosa, Jennifer F. (2011) 'Human Resources for Health in Southeast Asia: Shortages, Distributional Challenges, and International Trade in Health Services', *The Lancet*, vol. 337, no. 9767, pp. 769–781; and on tourism services in Kenya, see Akama, John S. and Kieti, Damiannah (2007) 'Tourism and Socio-economic Development in Developing Countries: A Case Study of Mombasa Resort in Kenya', *Journal of Sustainable Tourism*, vol. 15, no. 6, pp. 735–748.

[14] See e.g. Francois and Hoekman (2010).

[15] See before, Introduction and Part II.

3

New Approach to a Better Use of the Scope of Flexibilities

Chaudhuri and Karmakar (2008) constituted that, in general, developing countries 'have undertaken significant enhancement in both the width and the depth of the commitments they have entered into in PTAs'.[1] However, as these commitments were not reflected in their GATS offers, Chaudhuri and Karmakar (2008) suggest that developing countries bind commitments in services trade liberalisation not only in PTAs, but also in the WTO.[2]

According to le Pere (2009), more than 40 per cent of developing country exports are destined for other developing countries. This rate is growing annually by 11 per cent, with South-South services trade also growing 'dramatically'.[3] Particularly strong is also the growth of South-South investment flows, which are enabled and protected both by PTAs and by BITs. Important pull-factors for South-South FDI are geographic proximity, cultural ties and growing political and ideological affinities.[4] Thus, in other words, not *per se* simple considerations of trade opportunities and profit, but something one may call a more personal incentive to invest abroad.

Services trade liberalisation is of particular relevance for South-South investment flows. A study of the OECD showed in 2006, that privatisation in the services sectors generally provides great opportunities for developing country companies, and furthermore, the nature of the services sectors (requirement of proximity between producer and consumer), provides for synergies for developing country companies in neighbouring countries.[5] Thus, also the increasing FDI flows among developing

[1] Chaudhuri and Karmakar (2008, p. 220). [2] Ibid.

[3] Le Pere, Garth L. (2009) 'Exploring the promise of South-South Co-operation', In: Garth L. Le Pere and Lyal White (eds.), *Strengthening the Bilateral*, Edited Proceedings of the first Academic Seminar on Bilateral Relations between Argentina and South Africa, 12–14 May 2008, Institute for Global Dialogue, Midrand, pp. 67–84, p. 68.

[4] Le Pere (2009, p. 69). [5] Aykut and Goldstein (2006, p. 18).

countries clearly is an indicator for the convergence of the services sectors in the South.

While trade among developing countries is increasing, the number of PTAs among developing countries is growing steadily, too. The following paragraphs are looking in detail at the existing level of liberalisation in the thirty PTAs among developing countries, which include commitments in services trade liberalisation. It is, however, by no means guaranteed that the growth of trade among developing countries is in fact caused by the depth of commitments in South-South PTAs. Unilateral and multilateral trade liberalisation may encourage and increase South-South trade in services equally.[6]

At the same time, it economic studies suggest that if the initial level of restrictiveness with respect to trade liberalisation in services is high, a moderate attempt for liberalisation will not achieve to have an impact on the actual performance of service suppliers.[7] Therefore, comparing the depth of liberalisation in South-South PTAs with the level of liberalisation already established by commitments under GATS has implications for the expected performance of a PTA: the deeper commitments in trade liberalisation in services are compared to the level of liberalisation prior to the establishment of the PTA, the more likely it is that South-South trade in services indeed will see an increase related to preferential services trade regulation.

In order to establish the level of liberalisation in South-South PTAs, the following paragraphs are based on the analysis of the main treaty texts and the schedules of the thirty South-South PTAs with substantial trade liberalising commitments found in the dataset. The level of liberalisation is empirically established through coding of the different liberalising commitments undertaken in services sectors. According to the same coding scheme, the commitments of the countries involved in South-South PTAs in services under GATS are taken as an indicator for the level of liberalisation prior to the establishment of the PTA.[8] This allows both to analyse the compliance with GATS Art. V requirements of South-South PTAs and the actual expected liberalising impact of the PTAs on South-South trade in services.

6 On unilateral and multilateral liberalisation, see Krueger (1999, p. 917); Trebilcock, Howse and Eliason (2012).

7 Dihel et al. (2008, p. 67).

8 The entire list of codified commitments can be found in the Annex Table of Coded Data, at the end of this thesis.

I. Depth of Regulation

Not all South-South PTAs have already concluded their schedules of commitments in services trade liberalisation. Given that the general structure of services trade regulation – unless full market access and national treatment is granted – requires further clarifications on the individual commitments in the individual sectors, PTAs, which have not yet concluded a schedule of commitments, are basically restricted to the level of liberalisation under the GATS – in addition to a stand-still obligation.

This is a consequence of the general structure of services trade liberalisation: the main treaty text establishes the basic rules with reference to the list of commitments in the schedule. The actual liberalising commitments are generally limited to the schedule. Thus, while the main treaty text provides for the basic rules in trade in services to which the members of a PTA are committed, these rules generally only apply to areas of services trade, in which liberalising commitments have been undertaken. As long as the schedule is still under negotiation, the services provisions in main treaty text are of limited legal consequence, because members have not yet established the list of liberalising commitments to which these provisions apply.

The result of such a constellation is that the general commitments under the GATS apply among members of a PTA. Furthermore, increasing the barriers to trade in services among the members of a PTA is prevented through on the one side the binding commitments under GATS, and on the other side a general reference to a stand-still obligation, usually located in the article regulating the establishment of the schedules. In *Colombia – Mexico – Venezuela (1994)* the relevant provision was phrased like follows:[9]

> (1) Ninguna Parte incrementará el grado de disconformidad de sus medidas existentes [. . .]. Cualquier reforma de estas medidas no disminuirá el grado de conformidad de la medida tal como estaba en vigor inmediatamente antes de la reforma.
> (2) Dentro de los ocho meses siguientes a la firma del Tratado, las Partes suscribirán un Protocolo que constará de dos listas que contendrán los acuerdos de las negociaciones que las Partes realicen durante esos ocho meses.
> [. . .]

[9] *Colombia – Mexico – Venezuela (1994)*, Art. 10–07.

Thus, usually, a stand-still obligation is introduced with respect to the general rules as established by the main treaty text until the schedules of commitments are implemented. PTAs in services, which are implemented prior to the establishment of the schedules of commitments, tend to include separate services chapters in the main treaty text. These separate chapters establish liberalising commitments independent from the schedule in sectors of particular economic and political interest. Table 12 illustrates the South-South PTAs, which were implemented before the schedule of commitments was adopted and depicts the liberalising impact.

The table illustrates well that, even if the schedule of commitments in the area of services trade liberalisation has not yet been adopted, these PTAs in services nevertheless create a certain level of minimal additional trade liberalisation in services. The sectors of services trade, which are considered to be of most relevance, are included in the main treaty and establish liberalising commitments independent from the schedule.

In this respect, it is of particular interest is that all South-South PTAs in services in this sample include a separate chapter on investment and financial services. The Mexican PTAs[10] actually establish National Treatment for investment and financial services, while for other services sectors only the GATS level of liberalisation applies at the time of entry into force of the PTAs. Thus, most likely, Mexico and its partner countries in the two PTAs agreed that the regulation and liberalisation of investment and trade in financial services was of superior interest. Arguably, in addition of the GATS level of liberalisation prior to the establishment of these Mexican South-South PTAs in services, together with the liberalisation of trade in financial services already provides for a considerable economic push among the member to these PTAs, given the key role attributed to South-South investment and trade in services to economic growth.[11]

Furthermore, the fact that binding, individual lists of liberalising commitments in services trade are yet missing, does not prevent the members of a PTA in services to include binding provisions on labour migration into the main treaty text, therewith liberalising mode 4 supply of services to a limited extent. Three out of five South-South PTAs yet waiting to implement the Schedule, establish liberalising commitments in mode

[10] *Colombia – Mexico – Venezuela (1994)* and *Mexico – Uruguay (2003).*

[11] See Table 12.

Table 12 *South-South PTAs without schedules*[a]

PTAs in services (no schedule)	Services chapter	Transportation	Communication	Financial services	Movement of persons
Colombia – Mexico – Venezuela (1994)	GATS level	Shall be liberalised bilaterally, cooperation agreement	Right to access, cooperation for interoperability	National Treatment	Liberalising commitments for groups of persons
CARICOM Services (1997)	Stand-still obligation/ GATS level	–	–	Stand-still obligation	–
Mexico – Nicaragua (1997)	GATS level	–	Right to access, cooperation for interoperability	MFN treatment	Liberalising commitments for groups of persons
*CARICOM – Cuba (2000)**	GATS level, exchange of information	Cooperation	–	Cooperation	–
CARICOM revised (2001)	Stand-still obligation/ GATS level	–	–	Stand-still obligation	Full liberalisation for skilled persons
Mexico – Uruguay (2003)	GATS level	–	Right to access, cooperation for interoperability	National Treatment	Liberalising commitments for groups of persons

* *CARICOM – Cuba (2000)* furthermore includes a special paragraph on the cooperation in the area of tourism.

[a] Derived from dataset.

4 supply of services.[12] While these commitments are indeed restricted to a number of categories of people, service suppliers are generally included in these categories. Indirectly, these commitments, thus, liberalise services trade in many sectors, in which mode 4 provision of a service is common.

Finally, next to tourism, which was only separately listed by *CARICOM – Cuba (2000)*, the services sectors of transportation and telecommunication rank high with respect to economic interests of the members of South-South PTAs.[13] As services are linked to other economic activities, their impact on value-added production is particularly highlighted in these separate paragraphs. Arguably, the services sectors, which are considered to be the most directly linked to the productivity in other economic sectors, may thus be transportation, telecommunication and financial services. Mode 4 supply of services – provided that in these South-South PTAs in services, mode 4 labour migration is only included in the liberalising commitments as a consequence of the nature of mode 4 labour migration – may be justified through the key role that labour migration plays in the process of successful convergence of two economies.

The particular interest of members to a South-South PTA in services in these three sectors in addition to mode 4 labour migration is only partially confirmed by the analysis of the level of commitments in the schedules of the rest of the South-South PTAs in services.

The initial analysis of the sectors covered by substantial South-South PTAs in services showed that all of them cover at least a majority of the services sectors. *MERCOSUR Services (1997)*, *Chile – MERCOSUR (2009)* and the *EAC (2009)* cover the least sectors, with only seven of them listed in the schedules. While in *EAC (2009)* all members entered commitments in the same sectors, in *MERCOSUR Services (1997)* and in *Chile – MERCOSUR (2009)* each member entered a different number and choice of sectors in its schedule, none of them, however, includes more than eight sectors.

Furthermore, *Chile – China (2008)* is listing eight sectors in the schedule, while *China – Peru (2009)* lists ten sectors. Considering, the binding commitments then entered by the members, this lower number of listed sectors may decrease further: e.g. in *MERCOSUR Services (2007)* basically no commitments are entered in the sector of educational services, which

[12] *Colombia – Mexico – Venezuela (1994)*, *CARICOM revised (2001)* and *Mexico – Uruguay (2003)*.

[13] Transportation: *Colombia – Mexico – Venezuela (1994)* and *CARICOM – Cuba (2000)*; Telecommunication: *Colombia – Mexico – Venezuela (1994)* and *Mexico – Uruguay (2003)*.

makes commitments in trade liberalisation in services further decrease to only six sectors. However, even taking actual commitments entered in the schedules into consideration, none of the South-South PTAs in services lists commitments in less than six services sectors (see Table 13).

Generally, of the sectors codified, the sectors with the highest level of liberalisation are construction services (with an average level of 2.08 in NT and 1.86 in MA), educational services (with an average level of 2.04 in NT and 1.95 in MA), and tourism services (with an average level of 1.60 in NT and 1.65 in MA). Interestingly, the sectors with arguably the greatest economic interest for members of South-South PTAs in services, transportation, communication and financial services have a slightly higher level of average liberalisation (see Table 13). Arguably this may mirror the economic relevance of the sectors, in which commitments are more sensitive than in other services sectors.

The only South-South PTA in services, which establishes full market integration in trade in services is *WAEMU (1994)*: it provides for full liberalisation in trade in services in general, with a commitment to policy cooperation in transportation and communication. In addition, *WAEMU (1994)* establishes full market integration for investment and trade in services and free movement of labour.[14]

Thus, in conclusion, not all South-South PTAs have since their entry into force adopted a schedule of commitments in services trade liberalisation. This leaves trade liberalisation in services among the members of these PTAs on the general level of GATS commitments with the exception of individual sectors explicitly listed in the main treaty text. Of particular interest seem the sectors of transportation, communication and financial services, in addition to mode 4 labour migration.

South-South PTAs, which have adopted a schedule of commitments in trade liberalisation in services, tend to list the majority of services sectors, while not all of them enter commitments in all of the services sectors. There is, however, no South-South PTA in services, which has entered commitments in less than six services sectors.

The only South-South PTA establishing a full market for trade in services is the *WAEMU (1994)*. Considering the time in which this agreement was adopted, the strong commitment to both the movement of persons and trade liberalisation in services is remarkable – it even was introduced prior to the entry into force of the GATS, and just shortly after the establishment of the EU single market for services in 1992. Given that the

[14] *WAEMU (1994)*, Art. 91–100.

Table 13 *Level of liberalisation in particular sectors and modes of supply*[a]

PTA	appr	sects	bus NT	bus MA	com NT	com MA	cons NT	cons MA	edu NT	edu MA	fin NT	fin MA	tou NT	tou MA	tran NT	tran MA	lab NT	lab MA	horiz
Bolivia – Mexico (1994)	*neg*	11	2	2	3	3	3	3	2	2	2	2	2	2	3	3	2	2	1
Costa Rica – Mexico (1994)	*neg*	all	2	1	3	2	2	1	2	1	4	4	1	1	3	2	2	2	2
MERCOSUR services (1997)	*pos*	7	2	2	2	2	3	3	4	4	4	4	3	3	3	3	2	2	2
Central America – Domin. Republic (1998)	*neg*	all	2	2	NA	NA	NA	NA	NA	NA	NA	NA	NA	NA	NA	NA	2	2	NA
Chile – Mexico (1998)	*neg*	all	2	2	3	2	1	1	1	1	4	4	1	1	2	2	3	3	2
Central America – Chile (1999)	*neg*	all	3	2	3	3	2	1	2	2	1	1	1	1	3	3	2	2	2
Mexico – Northern Triangle (2000)	*neg*	all	2	1	2	1	2	1	1	1	4	4	2	1	2	1	2	2	1
Central America – Panama (2002)	*neg*	all	1	1	1	1	2	1	1	1	4	4	1	1	2	2	2	2	
India – Malaysia (2005)	*pos*	11	2	3	2	3	2	3	3	3	NA	NA	2	3	2	3	2	2	2
Chile – Colombia (2006)	*neg*	all	2	1	3	3	2	2	2	2	4	4	1	1	2	2	3	2	2
Chile – Panama (2006)	*neg*	all	2	2	3	2	2	1	2	2	4	4	1	1	3	3	2	2	2
Chile – Peru (2006)	*neg*	all	2	1	3	1	1	1	1	1	4	4	1	1	3	2	2	2	2
ASEAN – China (2007)	*pos*	11	2	3	2	2	2	2	2	2	3	3	2	2	2	2	3	3	2
Colombia – Northern Triangle (2007)	*neg*	all	2	2	3	2	2	1	1	2	4	4	1	2	2	2	2	2	2
Malaysia – Pakistan (2007)	*pos*	11	3	3	2	3	2	3	2	2	4	4	2	2	2	2	2	2	2
Chile – China (2008)	*pos*	8	2	2	2	2	4	4	2	2	4	4	4	4	3	3	3	3	3
Chile – MERCOSUR (2009)	*pos*	7	3	3	2	2	2	2	4	4	4	4	2	2	2	2	2	2	2
China – Pakistan (2009)	*pos*	11	2	3	2	3	3	3	3	3	2	3	2	2	2	2	2	3	2
China – Peru (2009)	*pos*	11	2	3	2	3	3	3	3	3	2	3	2	2	2	3	2	2	2
EAC (2009)	*pos*	7	1	2	3	3	4	4	2	2	3	3	2	2	1	2	1	1	NA
China – Costa Rica (2010)	*pos*	10	2	3	2	2	1	1	3	3	4	4	2	2	3	3	3	2	3
Mexico – Peru (2011)	*neg*	all	3	2	3	2	2	1	2	1	4	4	1	1	3	2	3	3	1
Panama – Peru (2011)	*neg*	all	3	2	3	2	1	1	2	1	4	4	1	1	3	2	2	2	2
			2.13	**2.08**	**2.34**	**2.13**	**2.08**	**1.86**	**2.04**	**1.95**	**3.17**	**3.26**	**1.6**	**1.65**	**2.3**	**2.21**	**2.21**	**2.17**	**1.69**

[a] Derived from dataset.

Legend: appr = approach; neg = negative list approach; pos = positive list approach; sects = number of in which commitments have been made; bus NT/MA = business services, National Treatment and Market Access; com NT/MA = communication services, National Treatment and Market Access; cons NT/MA = construction services, National Treatment and Market Access; edu NT/MA = education services, National Treatment and Market Access; fin NT/MA = financial services, National Treatment and Market Access; tou NT/MA = tourism services, National Treatment and Market Access; tran NT/MA = transportation services, National Treatment and Market Access; lab NT/MA = mode 4 supply of services, National Treatment and Market Access; horiz = horizontal commitments; for all sectors, 1 = full commitment, 2 = 1–2 limitations, 3 = more than 3 limitations, 4 = unbound or very few commitments, NA = not available.

WAEMU (1994) abstains from detailed regulation – including schedules of individual liberalising commitments – but opens the market for trade liberalisation in services with relatively simple words, *WAEMU (1994)* can be considered a pioneer for creating a fully integrated single market for services.

II. GATS-Plus, GATS-Extra and GATS-Minus

Dihel, Eschenbach and Sheperd (2008) characterise the different levels of commitments in services trade liberalisation under the GATS as follows:[15]

> [. . .] least-developed countries [. . .] have on average made commitments in twenty-four sub-sectors and developing economies in forty-two sub-sectors [. . .]. By contrast, transition economies have made commitments in more sectors than even developed countries.

The following paragraphs look at the level of GATS-plus (GATS+) and GATS-extra (GATSx) commitments in South-South PTAs in services. GATS-plus is defined as commitments, which go beyond the commitments entered in the GATS schedule. GATS-extra are commitments in or related to trade in services, which go beyond the scope of regulation of the GATS. This may be for instance in the area of new technologies, in investment or in labour migration. As a preliminary analysis showed, the category of GATS-minus (GATS−) also needs to be introduced: GATS-minus are the PTAs, in which the schedules list less commitment than the members have listed under the GATS. Thus, these agreements would establish a lower level of liberalisation among its members in theory, while in practice the GATS commitments should prevail as a minimum standard.

The fact that a number of countries have entered into GATS-minus commitments in their PTAs in services has sparked a relatively recent discussion on the implications of such commitments. It is unclear whether the more recent, more specific provision in the PTA prevails over the commitments under GATS according to VCLT Art. 30 on successive treaties relating to the same subject matter. It is to be expected that among the members of a GATS-minus PTA in services, the GATS-minus level of liberalisation prevails in practice. However, the parties to such an agreement could file a complaint with the DSB against the party, which has only

[15] Dihel et al. (2008, p. 40).

offered GATS-minus commitments in the PTA, for not fulfilling the obligations under GATS. It would, thus, be possible to enforce the GATS level of liberalisation despite GATS-minus commitments in a PTA. However, this is of course rather theoretical since the members of a PTA are unlikely to be expected to file a complaint against each other on this basis.

It has been suggested that the GATS-minus level in the PTA may be closer to the openness of the services markets in practice, since it is well known that oftentimes GATS commitments only exist on paper and have not translated to liberalisation in practice.[16] Furthermore, the dispute settlement system of a PTA has to be taken into consideration: it only applies to commitments under the PTA. Thus, a violation of commitments outside the scope of the PTA cannot be claimed under the dispute settlement procedures of a PTA but would have to be brought to the WTO DSB. Possibly it is less likely that such a claim is filed with the WTO DSB than with the dispute settlement of the PTA. Filing GATS-minus commitments under the PTA may, thus, furthermore be related to a choice of fora.

Of the thirty substantial South-South PTAs in services in the dataset, six have not yet adopted a schedule of commitments.[17] These six agreements are not going beyond the level of GATS commitments and are, therefore, not of interest to this analysis. Furthermore, *WAEMU (1994)* establishes a single market for trade in services, while not providing for detailed regulation in the area of services trade regulation. It can be considered to be GATS-plus as a whole, while GATS-extra information may be rare. *WAEMU (1994)* will, therefore, only be discussed with reference to potential GATS-extra regulation. This leaves twenty-three South-South PTAs in services for the discussion of GATS-plus and GATS-extra commitments. In Table 14, the number of subsectors in which commitments are undertaken is compared with respect to GATS schedules and the schedules of PTAs (as available). While, particularly in the case of a negative list approach, the numbers of committed subsectors itself does not provide for a finite analysis of the scope of liberalisation, it nevertheless substantiates general tendencies and helps to identify the most interesting PTAs for a discussion in more detail.

A third of the here assessed substantial South-South PTAs establishes trade liberalisation in services exceeding the GATS level (GATS+).[18]

[16] Adlung and Miroudot (2012). [17] See Table 12 .

[18] Based on this assessment, the PTAs establishing trade liberalisation in services beyond GATS levels are *Chile – Mexico (1998)*, *Chile – Panama (2006)*, *Chile – Peru (2006)*,

Table 14 *Depth of overall liberalisation*[a]

Name of PTA	Countries	GATS	PTA	Evaluation
Costa Rica – Mexico (1994)	Costa Rica	23	100 (neg)	GATS
	Mexico	127	273 (neg)	GATS−
Colombia – Mexico (1994)	Colombia	150	72 (neg)	GATS+
	Mexico	127	134 (neg)	GATS
Chile – Mexico (1998)	Chile	86	75 (neg)	GATS+
	Mexico	127	75 (neg)	GATS+
Central America – Chile (1999)	Chile	86	70 (neg)	GATS+
	Costa Rica	23	97 (neg)	GATS−
	El Salvador	40	55 (neg)	GATS
	Guatemala	23	22 (neg)	GATS
	Honduras	22	90 (neg)	GATS−
Mexico – N. Triangle (2000)	El Salvador	40	61 (neg)	GATS−
	Honduras	22	104 (neg)	GATS−
	Guatemala	23	55 (neg)	GATS−
	Mexico	127	235 (neg)	GATS−
Central America – Panama (2002)	Costa Rica	23	75 (neg)	GATS−
	El Salvador	40	71 (neg)	GATS−
	Honduras	22	85 (neg)	GATS−
	Panama	94	76 (neg)	GATS+
India – Malaysia (2005)	India	42	91	GATS+
	Malaysia	157	121	GATS−
Chile – Colombia (2006)	Chile	86	69 (neg)	GATS+
	Colombia	150	102 (neg)	GATS
Chile – Panama (2006)	Chile	86	62 (neg)	GATS+
	Panama	94	68 (neg)	GATS+
Chile – Peru (2006)	Chile	86	69 (neg)	GATS+
	Peru	55	83 (neg)	GATS+
ASEAN – China (2007)	Brunei	28	4	GATS−
	Cambodia	93	115	GATS+
	Indonesia	79	20	GATS−
	Laos	72	10	GATS−
	Malaysia	157	44	GATS−
	Myanmar	5	11	GATS+
	Philippines	111	47	GATS−
	Singapore	79	84	GATS+
	Thailand	109	14	GATS−
	Vietnam	125	138	GATS+
	China	104	57	GATS−

(*cont.*)

Table 14 (*cont.*)

Name of PTA	Countries	GATS	PTA	Evaluation
Colombia – N. Triangle (2007)	Colombia	150	104 (neg)	GATS
	El Salvador	40	58 (neg)	GATS+
	Honduras	22	57 (neg)	GATS+
	Guatemala	23	26 (neg)	GATS+
Chile – China (2008)	Chile	86	80	GATS–
	China	104	66	GATS–
China – Pakistan (2009)	China	104	104	GATS
	Pakistan	63	152	GATS+
China – Peru (2009)	China	104	148	GATS+
	Peru	55	118	GATS+
EAC (2009)	Burundi	23	58	GATS+
	Kenya	56	52	GATS–
	Rwanda	7	59	GATS+
	Tanzania	1	32	GATS+
	Uganda	11	55	GATS+
China – Costa Rica (2010)	China	104	132	GATS+
	Costa Rica	23	52	GATS+
Mexico – Peru (2011)	Mexico	127	115 (neg)	GATS
	Peru	55	84 (neg)	GATS+
Panama – Peru (2011)	Panama	94	87 (neg)	GATS
	Peru	55	87 (neg)	GATS+

[a] Derived from dataset (estimation based on coding of commitments) and the WTO Integrated Trade Intelligence Portal (I-TIP) [Online], available at: http://i-tip.wto.org/services/. This is a general assessment and does not consider the listed scope of commitments, nor the listed numbers of services classification lists. A detailed analysis of the depth of commitments vis-à-vis GATS commitments would require a textual analysis of each commitment, along with a comparison of the listed services according to the relevant services classification list.

However, in another third, members have entered a lower level of liberalisation in their PTA schedules than under GATS (GATS–).[19] This

and *Colombia – Northern Triangle (2007)*, although these four agreements are based on a negative list approach which is difficult to compare with commitments under GATS (positive list approach), and *China – Peru (2009)*, *EAC (2009)* and *China – Costa Rica (2010)*.

19 Based on this assessment, the PTAs establishing less trade liberalisation in services than GATS across its members are *Costa Rica – Mexico (1994)*, *Central America – Chile (1999)*,

is surprising, given that the general level of liberalisation as established under the GATS is applicable to the members of these PTAs nevertheless, as they are all members of the WTO and multilaterally bound to the level entered in their GATS schedules. Thus, entering a lower level of liberalisation in the schedule of a PTA in services is generally of limited legal consequence.

In addition, an equally large number of PTAs comes along with schedules, which essentially copy the level of commitments under the GATS (GATS).[20] These PTAs, thus, create the general basis for substantial trade liberalisation on a preferential basis, but do not yet establish additional liberalisation to the one already implemented among the members of the PTA through the GATS commitments. The question that one wishes to find an answer to is, thus, why these countries decided to enter into a South-South PTA in services when finally they were not prepared to commit to additional liberalisation?

While the individual reasons that led to such a limited liberalising result may differ, it can generally be said that the inclusion of services trade regulation together with a schedule of commitments in a PTA, is – irrespective of the depth of liberalisation in the individual schedules – contributing to the convergence of markets, to transparency and to strengthening legal certainty. It is, thus, not entirely pointless to enter a copy of the GATS commitments in a PTA schedule.

The analysis also shows that GATS-extra commitments and regulation are rare among South-South PTAs in services. They are usually restricted to the definition of the objective of services trade liberalisation, to labour migration, investment, and in some unique cases, to new and modern services. The Table 15 illustrates the GATS-extra commitment that was discovered in the thirty South-South PTAs in the dataset.

In conclusion, the analysis of the general level of GATS-plus and GATS-extra commitments in South-South PTAs in services showed that only a limited number of the existing substantial South-South PTAs in services establish GATS-plus commitments, with just a handful of PTAs further establishing GATS-extra commitments. An equally large group of South-South PTAs in services is more or less restricted to the respective level of

Mexico – Northern Triangle (2000), *Central America – Panama (2002)*, *ASEAN – China (2007)* and *Chile – China (2008)*.

20 Based on this assessment, the PTAs remaining more or less on GATS level of market access and trade liberalisation in services are *Colombia – Mexico (1994)*, *India – Malaysia (2005)*, *Chile – Colombia (2006)*, *China – Pakistan (2009)*, *Mexico – Peru (2011)* and *Panama – Peru (2011)*.

Table 15 *GATS-extra commitments*[a]

Name of the PTA	GATSx commitment
WAEMU (1994)	Labour migration
CARICOM – Cuba (2000)	Computer services and entertainment
CARICOM revised (2001)	Labour migration, economic hardships
Chile – Colombia (2006)	E-commerce, labour migration, environment
ASEAN (2008)[b]	Mutual recognition agreements of professional certificates and diplomas, no services chapter
Colombia – Northern Triangle (2007)	E-commerce
EAC (2009)	Labour migration

[a] Derived from dataset.

[b] Not in the dataset, since *ASEAN (2008)* has not yet liberalised services trade.

liberalisation of its members under the GATS, or members even entered fewer commitments in trade liberalisation in services in the schedule of the PTA, than they did in their GATS schedule.

Thus, with the exception of the *WAEMU (1994)*, which refrained from regulating liberalising commitments through additional schedules, none of the other South-South PTAs in services is establishing a single market for services, or even abolishing substantially all the barriers to trade. Rather, South-South PTAs in services tend to provide a basis for a future single market, they provide for increased transparency in the area of services trade regulation and they contribute to the convergence of markets, if, however, not typically at high speed.

III. Sectors of Interest

Of particular interest are the commitments in the identified sectors of interest as established previously in Part II of this study. Economic and political theory suggests that in the context of a regional South-South PTA, in particular business and professional services, construction services and educational services are most suitable for preferential liberalisation. This is linked with the geographical proximity, the cultural ties, shared history and similar language. Of the thirty South-South PTAs in the dataset,

Table 16 *Fully liberalised sectors of interest*

Name of PTA	Sector(s) fully liberalised
Chile – Mexico (1998)	Construction, education
Central America – Chile (1999)	Financial services
Mexico – Northern Triangle (2000)	Education
Central America – Panama (2002)	Business and professional services, communication, education
Chile – Peru (2006)	Construction, education
China – Costa Rica (2010)	Construction
Panama – Peru (2011)	Construction

arguably the members of only five PTAs are not sufficiently closely related to suggest a specific focus on said sectors.[21]

Another group of sectors of particular interest is the group of services sectors, which are expected to yield the largest economic benefits when liberalised. Ideally, according to economic and political theory, these sectors should be fully liberalised unilaterally. Since developing countries are reluctant to fully liberalising services sectors unilaterally, given the potential social costs of such liberalisation and increasing competition, full liberalisation under the GATS is equally not the preferred avenue. However, in PTAs, particularly when the expected increasing competition is relatively limited considering the South-South context, theory of economic development strongly advocates full liberalisation in transportation, communication, financial services and business and professional services. These sectors are attributed with the greatest impact on economic growth and value-added production. Full liberalisation in these sectors is, thus, recommended for all South-South PTAs in the dataset.

Table 16 shows the PTAs and sectors of particular interest, which indeed are fully liberalised, both with respect to Market Access and National Treatment.[22]

[21] *Chile – China (2008)*, *Peru – China (2009)*, *ASEAN – China (2007)*, *China – Pakistan (2009)* and *Malaysia – Pakistan (2007)*. It is interesting to note that China is most active in promoting cross-cultural and cross-regional trade relations with other developing countries. Pakistan – considering also its limited number of PTAs in services – appears to be particularly open to cross-cultural and cross-regional services trade liberalisation, as well.

[22] See Part II of this thesis, Table 3.

Only seven out of thirty South-South PTAs in services open at least one services sector entirely. In these seven agreements, construction and education are the sectors, which are fully liberalised most of the times (each four times). Thus, if at all, developing countries seem to be most likely to open these two sectors entirely, while they tend to insist on a number of limitations in other sectors. It is interesting to note that one of the PTAs opening the construction sector entirely, is *China – Costa Rica (2010)*, a cross-continental and cross-cultural PTA. According to the economic and political theory, the focus of a cross-continental PTA would be expected to rest on other services sectors, which promise more economic growth and are not depending on regional proximity or local presence as much as construction.

The picture looks slightly different if full commitment in either Market Access or National Treatment (or both) is taken into account. Table 17 illustrates the PTAs and sectors of interest, in which at least one full commitment has been undertaken.[23]

Almost half of the thirty South-South PTAs in services (thirteen) indeed have entered at least one full commitment in either Market Access or National Treatment in one of the sectors of particular interest. The most liberal agreements are (a) *Mexico – Northern Triangle (2000)* with no limitations to Market Access in five out of six sectors of particular interest and to National Treatment in one out of six, (b) *Central America – Panama (2002)* with no limitations to either Market Access or National Treatment in three out of six sectors of particular interest and to Market Access in one additional one sector, and (c) *Chile – Peru (2006)* with two out of six sectors of particular interest which have no limitations in either Market Access or National Treatment and additional two sectors with no limitations in Market Access. This indicates that, overall, the Central and Latin American South-South PTAs in services tend to be most substantial.

On the other hand, however, none of the thirty South-South PTAs in the dataset opens all of the sectors of particular interest and, generally, liberalisation appears limited. While the sectors of construction and education services tend to rank highest in terms of level of liberalisation in South-South PTAs, financial services and transportation are at the lower end of liberalising commitments. Possibly, this could be an indicator for political objective of these PTAs: rather than using services trade liberalisation as a motor for economic growth, liberalisation of services trade

[23] See Part II of this study.

Table 17 *Full commitments to one or more sectors of interest*[a]

Name of PTA	Sector MA						Sector NT					
	Business and professional	Communication	Construction	Education	Financial services	Transportation	Business and professional	Communication	Construction	Education	Financial services	Transportation
Costa Rica – Mexico (1994)	X		X	X								
Chile – Mexico (1998)			X	X					X	X		
Central America – Chile (1999)			X		X						X	
Mexico – Northern Triangle (2000)	X	X	X	X		X				X		
Central America – Panama (2002)	X	X	X	X			X	X		X		
Chile – Colombia (2006)	X											
Chile – Panama (2006)			X									
Chile – Peru (2006)	X	X	X	X					X	X		
Colombia – Northern Triangle (2007)			X							X		
EAC (2009)							X					X
China – Costa Rica (2010)			X						X			
Mexico – Peru (2011)			X	X								
Panama – Peru (2011)			X	X					X			

[a] Derived from dataset.

Legend: MA = Market Access, NT = National Treatment, (none) = no limitations, **X** = full commitment in both MA and NT.

serves primarily the purpose of contributing to market integration in a South-South PTA in services. Since the two main sectors having experienced substantial liberalisation efforts in South-South PTAs, construction and education, are attributed with more suitability for preferential liberalisation than for multilateral liberalisation, arguably, countries choose to liberalise the sectors that are more suitable for multilateral liberalisation primarily under the GATS and in North-South PTAs.

In conclusion, even when looking at the level of the sectors of particular interest, generally, the depth of commitments is limited. While there seems to be a trend towards opening up the services sectors of construction and education, the results from the analysis of the dataset do not indicate a clear sectorial preference in South-South PTAs with respect to liberalising commitments in any of the six sectors of particular interest.

IV. Modes of Supply

According to Dihel, Eschenbach and Sheperd (2008), developing countries already commit to the least of all groups of countries under the GATS to trade liberalisation in mode 3 supply of services. Therefore, a particularly great potential for economic growth is seen in relaxing restrictions on foreign establishment.[24] They are in good company, as has been shown previously in Part II of this thesis. While mode 3 supply of services is attributed with particularly strong potential for fostering economic growth and it is equally well suited to any level of regulation, be it the bilateral, regional or multilateral level.[25]

GATS mode 3 supply of services, the right to establishment and investment protection and regulation are all closely linked. Since finance is key to economic growth in developing countries,[26] and, since particularly much potential for economic development is attributed to the liberalisation of mode 3 supply of services and investment in South-South PTAs, one might be tempted to expect particular openness in and a particular focus on mode 3 supply of services and the right to establishment.

In addition to mode 3 supply of services and investment, mode 4 supply of services is also attributed with a central role for economic development, in particular in a South-South context. It is both seen as an important

[24] Dihel et al. (2008, pp. 40, 72). [25] See Part II.

[26] See e.g. Hansen, Henrik and Rand, John (2006) 'On the Causal Links between FDI and Growth in Developing Countries', *The World Economy*, vol. 29, no. 1, pp. 21–41.

factor for economic growth, and as particularly suitable for preferential liberalisation.[27]

Table 18 provides an overview of the different commitments undertaken with respect to mode 3 and mode 4 supply of services South-South PTAs in services. It furthermore provides for general information on the regulatory structure and the depth of the commitments related to both mode 3 and mode 4 supply of services.

With respect mode 3 supply of services, the analysis generally shows a commitment to the right to establishment and mode 3 supply of services, along with investment regulation and protection in South-South PTAs in services. The majority of the South-South PTAs in services in the dataset provides for mode 3 supply of services (in seventeen PTAs it is included in the services chapter, and in eleven it is excluded from the services chapter, but included in the investment chapter). Primarily linked with the regulatory structure of the PTA – in particular if it is similar to the NAFTA model of PTAs in services – mode 3 supply is excluded from the scope of application of the services chapter in eleven South-South PTAs, but covered in the investment chapter. Six South-South PTAs in the dataset do not include an investment chapter in the same agreement. In these cases, mode 3 supply of services is included in the scope of application of the services chapter. Therewith, investment is also protected and regulated as long as it is related to the provision of services.

With respect to mode 4 supply of services, the temporary stay of service providers from one member in the territory of another member of a South-South PTA in services appears to be undisputed: twenty-eight out of thirty South-South PTAs in services provide in general for a commitment to mode 4 supply in services.[28] Even more so, sixteen South-South PTAs provide for GATS-extra commitments with respect to temporary labour migration, while five agreements go beyond GATS levels of commitment. Thus, evidence from the dataset suggests that at least with respect to mode 4 supply of services and the temporary labour migration, South-South PTAs tend to go substantially beyond their levels of commitment under the GATS.

This is further emphasised by the fact that, out of thirty South-South PTAs in services, twenty-six agreements include regulation on the mutual

[27] See Part II.

[28] The only two PTAs in the dataset, which do not provide for a clear commitment to mode 4 supply of services are *CARICOM Services (1997)*, which is a Stand-Still Agreement, and *CARICOM – Cuba (2000)*, which is a Cooperation Agreement.

Table 18 *Commitments made in mode 3 and mode 4 supply of services*[a]

PTA	type	inv-chap	mode 3	mode 4	move-plus	recogn
Bolivia – Mexico (1994)	NAFTA	incl	incl	allowed	extra	incl
Colombia – Mexico (1994)	GATS	incl	incl	allowed	extra	incl
Costa Rica – Mexico (1994)	NAFTA	incl	incl	allowed	plus	incl
WAEMU (1994)	Customs Union	incl	incl	allowed	extra	NA
CARICOM Services (1997)	Stand-still	no	NA	NA	NA	incl
MERCOSUR services (1997)	Protocol	no	incl	allowed	no	NA
Mexico – Nicaragua (1997)	GATS	incl	incl	allowed	extra	incl
Central America – DR (1998)	GATS	incl	incl	allowed	extra	incl
Chile – Mexico (1998)	NAFTA	incl	sep	allowed	plus	incl
Central America – Chile (1999)	NAFTA	incl	sep	allowed	extra	incl
CARICOM – Cuba (2000)	Cooperation	incl	NA	NA	no	NA
Mexico – Northern Triangle (2000)	NAFTA	incl	sep	allowed	plus	incl
CARICOM revised (2001)	EU/GATS	incl	incl	allowed	extra	incl
Central America – Panama (2002)	NAFTA	incl	sep	allowed	extra	incl
Mexico – Uruguay (2003)	NAFTA	incl	sep	allowed	extra	incl
India – Malaysia (2005)	GATS	incl	incl	allowed	no	incl
Chile – Colombia (2006)	NAFTA	incl	sep	allowed	extra	incl
Chile – Panama (2006)	NAFTA	incl	sep	allowed	no	incl
Chile – Peru (2006)	NAFTA	incl	sep	allowed	extra	incl
ASEAN – China (2007)	GATS	no	incl	allowed	no	incl
Colombia Northern – Triangle (2007)	NAFTA	incl	sep	allowed	extra	incl

Malaysia – Pakistan (2007)	GATS	incl	incl	allowed	no	incl
Chile – China (2008)	GATS	no	incl	allowed	no	incl
Chile – MERCOSUR (2009)	Protocol	no	incl	allowed	extra	incl
China – Pakistan (2009)	Protocol	no	incl	allowed	no	incl
China – Peru (2009)	GATS	incl	incl	allowed	plus	incl
EAC (2009)	Protocol	incl	incl	allowed	extra	NA
China – Costa Rica (2010)	GATS	incl	incl	allowed	plus	incl
Mexico – Peru (2011)	GATS	incl	sep	allowed	extra	incl
Panama – Peru (2011)	NAFTA	incl	sep	allowed	extra	incl

[a] Derived from dataset.

Legend: type = to what model-treaty does the PTA refer to?; inv-chap = is there a chapter on investment in the main treaty text?; mode 3 = is mode 3 supply of services included in the services chapter of the PTA?; mode 4 = is mode 4 supply of services allowed?; move-plus = do commitments in mode 4 supply of services go beyond GATS commitments? no = GATS level, plus = GATS-plus, extra = GATS-extra; recogn = does the PTA include regulation on mutual recognition of certificates and diplomas?

recognition of professional certificates and diplomas. With respect to the implementation of commitments in mode 4 supply of services, mutual recognition agreements are key: if professional certificates and diplomas are not mutually recognised, mode 4 supply of services can turn out to be facing considerable obstacles, and at times even be impossible to implement.[29] Thus, the inclusion of provisions on the mutual recognition of professional certificates and diplomas can serve as an indicator for the intended depth of liberalisation and implementation of commitments in practice.

Compared with the commitments in the sectors of particular interest, commitments in the modes of supply of particular interest appear to be closer aligned with economic and political theory. In particular with respect to commitments in mode 4 supply of services, South-South PTAs in services can generally be characterised as going substantially beyond GATS levels of commitments, at times even introducing new regulation. Arguably, the commitment to mode 4 supply of services in South-South PTAs in services is a stronger one, than can generally be found in North-South PTAs in services and even in North-North PTAs in services.

Liberalisation in mode 3 supply and investment in South-South PTAs generally appears to be relevant and important, given that the majority of the agreements in the dataset cover them. However, since political and economic theory particularly encourages South-South mode 3 supply of services and liberalisation of FDI, the overall commitments are nevertheless lagging slightly behind the recommended levels.

V. Compliance with GATS

As has been discussed in detail previously, parallel to GATT Art. XXIV, GATS Art. V is generally perceived as ill-equipped to enforce compliance, and compliance with both provisions is generally perceived as low. One of the reasons for the low compliance with both GATT Art. XXIV and GATS Art. V is seen in the institutional setting of the WTO, and the requirement of consensus among all members for any action taken by the WTO.[30] Thus, a country that violates its commitments under GATT Art. XXIV or GATS Art. V can veto actions taken against itself. Furthermore, since

[29] Related, see Nicolaïdis, Kalypso and Schmidt Susanne, K. (2007) 'Mutual Recognition "on trial": The long Road to Services Liberalisation', *Journal of European Public Policy*, vol. 14, no. 5, pp. 717–734.

[30] Picker (2005, p. 282).

most members of the WTO are a party to a partially compliant PTA in services, it is not in their interest to criticise others, since they may have done more or less the same themselves.[31]

As has further been shown previously, the scope of flexibility in GATS Art. V for South-South PTAs remains unclear and requires legal interpretation. Therefore, the legal analysis of the compatibility of the South-South PTAs in services in the dataset with the requirements of GATS Art. V foremost emphasises one factor: the scope of flexibility for South-South PTAs in services is not yet fathomed.

Table 19 shows the general level of compliance with the requirements of GATS Art. V, based on what the South-South PTAs in services generally provide for.

If GATS Art. V was read from a positivist approach, it would normally require that all sectors are covered by the agreement, as well as all modes of supply, and that services sectors are basically fully liberalised (GATS Art. V:1). Arguably, it establishes the requirement to grant MFN to the members of the PTA (see *Canada – Autos*, Report of the Panel)[32] and with respect to the overall depth of liberalisation, PTAs in services have to be at least GATS+ (GATS Art. V:1, including Footnote). If a reference to GATS Art. V is included in the PTA, this can be interpreted as an indicator of the willingness to comply with GATS Art. V, since, according to VCLT Art. 30:2 such a reference introduces the superiority of the GATS over the subsequent PTA in services.[33]

The general results from the analysis of the South-South PTAs in services are more or less in line with findings of other scholars, which have looked at North-South or North-North PTAs in services. PTAs in services have been found to rarely go substantially beyond the level of GATS commitments,[34] oftentimes they even turned out to be GATS–,[35] and overall, they are generally not considered fit to pass a strict application of the requirements of GATS Art. V. Surprisingly enough, however, South-South PTAs in services tend to be slightly more compliant with GATS

31 See the discussion in more detail in Part II.

32 The Appellate Body did not elaborate on this aspect of the Report of the Panel. The finding of the Panel may, therefore, be disputable, see *Canada – Autos*, WT/DS 139 (11 February 2000), Report of the Panel, para. 10.270.

33 VCLT Art. 30:2 says: When a treaty specifies that it is subject to, or that it is not to be considered as incompatible with, an earlier or later treaty, the provisions of that other treaty prevail.

34 See e.g. Roy, Marchetti and Lim (2007).

35 See e.g. Adlung and Miroudot (2012).

Table 19 *Level of compliance with GATS Art. V requirements*[a]

PTA	MFN	Modes covered	Sectors covered	Depth of lib	NT	Sectors full lib	GATS ref
Bolivia – Mexico (1994)	X	all	11	GATS+	X	none	X
Colombia – Mexico (1994)	X	all	NA	GATS	X	none	no
Costa Rica – Mexico (1994)	X	all	all	GATS–	X	none	X
WAEMU (1994)	no	all	NA	NA	X	none	no
CARICOM Services (1997)	no	NA	NA	NA	X	none	no
MERCOSUR Services (1997)	X	all	7	NA	X	none	X
Mexico – Nicaragua (1997)	X	all	NA	NA	X	none	X
Central America – DR (1998)	X	all	all	NA	X	none	X
Chile – Mexico (1998)	X	all	all	GATS+	X	2	X
Central America – Chile (1999)	X	all	all	GATS–	X	1	X
CARICOM – Cuba (2000)	X	NA	8	NA	no	none	X
Mexico – Northern Triangle (2000)	X	all	all	GATS–	X	1	X
CARICOM revised (2001)	X	all	NA	NA	X	none	X
Central America – Panama (2002)	X	all	all	GATS–	X	3	X
Mexico – Uruguay (2003)	X	all	all	NA	X	none	X
India – Malaysia (2005)	X	all	11	GATS	X	none	X
Chile – Colombia (2006)	X	all	all	GATS	X	none	X
Chile – Panama (2006)	X	all	all	GATS+	X	none	X
Chile – Peru (2006)	X	all	all	GATS+	X	2	X
ASEAN – China (2007)	no	all	11	GATS–	X	none	X
Colombia – Northern Triangle (2007)	X	all	all	GATS+	X	none	X

Malaysia – Pakistan (2007)	X	all	11	GATS+	X	none	X
Chile – China (2008)	no	all	8	GATS	X	none	X
Chile – MERCOSUR (2009)	no	all	7	NA	X	none	X
China – Pakistan (2009)	no	all	11	GATS	X	none	X
China – Peru (2009)	no	all	11	GATS+	X	none	X
EAC (2009)	X	all	7	GATS+	X	none	no
China – Costa Rica (2010)	no	all	10	GATS+	X	1	X
Mexico – Peru (2011)	X	all	all	GATS	X	none	X
Panama – Peru (2011)	X	all	all	GATS	X	1	X

[a] Derived from dataset.

Legend: MFN = does the PTA provide for MFN treatment?; modes = covered no. of modes of supply covered by the PTA; sectors covered = no. of services sectors covered by the PTA; depth of lib = how deep is the general level of liberalisation? See Table 14); NT does the PTA provide for National Treatment?; sectors full lib = no. of sectors which are fully liberalised in the PTA (See Table 16); GATS ref = does the PTA refer to the GATS?; NA = information not available.

Art. V overall than other PTAs are: most of the South-South PTAs cover almost all sectors, all but one provide for National Treatment in general, basically all of them cover all modes of supply, and fourteen out of twenty-three analysed treaties are considered to be GATS+ with respect to the overall depth of liberalisation.

Nevertheless, a strictly positivist interpretation of the requirements of GATS Art. V to the South-South PTAs in services in the dataset would mean that a number of them would not turn out to be in compliance with WTO law. The main stumbling block in this respect is the number of sectors covered by the agreement, and the overall depth of liberalisation. Since GATS Art. V does not explicitly require MFN treatment among the parties to a PTA in services, the fact that a number of South-South PTAs in services does not provide for MFN treatment can be ignored for the time being. Based on a narrow interpretation, excluding services sectors from the scope of application of a PTA is only to the extent possible, that no major trade-flows are concerned, and that the number of services sectors excluded is not more than two (see also *Turkey – Textiles*).[36] If sectors are not yet fully liberalised, this can be balanced by the flexibility in GATS Art. V:1, which provides for a reasonable time frame for the implementation of the requirements, in particular in a South-South context. Thus, a South-South PTA arguably still complies with WTO law, even if services market integration is not yet fully established, as long as subsequent rounds of negotiations on liberalisation are planned.

Table 20 shows the PTAs, which would not comply with the requirements of GATS Art. V, if the flexibility in the provision was to be interpreted narrowly, the PTAs, which arguably comply with WTO law, as well as the PTAs, for which compliance is unclear.

The analysis shows that not even a third of the South-South PTAs in services in the dataset complies with the requirements as established by GATS Art. V, even if a generous – unlimited – time frame for the implementation of the requirements is taken into account.[37] An additional three PTAs would furthermore no longer qualify as "WTO-compliant", if the requirement to provide for MFN treatment in a PTA was taken into

[36] *Turkey – Textiles* WT/DS34/AB/R (22 October 1999), Report of the Appellate Body, para. 48.

[37] This analysis is based on the previously established 'medium legal interpretation' of the scope of flexibility for South-South PTAs, see Part IV.

Table 20 *PTAs not complying with narrow interpretation of GATS Art. 5*[a]

PTA	Non-compliance
Costa Rica – Mexico (1994)	Not more than GATS, no fully liberalised sector
MERCOSUR services (1997)	Only seven sectors covered, no fully liberalised sector
Central America – Chile (1999)	Not more than GATS
CARICOM – Cuba (2000)	Only eight sectors covered, no fully liberalised sector, no general National Treatment
Mexico – Northern Triangle (2000)	Less than GATS
Central America – Panama (2002)	Less than GATS
India – Malaysia (2005)	Not more than GATS, no fully liberalised sector
Chile – China (2008)	Less than GATS, only eight sectors covered, no fully liberalised sector
Chile – MERCOSUR (2009)	Not more than GATS, only seven sectors covered, no fully liberalised sector
China – Peru (2009)	Not more than GATS, no fully liberalised sector
EAC (2009)	Not more than GATS, only seven sectors covered, not fully liberalised sector
PTA	**Compliance**
Bolivia – Mexico (1994)	More than GATS, eleven sectors covered, deeper integration planned
Chile – Mexico (1998)	More than GATS, all sectors covered, two fully liberalised sectors, deeper integration planned
Chile – Panama (2006)	More than GATS, all sectors covered, deeper integration planned
Chile – Peru (2006)	More than GATS, all sectors covered, two fully liberalised sectors, deeper integration planned
ASEAN – China (2007)	More than GATS, eleven sectors covered, deeper integration planned
Malaysia – Pakistan (2007)	More than GATS, eleven sectors covered, deeper integration planned
China – Pakistan (2009)	More than GATS, eleven sectors covered, deeper integration planned

(*cont.*)

Table 20 *(cont.)*

PTA	Compliance
China – Costa Rica (2010)	More than GATS, ten sectors covered, one fully liberalised sector, deeper integration planned
Panama – Peru (2011)	More than GATS, all sectors covered, one sector fully liberalised, deeper integration planned
PTA	**Unclear**
Colombia – Mexico (1994)	Unknown covered sectors
WAEMU (1994)	Unknown covered sectors, unknown depth of commitments
CARICOM Services (1997)	Unknown covered modes of supply and sectors, unknown depth of commitments
Mexico – Nicaragua (1997)	Unknown covered sectors, unknown depth of commitments
Central America – DR (1998)	Unknown depth of commitments
CARICOM revised (2001)	Unknown covered sectors, unknown depth of commitments
Mexico – Uruguay (2003)	Unknown depth of commitments
Chile – Colombia (2006)	More than GATS, all sectors covered, but no deeper integration planned
Colombia – Northern Triangle (2007)	More than GATS, all sectors covered, but no deeper integration planned
Mexico – Peru (2011)	More than GATS, all sectors covered, but no deeper integration planned

[a] Derived from dataset, GATS Art. V.

consideration, since the majority of the Chinese South-South PTAs in services does not provide for MFN treatment.[38]

Turning to the suggested broad legal interpretation of the scope of flexibility in GATS Art. V for South-South PTAs, which is linked with SDT and graduation theory,[39] evidence from the analysis of the South-South

[38] *ASEAN – China (2007)*, *China – Pakistan (2009)* and *Costa Rica – China (2010)* would no longer comply with GATS Art. V if the MFN requirement is considered to be inherent in GATS Art. V.

[39] See previously.

PTAs in services in the dataset shows a more differentiated picture. Based on the broad interpretation, in a South-South context, flexibility can be provided for sectorial agreements, which fully liberalise sectors of particular interest for preferential agreements and relevance for the overall expected economic impact. There are two South-South PTAs in services in the dataset, which show particular similarities with the suggested interpretation of the scope of flexibility: *Mexico – Northern Triangle (2000)* and *Central America – Panama (2002)*.

Mexico – Northern Triangle (2000) covers basically all sectors and all modes of supply, while it fully liberalises education services. The overall assessment of the depth of commitments turns out to be GATS-minus. Thus, arguably, the main focus of the agreement is on education services, which indeed is fully liberalised. Based on the broad interpretation, this would not necessarily qualify as a violation of GATS commitments: it is unlikely that the full liberalisation of education services in the context of *Mexico – Northern Triangle (2000)* will distort competition on the global market for education services. Furthermore, since education services are particularly suitable for preferential liberalisation, and since subsequent rounds of liberalisation are planned in *Mexico – Northern Triangle (2000)*, the market integration in education services arguably serves the purpose of strengthening education services among the members, and of facilitating future liberalisation in services trade. Even though the PTA is not labelled as such, *Mexico – Northern Triangle (2000)* could, thus, *de facto* be considered a partially sectorial PTA in services.

Even more distinct is *Central America – Panama (2002)*. The agreement liberalises business and professional services, communication services and education services fully, while the overall assessment of the depth of commitments turns out to be GATS-minus. Arguably, in other sectors, members have only entered limited commitments, even below GATS levels of commitments. Thus, the focus of *Central America – Panama (2002)* appears to be on market integration in three services sectors. All of the sectors fully liberalised in the agreement are attributed with a high potential of fostering economic growth in developing countries, and with particular suitability for preferential liberalisation. Thus, from a policy perspective, the choice of sectors, which are fully liberalised, can be justified with the objective of promoting economic growth. Furthermore, it is unlikely that liberalising business and professional services, communication services and education services in the context of *Central America – Panama (2002)* will develop a distorting impact on the global market of these services. Both aspects would on the one hand justify compatibility with WTO law under the broad interpretation of the legal scope of flexibility in GATS Art. V, and on the other hand suggest that *Central America – Panama (2002)* is in fact a partially sectorial agreement, with a particular focus on three services sectors.

There are a number of additional South-South PTAs in services in the dataset, which demonstrate a particular focus on a limited number of fully liberalised services sectors.[40] While the contrast between fully liberalised sectors and the overall depth of commitments is less stark, arguably these PTAs potentially also qualify as partially sectorial agreements, depending on the intent of their members.

In conclusion, while the general compliance with the requirements of GATS Art. V appears to be similarly unambitious in a South-South context to the level of compliance in North-South or North-North PTAs, South-South PTAs generally tend to be broad in coverage. Under none of the suggested interpretations of the legal scope of flexibility for South-South PTAs in services in GATS Art. V would all of the PTAs in the dataset comply with WTO law. However, since a limited number of PTAs shows a particular focus on a limited number of fully liberalised services sectors, arguably there are *de facto* partially sectorial South-South PTAs in services already in place today.

VI. Implementation of GATS Art. V Requirements

The analysis of the level of compliance – also of other studies[41] – shows that PTAs in services do not generally provide for actual market integration in services trade. Rather, they tend to go to a differing degree beyond the liberalising commitments of the GATS, but do not fully liberalise trade in services. Thus, generally, the requirement of covering substantially all the trade in a PTA as established in GATS Art. V:1, while also eliminating substantially all discrimination, is generally only to a limited degree complied with.

On the other hand, analysis also shows that PTAs in services generally tend to be broad in coverage and that generally most or all services sectors are covered, as well as all of the modes of supply. Thus, these requirements as established in GATS Art. V:1 are generally well implemented in IEL.

[40] See previously.

[41] See Evans et al. (2006); Marchetti and Roy (2008); Chanda, Rupa (2011) Mapping the Universe of Services Disciplines in Asian PTAs, Working Paper No. 2011/33, NCCR trade regulation, Bern.

This is interesting, because it points to another aspect related to the implementation of the requirements of GATS Art. V: the general structure and regulatory scope of the GATS as a whole are well acknowledged and oftentimes copied in PTAs in services. The fear that the regulatory impact of the GATS may diminish over time by large numbers of PTAs, which do not fully comply with GATS Art. V, appears, therefore, to be less substantiated.

It has to be taken into consideration that the GATS is the first agreement worldwide which introduced coherent, substantial and encompassing regulation of services trade. Given that the GATS has been criticised strongly in recent years for not achieving all its objectives,[42] it is all the more important to point out that the regulatory framework of trade in services as established by the GATS has not yet been replaced by a different scheme.

While there are different models with respect to the structure of services trade regulation – such as the GATS model and the NAFTA model or the newer EU model – differences in regulation are minor and rather a structural question, than a systemic one. South-South PTAs tend to be more or less equally spread to both the GATS model and the NAFTA model. To date, the newer EU model, which separates both the regulation of mode 3 supply of services and mode 4 supply of services from the services chapter, has not yet been copied in a South-South PTA in services.

Furthermore, while there have been calls for a fifth mode of supply in order to better capture services that are inherent in the process of the production of a good,[43] PTAs in general, but also South-South PTAs in particular are not (yet) introducing regulatory inventions in the field of services trade regulation. Thus, the GATS in general and with it GATS Art. V can be considered to be generally well implemented in IEL.

On the other hand, however, it is striking that from a strictly legal perspective, few PTAs worldwide do comply with all the requirements of GATS Art. V. From this study and others, a general consensus on the scope of the requirements of GATS Art. V appears to emerge: WTO members expect from a PTA in services that it covers more or less all services sectors and all modes of supply while establishing a deeper level of liberalisation than the GATS (GATS+). This emerging consensus may not be entirely in line with the scope of the legal provisions in GATS Art. V, but since it

[42] See, e.g. Kelsey, Jane (2003) 'Legal Fetishism and the Contradictions of the GATS', *Globalisation, Societies and Education*, vol. 1, no. 3, pp. 267–280.

[43] See Cernat and Kutlina-Dimitrova (2014).

seems to reflect a generally accepted interpretation of the requirements for an MFN exemption under GATS, arguably it is the most realistic interpretation.

However, while a consensus emerges on the scope of the requirements of GATS Art. V, there is little evidence of an emerging consensus with respect to the flexibilities as established in GATS Art. V. This is particularly regrettable with respect to South-South PTAs in services, since the scope of flexibilities is potentially larger for developing countries and LDCs than generally known. Clarification on the scope of flexibility would empower developing countries to enter into more tailor-made PTAs in services, which are actually capable of delivering the intended policy goals.

One way of promoting clarification of the scope of flexibilities for South-South PTAs would be in actually establishing South-South PTAs that are based on a possible interpretation of the scope of flexibilities. Through fathoming of the scope of flexibilities, a new consensus could be achieved with other countries following or protesting. While this study has shown some rather hidden examples of a potential fathoming of the flexibilities for South-South PTAs in GATS Art. V, these remain isolated cases and South-South PTAs in general do not appear to be more welcoming to regulatory experiments than other PTAs in services are.

In conclusion, while there is a general consensus emerging with respect to the scope of the requirements in GATS Art. V, this study did not discover evidence of an emerging consensus on the scope of flexibilities for South-South PTAs in services. This is regrettable, since the requirements for South-South PTAs in services ought to be less strict than for other PTAs in services. But since the degree of relaxation with respect to the requirements in GATS Art. V for South-South PTAs in services remains unclear, developing countries and LDCs may remain reluctant to fully make use of the potential for economic development slumbering in tailor-made South-South PTAs in services.

VII. Implications for the Scope of GATS Art. V

While the requirements as established in GATS Art. V:1 appear to be generally agreed upon and PTAs appear to generally attempt to comply with the emerging consensus, the scope of flexibilities for South-South PTAs – and therewith the minimal requirements for a South-South PTA – remains unclear. South-South PTAs are widely disregarding the potential of additional flexibilities with respect to the compliance with GATS Art. V requirements.

This study showed that South-South PTAs are to a similar degree complying with GATS Art. V as are other PTAs. Thus, the flexibilities as they are clearly stated in GATS Art. V:1 and GATS Art. V:3 are not implemented in practice. This may have a number of reasons, which for the moment can only be guessed: developing countries may not be aware of the flexibilities, or they may not trust them; such flexibilities may not be desired by developing countries; or, they may not be necessary since PTAs in services are not expected to actually deliver an impact on trade-flows.

If developing countries intended to fully integrate their services markets, they could already have done so under the relatively uncertain regime by GATS Art. V requirements. However, none of the analysed South-South PTAs does endeavour to do so. Thus, the scope of flexibilities becomes more relevant, all the more since a few South-South PTAs *de facto* establish quasi-sectorial agreements by fully liberalising a strongly limited number of services sectors while leaving the level of liberalisation in other sectors more or less at the GATS level.

The legal analysis has furthermore shown that economic and political theory on the potential of economic development in South-South PTAs in services is not widely mirrored in the agreements. At this stage, it is only possible to provide guesswork on the reasons for the discrepancy between economic and political theory and the *de facto* structure and scope of South-South PTAs in services. What appears safe to say, however, is that given the discrepancy between theory of economic development and *de facto* legal reality in South-South PTAs in services, it is unlikely that these agreements will indeed promote economic development as predicted by economic theory.[44]

It is important to point out that LDCs are only to a limited degree engaged in South-South PTAs in services. Since poverty is most fundamental in LDCs, improving the income of the people living in LDCs is key. The reasons for sluggish economic development in LDCs cited by Lee (2011) are all related in one way or another to the services sector:[45]

> Poor social and industrial infrastructure, insufficient capital and low levels of technology, low literacy and education levels, lack of entrepreneurship and management expertise, insufficient political leadership for economic

[44] See also Dihel, Eschenbach and Sheperd (2008, p. 73), where they state: 'The impact of lifting restrictions on performance may increase more than proportionally with the scale of the liberalisation measure. This may mean that moderate liberalisation is not enough to achieve an impact on performance if the initial degree of restrictiveness is high'.

[45] Lee (2011a, pp. 10–11).

> development coupled with political instability, corruption and weak government institutions with absence of effective administrative support, and even some cultural issues that are deterrents to economic development.

Therefore, it appears all the more regrettable that only a handful of LDCs are engaged in South-South trade liberalisation in services today. Since, economic and political theory as cited in this study is not taking into account the particular circumstances and conditions for trade in services in LDCs, the same theory, which tends to hold true for developing countries in general, may not apply to some LDCs.

However, while this study shows the importance of clarification with respect to the scope of flexibilities in GATS Art. V for South-South PTAs, neither the legal analysis nor the analysis of the South-South PTAs in services in the dataset provides for a reliable indicator. Since this question is related to the general discussion on the modernisation of SDT, the role of developing countries in the WTO and the role of WTO law in IEL, clarification with respect to the scope of flexibilities for South-South PTAs in services may be found if these larger questions are tackled by the members of the WTO first.

VIII. Lessons to be Learned

One problem of both GATT Art. XXIV and GATS Art. V is their focus on the economic implications of PTAs while more or less neglecting the impact of PTAs on the institutional logic of IEL.[46] Not only does their focus on the economic implications cause difficulties in establishing whether a violation has occurred, it also renders the WTO toothless when aiming at invigorating the inner systemic logic of IEL as – at least in theory – embodied in GATT Art. XXIV and GATS Art. V.

On the other hand, the focus on the economic implications arguably leaves more scope of flexibility for PTAs in general and South-South PTAs in particular: it may be more of a challenge to prove that not 'substantially all the trade' is covered by a PTA, than it would be to show that, e.g. MFN treatment is missing. Thus, the focus on economic implications contributes to a more flexible interpretation of the requirements established by both GATT Art. XXIV and GATS Art. V.

It is of course true that we are closing in on a so-called spaghetti-bowl effect with respect to PTAs in services. The risk of overlapping and

[46] See also Picker (2005, p. 284).

contradictory commitments and regulation in services trade has increased overtime.[47] Since it is essentially in the interest of any country involved in preferential services trade that the liberalising commitments remain meaningful and enforceable, given time, history suggests that the current cobweb will most likely create an incentive to return to a plurilateral or multilateral forum in order to re-establish regulatory coherence.[48] The law in practice – particular international law – is essentially what states are prepared to do with it. Since the emerging consensus on the requirements of GATS Art. V is only to the extent of the depth of commitments not fully in line with the law, there is little evidence of WTO members being prepared to leave the regulatory realms of the GATS.

However, the focus on economic implications of PTAs in both GATT Art. XXIV and GATS Art. V suggests that in particular the economic implications in the context of South-South PTAs should also be taken into account. Regrettably, the scope of flexibility for developing countries and LDCs with respect to the conclusion of PTAs has not yet been clarified. Given the economic focus, the answer to this question may be linked with ideas stemming from the graduation theory: graduation theory essentially links flexibility to the level of economic development in a country.[49]

This takes the specific discussion on the flexibilities in GATS Art. V for South-South PTAs in services to a higher level: since SDT in other areas of trade law and the system of flexibilities in the GATS appear to be more and more inefficient, a new, more modern system may be required. After all, one of the key issues in the Doha Round is related to the role of developing countries and LDCs in the WTO. Quite clearly, the WTO requires a new consensus with respect to the flexibilities for developing countries and LDCs in order to revive multilateral negotiations. This need is further substantiated by the study on the flexibilities in GATS Art. V for South-South PTAs, which has shown that the scope of flexibilities remains unknown.

The need for more efficient and meaningful SDT also stems from the current emergence of the so-called mega-regionals, the plurilateral agreements between either two or more major economic blocs[50] or a large number of countries.[51] Those agreements are based on a negotiating mandate, which covers regulatory convergence and substantial trade

[47] Agu (2009). [48] See Cottier et al. (2015). [49] See previously, Foundations.

[50] In 2015, these are the Transpacific Partnership (TPP) and the Transatlantic Trade and Investment Partnership (TTIP).

[51] In 2015, this is the Trade in Services Agreement (TiSA).

liberalisation. They have the economic weight and geographic scope – if successfully concluded – to introduce new, quasi-global standards. In third countries, these mega-regionals will harm economic growth through trade-diversion linked with discriminatory tariffs, and discriminatory rules of origin. Should they succeed in establishing new emerging global standards, however, the mega-regionals will create substantial economic opportunities through spill-over effects for third countries, which are able to adopt these standards.

Thus, mega-regionals are doubly threatening to economic growth in developing countries and LDCs: (1) they will inevitably suffer from trade diversion as will all other third countries and (2) they might not be able to adopt the new emerging standards, and therewith not be able to compensate trade diversion with spill-over effects – to the contrary of other third countries, which will gain from spill-over effects. The gap between the richest and the poorest WTO members is therefore likely to increase as a consequence of the mega-regionals.[52] Developing countries are, thus, well advised in investigating new approaches to a modernisation of SDT, which links flexibilities to individual levels of economic development and helps to counteract the economic disadvantages linked with mega-regionals. The here proposed large scope of flexibility in GATS Art. V could be such a possible approach.

IX. Innovation in South-South Agreements

Because of their integrative approach and particularly when a negative list approach is chosen, (1) PTAs ought to be more transparent than the GATS;[53] (2) if a system to guarantee the implementation of the commitments is established, the enforcement of commitments ought to be more feasible for developing countries than it is through the WTO system of dispute settlement;[54] and (3) finally, the greater ease and ability to arrive at consensus in a smaller group of countries[55] ought to allow for more innovative regulation.

Nevertheless, as previous analysis showed, regulatory innovations are scarce in South-South PTAs in services. And this is the case despite the fact that there are a number of regulatory innovations in services trade

[52] For a comprehensive discussion of trade diversion and spill-over effects in TTIP, see Sieber-Gasser, Charlotte (2016).

[53] Stephenson (2001, p. 21).

[54] See Van der Borght (1999).

[55] Stephenson (2001, pp. 32–34).

regulation that could be tested in a PTA. Such are: (a) more transparency through abstaining from annexes and schedules, e.g. by regulating all commitments in the main treaty text, (b) more coherence through regulating non-tariff barriers to trade in both goods and services in the same chapter, (c) introducing a separate chapter on value-added production or (d) introducing a definition of 'services trade', which clearly defines how services provided during the production process of a good should be treated. Furthermore, new services sectors related to technological advancement could be introduced, as well as services provided by low-skilled labour.

On the plurilateral level, a potentially innovative initiative for the future regulation of services trade is under way, the Trade in Services Agreement (TiSA).[56] A number of developing countries are part of the coalition, which is negotiating TiSA.[57] Since, however, negotiations are taking place behind 'closed doors', no documents on the regulatory structure and content of the negotiations are yet available. Thus, at this point, no reliable predictions on the regulatory innovation promoted by TiSA can be made.

This is similarly the case for the TPP and the TTIP. If in the services chapters of those two mega-regionals regulatory innovation is introduced, it is likely that this will spread to other countries over time. From what is known to date, the future of services trade liberalisation and regulation is likely to be structured in an – arguably – more transparent manner and divided into separate chapters (modes 3 and 4 supply of services and financial services and other key services sectors in separate chapters in the main treaty text). Furthermore, the negative list approach along with a number of minor amendments to the rules of scheduling commitments appear to be the new basic approach to services trade liberalization. None of these regulatory innovations departs entirely from the basic regulatory concept of GATS. Given that the main negotiating partners in both negotiations are also part of the TiSA negotiations, and given that neither the EU nor the US were particularly innovative in the past with respect to services trade regulation, it is rather unlikely that the TPP or the TTIP will introduce substantial new regulation in the area of services trade.[58]

[56] See [Online] https://servicescoalition.org/negotiations/trade-in-services-agreement (last visited 7 April 2014).

[57] In April 2014, these are Chile, Colombia, Costa Rica, Mexico, Pakistan, Panama, Paraguay, Peru and Turkey.

[58] See also Cottier et al. (2014, pp. 50–71).

Thus, rather than on the pluri- or multilateral level, regulatory innovation in services trade may continue to evolve rather on a unilateral basis or domestically and subsequently translate into PTAs. As it looks, it is rather unlikely that South-South PTAs in services will become the main birthplace of innovative initiatives in services trade regulation.

A. *GATS-Extra: Emerging Patterns*

Regulatory innovation is most likely to be found in the main treaty text, since this is binding for all members of a PTA, while commitments in the schedule or annex are only binding for one member. While many South-South PTAs in the dataset include a separate paragraph or even sub-chapter on one or two services sectors in the main treaty text,[59] four agreements in the dataset introduce a new chapter on services trade-related issues. These additional chapters are therefore interesting, because they are *per se* GATSx, notwithstanding their actual scope and regulatory structure.

CARICOM – Cuba (2000) introduces separate sub-chapters on computer services and entertainment services. *CARICOM revised (2001)* includes a separate provision on economic hardships and on labour migration. *Chile – Colombia (2006)* has separate sub-chapters on e-commerce, labour migration and environment. And *Colombia – Northern Triangle (2007)* also introduces a separate sub-chapter on e-commerce. Furthermore, *WAEMU (1994)* and *EAC (2009)* both establish provisions on labour migration. Finally, *ASEAN – China (2007)* provides for limited commitments in mode 4 supply of service, but builds on a considerably large body of mutual recognition agreements of professional certificates and diplomas.

Therefore, the additional provisions in the main treaty text on specific services sectors and modes of supply deserve closer attention. Of the six services sectors of particular interest, in four sectors additional provisions have been entered in the main treaty text. Table 21 illustrates the South-South PTAs, which provide for more specific regulation for at least one of the six services sectors of particular interest, and/or for mode 4 supply of services.

[59] Out of the thirty South-South PTAs in services in the dataset, twenty agreements provide for additional provisions on one or more services sectors or modes of supply in the main treaty text.

Table 21 *Agreements with specific regulation for sectors of interest or mode 4 supply*[a]

PTA	Business and professional services	Communication	Financial services	Transportation	Mode 4 supply
Bolivia – Mexico (1994)	X	X	X		X
Colombia – Mexico (1994)	X	X	X	X	X
Costa Rica – Mexico (1994)	X				
WAEMU (1994)					X
Mexico – Nicaragua (1997)		X	X		X
Central America – DR (1998)	X				X
Chile – Mexico (1998)	X	X		X	
Central America – Chile (1999)	X	X		X	X
Mexico – Northern Triangle (2000)		X	X		
CARICOM revised (2001)					X
Central America – Panama (2002)		X	X	X	X
Mexico – Uruguay (2003)	X	X			X
India – Malaysia (2005)			X		
Chile – Colombia (2006)	X				X
Chile – Peru (2006)	X				X
Colombia – Northern Triangle (2007)	X			X	X
Chile – MERCOSUR (2009)					X
EAC (2009)					X
Mexico – Peru (2011)	X		X		X
Panama – Peru (2011)	X	X	X		X
20 PTAs	***12***	***9***	***8***	***5***	***16***

[a] Derived from dataset.

Table 21 shows that most clarifications in South-South PTAs in the main treaty text are to be found with respect to mode 4 supply of services. Closely related are the provisions on business and professional services, because the provision of these services oftentimes depends on mode 4 supply of services. Communication and financial services are furthermore more specifically regulated in the main treaty text, while Transportation only appears as a separate sub-chapter in five out of thirty South-South PTAs in services.

Analysis of the chapters shows, however, little innovation. Arguably, the separate provisions in the main treaty text are rather considered to be serving the establishment of binding commitments for all parties to the agreement, than a means of developing new regulation. Also with respect to the regulation of computer services, e-commerce and entertainment, South-South PTAs in services are merely copying other agreements and are not yet endeavouring into the development of new regulation.

But, there are two exceptions to this rule: the provisions relating to labour migration in *CARICOM revised (2001)* and the structure of indirect mode 4 supply of services in *ASEAN (2008)*. In *CARICOM revised (2001)* a form of free movement of persons is introduced, which initially was provided to a relatively limited group of skilled people, and has been extended to other groups of people through successive rounds of negotiations. Currently it is debated, whether the rights should be extended to household workers.[60] In *ASEAN (2008)*, on the other hand, a services chapter has not yet been concluded. Nevertheless, indirectly, ASEAN members liberalise mode 4 supply of services through a number of mutual recognition agreements for professional certificates and diplomas.[61] This can be considered as an innovative approach to services trade liberalisation (with an emphasis on investment and temporary movement of service suppliers) and to the regulation of labour migration.[62]

[60] See CARICOM [Online], available at: www.caribbean360.com/news/jamaica_news/jamaica-to-expand-free-movement-categories#axzz2z66IQO7X.

[61] See ASEAN [Online], available at: www.asean.org/communities/asean-economic-community/item/asean-framework-agreement-on-mutual-recognition-arrangements-3.

[62] For a more detailed discussion of innovative regulation of labour migration in a South-South context, see Sieber-Gasser, Charlotte (2013) 'Variationen der regionalen Personenfreizügigkeit', *Jusletter*, 18 March.

4

Systemic Considerations

Before turning to the systemic considerations of the different options for South-South PTAs, it has to be noted that the challenges already start at the term 'developing country'. Developing countries are not defined by WTO law and, thus, whether or not a South-South PTA is eligible for more flexibility is debatable already based on the members to it.[1] Furthermore, the level of notifications to the WTO is relatively low.[2] Thus, many PTAs remain entirely unspoken of in a global context. The lack of case law and absence of disputes on the basis of GATS Art. V, therefore, point towards *de facto* consensus that members are free to conclude PTAs in various forms, given that the PTA does not too overtly infringe upon WTO law. The evaluation of the options inherent in GATS Art. V for South-South PTAs is, thus, most of all relevant for more legal certainty and for elaborating a new approach to a more modern SDT.

The narrow interpretation (no additional flexibility) may not be in line with the general spirit of WTO law and cause contradictions with GATS Art. V:3 lit. a, as well as with the principle of SDT. Furthermore, not attributing more flexibility to South-South PTAs may – at least in the case of LDCs – not be in the interest of the WTO: given that economists appoint a central role to the services industry in bringing about sustainable economic growth in the global South, attributing more flexibility to LDCs and therewith strengthening their services sectors is of eminent importance for reducing global inequality.

The medium interpretation of allowing for little extra flexibility in terms of numbers of sectors and level of liberalisation arguably follows the spirit of WTO law, the principle of SDT and is in line with the legal

[1] For more information on the general discussion, see, e.g. Jessen, Henning (2006) "*Special and Differential Treatment for Developing Countries" im multidimensionalen Wandel des Wirtschaftsvölkerrechts*, Berliner Wissenschafts-Verlag, Berlin.

[2] The DESTA database indicates 156 South-South PTAs in services, whereas the WTO lists only 31.

text of GATS Art. V. However, in practice, this interpretation may develop limited impact on the actual level of liberalisation in trade in services and on the global process of economic integration, contributing to trade diversion and legal uncertainty rather than promoting global free trade. The clear goal of GATS Art. V might, thus, be missed. Evidence from stocktaking of South-South PTAs in services shows that most members to a South-South PTA do not exceed their commitments under GATS and the overall impact of PTAs on trade liberalisation in services in the South is often negligible.[3] There are two ways of interpreting this data: (1) there is no demand for veritable trade liberalisation in services in the South and (2) the legal provision of GATS Art. V is insufficient in creating the right set of boundaries and incentives to allow for trade creation through PTAs.

Given the assessment in this study, the large scope of flexibility for South-South PTAs in GATS Art. V appears the most promising, while also the most revolutionary option: Tailored PTAs between developing countries and LDCs, which aim at promoting sustainable economic growth among its members by focusing on the relevant key services sectors but bind its members to liberalise fully those sectors, are in line with SDT in general, and with the GATS preamble in particular. They are in line with GATS Art. V as was discussed previously, and they should indeed serve as a meaningful trade policy instrument in fostering sustainable economic growth.[4] In particular with regard to the economic challenges of LDCs and developing countries emerging from potential mega-regionals in the near future, focusing on how to use the existing flexibilities in WTO law to the benefit of poorer economies is timely.

The main systemic concern with regard to the large scope of interpretation refers to the potential trade-diverting impact for other LDCs and developing countries. While the necessary repercussions to prevent trade diversion for other poorer economies will have to be assessed on a case-by-case basis and is neither solved with the other two options of the scope of interpretation, considerable trade diversion could also develop the side effect that LDCs and developing countries increasingly engage in South-South PTAs as a consequence. That would *per se* be considered a positive development since these agreements benefit generally from a large scope of flexibility under WTO law and their potential remains hitherto untapped.

[3] For more detail, see previously in this Part III.

[4] Optimistic about the trade-creating effect of PTAs in services: Fink and Jansen (2007).

I. Legal Uncertainty

Given the different possible interpretations of the scope of GATS Art. V from a strictly legal view, the resulting legal uncertainty is considerable.[5] As has been shown before, this legal uncertainty does not necessarily imply uncertainty in other areas, such as foreign relations. Since the compatibility of a PTA in services with GATS Art. V has so far not been subject to dispute settlement, and since the WTO members have to date only once come to a conclusion on the compatibility of a PTA (and clearly to acknowledged compatibility) under the CRTA procedures,[6] *de facto* certainty appears to be stable. Generally members respect the basic guidelines of GATS Art. V and attempt to at least establish a level of liberalisation that goes slightly beyond their GATS schedules.

This *de facto* certainty can, however, easily be shaken by just one dispute on the compatibility of a PTA in services with GATS Art. V being brought to the DSB. Since most countries are engaged in economic integration agreements in services with more or less questionable depth, it seems unlikely that such a dispute would be brought to the DSB anytime soon. Such a prediction is based on the assumption that those standing in a glass house should not be tempted to cast stones. Nonetheless, history shows that in the end, more often than not someone ended up throwing a stone anyway.[7] Therefore, considering ways to strengthen legal certainty with respect to the interpretation of GATS Art. V may indeed translate into longer-term stability in IEL.

The most obvious way of strengthening legal certainty with respect to the interpretation of GATS Art. V would consist in bringing a dispute on GATS Art. V to the DSB. In particular with respect to the flexibilities attributed to South-South PTAs in services, such an undertaking would greatly enhance the clarity and enforceability of GATS Art. V.

Broude (2011) elaborates that the WTO would be the ideal and most obvious forum for disputes in international development.[8] However,

[5] On how regulatory flexibility can contribute to legal certainty, see Krajewski (2013).

[6] The Customs Union between the Czech and the Slovak Republics; see also Mavroidis, Petros C. (2010) Always Look at the Bright Side of Non-Delivery: WTO and Preferential Trade Agreements, Yesterday and Today [Online], available at: www.wto.org/english/res_e/publications_e/wtr11_forum_e/wtr11_14dec10_e.pdf.

[7] Considering the new dimension of economic implications for third countries inherent in mega-regionals, this day could come sooner than expected.

[8] Broude, Tomer (2011) 'Development Disputes in International Trade', In: Y-S. Lee, G. N. Horlick, W-M. Choi and T. Broude (eds.), *Law and Development Perspective on International Trade Law*, Cambridge University Press, New York, pp. 29–48.

'WTO jurisprudence only partially reflects the potential coverage of development disputes in the WTO'. This is because developing countries have generally proved to be dispute-averse, while LDCs – with the exception of Bangladesh – still have to participate in a dispute for the first time at all. This has an adverse impact on the selection of development-related disputes: not the most urgent disputes over poverty alleviation are brought to the WTO, but those involving countries that are already quite well integrated into the world economy.[9]

Remarkably, development-related disputes in the WTO are often directed against a policy, which intends to foster development, e.g. by protecting infant industries, developing countries fail to meet the commitments under WTO law.[10] At first this may seem unfortunate for developing countries, as WTO law restricts their ability to implement the policies, which they conceive as most promising for their economic development. However, such policies are often criticised as inefficient, and government intervention in development 'represents a legitimate controversy in development economics'.[11] The problem with these cases is, however, that they strictly focus on the compliance with WTO law, without further considering the development impact of these – questionable – policies. If the development objective of WTO law were to be strongly embedded in the legal body of the WTO, it might in the future be possible that economic policies intending to promote economic development are more often considered legitimate.

There are, of course, also other disputes that were initiated by developing members against harmful policies of developed countries. The poster child for this kind of disputes is *US – Upland Cotton*,[12] in which Brazil challenged the US subsidies for cotton producers, which had a depressing effect on world prices and thereby robbed developing countries of their competitive advantages in this sector. Interestingly, these cases[13] focus more on the development effects of the policies in question than on the

[9] Broude (2011, pp. 40–41).

[10] See, e.g. *Indonesia – Autos*, WT/DS54/R, WT/DS545/R, WT/DS59/R, WT/DS64/R (2 July 1998) Report of the Panel; *India – Quantitative Restrictions*, WT/DS90/AB/R (23 August 1999) Report of the Appellate Body; *China – Auto Parts*, WT/DS339, 340, 342/AB/R (15 December 2008), Report of the Appellate Body.

[11] Broude (2011, p. 42).

[12] *US – Upland Cotton*, WT/DS267/AB/R (3 March 2005), Report of the Appellate Body.

[13] Others involve *EC – Bananas III*, WT/DS27/RW2/ECU and WT/DS27/RW/USA (26 November 2008), Reports of the Appellate Body; *US – Wool Shirts and Blouses*, WT/DS33/AB/R (25 April 1997), Report of the Appellate Body; *EC – Sardines*, WT/DS231/AB/R (26 September 2002), Report of the Appellate Body.

compliance with WTO regulation.[14] Thus, it may be possible for complaining countries to strengthen the focus of the dispute settlement on the development objective of WTO law.

Broude (2011) puts forward that many of the WTO disputes are strongly related to development. However, instead of avoiding to discuss the strong link between trade law and economic development, the WTO prefers to treat disputes of all kinds 'as if they were simply run-of-the-mill trade disputes driven by regular political economy factors relating to international competitiveness'. He suggests that development disputes should be treated differently because the underlying issue is not related to compliance with WTO law alone, but is merely related to the development objective embedded in the legal body of the WTO in several places.[15] It submitted that as *EC – Bananas*[16] or *US – Upland Cotton*[17] have shown, increasing participation of developing countries in the dispute settlement system of the WTO may already increase the awareness for development objectives in trade law, as well as bring more legal certainty to the interpretation of the development goal embedded in trade law. The main question is, thus, how to increase participation of developing countries rather than how to influence the DSB towards increased awareness for development.

II. Political and Economic Effect

A general flaw in GATS Art. V arguably can be attributed to the lack of distinction with respect to the different services sectors: the provision applies to all modes of supply and all services sectors equally. As has been shown before the different services sectors included in the GATS contribute to economic development and to economic integration to varying degrees. The priorities attributed to growth and preferentialism as established in economic and political literature has been summarised in Table 3.

In addition, the general understanding, according to which some services sectors are more suitable for multilateral regulation than others, gains attention. Thus, from an economic or political science approach to preferentialism among developing countries, GATS Art. V arguably does not sufficiently differentiate among the different services sectors and

[14] See also Broude (2011, pp. 44–45). [15] Broude (2011, p. 46).

[16] Complainants were Ecuador, Guatemala, Honduras, Mexico and the US.

[17] Complainant was Brazil.

does not necessarily take into full consideration the implications of the different levels of regulation. In consequence, applying GATS Art. V on South-South PTAs in services in a very strict sense of the provision (see narrow interpretation above) contradicts economic and political theory of South-South preferential trade in services.

On the other hand, however, it is well established that partial liberalisation of services sectors may even have a counterproductive impact on trade: since services trade liberalisation is primarily related to regulatory, behind-the-border barriers to trade, efforts to open services sectors for trade in services may overall be more costly compared to the gains from liberalisation if liberalisation is only partial.[18] Therefore, in addition to more flexibility with respect to the number of sectors and modes of supply that have to be covered by a PTA in services, economic and political theory suggests that the level of liberalisation in covered sectors should be less flexible and National Treatment should be mandatory.

Finally, general economic theory of trade liberalisation attributes the greatest benefits of liberalisation of services trade to liberalisation between equal competitors. Particularly in services trade, spill-over effects of liberalisation are substantial, but depend on the right level of competition. Trade liberalisation in services in a South-South context may not always and in all sectors equally promise spill-over effects, because of unequal competition at the outset. Liberalisation as required by the positivist interpretation of GATS Art. V may therefore only be beneficial to one side of the PTA and not promote the necessary spill-over effects needed for sustainable economic growth.[19] The suggested large scope of flexibility in GATS Art. V for South-South PTAs would allow tailoring more beneficial liberalisation also in this regard.

On a side note, what also needs to be taken into consideration are the economic implications of legal uncertainty: it appears that the economic costs of the legal uncertainty embedded in GATS Art. V have not yet been investigated. Other case studies, however, have shown a considerable economic effect linked with legal uncertainty.[20] Thus, arguably, countries do not tailor their services trade commitments in PTAs to their best benefit because they are afraid of the consequences of not entirely meeting WTO requirements as established in GATS Art. V. This, on the other hand, leaves service suppliers with weak protection and regulation. In return,

[18] Nielson and Taglioni (2004). [19] See Francois and Hoekman (2010).

[20] See, e.g. Wagner, Helmut (2004) Economic Analysis of Cross-Border Legal Uncertainty: The Example of the European Union, Discussion Paper, Maastricht.

this may to a certain extent explain the relatively low shares of global trade in services in mode 4 supply of services and mode 2 supply.

III. Number of Notifications

The low level of notifications of South-South PTAs[21] in services to the WTO is linked with the legal uncertainty related to the interpretation of the scope of flexibility in GATS Art. V. To a certain extent, this is paradoxical, since it is well known that the evaluation of the PTA by the WTO secretariat and the CRTA will most likely not pose a challenge to the implementation of the PTA.

As was shown, South-South PTAs in services tend to be more concerned with the requirements of GATS Art. V than North-South or even North-North PTAs in services are.[22] This finding also points to a general culture of acceptance of the constitutional character of WTO law in relation to MFN-exemptions. For South-South PTAs in services, in which weak economies with limited geopolitical clout are involved, confirmation of the PTA by the WTO is important. Thus, arguably members of a South-South PTA in services are particularly aware of the legal uncertainties linked with the requirements of GATS Art. V. Comparing South-South PTAs in services with other PTAs in services, it appears that developing countries do their best to comply with the requirements in the first place. With respect to notifying their PTAs to the WTO, their track-record is equally mixed as for other groups of countries.

Do developing countries feel less inclined to notify their PTAs to the WTO since the result of the examination following the notification could potentially question the legality of their PTAs? To my knowledge, this phenomenon has not yet been discussed in literature, but would have to be studied in more detail by political scientists, since the underlying dynamics appear to be complex.

IV. Level of Liberalisation

While literature on the exact circumstances of the drafting and negotiation of GATS Art. V is scarce, the judgment of senior GATS specialists of GATS Art. V as being a 'political animal' can easily be agreed to. It is

[21] Twenty-two of the thirty substantial South-South PTAs in services in the dataset are notified to the WTO.

[22] See previously, in this Part III.

of course no coincidence that GATS Art. V turned out the way it has: the remaining need for legal interpretation of the meaning and the scope of the provision of GATS Art. V have been introduced into the GATS arguably on purpose. Being aware of the regulatory deficiencies of GATS Art. V allows the members of the GATS to work with the provision. The need for legal interpretation creates a larger scope for political action. It leaves members freer in the conclusion of PTAs in services than a more precise GATS Art. V would.

On the other hand, this freedom comes at a cost: the majority of PTAs in services – in particular also South-South PTAs in services – do not substantially go beyond the level of commitments undertaken under the GATS. Thus, the liberalising impact of the majority of PTAs in services is limited. A more precise GATS Art. V arguably would have limited the freedom of members in policymaking on the preferential level, but it would have increased the depth of commitments in PTAs in services. As it stands now, the provision is encouraging deep to full liberalisation, but given the flexibilities provided for South-South PTAs in services, there is no clear, unambiguous obligation to full liberalisation to be found in GATS Art. V. Thus, the flexibilities attributed under GATS Art. V to South-South PTAs in services – while in the right place and targeting the right group of countries in theory – are too 'flexible' in practice to ascertain full liberalisation in the sectors which are opened on a preferential basis.

In this context, it is important to point out that the focus of liberalising commitments under GATS Art. V is not on Market Access, but on National Treatment. This can be explained by the historical context of the GATS: when negotiations on the GATS began, the world was divided into capitalist countries and communist countries. The former Soviet Union collapsed in 1991, very shortly before the conclusion of the negotiations on the GATS. Thus, in a considerable number of future members of the GATS, services trade as a whole was not liberalised: major services sectors were entirely controlled by the government and state-owned service providers were largely operating outside of competition.[23] Based on this market analysis, non-discrimination should be provided in the services sectors, which are liberalised, while members should not be forced to liberalise immediately all of their services sectors (Market Access). The

[23] See, e.g. Eschenbach, Felix and Hoekman, Bernard (2005) Services Policy Reform and Economic Growth in Transition Economies, 1990–2004, World Bank Policy Research Working Paper, World Bank, Washington DC.

focus on non-discrimination rather than Market Access can be found in GATS Art. V:1 lit. b, which states:

> (b) provides for the absence or elimination of substantially all discrimination, in the sense of Article XVII, between or among the parties, in the sectors covered under subparagraph (a), through:
> (i) elimination of existing discriminatory measures, and/or
> (ii) prohibition of new or more discriminatory measures,
> either at the entry into force of that agreement or on the basis of a reasonable time-frame, except for measures permitted under Articles XI, XII, XIV and XIV bis.

Instead of Market Access, which is defined in GATS Art. XVI, the focus of the requirements established by GATS Art. V, thus, lie on National Treatment as defined in GATS Art. XVII. It is true that GATS Art. V:1 lit. a requires substantial sectorial coverage, but GATS Art. V in general does not require full Market Access in the services sectors covered by a PTA in services. However, National Treatment is required if a commitment in Market Access is undertaken.[24]

This structure is enabled for formerly communist countries with only limited liberalisation in services trade to join the GATS, and to conclude PTAs in services that are compatible with GATS Art. V. At the time, requiring full Market Access in a PTA in services would have made it impossible for a considerable number of countries to enter into a PTA in services, since their services industries had not yet undergone the necessary structural change.

While prioritising commitments in National Treatment over commitments in Market Access may have been reasonable when the GATS was negotiated, this thesis puts forward that in the global economy of the 21st century, the focus should shift to commitments in Market Access: the depth of liberalisation in a PTA in services primarily depends on the scope of Market Access. National Treatment ought to be the natural consequence following commitments in Market Access. But since National Treatment can only be granted in sectors in which Market Access commitments have been undertaken, encouraging – and obliging – substantial liberalisation in a PTA in services primarily requires substantial commitments to be made in Market Access.

This is particularly true for the line of argumentation and legal interpretation brought forward earlier in this part of the study, which relates the scope of flexibility for South-South PTAs in services to the economic

[24] See GATS Art. V:1.

development potential of such agreements. The argument has more validity when the depth of liberalisation in a South-South PTA in services is indeed substantial. Thus, the focus on commitments in National Treatment is insufficient in this respect and a shift also to a primary focus on Market Access commitments in South-South PTAs in services would serve the economic development potential of these agreements.

5

In Summary

GATS Art. V is considered to be of the regulatory quality of a 'political animal', thus providing for considerable policy space for members of the GATS with respect to the conclusion of PTAs. However, GATS Art. V does not only provide for policy space, it also provides for considerable room for legal interpretation of the scope of its provisions. The need for legal interpretation of the scope of GATS Art. V – in particular with respect to the flexibility attributed to South-South PTAs in services – encourages taking into consideration the broader regulatory context and the systemic role of GATS Art. V. While there is general agreement to the extent that South-South PTAs in services are meant to be provided with more flexibility with respect to the implementation of the requirements of GATS Art. V, little has been established in case law or in legal literature on the scope of such flexibility. This study therefore presents the potential breadth of the scope of flexibility in GATS Art. V for South-South PTAs in services by introducing three different legal interpretations:

(1) The narrow legal interpretation of the scope of flexibility is based on a positivist approach and remains close to the legal wording of GATS Art. V. Following this interpretation flexibility for South-South PTAs in services would consist (a) in a more generous time frame for full implementation of the commitments under GATS Art. V and a corresponding PTA in services (GATS Art. V:1), (b) in more flexibility attributed to the requirements as established in GATS Art. V:1 (GATS Art. V:3 lit. a) potentially allowing for the exclusion of a less trade-relevant services sector from the scope of application of a PTA and (c) in the right to treat third country legal persons on a discriminatory basis even if they were established in the country pre-conclusion of the PTA (GATS Art. V:3 lit. b).

(2) The medium legal interpretation attributes a broader scope of flexibility to the flexibility established in GATS Art. V:3 lit. a with respect

to the sectorial coverage and the coverage of substantially all the trade as required by GATS Art. V:1. By slightly broadening the interpretation of the scope of flexibility in GATS Art. V:3 lit. a, the broader objective of GATS Art. V is taken into account. This interpretation would, in addition to the flexibilities established in the narrow legal interpretation, allow excluding a number of services sectors from the scope of application in a South-South PTAs, and possibly also one of the modes of supply.

(3) Finally, the broad legal interpretation of the scope of flexibilities in GATS Art. V for South-South PTAs would even allow for sectorial agreements. Such an interpretation attributes a particularly large scope of flexibility to South-South PTAs with respect to the requirements established in GATS Art. V.1. It is based on the interpretation of GATS Art. V:3 lit. a in the light of a South-South PTA in services and takes into consideration the general objective of the GATS, the underlying legal philosophy of non-reciprocal commitments inherent in the positive list approach and in SDT, the literature on economic development, as well as elements of the graduation theory. It advocates relative freedom for South-South PTAs in services in terms of numbers of services sectors covered by the agreement, but balances this freedom with the requirement to establish full liberalisation and market integration in the sectors covered by such an agreement.

This study brings the broad interpretation of the scope of flexibility of GATS Art. V forward as the most innovative and promising option. In order to balance increasing trade diversion for developing countries and LDCs, it is timely to investigate new approaches to the existing SDT framework at the WTO. Substantiating the existing flexibility of GATS Art. V for South-South PTAs with meaningful interpretation is one avenue to pursue when attempting to promote economic development through trade liberalisation in poorer economies.

On the one hand, the current system appears, however, to be working relatively well since members of the WTO refrain from bringing cases related to the WTO-compatibility of PTAs to the DSB, and PTAs notified to the WTO are generally accepted. On the other hand, this *de facto* certainty can be shaken quickly when a member to the WTO decides to file a complaint against another member based on a violation of MFN. Thus, clarification through the DSB on the scope of the flexibilities for South-South PTAs in services would indeed also contribute to more policy coherence and certainty.

Furthermore, given the development aspects inherent in GATS Art. V, it is unfortunate from a developing country perspective, that no disputes related to the development aspects of the GATS have yet been brought to the DSB. Overall, a clarification of the status of 'economic development' in WTO law would greatly help developing countries in aligning their trade policies to their maximal benefit.

It is unfortunate that GATS Art. V does not distinguish between the different services sectors. The services sectors are not all equally well suited for multilateral regulation, and they are not all equally relevant for economic development and for the fostering of value-added production. Introducing a means to take into consideration the characteristics of the different services sectors, would, arguably, have contributed to deeper and more meaningful preferential liberalisation.

Finally, the flexibilities in GATS Art. V for South-South PTAs appear to be too large with respect to the obligation to full market integration in a number of services sectors. Since GATS Art. V historically focuses on National Treatment rather than on Market Access, it has been brought forward that this focus is outdated in the global economy of the 21st century. In the interest of substantial depth of liberalising commitments – particularly in South-South PTAs – the focus should shift to commitment in Market Access with National Treatment as the standard of any commitment.

Conclusion

> "True happiness comes from the joy of deeds well done, the zest of creating things new."
>
> *Antoine de Saint-Exupéry*

This study explores the legal scope for accommodating development in International Economic Law (IEL). It does so by focusing on the relationship between the GATS and South-South Preferential Trade Agreements (PTAs) in services. South-South trade liberalisation in services is generally attributed in economic and political theory with a considerable potential for economic development in poorer countries. However, little is known to date on the regulatory structure and the scope of liberalising commitments in South-South PTAs in services. With a view to complementing economic and political literature on the topic, this study provides for an empirical assessment of the legal aspects of South-South preferential services trade and a comprehensive discussion of the scope of legal flexibilities for South-South preferential services trade liberalisation with a view to its development potential.

Based on the empirical legal analysis of in total 298 PTAs in services, this study was able to uncover a number of issues concerning the scope for development as it is embedded in IEL. It has been brought forward that the distinction in WTO law between LDCs, developing countries and developed countries is essentially arbitrary, arguably with the exception of the group of LDCs. Even though the groups of developing and developed countries are not legally defined categories, WTO law is nevertheless building upon these distinctions. In an age of emerging and transforming economies alongside with countries with highly developed and competitive industries in one sector and industries heavily depending on subsidies and imports in another sector, such distinctions are increasingly difficult to substantiate and justify.

The study, thus, argues in favour of the concept of interdependent, internally heterogeneous countries and departs from the perception of single and uniform nation states. It takes into consideration that nation states are no longer single, uniform units and that when discussing trade liberalisation in services, foremost the level of development of individual services sectors is decisive, much more than the general economic situation of a country.

The categories of 'developing country' and 'LDC' are frequently referred to in WTO law. They receive more favourable treatment and preferences granted with the objective of promoting economic development. It is, however, questionable, whether the measures addressing the special needs of LDCs and developing countries deliver the intended results: despite WTO membership and manifold preferences in the world trading system, the number of LDCs keeps growing.

The basic level of liberalisation in services provided by the GATS was initially understood as a starting point for further liberalisation at the multilateral level. Negotiations at the multilateral level have not yet resulted in further commitments in trade liberalisation in services, but the global economy has evolved and services are becoming more important, especially for cross-border value-added chains. Hence, PTAs constitute an instrument for further liberalisation in trade in services both at the regional and bilateral level.

Preferential services trade is no longer driven solely by the United States and the EU. Many developing countries have undertaken considerable efforts to establish a broad framework of PTAs for trade in services. Some developing countries in Asia and Central and Latin America have even concluded more PTAs in services than most industrialised countries have, and many of the PTAs of developing countries are with other developing countries.

The empirical legal study of South-South PTAs in services is based on a dataset of PTAs in services, which encompasses in total 298 agreements from all over the world. All of the PTAs in the dataset have been empirically assessed through an exhaustive coding exercise based on a coding scheme, which was initially developed by Dür et al. of the Design of Trade Agreements (DESTA) project. The coding scheme was subsequently complemented and further developed to allow for a more precise data collection.

On the background of the general assessment of the entire dataset, this study was able to discuss the evolution and development of South-South PTAs in services in a broader, global context of preferential services trade liberalisation. In order to differentiate between North-South, North-North and South-South PTAs, the definition and role of developing countries in WTO law had to be assessed. Since a general definition of 'developing country' is missing in WTO law, this thesis is taking the OECD list of ODA recipients as the benchmark for qualifying as a South-South PTA.

All countries engaged in South-South PTAs in services are members of the WTO. Thus, they have a commitment to comply with GATS Art. V, which establishes requirements for PTAs in services in order to qualify for an MFN exemption under WTO law. The exact scope of the requirements established in GATS Art. V is, however, not self-explanatory. Since literature on the legal interpretation of GATS Art. V is generally scarce; this study endeavoured to provide for a substantive overview on the objective, scope and history of GATS Art. V in general. The general discussion of the legal interpretation of GATS Art. V shows that PTAs in general are expected to cover substantially all services sectors, all the trade in services and all modes of supply. Furthermore, they are expected to eliminate substantially all barriers to trade.

However, according to recent economic literature, certain services sectors are of particular importance for economic development in developing countries, while other sectors are particularly suitable for regional and bilateral liberalisation. The same holds true for modes of supply, as not all modes of supply are equally relevant for economic development and are equally suitable for regional and bilateral liberalisation. The study, thus, focuses its analysis on a number of services sectors and modes of supply of particular interest for South-South PTAs, in order to substantiate the assessment of their potential of promoting economic development.

GATS Art. V does provide for flexibilities with respect to South-South PTAs in services. Developing countries are, thus, not expected to fully comply with all of the requirements otherwise effective. The scope of these flexibilities is disputed in legal literature and has to date not been clarified by case law. By means of legal interpretation and comparative legal analysis, this study shows that potentially a scope of flexibility embracing even sectorial agreements in a South-South context can be covered by GATS Art. V.

The legal analysis of PTAs in services in general and of South-South PTAs in services in particular shows evidence of an emerging global consensus on the scope of the requirements of GATS Art. V: PTAs in services appear to be expected to cover basically all services sectors and all modes of supply, while with respect to the depth of liberalising commitments, a more liberal level than the GATS level (GATS-plus) is sufficient. However, no evidence on using the scope of flexibility for South-South PTAs in services could be detected: South-South PTAs in services appear to be equally compliant with the general requirements of WTO law in comparison with other PTAs. Thus, developing countries do not yet fully make use of the flexibilities provided to them in GATS Art. V.

Furthermore, economic theory suggests that the liberalisation of a number of services sectors is key to economic growth in developing countries, and that some services sectors may be more suitable for preferential liberalisation than for multilateral liberalisation. Despite these compelling arguments, however, the regulatory scope and structure of South-South PTAs in services is not in line with the suggestions derived from economic and political theory. Thus, it is to be expected that the South-South PTAs in the dataset develop little impact on economic development. This is regrettable, since the GATS arguably would provide for sufficient flexibilities allowing developing countries to tailor their PTAs in services to meet their economic needs.

The reasons why developing countries are not making use of the flexibilities in GATS Art. V today may be manifold. It is suggested that the need for clarification of the scope of flexibilities in GATS Art. V for South-South PTAs in services needs to be seen in the context of a larger debate on WTO law. The stalling of the Doha Round has shown that it is high time for a modernisation of Special and Differential Treatment (SDT), that it is necessary to clarify the role of developing countries in the WTO and, furthermore, that the constitutional character of WTO law needs to be strengthened.

The need for more efficient SDT in WTO law is further substantiated by the imminent increase of inequality among WTO members as a consequence of trade diversion for developing countries and LDCs emanating from the currently negotiated mega-regionals, e.g. TPP and TTIP. It is suggested to substantiate the existing SDT in WTO law with a consistent focus on increasing economic spill-over effects from liberalisation for developing countries and LDCs. The study, thus, emphasises the legal arguments for a large scope of flexibility for South-South PTAs in services, up to the extent that sectorial agreements are covered by the GATS.

1

Lessons for the WTO

Kennes (2000) rightly points out that South-South economic integration can actually be crucial for the functioning of the world trading system: particularly small developing countries cannot afford to invest the required time, competence and finance in their representation at the WTO, as would be required to ensure effective participation in the world trading system. Through regional economic integration, a basis for collaboration in the WTO is established, which may lead to more effective – and inherently necessary – participation of developing countries in the member-driven WTO.[1] Therefore, encouraging South-South economic integration through the provision of particular flexibility with respect to GATS Art. V and GATT Art. XXIV is in the overall interest of the WTO.

However, to date – despite the large cobweb of SDT provisions in WTO law – no particular regulation and encouragement of South-South economic integration and cooperation is to be found in WTO law. Arguably, this is a deficiency, which ought to be taken up by the secretariat. Such awareness for the central role of South-South economic integration for the WTO, and for global trade in general, does not necessarily need to translate into new legal provisions. A general discussion on the issue and encouragement to engage in South-South economic integration by the secretariat may already be a step in the right direction.

The analysis of the level of notifications of PTAs in services to the WTO in this study showed that a considerable share of PTAs is not notified despite the obligation of WTO members to do so. Furthermore, with respect to PTAs in services, some confusion on the notification process was discovered: while generally only PTAs in services that actually liberalise services trade among its members would have to be notified, still a relatively large number of PTAs, which only provide for an intention to liberalise services trade sometime in the future were notified to the WTO. Reaffirming that only PTAs providing for actual liberalisation need to be

[1] Kennes, Walter (2000, p. 21).

notified to the WTO, arguably, would strengthen the awareness for the process and ensure that WTO members are reminded of its purpose.[2]

In general, this study emphasised that the purpose and structure of the notification process requires amendment. As it is today, the process can be labelled a more or less toothless exercise with limited impact on the overall regulatory coherence in IEL. Since the legal uncertainty about the scope of the requirements of GATS Art. V appears to contribute to the reluctance of members to notify their PTAs, clarification in this aspect could – or should even– be provided by the Committee on Regional Trade Agreements (CRTA). It is rather unlikely that GATS Art. V will be at the core of a dispute soon, thus, clarification on the scope of GATS Art. V has to be sought through other means. It would appear reasonable that the CRTA provides for such clarification.

Interestingly enough, despite the fact that the notification process is considered inefficient, members nonetheless mostly respect the notification obligations for PTAs. Even though, to date, the compliance of PTAs with WTO law has not yet been the main cause for a dispute, this cannot be excluded in the future. This eventuality seems to be a powerful enough a threat, ensuring that WTO members carefully draft their PTAs – in compliance with WTO law to the extent possible. This thesis, thus, did not argue for strengthening the CRTA in a way that would allow them to more effectively disapprove of PTAs, as this was not deemed necessary.

[2] On a side note, it was observed that it is not quite clear why the PTAs which do not liberalise yet services trade among its members are even in the list of notified PTAs of the WTO.

2

Lessons for the Architecture of International Economic Law

The flexibilities in GATS Art. V for South-South PTAs in services are in good company: a vast number of flexibilities and preferences for developing countries and LDCs is scattered around the legal texts of the WTO. This study wishes to emphasise that the current regime appears both incoherent and inefficient, and may negatively affect the ability of developing countries and LDCs to apply these flexibilities and preferences in their best interest. Based on the case study of the flexibilities in GATS Art. V, the thesis suggests a modern understanding of SDT, which is based on ideas from graduation theory.

The addressees of IEL are the member states. Generally, countries are treated as a single, distinct unit in IEL. In a world of economic convergence, however, it is brought forward that the subject of IEL cannot anymore be divided into isolated aspects of single member states. This is equally true for the labelling or classification of WTO members into different groups, such as LDCs or developing countries. In order to bring more meaning back to SDT, it is therefore suggested that the ability to compete on the global market is the main benchmark for flexibilities in IEL.[1] Such ability, furthermore, should not be assessed at the country level, but at the level of individual economic sectors wishing to benefit from SDT. This would render the labelling of countries obsolete and allow for sector-specific – and therewith arguably better accepted and more efficient – SDT.[2]

While this study suggested that the idea of graduation should be introduced in one way or another in IEL with respect to the classification of

[1] It may of course be both a practical and a theoretical challenge to define these benchmarks. However, it does not appear to be unfeasible.

[2] One concern today is the fact that some 'developing countries' actually have a few competitive and developed industries, while the rest of the economy is still pre-industrial. Treating the industries according to their level of competitiveness would allow balancing these inequalities with respect to economic development in the sense of fair treatment.

developing countries, this could also be achieved through treaty interpretation. Arguably, a number of the deficiencies of SDT today could be balanced by graduation in treaty interpretation. This would mean that the scope of flexibilities would be broader, the less developed an industry is. Thus, even the scope of flexibilities as established in WTO law would not be static, but adjust to the single case.

On a more general note, this study encouraged to critically assess the ability of the GATS to serve as the main regime for services trade regulation. It may be that the same philosophy of progressive liberalisation, which served its cause so well under the GATT,[3] was not suitable for services trade liberalisation: the main barriers to services trade are not tariffs, but behind-the-border issues such as national legislation. Thus, multilateralisation of services trade – very much like further multilateralisation of goods trade considering that most tariffs have been successfully abolished – may require a new philosophy, different from the initial GATT philosophy of gradual, progressive liberalisation through subsequent rounds of multilateral trade negotiations.

Depending on the outcome of the negotiations on the Trade in Services Agreement (TiSA), and the mega-regionals, the Transpacific Partnership (TPP) and the Transatlantic Trade and Investment Partnership (TTIP), as well as on the outcome of future rounds of multilateral negotiations in the WTO, we may, sooner rather than later, see a regulatory shift in services trade regulation. This is an interesting time for IEL, with parallel regulatory initiatives taking place in a number of different multilateral, plurilateral and preferential fora. After the stalling of the Doha Round, suddenly IEL has come to life again and services trade regulation is right in the middle of the global struggle for meaningful, coherent and fair trade regulation that lives up to the realities of the 21st century.

[3] See Cottier (2006, p. 779).

3

Critical Issues for Future Research

A number of issues of interest for future research have been uncovered. Political scientists may want to look into the reasons why certain PTAs are not readily notified to the PTA: What are the underlying political dynamics that lead to notification? Insights could help rendering the notification process more meaningful. Economists, on the other hand, could look into establishing a practical and objective framework for assessing the global competitiveness of individual industries, irrespective of the country's income level. The discussion of such a system of economic benchmarks would provide meaning and substance to the ideas of sector-level graduation in SDT. Furthermore, considering the weak implementation of services trade regulation in general, it appears necessary to study the economic costs of the legal uncertainty attributed with services trade regulation. Such insights could provide the basis for developing more coherent, transparent and effective services trade regulation in the future. Finally, further legal analysis is required on the phenomenon of PTAs that establish a GATS-minus level of liberalisation. Even though GATS-minus commitments are relatively widespread, it remains unclear to date, which commitments prevail in legal practice. Given that regulatory evidence of partially sectorial agreements was discovered, the regulatory scope for liberalising individual sectors more than others observed in some PTAs in services requires further research. Insights from such studies would inform the legal discussion on the scope of flexibilities in GATS Art. V. It would also provide further insights into how – and if – WTO members use IEL as an instrument for fostering economic development.

BIBLIOGRAPHY

Documents

Communication from Brazil, Chile, Colombia, Cuba, Honduras, Jamaica, Nicaragua, Mexico, Peru, Trinidad and Tobago, and Uruguay, Structure of a Multilateral Framework for Trade in Services, GATT Doc. No. MTN.GNS/W/95 (26 February 1990).

Communication from New Zealand, Structure and Mechanism for a General Agreement on Trade in Services, reprinted in 7 Inside US Trade (28 September 1989).

Communication from Peru, Elements of a Framework Agreement in Trade on Services, GATT Doc. No. MTN.GNS/W/84 (20 November 1989).

Communication from the Republic of Korea, On the Structure of General Agreement on Trade in Services (25 October 1989).

Communication from the United States, Agreement on Trade in Services, GATT Doc. No. MTN.GNS/W/75 (17 October 1989).

Contracting Parties, Generalised System of Preferences, Decision of 25 June 1971, L/3545 (28 June 1971).

Contracting Parties, Trade Negotiations among Developing Countries, Decision of 26 November 1971, L/3636 (30 November 1971).

Draft Final Act Embodying the Results of the Uruguay Round of Multilateral Trade Negotiations, GATT Doc. No. MTN.TNC/W/FA (20 December 1991).

Draft Multilateral Framework for Trade In Services, GATT Doc. No. MTN.GNS/35 (23 July 1990).

GATT Council, Minutes of the Meeting on 25 May 1971, C/M/69 (28 May 1971).

GATT, Draft Text of Services Compromise, paras. III(A)(1)(b)(i) and (ii) XX; *Declaration of the Countries of Latin America and the Caribbean*, at the V Latin American Consultation Meeting of SELA on the Uruguay Round of Multilateral Trade Negotiations, GATT Doc. No. MTN.TNC/W/22 (23 July 1990).

Global System of Trade Preferences among Developing Countries, UNCTAD, GSTP/MM/BELGRADE/10 (12 April 1988).

Group of Negotiations on Services, Note on the Meeting of 18–22 July 1988, GATT Doc. MTN.GNS/16 (8 August 1988).

Group of Negotiations on Services, Note on the Meeting of 19–23 September 1988, GATT Doc. MTN.GNS/17 (18 October 1988).

Group of Negotiations on Services, Note on the Meeting of 31 October – 3 November 1988, GATT Doc. MTN.GNS/16 (18 October 1988).

Guidelines for the Scheduling of Specific Commitments under the General Agreement on Trade in Services (GATS), S/L/92 (28 March 2001).

Havana Charter, United Nations Conference on Trade and Employment, Havana, 21 November 1947 – 24 March 1948, Final Act and Related Documents, UN Doc E/CONF.2/78 (April 1948).

Ministerial Conference, Preferential Treatment to Services and Service Suppliers of Least-Developed Countries, Decision of 17 December 2011, WT/L/847, Geneva.

Ministerial Declaration on the Uruguay Round, GATT Doc. No. MIN.DEC (September 20 1986).

United Nations, General Assembly, Resolution, Programme of Action on the Establishment of a New International Economic Order, A/RES/S-6/3202 (1 May 1974).

WTO, Committee on Regional Trade Agreements, Examination of the European Communities – Hungary Europe Agreement, Services; The European Communities – Poland Europe Agreement, Services; and The European Communities – Slovak Europe Agreement, Services, Note on the Meeting of 18 February 1998, WT/REG50/M/2, WT/REG51/M/2, WT/REG52/M/2 (19 March 1998).

WTO, Committee on Regional Trade Agreements, Systemic Issues Related to 'Substantially all Trade' – Background Note by the Secretariat, Revision, WT/REG/W/21/Rev.1 (5 February 1998).

WTO, Committee on Regional Trade Agreements, Council for Trade in Services, Communication from the European Communities and their Member States, Article V of the GATS: Systemic Issues, WT/REG/W/35, S/C/W/124 (21 September 1999.

WTO, Committee on Regional Trade Agreements, Note on the Meetings of 29–30 April and 3 May 1999, WT/REG/M/22 (4 June 1999).

WTO, Committee on Regional Trade Agreements, Note on the Meetings of 1–2 July 1999, WT/REG/M/23 (2 August 1999).

WTO, Committee on Regional Trade Agreements, Systemic Issues Arising from Article V of the GATS, Communication from Hong Kong, China, WT/REG/W/34 (19 February 1999).

WTO, Committee on Regional Trade Agreements, Synopsis of 'Systemic' Issues Related to Regional Trade Agreements, Note by the Secretariat, WT/REG/W/37 (2 March 2000).

WTO Committee on Trade and Development, 'Gulf Co-operation Council Customs Union – Saudi-Arabia's Notification: Communication from the European

Communities', November 25 2008, WT/COMTD/66/Add.2 (25 November 2008).

WTO, Negotiating Group on Rules, Compendium of Issues Related to Regional Trade Agreements, Background Note by the Secretariat, Revision, TN/RL/W8/Rev.1 (1 August 2002).

WTO, Services Sectoral Classification List, Note by the Secretariat, MTN.GNS/W/120 (10 July 1991).

WTO, Transparency Mechanism for Regional Trade Agreements, Decision of 14 December 2006, WT/L/671 (18 December 2006).

References

Abu-Akeel, Aly K. (1999) 'Definition of Trade in Services under the GATS: Legal Implications', *George Washington Journal of International Law and Economics*, vol. 32, no. 2, pp. 189–210.

Adlung, Rudolf (2006a) 'Services Negotiations in the Doha Round: Lost in Flexibility?', *Journal of International Economic Law*, vol. 9, no. 4, pp. 865–893.

(2006b) 'Public Services and the GATS', *Journal of International Economic Law*, vol. 9, no. 2, pp. 455–485.

(2007) *The Contribution of Services Liberalisation to Poverty Reduction: What Role for the GATS?*, Economic Research and Statistics Division, WTO, Geneva.

(2009) Services Liberalisation from a WTO/GATS Perspective: In Search of Volunteers, Staff Working Paper ERSD-2009–05, WTO, Geneva.

Adlung, Rudolf and Carzaniga, Antonia (2009) 'MFN Exemptions under the General Agreement on Trade in Services: Grandfathers Striving for Immortality?', *Journal of International Economic Law*, vol. 12, no. 2, pp. 357–392.

Adlung, Rudolf and Mamdouh, Hamid (2014) How to Design Trade Agreements in Services: Top Down or Bottom Up?, Staff Working Paper ERSD-2013-08, WTO, Geneva.

Adlung, Rudolf and Miroudot, Sébastien (2012) Poison in the Wine? Tracing GATS-minus Commitments in Regional Trade Agreements, Staff Working Paper, ERSD No. 2012-04, World Trade Organisation, Geneva.

Adlung, Rudolf and Morrison, Peter (2010) 'Less than the GATS: 'Negative Preferences' in Regional Services Agreements', *Journal of International Economic Law*, vol. 13, no. 4, pp. 1103–1143.

Adlung, Rudolf and Roy, Martin (2005) Turning Hills into Mountains? Current Commitments under the GATS and Prospects for Change, Staff Working Paper, Economic Research and Statistics Division, WTO, Geneva.

Agu, Chukwuma (2009) 'Multilateralism, Regionalism and the Paradox of the "Spaghetti Bowl" in Developing Countries', *Aussenwirtschaft*, 64, pp. 293–316.

AIZENMANN, JOSHUA AND JINJARAK, YOTHIN (2009) 'Globalisation and Developing Countries – a Shrinking Tax Base?', *The Journal of Development Studies*, vol. 45, no. 5, pp. 653–671.

AKAMA, JOHN S. AND KIETI, DAMIANNAH (2007) 'Tourism and Socio-economic Development in Developing Countries: A Case Study of Mombasa Resort in Kenya', *Journal of Sustainable Tourism*, vol. 15, no. 6, pp. 735–748.

AUSTRALIAN GOVERNMENT (2004) *South-South Trade: Winning from Liberalisation*, Department of Foreign Affairs and Trade, Barton.

AVILA, JOHN L. (2003) 'EU Enlargement and the Rise of Asian FTAs: Implications for Asia-Europe Relations', *Asia Europe Journal*, vol. 1, no. 2, pp. 213–222.

AYKUT, DILEK and GOLDSTEIN, ANDREA (2006) Developing Country Multinationals: South-South Investment Comes of Age, Working Paper, OECD Development Centre, Paris.

AYKUT, DILEK AND RATHA, DILIP (2004) 'South-South FDI Flows: How Big Are They?', *Transnational Corporations*, vol. 13, no. 1, pp. 149–176.

BALDWIN, RICHARD (2006) 'Multilateralising Regionalism: Spaghetti Bowls as Building Blocs on the Path to Global Free Trade', *The World Economy*, vol. 29, no. 11, pp. 1451–1518.

(2011) Trade and Industrialisation after Globalisation's 2nd Unbundling: How Building and Joining a Supply Chain Are Different and Why It Matters, Working Paper 17716, NBER, Cambridge.

BARTELS, LORAND (2009) 'Interim Agreements' under Article XXIV GATT', *World Trade Review*, vol. 8, no. 2, pp. 339–350.

(2012) 'Regional Trade Agreements', In: R. Wolfrum (ed.), *The Max Planck Encyclopedia of Public International Law*, Vol. VIII, Oxford University Press, Oxford, pp. 853–863.

BARTH, DIETRICH (1999) *The Prospects of International Services Trade*, Friedrich Ebert Stiftung, Bonn.

BATT, ROSEMARY (2002) 'Managing Customer Services: Human Resource Practices, Quit Rates, and Sales Growth', *The Academy of Management Journal*, vol. 45, no. 3, pp. 587–597.

BAYER, FRANK (2004) *Das System der deutschen Handelsverträge von 1853 und 1914*, Berliner Wissenschafts-Verlag, Berlin.

BHAGWATI, JAGDISH(1987) 'Trade in Services and the Multilateral Trade Negotiations', *The World Bank Economic Review*, vol. 1, no. 4, pp. 549–569.

(1992) 'Regionalism versus Multilateralism', *The World Economy*, vol. 15, no. 5, pp. 535–556.

BHAGWATI, JAGDISH, GREENAWAY, DAVID, AND PANAGARIYA, ARVIND (1998) 'Trading Preferentially: Theory and Policy', *The Economic Journal*, vol. 108, no. 449, pp. 1128–1148.

BLOOM, DAVID E. (2004) 'Globalisation and Education', In: M. M. Suarez-Orozco and D. B. Qin-Hilliard (eds.), *Globalisation, Culture and Education in the*

New Millennium, University of California Press, Berkeley and Los Angeles, pp. 56–78.

Bosco, David (2011) 'Who's a "Developing Country"? You'd Be Surprised.', 18 February, FP Voices [online], available at: http://bosco.foreignpolicy.com/posts/2011/02/16/whos_a_developing_country_youd_be_surprised#sthash.sgQoVPtA.dpbs (last visited 29 December 2013).

Bosworth, Barry and Collins, Susan M. (2007) Accounting for Growth: Comparing China and India, NBER Working Paper, National Bureau of Economic Research, Cambridge MA.

Brennan, Anna Marie (2011) 'The Special and Differential Treatment Mechanism and the WTO: Cultivating Trade Inequality for Developing Countries?', *Trinity College Review*, vol. 14, pp. 143–160.

Broude, Tomer (2011) 'Development Disputes in International Trade', In: Y-S. Lee, G. N. Horlick, W-M. Choi and T. Broude (eds.), *Law and Development Perspective on International Trade Law*, Cambridge University Press, New York, pp. 29–48.

Burgos, Sigfrido and Ear, Sophal (2012) 'China's Oil Hunger in Angola: History and Perspective', *Journal of Contemporary China*, vol. 21, no. 74, pp. 351–367.

Carzaniga, Antonia G. (2003) 'The GATS, Mode 4 and Pattern of Commitments', In: A. Mattoo and A. Carzaniga (eds.), *Moving People to Deliver Services*, The World Bank and Oxford University Press, Oxford, pp. 21–26.

Cernat, Lucian (2003) *Assessing South-South Regional Integration: Same Issues, Many Metrics*, Study Series No. 21, UNCTAD, Geneva.

Cernat, Lucian and Kutlina-Dimitrova, Zornitsa (2014) Thinking in a Box: A 'Mode 5' Approach to Service Trade, Chief Economist Note, European Commission [Online], available at: http://trade.ec.europa.eu/doclib/docs/2014/march/tradoc_152237.pdf (last visited 15 April 2014).

Chanda, Rupa (1999) *Movement of Natural Persons and Trade in Services: Liberalising Temporary Movement of Labour under the GATS*, Indian Council for Research on International Economic Relations, New Delhi.

(2004) Movement and Presence of Natural Persons and Developing Countries: Issues and Proposals for the GATS Negotiations, Working Paper 19, South Centre, Geneva.

(2011) Mapping the Universe of Services Disciplines in Asian PTAs, Working Paper No. 2011/33, NCCR trade regulation, Bern.

Chaudhuri, Sumanta and Karmakar, Suparna (2008) 'The Liberalisation of Cross-Border Trade in Services: A Developing Country Perspective', In: J. A. Marchetti and M. Roy (eds.), *Opening Markets for Trade in Services*, Cambridge University Press, Cambridge, pp. 184–223.

Choi, Won-Mog (2005) 'Legal Problems of Making Regional Trade Agreements with Non-WTO-Member States', *Journal of International Economic Law*, vol. 4, no. 8, pp. 825–860.

Civan, Abdülkadir, Genç, Savas, Taser, Davut and Atakul, Sinem (2013) 'The Effect of New Turkish Foreign Policy on International Trade', *Insight Turkey*, vol. 15, no. 3, pp. 107–122.

Clancy, Michael (1998) 'Commodity Chains, Services and Development: Theory and Preliminary Evidence from the Tourism Industry', *Review of International Political Economy*, vol. 5, no. 1, pp. 122–148.

Collier, Paul (2006) 'Why the WTO Is Deadlocked: And What Can Be Done about It', *The World Economy*, vol. 29, no. 10, pp. 1423–1449.

Corbet, Hugh (1977) 'Prospect of Negotiations on Barriers to International Trade in Services', *Pacific Community*, vol. 8, no. 3, pp. 454–469.

Cornford, Andrew (2004) Variable Geometry for the WTO: Concept and Precedents, Discussion Paper, UNCTAD, Geneva.

Cottier, Thomas (1993) 'Constitutional Trade Regulation in National and International Law: Structure-Substance Pairings in the EFTA Experience', In: M. Hilf and E-U. Petersmann (eds.), *National Constitutions and International Economic Law*, Kluwer Law and Taxation Publishers, Boston, pp. 409–442.

(2006) 'From Progressive Liberalisation to Progressive Regulation in WTO Law', *Journal of International Economic Law*, vol. 9, no. 4, pp. 779–821.

Cottier, Thomas and Foltea, Marina (2006) 'Constitutional Functions of the WTO and Regional Trade Agreements', In: Bartels, L. and Ortino, F. (eds.), *Regional Trade Agreements and the WTO Legal System*, Oxford University Press, Oxford.

Cottier, Thomas and Molinuevo, Martin (2008) 'Article V GATS', In: Wolfrum, R., Stoll, P-T. and Feinäugle, C. (eds.), *WTO – Trade in Services*, Max Planck Institute, Martinus Nijhoff Publishers, Leiden, pp. 125–151.

Cottier, Thomas and Nadakavukaren Schefer, Krista (1998) 'The Relationship between World Trade Organisation Law, National and Regional Law', *Journal of International Economic Law*, vol. 1, no. 1, pp. 83–122.

Cottier, Thomas and Oesch, Matthias (2001) 'WTO Law, Precedents and Legal Change', *Turku Law Journal*, vol. 3, pp. 27–41.

(2005) *International Trade Regulation*, Staempfli Publishers and Cameron May, Bern and London.

Cottier, Thomas, Sieber-Gasser, Charlotte, and Wermelinger, Gabriela (2015) 'The Dialectical Relationship of Preferentialism and Multilateralism', In: M. Elsig and A. Dür (eds.), *Trade Cooperation: The Purpose, Design and Effects of Preferential Trade Agreements*, Cambridge University Press, Cambridge, pp. 465–496.

Cottier, Thomas, Egger, Peter, Francois, Joseph, Manchin, Miriam, Shingal, Anirudh and Sieber-Gasser, Charlotte (2014) Potential Impacts of a EU-US Free Trade Agreement on the Swiss Economy and External Economic Relations, Rechtsgutachten erstattet Staatssekretariat für Wirtschaft

SECO, WTI, Bern [Online], available at: www.wti.org (visited August 17 2015).

Cowhey, Peter F. and Aronson, Jonathan D. (2008) 'Trade in Services Telecommunications', In: A. Mattoo, R. M. Stern and G. Zanini (eds.), *A Handbook of International Trade in Services*, Oxford University Press, Oxford, pp. 389–436.

Crawford, Jo-Ann and Fiorentino, Roberto V. (2005) The Changing Landscape of Regional Trade Agreements, Discussion Paper, World Trade Organisation, Geneva.

Crawford, Jo-Ann and Laird, Sam (2001) 'Regional Trade Agreements and the WTO', *The North American Journal of Economics and Finance*, vol. 12, no. 2, pp. 193–211.

Cullet, Philippe (2003) *Differential Treatment in International Environmental Law*, Aldershot, Ashgate.

Das, Kasturi (2006) *GATS Negotiations and India: Evolution and State of Play*, Centre for Trade and Development (Centad), New Delhi.

Davey, William J. (2005) 'The WTO Dispute Settlement System: The First Ten Years', *Journal of International Economic Law*, vol. 8, no. 1, pp. 17–50.

Dawson, Laura Ritchie (2012) 'Labour Mobility and the WTO: The Limits of GATS Mode 4', *International Migration*, vol. 51, no. 1, pp. 1–23.

Dee, Philippa (2005) A Compendium of Barriers to Services Trade, Paper prepared for the World Bank, Asia-Pacific School of Economics and Government, Canberra.

De Haas, Hein (2007) 'Turning the Tide? Why Development Will Not Stop Migration', *Development and Change*, vol. 38, no. 5, pp. 819–841.

Delimatsis, Panagiotis (2012) 'The WTO Outlaws the Privileges of the Chinese Payment Services Giant', *American Society of International Law*, vol. 16, no. 31, insights, September 28.

De Melo, Jaime (2007) 'Regionalism and Developing Countries: A Primer', *Journal of World Trade*, 41, no. 2, pp. 351–369.

(2015) Trade in Services and Regulatory Flexibility – 20 Years of GATS, 20 Years of Critique, TILEC Discussion Paper, DP 2015-016, August 2015, Tilburg.

Devuyst, Youri and Serdarevic, Asja (2007) 'The World Trade Organisation and Regional Trade Agreements: Bridging the Constitutional Credibility Gap', *Duke Journal of Comparative & International Law*, vol. 18, no. 1, pp. 1–75.

Diebold, Nicolas F. (2010) *Non-discrimination in International Trade in Services: 'Likeness' in WTO/GATS*, Cambridge University Press, Cambridge.

(2013) *Non-discrimination in International Trade in Services: 'Likeness' in WTO/GATS*, 1st paperback ed., Cambridge University Press, Cambridge.

Dihel, Nora, Eschenbach, Felix and Sheperd, Ben (2008) 'South-South Services Trade', In: M. Panizzon, N. Pohl and P. Sauvé (eds.), *GATS and the Regulation of International Trade in Services*, Cambridge University Press, Cambridge, pp. 23–76.

Dingwerth, Klaus, Blauberger, Michael and Schneider, Christian (2011) *Postnationale Demokratie*, VS Verlag, Wiesbaden.

Dissou, Yazid (1998) *Dynamic Effects in Senegal of the Regional Trade Agreement among UEMOA Countries*, CREFA, Québec.

Dobson, Wendy (2008) 'Financial Services and International Trade Agreements: The Development Dimension', In: A. Mattoo, R. M. Stern and G. Zanini (eds.), *A Handbook of International Trade in Services*, Oxford University Press, Oxford, pp. 289–337.

Dornbusch, Rudiger (1992) 'The Case for Trade Liberalisation in Developing Countries', *The Journal of Economic Perspectives*, vol. 6, no.1, pp. 69–85.

Dossani, Rafiq (2007) 'The Next Wave of Globalisation: Relocating Service Provision to India', *World Development*, vol. 35, no. 5, pp. 772–791.

Dunning, John H. (2015) *The Globalization of Business: The Challenge of the 1990s*, Routledge Revivals, Routledge, New York.

Dunoff, Jeffrey L. and Trachtman, Joel P. (eds.) (2009) *Ruling the World? Constitutionalism, International Law, and Global Governance*, Cambridge University Press, Cambridge.

Dür, Andreas, Baccini, Leonardo, Elsig, Manfred and Milewicz, Karolina (2011) The Design of Preferential Trade Agreements: A New Dataset in the Making, Staff Working Paper ERSD-2011-10, World Trade Organisation, Geneva.

Eberhard, Torsten (2008) *Diskriminierende Gleichbehandlung von Entwicklungsländern in der WTO?*, Mendel Verlag, Witten.

Erixon, Fredrik and Lee-Makiyama, Hosuk (2010) Stepping into Asia's Growth Markets: Dispelling Myths about the EU-Korea Free Trade Agreement, Policy Brief No. 03/2010, ECIPE, Brussels.

Eschenbach, Felix and Hoekman, Bernard (2005) Services Policy Reform and Economic Growth in Transition Economies, 1990–2004, World Bank Policy Research Working Paper, World Bank, Washington DC.

European Commission (2015) Enlargement: Countries preparing to join [Online], available at: http://ec.europa.eu/enlargement/countries/check-current-status/index_en.htm (last visited 19 September 2015).

Evans, David, Gasiorek, Michel, Ghoneim, Ahmed, Haynes-Prempeh, Michanne, Holmes, Peter, Iacovone, Leo, Jackson, Karen, Iwanow, Tomasz, Robinson, Sherman and Rollo, Jim (2006) Assessing Regional Trade Agreements with Developing Countries: Shallow and Deep Integration, Trade, Productivity, and Economic Performance, DFID Project Number 04 5881, University of Sussex.

Feichtner, Isabel (2012) *The Law and Politics of WTO Waivers: Stability and Flexibility in International Law*, Cambridge University Press, Cambridge.

Feketekuty, Geza (1988) *International Trade in Services: An Overview and Blueprint for Negotiations*, Ballinger Publishing Company, Cambridge.

(2000) 'Assessing and Improving the Architecture of GATS', In: P. Sauvé and R. Stern (eds.), *GATS 2000: New Direction in Services Trade Liberalisation*, The Brookings Institution, Washington DC, pp. 85ff., p. 98.

Findlay, Christopher (2008) 'Transport Services', In: A. Mattoo, R. M. Stern and G. Zanini (eds.), *A Handbook of International Trade in Services*, Oxford University Press, Oxford, pp. 356–387.

Fink, Carsten (2007) *Preferential Trade Agreements in Services: Friends or Foes of the Multilateral Trading System?*, GEM, Paris, pp. 11–12.

Fink, Carsten and Jansen, Marion (2007) Services Provisions in Regional Trade Agreements: Stumbling or Building Blocks for Multilateral Liberalisation?, paper presented at the Conference on Multilateralising Regionalism, organised by WTO, HEI and CEPR, 10–12 September 2007, Geneva.

(2008) 'Services Provisions in Regional Trade Agreements: Stumbling Block or Building Blocks for Multilateral Liberalisation?', In: R. Baldwin and P. Low (eds.), *Multilateralising Regionalism: Challenges for the Global Trading System*, Cambridge University Press, New York, pp. 221–261.

Fink, Carsten, Mattoo, Aaditya and Rathindran, Randeep (2002) 'An Assessment of Telecommunications Reform in Developing Countries', *Information Economics and Policy*, vol. 15, no. 4, pp. 443–466.

Francois, Joseph and Hoekman, Bernhard (2010) 'Services Trade and Policy', *Journal of Economic Literature*, vol. 48, September, pp. 642–692.

Francois, Joseph and Wooton, Ian (2002) 'Trade in International Transport Services: The Role of Competition', *Review of International Economics*, vol. 9, no. 2, pp. 249–261.

Fugazza, Marco and Vanzetti, David (2006) A South-South Survival Strategy: The Potential for Trade among Developing Countries, Study Series No. 33, UNCTAD, Geneva.

Gabriele, Alberto (2004) Exports of Services and Economic Growth in Developing Countries, Report, UNCTAD [Online], available at: http://unctad.org/en/docs/ditctncdmisc20036_en.pdf (last visited 11 April 2014).

Garbacz, Christopher and Thompson, Herbert G. (2007) 'Demand for Telecommunication Services in Developing Countries', *Telecommunications Policy*, vol. 31, no. 5, pp. 276–289.

Geddes, Barbara (1995) 'The Politics of Economic Liberalisation', *Latin American Research Review*, vol. 30, no. 2, pp. 195–214.

George, Clive and Kirkpatrick, Colin (2004) 'Trade and Development: Assessing the Impact of Trade Liberalisation on Sustainable Development', *Journal of World Trade*, vol. 38, no. 3, pp. 441–469.

Goldberg, Pinelopi K. and Pavcnik, Nina (2007) 'Distributional Effects of Globalization in Developing Countries', *Journal of Economic Literature*, vol. XLV, March, pp. 39–82.

GOLUB, STEPHEN (2010) The Role of Transit and Re-export Trade in Togo's Economy [Online], available at: www.swarthmore.edu/Documents/academics/economics/Golub/Togo-reexports.pdf (last visited 11 April 2014).

GOOTIIZ, BATSHUR AND MATTOO, AADITYA (2009) Services in Doha: What's on the Table?, Policy Research Working Paper No. 4903, The World Bank, Washington DC.

GRIFFITHS, BRIAN (1975) *Invisible Barriers to Invisible Trade*, Trade Policy Research Centre, Macmillan, London.

GROVER GOSWAMI, ARTI, MATTOO, AADITYA AND SAEZ, SEBASTIAN (2012) 'Exporting Services: A Developing-Country Perspective', In: A. Grover Goswami, A. Matto and S. Saez (eds.), *Exporting Services: A Developing Country Perspective*, The World Bank, Washington DC, pp. 1–24.

GRYNBERG, ROMAN (2000) The Pacific Island States and the WTO: Towards a Post-Seattle Agenda for the Small Vulnerable States, Global Conference on the Development Agenda for Small States, London.

HANSEN, HENRIK AND RAND, JOHN (2006) 'On the Causal Links between FDI and Growth in Developing Countries', *The World Economy*, vol. 29, no. 1, pp. 21–41.

HAWTHORNE, HELEN (2013) *Least Developed Countries and the WTO: Special Treatment in Trade*, Palgrave Macmillan, Basingstoke.

HELBLE, MATTHIAS AND WIGNARAJA, GANESHAN (2013) Bali Ministerial a Turning Point for the WTO? [Online], available at: www.eastasiaforum.org/2013/11/03/bali-ministerial-a-turning-point-for-the-wto/ (last visited 7 November 2013).

HERON, TONY AND SILES-BRÜGGE, GABRIEL (2012) 'Competitive Liberalisation and the 'Global Europe' Services and Investment Agenda: Locating the Commercial Drivers of the EU-ACP Economic Partnership Agreements', *Journal of Common Market Studies*, vol. 50, no. 2, pp. 250–266.

HESTERMEYER, HOLGER (2008) 'Preamble General Agreement on Trade in Services', In: R. Wolfrum, P-T. Stoll, and C. Feinäugle (eds.), *WTO – Trade in Services*, Max Planck Institute, Martinus Nijhoff Publishers, Leiden, pp. 17–29.

HEYDON, KENNETH (1990) 'Developing Country Perspectives, in the Uruguay Round: Services in the World Economy', P. A. Messerli and K. P. Sauvant (eds.), *The Uruguay Round: Services in the World Economy*, The World Bank, Washington DC, pp. 159–165.

HODGE, JAMES (2002) 'Liberalisation of Trade in Services in Developing Countries', In: B. M. Hoeckman, A. Mattoo and P. English (eds.), *Development, Trade and the WTO: A Handbook*, The World Bank, Washington DC, pp. 221–234.

HOEKMAN, BERNARD (2000) 'The Next Round of Services Negotiations: Identifying Priorities and Options', Review, Federal Reserve Bank of St. Louis, pp. 31–48.

(2001) Strengthening the Global Trade Architecture for Development: The Post Doha Agenda, PSIO Occasional Paper, WTO Series No. 11, Geneva.

(2005a) 'Operationalising the Concept of Policy Space in the WTO: Beyond Special and Differential Treatment', *Journal of International Economic Law*, vol. 8, no. 2, pp. 405–424.

(2005b) 'Transfer of Technology to Developing Countries: Unilateral and Multilateral Policy Options', *World Development*, vol. 33, no. 10, pp. 1587–1602.

Hoekman, Bernard and Kostecki, M. M. (2009) *The Political Economy of the World Trading System: From GATT to WTO*, Oxford University Press, Oxford.

Hoekman, Bernard and Mattoo, Aaditya (2007a) 'International Trade: Trade in Services', In: A. T. Guzman and A. O. Sykes (eds.), *Research Handbook in International Economic Law*, Edward Elgar Publishing Limited, Cheltenham, pp. 113–150.

(2007b) Services Trade and Growth, Paper prepared for a meeting of the Commission in Growth and Development, World Bank, Washington DC.

(2008) 'Services Trade and Growth', In: J. A. Marchetti and M. Roy (eds.), *Opening Markets for Trade in Services*, Cambridge University Press, Cambridge, pp. 21–57.

Hoekman, Bernard, Mattoo, Aaditya and Sapir, André (2007) 'The Political Economy of Services Trade Liberalisation: A Case for International Regulatory Cooperation?', *Oxford Review of Economic Policy*, vol. 23, no. 3, pp. 367–391.

Hoekman, Bernard, Michalopoulos, Constantine, and Winters, Alan L. (2003) More Favorable and Differential Treatment of Developing Countries: Towards a New Approach in the WTO, World Bank Policy Research Working Paper, World Bank, Washington DC.

Holmes, Frank (1990) 'ANZCERTA, Trade in Services, and ASEAN', *ASEAN Economic Bulletin*, vol. 7, no. 1, pp. 1–10.

Horn, Henrik and Mavroidis, Petros C. (2001) 'Economic and Legal Aspects of the Most-Favoured-Nation Clause', *European Journal of Political Economy*, vol. 17, no. 2, pp. 233–279.

Horn, Henrik and Weiler, Joseph (2005) 'European Communities – Trade Description of Sardines: Textualism and its Discontent', In: H. Horn and P. C. Mavroidis (eds.), *The WTO Case Law of 2002*, Cambridge University Press, Cambridge, pp. 551–578.

Horn, Henrik, Mavroidis, Petros C. and Sapir, André (2010) 'Beyond the WTO? An Anatomy of EU and US Preferential Trade Agreements', *The World Economy*, vol. 33, no. 11, pp. 1565–1588.

Hudec, R. E. (1975) *The GATT Legal System and World Trade Diplomacy*, Praeger, New York.

Hufbauer, Gary and Stephenson, Sherry (2007) 'Services Trade: Past Liberalisation and Future Challenges', *Journal of International Economic Law*, vol. 10, no. 3, pp. 605–630.

IPC (2004) A New Approach to Special and Differential Treatment, 15 September 2004, IPC Position Paper, Washington and Brussels.

Islam, Rizwanul and Alam, Shawkat (2009) 'Preferential Trade Agreements and the Scope of GATT Article XXIV, GATS Article V and the Enabling Clause: An Appraisal of GATT/WTO Jurisprudence', *Netherlands International Law Review*, vol. 56, no. 1, pp. 1–34.

Ismail, Faizel (2006) 'How Can Least-Developed Countries and Other Small, Weak and Vulnerable Economies Also Gain from the Doha Development Agenda on the Road to Hong Kong?', *Journal of World Trade*, vol. 40, no. 1, pp. 37–68.

(2011) 'Rediscovering the Role of Developing Countries in the GATT', In: Y.-S. Lee, G. N. Horlick, W.-M. Choi and T. Broude (eds.), *Law and Development Perspective on International Trade Law*, Cambridge University Press, New York, pp. 130–160.

Ismail, Faizel and Vickers, Brendan (2011) 'Towards Fair and Inclusive Decision-Making in the WTO Negotiations', In: Carolyn Deere Birkbeck (ed.), *Making Global Trade Governance Work for Development*, Cambridge University Press, Cambridge, pp. 461–485.

Jackson, John H. (1997) *The World Trading System: Law and Policy of International Economic Relations*, 2nd edition, The MIT Press, London.

Jacobsson, Johanna and Stocchetti, Marikki (2013) The WTO Under Pressure: Tackling the Deadlock in Multilateral Trade, Briefing Paper, Finnish Institute of International Affairs, Helsinki.

Jean, Sébastien (2013) WTO: Rethinking the Special and Differential Treatment Granted to Developing Countries, CEPII, le blog, 8 October 2013 [online], available at: www.cepii.fr/blog/bi/post.asp? IDcommunique = 249 (last visited 7 November 2013).

Jessen, Henning (2006) '*Special and Differential Treatment for Developing Countries' im multidimensionalen Wandel des Wirtschaftsvölkerrechts*, Berliner Wissenschafts-Verlag, Berlin.

J. M. (1992) 'GATT, the Dunkel Draft and India', *Economic and Political Weekly*, vol. 27, no. 4, pp. 140–142.

Kanchanachitra, Chumrurtai, Lindelow, Magnus, Johnston, Timothy, Hanvoravongchau, Piya, Lorenzo, Fely M., Huong, Nguyen L., Wilopo, Siswanto A. and Dela Rosa, Jennifer F. (2011) 'Human Resources for Health in Southeast Asia: Shortages, Distributional Challenges, and International Trade in Health Services', *The Lancet*, vol. 337, no. 9767, pp. 769–781.

Karsenty, Guy (2000) 'Assessing Trade in Services by Mode of Supply', In: P. Sauvé and R. M. Stern (eds.), *GATS 2000: New Directions in Services Trade Liberalisation*, The Brookings Institution, Washington DC, pp. 33–56.

Kasteng, Jonas, Karlsson, Arne and Lindberg, Carina (2004) *Differentiation between Developing Countries in the WTO*, Swedish Board of Agriculture, International Affairs Division, Jönköping.

Keck, Alexander and Low, Patrick (2004) Special and Differential Treatment in the WTO: Why, When and How?, Staff Working Paper ERSD-2004-03, World Trade Organisation, Geneva.

Keet, Dot (2006) *South-South: Strategic Alternatives to the Global Economic System and Power Regime*, Transnational Institute, Amsterdam.

Kelsey, Jane (2003) 'Legal Fetishism and the Contradictions of the GATS', *Globalisation, Societies and Education*, vol. 1, no. 3, pp. 267–280.

Kennes, Walter (2000) Strategies for Effective Participation of Developing Countries in the World Trading System, PSIO Occasional Paper, WTO Series No. 06, Geneva.

Keohane, Robert. O. (1986) 'Reciprocity in International Relations', *International Organisation*, vol. 40, no. 1, pp. 1–27.

Kessie, Edwini (1999) 'Developing Countries and the WTO – What Has Changed?', *World Competition*, vol. 22, no. 2, pp. 83–110.

(2007) 'The Legal Status of Special and Differential Treatment Provisions under the WTO Agreements', In: G. A. Bermann and P. C. Mavroidis (eds.), *WTO Law and Developing Countries*, Cambridge University Press, Cambridge, pp. 12–35.

Khor, Martin (2008) *Bilateral and Regional Free Trade Agreements: Some Critical Elements and Development Implications*, Third World Network, Penang.

Kim, Bongchul (2009) 'Development and Prospect of the CRTA in WTO System', *International Area Studies Review*, vol. 12, no. 1, pp. 3–15.

Kleen, Peter and Page, Sheila (2005) Special and Differential Treatment of Developing Countries in the World Trade Organisation, Global Development Studies No. 2, Overseas Development Institute and Ministry for Foreign Affairs Sweden, London.

Konan, Denise E. and Maskus, Keith E. (2006) 'Quantifying the Impact of Services Liberalisation in a Developing Country', *Journal of Development Economics*, vol. 81, pp. 142–162.

Krajewski, Markus (2003) *National Regulation and Trade Liberalisation in Services*, Kluwer Law International, The Hague.

(2013) Balancing Legal Certainty with Regulatory Flexibility, 1 March [Online], available at SSRN: http://ssrn.com/abstract=2419885 (last visited 24 September 2015).

Krancke, Jan (1999) Liberalisierung des internationalen Dienstleistungshandels: Analyse des GATS und Perspektiven für die zukünftige Handelsliberalisierung, Kieler Working Paper No. 954, Institut für Weltwirtschaft, Kiel.

Krueger, Anne O. (1998) 'Why Trade Liberalisation Is Good for Growth', *The Economic Journal*, vol. 108, pp. 1513–1522.

(1999) 'The Developing Countries and the Next Round of Multilateral Trade Negotiations', *The World Economy*, vol. 22, no. 7, pp. 909–132.

Krugman, Paul R. (1979) 'Increasing Returns, Monopolistic Competition, and International Trade', *Journal of International Economics*, vol. 9, no. 4, pp. 469–479.

(2008) 'Trade and Wages, Reconsidered', *Brookings Papers on Economic Activity*, Spring, pp. 103–37.

Langhammer, Rolf J. (2006) Service Trade Liberalisation as a Handmaiden of Competitiveness in Manufacturing: An Industrialised or Developing Country Issue?, Kiel Working Paper, The Kiel Institute for the World Economy, Kiel.

Larsen, Kurt and Vincent-Lancrin, Stéphan (2002) 'International Trade in Educational Services: Good or Bad?', *Higher Education Management and Policy*, vol. 14, no. 3, pp. 9–46.

Larsen, Kurt, Martin, John P. and Morris, Rosemary (2002) 'Trade in Educational Services: Trends and Emerging Issues', *The World Economy*, vol. 25, no. 6, pp. 849–868.

Lashley, Conrad and Morrison, Alison (2011) *In Search of Hospitality: Theoretical Perspectives and Debates*, 2nd edition, Routledge, New York.

Latrille, Pierre and Lee, Juneyoung (2012) Services Rules in Regional Trade Agreements: How Diverse and How Creative as Compared to the GATS Multilateral Rules?, Staff Working Paper ERSD-2012-19, World Trade Organisation, Geneva.

Lee, Yong-Shik (2011a) 'Law and Development for Least Developed Countries: Theoretical Basis and Regulatory Framework for Microtrade', In: Y-S. Lee, G. N. Horlick, W-M. Choi and T. Broude (eds.), *Law and Development Perspective on International Trade Law*, Cambridge University Press, New York, pp. 7–28.

Lee, Yong-Shik (2011b) 'World Trade Organisation and Developing Countries', In: Y-S. Lee, G. N. Horlick, W-M. Choi and T. Broude (eds.), *Law and Development Perspective on International Trade Law*, Cambridge University Press, New York, pp. 105–129.

Le Pere, Garth L. (2009) 'Exploring the Promise of South-South Co-operation', In: Garth L. Le Pere and Lyal White (eds.), *Strengthening the Bilateral*, Edited Proceedings of the first Academic Seminar on Bilateral Relations between Argentina and South Africa, 12–14 May 2008, Institute for Global Dialogue, Midrand, pp. 67–84.

Levy, Philippe I. (2006) 'Do We Need an Undertaker for the Single Undertaking? Considering Angles of Variable Geometry', In: S. J. Evenett and B. M. Hoekman (eds.), *Economic Development and Multilateral Cooperation*, The World Bank/Palgrave Macmillan, Washington DC, pp. 417–438.

Levy Yeyati, Eduardo, and Sturzenegger, Federico (2000) 'Is EMU a Blueprint for Mercosur?', *Cuadernos de Economia*, vol. 37, no. 110, pp. 63–99.

Lewis, David (2011) *Bangladesh: Politics, Economy and Civil Society*, Cambridge University Press, Cambridge.

Lewis, Patsy (2002) *Surviving Small Size: Regional Integration in Caribbean Ministates*, University of the West Indies Press, Kingston.

(2007) 'Is the WTO Doing Enough for Developing Countries?', In: G. A. Bermann and P. C. Mavroidis (eds.), *WTO Law and Developing Countries*, Cambridge University Press, Cambridge, pp. 324–357.

Low, Patrick and Mattoo, Aaditya (2000) 'Is There a Better Way? Alternative Approaches to Liberalisation under the GATS', In: P. Sauvé and R. M. Stern (eds.), *GATS 2000: New Directions in Services Trade Liberalisation*, The Brookings Institution, Washington DC, pp. 449–472.

Lusch, Robert F. (2011) 'Reframing Supply Chain Management: A Service-Dominant Logic Perspective', *Journal of Supply Chain Management*, vol. 47, no. 1, pp. 14–18.

Malmgren, Harald B. (1985) 'Negotiating International Rules for Trade in Services', *The World Economy*, vol. 8, no. 1, pp. 11–26.

Manger, Mark S. (2009) *Investing in Protection: The Politics of Preferential Trade Agreements between North and South*, Cambridge University Press, Cambridge.

Manrique Carpio, Claudia and Comas Mir, Jaume (2014) 'The Least-Developed Countries Services Waiver: Any Alternative Under the GATS?', *Goettingen Journal of International Law*, vol. 6, pp. 115–143.

Marchetti, Juan A. and Mavroidis, Petros C. (2011) 'The Genesis of the GATS (General Agreement on Trade in Services)', *The European Journal of International Law*, vol. 22, no. 3, pp. 689–721.

Marchetti, Juan A. and Roy, Martin (2008) 'Services Liberalisation in the WTO and in PTAs', In: J. A. Marchetti and M. Roy (eds.), *Opening Markets for Trade in Services*, World Trade Organisation, Cambridge University Press, Cambridge, pp. 61–112.

Martin, Philip and Abella, Manolo (2009) 'Migration and Development: The Elusive Link at the GFMD', *International Migration Review*, vol. 43, no. 2, pp. 431–439.

Mattoo, Aaditya (2000a) 'MFN and the GATS', In: T. Cottier and P. C. Mavroidis (eds.), *Regulatory Barriers and the Principle of Non-Discrimination in World Trade Law*, University of Michigan Press, Ann Arbor, pp. 51–99.

(2000b) Shaping Future Rules for Trade in Services: Lessons from the GATS, NBER Conference in Trade in Services, World Bank, Washington DC.

Mattoo, Aaditya and Fink, Carsten (2002) Regional Agreements and Trade in Services: Policy Issues, Policy Research Paper, World Bank, Washington DC.

Mattoo, Aaditya and Payton, Lucy (2007) 'Services Trade for Zambia's Development: An Overview', In: A. Mattoo and L. Payton (eds.), *Services Trade and Development*, Palgrave Macmillan and World Bank, New York and Washington DC, pp. 1–60.

Mattoo, Aaditya and Wunsch-Vincent, Sacha (2004) 'Pre-empting Protectionism in Services: The GATS and Outsourcing', *Journal of International Economic Law*, vol. 7, no. 4, pp. 765–800.

Mavroidis, Petros C. (2010) Always Look at the Bright Side of Non-Delivery: WTO and Preferential Trade Agreements, Yesterday and Today [Online], available at: www.wto.org/english/res_e/publications_e/wtr11_forum_e/wtr11_14dec10_e.pdf (last visited 16 April 2014).

McGuire, Greg (2002) Trade in Services – Market Access Opportunities and the Benefits of Liberalisation for Developing Economies, UNCTAD, Policy Issues in International Trade and Commodities, Study Series No. 19, New York/Geneva.

Melchior, Arne, Stevens, Christopher and Johnsen, Åshild (2010) Services and Development: The Scope of Special and Differential Treatment in the GATS, NUPI Report 2010, Norwegian Institute of International Affairs, Oslo.

Michalopoulos, Constantine (2000) Trade and Development in the GATT and WTO: The Role of Special and Differential Treatment for Developing Countries, Working Paper, World Bank, Washington DC.

Miles, Ian (2005) 'Innovation in Services', In: J. Fagerberg, D. C. Mowery and R. R. Nelson (eds.), *The Oxford Handbook of Innovation*, Oxford University Press, Oxford, pp. 433–457.

Morrissey, Oliver (2006) 'Aid or Trade, or Aid and Trade?', *Australian Economic Review*, vol. 39, no. 1, pp. 78–88.

Munin, Nellie (2010) *Legal Guide to GATS*, Kluwer Law International, Alphen aan den Rijn.

Murphy, Sophia (2013) The Road to Bali: The WTO's Ninth Ministerial, IATP [Online], available at: www.iatp.org/blog/201308/the-road-to-bali-the-wto%E2%80%99s-ninth-ministerial (last visited 7 November 2013).

Natens, Bregt and Wouters, Jan (2013) The Scope of GATS and of its Obligations, Working Paper, Leuven Centre for Global Governance Studies, Leuven.

Newfarmer, Richard (2006) 'Regional Trade Agreements: Designs for Development', In: R. Newfarmer (ed.), *Trade, Doha, and Development: A Window into the Issues*, The World Bank, Washington DC, pp. 243–253.

Nicolaïdis, Kalypso and Schmidt Susanne K. (2007) 'Mutual Recognition "On Trial": The Long Road to Services Liberalisation', *Journal of European Public Policy*, vol. 14, no. 5, pp. 717–734.

Nielsen, Hannah and Spenceley, Anna (2011) The Success of Tourism in Rwanda – Gorillas and More, Background Paper, World Development Report 2011, The World Bank, Washington DC.

NIELSON, JULIA AND CATTANEO, OLIVER (2003) 'Current Regimes for the Temporary Movement of Service Providers: Case Studies of Australia and the United States', In: A. Mattoo and A. Carzaniga (eds.), *Moving People to Deliver Services*, World Bank and Oxford University Press, Washington DC, pp. 113–156.

NIELSON, JULIA AND TAGLIONI, DARIA (2003) A Quick Guide to the GATS and Mode 4, Paper prepared for the OCED/World Bank/IOM Seminar on Trade and Migration, 12–14 November 2003, Geneva [Online], available at: www.iom.int/jahia/webdav/site/myjahiasite/shared/shared/mainsite/microsites/IDM/workshops/Trade_2004_04051004/related%20docs/quick_guide.pdf (last visited 14 April 2014).

(2004) Services Trade Liberalisation: Identifying Opportunities and Gains, OECD Trade Policy Papers, Paris.

NULLMEIER, FRANK (2009) 'Formen der Staatlichkeit: Zu einer Analytik politischer Einheiten', In: Nicole Deitelhoff and Jens Steffek (eds.), *Was bleibt vom Staat? Demokratie, Recht und Verfassung im globalen Zeitalter*, Campus Verlag, Frankfurt am Main, pp. 35–56.

NZZ (2011) Der grosse Trumpf des Restaurants ist die Gastfreundschaft [Online], available at: www.nzz.ch/aktuell/startseite/der-grosse-trumpf-des-restaurants-ist-die-gastfreundschaft-1.13603047 (last visited 28 December 2013).

O'Brien, Derek (2011) 'CARICOM: Regional Integration in a Post-Colonial World', *European Law Journal*, vol. 17, no. 5, pp. 630–648.

OECD (2008) 'The Interaction between Investment and Services Chapters in Selected Regional Trade Agreements', In: International Investment Law: Understanding Concepts and Tracking Innovations, OECD Trade Working Paper No. 55, Paris, pp. 241–340.

(2015) DAC List of ODA Recipients: Effective for Reporting on 2014, 2015 and 2016 Flows [Online], available at: www.oecd.org/dac/stats/daclist.htm (last visited 19 September 2015).

ORTINO, FEDERICO (2006) 'Treaty Interpretation and the WTO Appellate Body Report in US-Gambling: A Critique', *Journal of International Economic Law*, vol. 9, no. 1, pp. 117–148.

ORTINO, FEDERICO AND SHEPPARD, AUDLEY (2006) 'International Agreements Covering Foreign Investment in Services; Patterns and Linkages', In: L. Bartels and F. Ortino (eds.), *Regional Trade Agreements and the WTO Legal System*, Oxford University Press, Oxford, pp. 201–214.

PAGE, SHEILA, CALÌ, MASSIMILIANO AND TE VELDE, DIRK W. (2008) *Development Package at the WTO? What Do Developing Countries Want from the Doha Round?*, Overseas Development Institute, London.

PANEL ON DEFINING THE FUTURE OF TRADE (2013) *The Future of Trade: The Challenges of Convergence*, WTO, Geneva.

PANIZZON, MARION (2010) Trade and Labour Migration: GATS Mode 4 and Migration Agreements, Occasional Papers No. 47/January2010, Friedrich Ebert Stiftung, Geneva.

PARIKH, VAIBHAV (2003) 'Mode 4 and the Software Services Sector: An Indian View', In: A. Mattoo and A. Carzaniga (eds.), *Moving People to Deliver Services*, The World Bank and Oxford University Press, Oxford, pp. 163–170.

PARK, DONGHYUN AND NOLAND, MARCUS (2013) *Developing the Service Sector as and Engine of Growth for Asia*, Asian Development Bank, Manila.

PARK, INNWON AND PARK, SOONCHAN (2011) 'Regional Liberalisation of Trade in Services', *The World Economy*, vol. 34, no. 5, pp. 725–740.

PAUWELYN, JOOST (2008) *Optimal Protection of International Law: Navigating Between European Absolutism and American Voluntarism*, Cambridge University Press, Cambridge.

PICKER, COLIN B. (2005) 'Regional Trade Agreements v. the WTO: A Proposal for Reform fo Article XXIV to Counter This Institutional Threat', *Journal of International Economic Law*, vol. 26, no. 2, pp. 267–319.

POMFRET, RICHARD (2007) 'Is Regionalism an Increasing Feature of the World Economy?', *The World Economy*, vol. 30, no. 6, pp. 923–947.

POSNER, ERIC (2009) *The Perils of Global Legalism*, University of Chicago Press, Chicago.

POUND, ROSCOE (1923) *Interpretations of Legal History*, Cambridge University Press, Cambridge.

PRIMO BRAGA, CARLOS A. (1996) 'The Impact of the Internationalisation of Services on Developing Countries', *Finance & Development*, March, pp. 34–37.

PRIYADARSHI, SHISHIR AND RAHMAN, TAUFIQUR (2013) 'Build up to the Ninth WTO Ministerial Conference: Issues of Interest to LDCs', *Commonwealth Trade Hot Topics*, no. 98, Commonwealth Secretariat, London.

PROWSE, SUSAN (2002) 'The Role of International and National Agencies in Trade-related Capacity Building', *The World Economy*, vol. 25, no. 9, pp. 1235–1261.

QURESHI, A. H. AND WITTAYAWARAKUL, C. (2010) 'International Development Law and Preferential Trade Agreements involving Developing Countries', In: Y. Ngangjoh-Hodu and F. Matambalya (eds.), *Trade Relations between the EU and Africa*, Routledge, London, pp. 115–150.

RAJAMANI, LAVANYA (2006) *Differential Treatment in International Environmental Law*, Cambridge University Press, Cambridge.

RATHA, DILIP AND SHAW, WILLIAM (2007) South-South Migration and Remittances, Working Paper, World Bank, Washington DC.

REYNA, JIMMIE V. (1993) 'Services', In: T. P. Stewart (ed.), *The GATT Uruguay Round: A Negotiating History (1986–1992)*, vol. II, Kluwer Law and Taxation Publishers, Deventer, pp. 2335–2425.

RODRIK, DANI (1997) 'Has Globalisation Gone Too Far?', *California Management Review*, vol. 39, no. 3, pp. 29–53.

(2000) 'How Far Will International Economic Intergration Go?', *The Journal of Economic Perspectives*, vol. 14, no. 1, pp. 177–186.

(2011) *The Globalisation Paradox*, W. W. Norton & Company, Inc., New York.

Rodrik, Dani, Subramanian, Arvind and Trebbi, Francesco (2004) 'Institutions Rule: The Primacy of Institutions over Geography and Integration in Economic Development', *Journal of Economic Growth*, vol. 9, pp. 131–165.

Roy, Martin (2008) 'Out of Stock or Just in Time? Doha and the Liberalisation of Distribution Services', In: J. A. Marchetti and M. Roy (eds.), *Opening Markets for Trade in Services: Countries and Sectors in Bilateral and WTO Negotiations*, Cambridge University Press, Cambridge, pp. 224–263.

Roy, Martin, Marchetti, Juan and Lim, Hoe (2007) 'Services Liberalisation in the New Generation of Preferential Trade Agreements (PTAs): How Much Further than the GATS?', *World Trade Review*, vol. 6, no. 2, pp. 155–192.

(2008) 'The Race towards Preferential Trade Agreements in Services: How Much Market Access Is Really Achieved?', In: M. Panizzon, N. Pohl and P. Sauvé (eds.), *GATS and the Regulation of International Trade in Services*, Cambridge University Press, Cambridge, pp. 77–110.

Sauvé, Pierre (2002) 'Trade, Education and the GATS: What's In, What's Out, What's All the Fuss About?', *Higher Education Management and Policy*, vol. 14, no. 3, pp. 47–76.

(2008) 'Been There, Not Yet Done That: Lessons and Challenges in Services Trade', In: M. Panizzon, N. Pohl and P. Sauvé (eds.), *GATS and the Regulation of International Trade in Services*, Cambridge University Press, Cambridge, pp. 599–631.

(2013) A Plurilateral Agenda for Services? Assessing the Case for a Trade in Services Agreement (TISA), Working Paper No. 2013/29, NCCR trade regulation, Bern.

Sauvé, Pierre and Irace, Mary (2006) The Doha Development Agenda and GATS: The Benefits of Open Services Markets, Report for the National Foreign Trade Council, NFTC, Washington DC and New York.

Saxenian, AnnaLee (2002) *Local and Global Networks of Immigrant Professionals in Silicon Valley*, Public Policy Institute of California, San Francisco.

Schloeman, Hannes (2012) 'The LDC Services Waiver: Making It Work', *Bridges Africa Review*, vol. 1, no. 4 [Online], available at: http://ictsd.org/i/competitiveness/140321/ (last visited 11 April 2014).

Schwab, Susan C. (2011) 'After Doha: Why the Negotiations Are Doomed and What We Should Do about It', *Foreign Affairs*, vol. 90, no. 3, pp. 104–117.

Seyoum, Belay (2007) 'Revealed Comparative Advantage and Competitiveness in Services: A Study with Special Emphasis on Developing Countries', *Journal of Economic Studies*, vol. 34, no. 5, pp. 376–388.

Shingal, Anirudh and Sauvé, Pierre (2011) Reflections on the Preferential Liberalisation of Services Trade, MPRA Paper No. 32816, Munich.

SIEBER-GASSER, CHARLOTTE (2013) 'Variationen der regionalen Personenfreizügigkeit', *Jusletter*, 18 March.

(2016) 'TTIP and Swiss Democracy', In: M. Bungenberg, C. Herrmann, M. Krajewski and J. P. Terhechte (eds.), *European Yearbook of International Economic Law 2016*, European Yearbook of International Economic Law, vol. 7, Springer, Basel.

SIMO, REGIS Y. (2013) 'Integrating African Markets into the Global Exchange of Services: A Central African Perspective', *The Law and Development Review*, vol. 6, no. 2, pp. S255–S297.

SLAUGHTER, ANNE-MARIE (2004) *A New World Order*, Princeton University Press, Princeton.

SLAUGHTER, MATTHEW J. (2004) Infant-Industry Protection and Trade Liberalisation in Developing Countries, Research Report, USAID, Washington DC.

SNAPE, R. H. (1993) 'History and Economics of GATT's Article XXIV', In: K. Anderson and R. Blackhurst (eds.), *Regional Integration in the Global Trading System*, Harvester Wheatsheaf St. Martin's Press, London and New York, pp. 273–291.

SOUTH CENTRE (2011) Analysis of Draft Waiver Decision on Services and Services Suppliers of LDCs, Analytical Note, Geneva.

STEGER, DEBRA (2013) 'International Trade and Investment: Towards a Common Regime?', In: R. Echandi and P. Sauvé (eds.), *Prospects for International Investment Law and Policy*, Cambridge University Press, Cambridge, pp. 156–165.

STEINBERG, RICHARD H. (2002) 'In the Shadow of Law or Power? Consensus-Based Bargaining and Outcomes in the GATT/WTO', *International Organisation*, vol. 56, no. 2, pp. 339–374.

STEPHENSON, SHERRY M. (2000a) 'Regional Agreements on Services in Multilateral Disciplines: Interpreting and Applying GATS Article V', In: S. M. Stephenson (ed.), *Services Trade in the Western Hemisphere*, Brookings Institution Press, Washington DC, pp. 86–104.

(2000b) 'GATS and Regional Integration', In: P. Sauvé, and R. M. Stern (eds.), *GATS 2000: New Directions in Services Trade Liberalisation*, The Brookings Institution, Washington DC, pp. 509–529.

(2001) Services Liberalisation by Developing Countries: Is More Progress Possible Regionally than under the GATS?, PSIO Occasional Paper, WTO Series No. 08, Geneva.

(2002) 'Regional versus Multilateral Liberalisation of Services', *World Trade Review*, vol. 1, no. 2, pp. 187–209.

STEPHENSON, SHERRY AND PFISTER, ANNE-KATRIN (2013) 'The LDC Services Waiver beyond Bali', *Bridges Africa Review*, vol. 2, no. 8 [Online], available at: http://ictsd.org/i/news/bridges-africa-review/179028/ (last visited 11 April 2014).

STEVENS, CHRISTOPHER (2002) 'The Future of Special and Differential Treatment (S&D) for Developing Countries in the WTO', IDS Working Paper 163, Institute of Development Studies, Sussex.

STRANGE, SUSAN (2015) 'The Declining Authority of States', In: Frank J. Lechner and John Boli (eds.), *The Globalization Reader*, 5th edition, John Wiley & Sons, West Sussex, pp. 232–238.

THRASHER, RACHEL D. AND GALLAGHER, KEVIN P. (2009) '21st Century Trade Agreements: Implications for Development Sovereignty', *Denver Journal of International Law and Policy*, vol. 38, no. 2, pp. 313–350.

TRACHTMAN, JOEL P. (2011) 'The Limits of PTAs: WTO Legal Restrictions on the Use of WTO-Plus Standards Regulation in PTAs', In: K. W. Bagwell and P. C. Mavroidis (eds.), *Preferential Trade Agreements: A Law and Economics Analysis*, Cambridge University Press, Cambridge, pp. 115–149.

TREBILCOCK, MICHAEL, HOWSE, ROBERT AND ELIASON, ANTONIA (2012) *The Regulation of International Trade*, 4th edition, Routledge, New York.

UNCTAD (1999) Analysis of Experiences in Selected Services Sectors [Online], available at: http://unctad.org/en/Docs/c1d28.en.pdf (last visited 17 April 2014).

(2011) *Generalised System of Preferences: List of Beneficiaries*, UNCTAD, Geneva.

(2015) News Release, April 14 2015, Geneva [Online], available at: http://unctad.org/en/Pages/Statistics.aspx (last visited 19 September 2015).

VAN DER BORGHT, KIM (1999) 'The Advisory Center on WTO Law: Advancing Fairness Equality', *Journal of International Economic Law*, vol. 2, pp. 723–728.

VAN DER MAREL, ERIK AND MIROUDOT, SÉBASTIEN (2014) 'The Economics and Political Economy of Going beyond the GATS', *The Review of International Organisations*, vol. 9, no. 2, pp. 205–239.

WAGNER, HELMUT (2004) Economic Analysis of Cross-Border Legal Uncertainty: The Example of the European Union, Discussion Paper [Online], available at: www.netbased-university.de/hwagner/download/371-maastricht_181004_final_vers.pdf (last visited 16 April 2014).

WALSH, STEPHEN (2004) 'Addressing the Abuse of the WTO's Exemption for Regional Trade Agreements', ELSA Selected Papers on European Law, no. 1, pp. 62–106.

WEBER, ROLF H. AND BURRI, MIRA (2012) *Classification of Services in the Digital Economy*, Springer, Berlin and Heidelberg.

WHALLEY, JOHN (2003) Assessing the Benefits to Developing Countries of Liberalisation in Services Trade, NBER Working Paper, OECD, Paris.

(2004) 'Assessing the Benefits to Developing Countries of Liberalisation in Services Trade', *The World Economy*, vol. 27, no. 8, pp. 1223–1253.

WICKRAMASEKERA, PIYASIRI (2002) *Asian Labour Migration: Issues and Challenges in an Era of Globalisation*, International LabourOffice, Geneva.

Williams, Allan M. (2007) 'Listen to Me, Learn with Me: International Migration and Knowledge Transfer', *British Journal of Industrial Relations*, vol. 45, no. 2, pp. 361–382.

Winters, Alan L. (1999) 'Regionalism vs. Multilateralism', In: R. Baldwin et al. (eds.), *Market Integration, Regionalism and the Global Economy*, CEPR, London.

(2001) Trade Policies for Poverty Alleviation: What Developing Countries Might Do, PSIO Occasional Paper, WTO Series No. 10, Geneva.

(2002) 'Trade Liberalisation and Poverty: What Are the Links?', *The World Economy*, vol. 25, no. 9, pp. 1339–1367.

(2004) 'Trade Liberalisation and Economic Performance: An Overview', *The Economic Journal*, vol. 114, no. 493, pp. F4–F21.

(2005) Developing Country Proposals for the Liberalisation of Movements of Natural Service Suppliers, Working Paper, Sussex Centre for Migration Research, Sussex.

(2008) 'The Temporary Movement of Workers to Provide Services (GATS Mode 4)', In: A. Mattoo, R. M. Stern and G. Zanini (eds.), *A Handbook of International Trade in Services*, Oxford University Press, Oxford, pp. 480–541.

Wolf, Martin (2001) 'Will the Nation-State Survive Globalisation?', *Foreign Affairs*, vol. 80, no. 1, pp. 178–190.

Wolfe, Robert (2009) 'The WTO Single Undertaking as Negotiating Technique and Constitutive Metaphor', *Journal of International Economic Law*, vol. 12, no. 4, pp. 835–858.

Wolfrum, R. (2008) 'Article II GATS', In: R. Wolfrum, P-T. Stoll und C. Feinäugle (eds.), *WTO – Trade in Services*, Max Planck Institute, Martinus Nijhoff Publishers, Leiden, pp. 71–91.

Woolcock, Stephen and Sampson, Gary (2003) *Regionalism, Multilateralism and Economic Integration: The Recent Experience*, United Nations University Press, Tokyo.

WTO (2012) *International Trade Statistics 2012*, WTO, Geneva.

(2013a) Days 3, 4 and 5: Round-the-Clock Consultations Produce 'Bali Package', Ninth WTO Ministerial Conference, 5–7 December 2013 [Online], available at: www.wto.org/english/news_e/news13_e/mc9sum_07dec13_e.htm (last visited December 29 2013).

(2013b) Ninth WTO Ministerial Conference [Online], available at: www.wto.org/english/thewto_e/minist_e/mc9_e/mc9_e.htm (last visited 7 November 2013).

(2013c) Regional Trade Agreements Information System (RTA-IS) [Online], available at: http://rtais.wto.org/UI/PublicMaintainRTAHome.aspx (last visited 13 June 2013).

WTO Secretariat (2001) *Guide to the GATS: An Overview of Issues for Further Liberalisation of Trade in Services*, World Trade Organisation, Kluwer Law International, The Hague.

Yang, Yongzheng and Gupta, Sanjeev (2005) Regional Trade Arrangements in Africa: Past Performances and the Way Forward, Working Paper, International Monetary Fund, Washington DC.

Young, Margaret A. (2009) 'Fragmentation or Interaction: The WTO, Fisheries Subsidies and International Law', *World Trade Review*, vol. 8, no. 4, pp. 477–515.

Zahrnt, Valentin (2009) 'How States Perceive the Costs of Trade Liberalisation in the WTO', *Aussenwirtschaft*, 64, pp. 269–292.

Zdouc, Werner (2002) Legal Problems Arising Under the General Agreement on Trade in Services – Comparative Analysis of GATS and GATT, Dissertation, University of St. Gallen.

Zleptnig, Stefan (2010) *Non-economic Objectives in WTO Law*, Martinus Nijhoff Publishers, Leiden.

INDEX

Lightning Source UK Ltd.
Milton Keynes UK
UKOW04n1216100716

278000UK00003B/113/P

9 781107 147560